Reform and Recovery in East Asia

The role of the state in East Asian development has always been a controversial topic. The financial crisis in East Asia has rekindled the debate over the appropriate roles of the state and economic enterprise across the region. With extensive reform programmes underway in almost every economy, there is a renewed focus on the role that governments and governance can play both in determining future performance and preventing future catastrophe.

The excellent, international contributors to this book explore various aspects of the recent experience of East Asian economies and come to some surprising conclusions regarding the importance of market strengthening and government systems in the sustainability of economic recovery. *Reform and Recovery in East Asia* argues that the process of recovery is largely cyclical, but that reforms can play a major part in reducing future vulnerability. It concludes that successful structural reform is a central determinant of long-run growth performance, particularly as countries approach the technological frontier.

This exciting sequel to *East Asia in Crisis* offers a completely up-to-date assessment of the progress of East Asian recovery and provides a detailed review of the experience in the region's economies. It is stimulating and informative reading for all those interested in further understanding the dynamics of East Asian economic crisis and recovery.

Peter Drysdale is Executive Director of the Australia–Japan Research Centre, based at the Australian National University.

D0221689

Reform and Recovery in East Asia

The Role of the State and Economic Enterprise

Edited by Peter Drysdale

London and New York

First published 2000
by Routledge
11 New Fetter Lane, London EC4P 4EE

Simultaneously published in the USA and Canada
by Routledge
29 West 35th Street, New York, NY 10001

Reprinted 2002

Routledge is an imprint of the Taylor & Francis Group

Typeset in Garamond by Arawang Communication Group, Canberra
Printed and bound in Great Britain by
TJI Digital, Padstow, Cornwall

British Library Cataloguing in Publication Data
A catalog record for this book has been requested

Library of Congress Cataloging in Publication Data
Reform and recovery in East Asia: the role of the state and economic enterprise / edited
by Peter Drysdale.
    p. cm.
  Includes bibliographical references and index.
  ISBN 0-415-24095-6 (hardcover) – ISBN 0-415-24096-4 (pbk.)
  1. Asia–Economic conditions–1945–2. Asia–Economic policy. 3. Financial
crises–East Asia. I. Drysdale, Peter.

HC460.5.R43 2000
338.95–de21

                                                                          00-056028

ISBN 0–415–24095–6 (hbk)
ISBN 0–415–24096–4 (pbk)

Publisher's Note
This book has been prepared from camera-ready copy provided by the editor

Contents

PART III REFLECTIONS

Figures

Tables

Contributors

EDITOR

PETER DRYSDALE is a Professor in the Research School of Pacific and Asian Studies/Asia Pacific School of Economic Management and Executive Director of the Australia–Japan Research Centre, Australian National University. He is a member of the Order of Australia for his services to Australia–Asia relations.

CONTRIBUTORS

PREMA-CHANDRA ATHUKORALA, Senior Fellow, Economics Division, Research School of Pacific and Asian Studies/Asia Pacific School of Economics and Management, Australian National University.

CHENG YUK-SHING, Department of Economics, Hong Kong Baptist University.

CHIA SIOW YUE, Director, Institute of Southeast Asian Studies, Singapore.

CHRISTOPHER FINDLAY, Professor, Australia–Japan Research Centre and National Centre for Development Studies, Asia Pacific School of Economics and Management, Australian National University.

ROSS GARNAUT, Professor and Director of the Asia Pacific School of Management, Australian National University.

AKIYOSHI HORIUCHI, Dean, Faculty of Economics, University of Tokyo.

YIPING HUANG, Fellow, Department of Economics, Research School of Pacific and Asian Studies/Asia Pacific School of Economics and Management, Australian National University.

MASAHIRO KAWAI, Chief Economist and Manager, East Asia and Pacific Division, The World Bank.

ROSS H. MCLEOD, Fellow, Economics Division, Research School of Pacific and Asian Studies/Asia Pacific School of Economics and Management, Australian National University.

DAVID NELLOR, Assistant Director, Regional Office for Asia and The Pacific, International Monetary Fund.

BHANUPONG NIDHIPRABHA, Vice-Rector, Academic Affairs and Faculty of Economics, Thammasat University.

HEATHER SMITH, Postdoctoral Fellow, Economics Division, Research School of Pacific and Asian Studies/Asia Pacific School of Economics and Management, Australian National University.

HADI SOESASTRO, Executive Director, Centre for Strategic and International Studies, Jakarta.

LIGANG SONG, Fellow and Director of the China Economy and Business Program at the Asia Pacific School of Economics and Management, Australian National University. He has a joint appointment with Renmin University, Beijing.

MICHAEL J. SULLIVAN, Associate Professor, University of Nevada and Visiting Research Fellow, DLSU Angelo King Institute for Economic and Business Studies.

ANGELO A. UNITE, Associate Professor, Economics Department, College of Business and Economics, De La Salle University.

PETER G. WARR, John Crawford Professor of Agricultural Economics, Economics Division, Research School of Pacific and Asian Studies/Asia Pacific School of Economics and Management, Australian National University.

DOMINIC WILSON, research scholar at the Australia–Japan Research Centre/Asia Pacific School of Economics and Management, Australian National University.

Preface

This volume was put together following a conference of the same title held at the Australian National University in September 1999. It follows a conference on the impact of the East Asian crisis held in May 1998 from which the book *East Asia in Crisis: From being a miracle to needing one?* was brought together by Ross McLeod and Ross Garnaut.

Before the last book had gone to press, the conference from which this volume was drawn was in planning. That may have appeared to be a little brave at the time. There were signs of recovery in East Asia in September 1998. But the programs of reform are still being put into place. There is now a clearer picture of recovery and reform, although many questions remain about the relationship between reform and the recovery under way. These questions are the subject of this book.

The East Asia Office of the International Monetary Fund (IMF) in Tokyo provided financial support for the conference and research for this book. The Asia Centre of the Japan Foundation provided financial support for the preparation and publication of the book. I am particularly grateful to Kunio Saito, Christopher Morris and David Nellor for their encouragement of this continuing work on the East Asian economies and their interaction with international financial markets.

The project was coordinated through the Australia–Japan Research Centre in the Asia Pacific School of Economics and Management (APSEM) at the Australian National University. A number of people have assisted its completion greatly. Marilyn Popp, with characteristic efficiency, handled the organisation of the conference to discuss the papers that became the drafts of chapters for the book. Pam Hewitt and Jennifer Brewster did an excellent job in editing the manuscript. Minni Reis was responsible for pagemaking. And David Duke ably managed the whole project.

Craig Fowlie at Routledge was a keen supporter of the project and I thank him and his staff for their help in the timely publication of the book.

Ross Garnaut, David Vines, Max Corden, Chris Becker, Anne Booth, Junghoo Yoo, Hal Hill, Zanial-Abidin Mahani, Ron Duncan, George Fane, Ramkishen Rajan, Ian Hooper and Gordon de Brouwer made helpful comments on chapter drafts and I am most grateful to them and to the authors who have contributed to the book for their generous efforts in meeting the demanding publication schedule that was set for the publication.

Special thanks are due to Dominic Wilson whose substantial contribution in drawing the themes of the book together is inadequately reflected in his joint authorship of the introductory chapter.

Finally, I owe a particular debt to my wife, Liz, in this and in all my work, for her support and her encouragement when things seemed overwhelming.

Peter Drysdale
Canberra, January 2000

1 Perspectives

Dominic Wilson and Peter Drysdale

INTRODUCTION

The role of the state in East Asian development has always been a controversial issue. On the one hand, neoclassical economists argued that three decades of extraordinary East Asian growth were largely the consequence of policies that let the market function and kept distortions to a minimum (Krueger 1995). On the other, critics of the neoclassical approach maintained that the close ties between industry and government and selective government interventions were critical to the extraordinary growth performance of many East Asian economies (Amsden 1989; Wade 1990).

The financial crises in East Asia have rekindled the debate over the appropriate roles of the state and economic enterprise across the region. With the Korean, Malaysian and Thai economies now clearly in recovery – and signs of life in Japan – and with extensive reform programs underway in almost every economy, there is a renewed focus on the role that governments and governance can play both in determining future performance and preventing future catastrophe.

The debate over the appropriate role of governments has surfaced both as part of the diagnosis of the recent crises and as part of the suggested cure. Just as there was no single story of East Asian growth, there is no single set of problems that contributed to the different crises. As in the earlier debate, however, it is possible to identify a set of common features that make comparative analysis useful. Crises in many economies owed their severity in part to inadequate regulation, problems associated with close relationships between government, business and the financial sector, ineffective corporate governance and sometimes outright corruption. Resolution of these issues has proved problematic not only in the region's developing economies, but also in more developed countries like Korea and Japan, as it has in many other economies around the world.

As part of the response to the crisis and, in some countries, as a consequence of structural reform programs agreed with the International Monetary Fund (IMF), governments across the region are redefining the role of state in a whole range of areas of the economy. The focus of reforms is less on whether there should be more or less government involvement in the economy and more on what roles government should play and how it should fulfil them.

These reform processes are altering the boundaries between the government and the rest of the economy in complex ways. In some cases, governments are seeking to reduce the level of direct intervention in the economy, through privatisation, reduction of restrictions on foreign investment, or the dismantling of state-run businesses. In other areas, the crisis has seen increased government involvement. The intervention of the Hong Kong Monetary Authority in the local share market and the imposition of exchange controls in Malaysia are among the most dramatic instances of this renewed activism, but there are also less controversial examples. Widespread banking and corporate failures are prompting moves to strengthen government regulation of the financial and corporate sector and the resolution of non-performing assets and bank recapitalisation has involved the state, at least temporarily, taking effective ownership of large parts of the financial sector in several economies.

The interaction between these processes and reform and recovery poses some big questions about the role of the state and the economy in determining economic performance. This chapter is largely aimed at answering three central questions.

1. How essential were structural reforms to the current East Asian recovery?
2. What contribution can reforms make to reducing future vulnerabilities?
3. How important are reforms to the region's future performance?

To flag the conclusions at the outset, recent experience in East Asia suggests that the answer to the first question is that the process of recovery is largely cyclical, though some minimum commitment to reform appears to have been a precondition for recovery. The answer to the second question is that reforms can play a major part in reducing future vulnerability, though there are considerable problems in making the transition from where economies are now to where they want to be. And the answer to the third question is that successful structural reform *is* a central determinant of long-run growth performance, particularly as countries approach the technological frontier.

THE STORY SO FAR

Since late 1998, the East Asian region appears to have turned the corner in terms of macroeconomic performance, with the speed of recovery surprising most forecasters. Ross Garnaut (Chapter 2) gives a detailed commentary on the regional recovery. The Korean economy is now growing very strongly and significant positive growth has been recorded in Malaysia and Thailand. Recovery in Hong Kong and Singapore is lagging behind but a strong pick-up is imminent. Growth in the Chinese economy remains above 7 per cent, though there are concerns about a softening over the next year. Even the Japanese economy has pulled off three quarters of successive growth. Only in Indonesia are the prospects for a decisive recovery less clear, though there too the economy has stabilised.

The pace of reform, like the speed of recovery, has also varied across economies and across sectors. Masahiro Kawai (Chapter 13) provides an assessment of progress in financial and corporate sector restructuring. Much of the progress in reform to date has occurred in the financial sector. The Korean government has taken an aggressive approach to recapitalising the banking sector and the Thai and Malaysian governments have also made considerable progress with banking sector recapitalisation. Secondary markets for non-performing assets have been set up in Korea and Thailand and foreign bank involvement has increased. Regulatory oversight has also been tightened in some instances with new, independent regulatory authorities recently established in Japan and Korea. New regulations on loan classification have been introduced in Korea, Malaysia and Thailand, and new regulations on foreign exchange exposure have been introduced in Korea. In Japan, a more concerted effort towards banking reform was finally launched with a large capital injection in March 1999 in return for the submission of bank restructuring plans.

Outside the financial sector, progress with reform has been more mixed. There has been some progress with the removal of obstacles for mergers in Korea, liberalised foreign ownership laws in Korea and Thailand and new bankruptcy proceedings in Thailand in 1999 and in Indonesia. There has been progress too at the international level with proposals for a new capital accord published earlier this year and the OECD Task Force on Principles of Corporate Governance now complete. But significant obstacles to corporate restructuring remain in many of the crisis economies. In Korea, for instance, reform of the *chaebol* remains slow in comparison to the upheaval in the banking industry.

Overall, the story is one of considerable but patchy structural change. Once again, Indonesia's progress has been the most uncertain, with the political turmoil and the uncertainty surrounding the political transition impeding a coherent and rapid reform process. There are also indications that the Chinese authorities are adopting a more cautious attitude to reform, though renewed attention is being directed at financial sector weaknesses. Even in those economies where reform programs are most advanced, the process is a long way from completion and major challenges remain to be faced.

THE ROLE OF THE STATE IN THE ECONOMY

Although it is widely acknowledged that financial regulation, appropriate corporate structures, effective government and absence of corruption have important economic consequences, the links between governance and economic performance are not well understood. There is a growing realisation that institutions and policy processes matter, not just at a microeconomic level, but also in terms of their macroeconomic effects.

The recent experience of crisis and the ongoing process of reform and recovery in East Asia provides new material for this debate.

It is easily demonstrated that government intervention in markets can in many instances greatly worsen the allocation of resources. It is also true that governments can play important and constructive roles in addressing market failure and that shortcomings in government performance may consequently stem from sins of omission (failure to intervene) as well as sins of commission. Even in free market economies, governments play a central role in setting out the context in which markets operate. Although the analogy of the Robinson Crusoe' economy can be a helpful tool, it is increasingly clear that the institutional requirements for a properly functioning market economy are extensive. These requirements stretch beyond the guarantee of property rights and include the operation of an effective judicial system, the implementation of bankruptcy provisions, provision of a framework for competition policy and the regulation or supervision of a wide range of other economic activities. As David Nellor argues (Chapter 14), the smooth functioning of global markets suggests that rules of conduct are now required at the international as well as the national level.

In any market economy, the way in which governments provide this institutional setting creates the backdrop against which market incentives operate. In providing this backdrop, governments *can* fulfil several crucial functions, though the degree to which they actually *do* so varies enormously. They may provide public goods, regulate private activities to counteract other market failures, act to prevent or limit rent-seeking activities and the abuse of market power, and gather or disseminate information. At early stages of development, there may be a broader role for government to play in terms of coordinating investment activities, overcoming problems of asymmetric information, a role that Rodrik (1995) has argued was important in Korea and Taiwan.

The economic basis for governments to perform these functions lies in the field of welfare economics, which shows that markets may not always yield efficient outcomes where firms or individuals have market power, where externalities are important and where information is imperfect. Recent developments in the fields of asymmetric information, the theory of the firm and in regulatory economics have given us a clearer understanding of how these market failures can be important in reality. These developments also illustrate that appropriate intervention may allow governments to approximate the conditions under which market interactions do actually lead to optimal outcomes.

The importance of government behaviour stretches beyond institutions and policies to the processes of government. Policies and policy making need to be transparent and predictable to allow market participants to plan for the future. The risks associated with government action are an important part of the context in which investment, both foreign and domestic, is made. Public institutions must also be able to implement policy clearly and effectively. There is little point, for instance, in enacting sensible laws if the courts cannot enforce them.

The political arguments for effective governance are as important as the economic ones. Lack of transparency, arbitrary decision making, corruption and prolonged deadlock erode the legitimacy of governments. Where legitimacy is lost, the risks of widespread political and social instability, particularly at times of economic stress, are greatly increased, a point emphasised in Hadi Soesastro's analysis of governance problems in Indonesia (Chapter 6).

THE BUSINESS–GOVERNMENT NEXUS IN EAST ASIA

A large part of the task of providing effective governance lies in defining appropriate relationships between government, business and the financial sector. In most of the East Asian economies, close relationships between government and business have been common. Governments have often played significant roles, directly or indirectly, in the banking system and banks, in turn, have generally played a dominant role in corporate finance. In many economies, large, vertically integrated firms have also been common – sometimes explicitly encouraged by government. Aspects of these arrangements have been widely blamed for contributing to the financial crises. Yet it is important to remember that these arrangements also proved capable of supporting the extraordinary investment effort and the massive, unprecedented mobilisation of resources that characterised the period of outwardly oriented East Asian growth.

There are strengths as well as weaknesses to a system of close networks between business and government. At early stages of development, where there is great potential for large productivity gains, where investment returns are high and where market failures may be substantial, close relationships between firms, banks and governments may encourage investment by promoting long-term financing relationships and by lowering the cost of credit. Government involvement arguably helps to overcome problems of asymmetric information that can limit the ability of firms to finance projects and may have helped through coordination of the massive investment effort and provision of infrastructure. With ample scope for productive investment, the sheer quantity of investment may be the most important source of growth, particularly if the system is broadly market-conforming.

As development progresses, the risks of these kinds of arrangements appear to rise. As marginal returns fall and the scope for easy' productivity gains is exhausted, the costs of inefficient resource allocation may become relatively more important. With opportunities in the real sector decreasing in profitability, the temptation for more speculative ventures is likely to increase. As the costs of existing institutional arrangements grow, countries are then faced with the difficult task of making the transition to institutions that are needed for a more developed market economy, where innovation rather than factor accumulation takes over as the engine of growth.

In hindsight, it appears that three weaknesses arising from the system of business–government relationships in many East Asian countries have been particularly important. These problems are encountered everywhere, but have been particularly acute in some economies in the region.

1. Existing structures have not provided effective discipline for firms and banks. For market mechanisms to provide efficient outcomes, effective discipline is needed to prevent firms from abusing market power, to stop managers from exploiting privileged information and to ensure that resources are allocated to the most efficient firms and projects. In practice, this discipline can be provided in a number of ways. Vigorous competition from other firms, the threat of takeover through capital markets or monitoring by creditors can perform the function of ensuring that private decisions lead to efficient resource allocation. To the extent that monitoring has features of a public good, public authorities may also be required to play a regulatory role.

As Angelo Unite points out (Chapter 9), the tradition of family ownership in many East Asian economies and of large corporate groups in Korea and Japan has meant that capital markets have not been active in many of the region's economies. Much of the monitoring of firms has in practice been left to banks. Ideally, bank monitoring of firms through long-term relationships should prevent the kinds of agency problem that lead to inefficient investments. But in many cases, banks themselves have not faced sufficient incentives to discipline firms and related party lending has been common. Inadequate regulation and close links between government agencies and the corporate sector have made regulatory forbearance common. Akiyoshi Horiuchi (Chapter 3) provides a comprehensive diagnosis of the Japanese banking crisis, where these problems have been particularly prevalent.

With limited competition in the financial sector and government intervention to support weak institutions, the incentives to alter inefficient practices have often been low. The disastrous performance of the Japanese financial sector indicates the dangers this may pose. There is growing acceptance that competition can play an important role in providing the incentives for effective management in the corporate and financial sector. Particularly for economies where domestic markets are small, foreign involvement may be an important part of ensuring a competitive environment.

2. Institutional arrangements have encouraged inefficient management and allocation of risk. Much attention has been directed at the problems of implicit and explicit government guarantees to firms and banks, frequently grouped together under the general heading of moral hazard'. Exposure to risk is an important discipline in ensuring that firms face the consequences of their actions. By subsidising or suppressing the risks faced by firms, government involvement can encourage excessive risk-taking and over-investment. Problems of moral hazard have been most obvious in the banking sector but extend to other implicit guarantees of support and rescue. Heather Smith (Chapter 4) contrasts the problems that arose from these forms of government intervention in the Korean and Taiwanese economies.

Extensive government involvement in the financial sector, particularly where it underwrites risk, may also impede the development of alternative structures for risk management. Many of the region's economies have underdeveloped financial markets. In some instances, governments actively discouraged development of futures markets. Thin equity markets, narrow fixed-income markets and the absence of simple derivatives make it difficult for the private sector to engage in effective risk management and to hedge effectively.

   3. The interrelationship between government and business has sometimes increased opportunities for rent seeking. Where governments are closely involved in business activities, there is a risk that rent seeking or outright corruption becomes entrenched. Ross McLeod (Chapter 7) presents a strong critique of the Soeharto regime as government by franchise', by way of example. While McLeod may overstate the case, there is no doubt that increased rent seeking or corruption not only increases the inefficiency of resource allocation, but may also undermine the legitimacy of government and weaken the prospects for transparent and predictable policy making. In practice, the degree of competence and honesty in the civil service varies greatly across the region. The development of an entrenched and privileged group of rent seekers can increase the fragility of the political system and may inhibit the smooth transfer of political power in crises or a vigorous reform process. The Korean and Thai cases where that transfer occurred naturally through the electoral process provide a stark contrast to the painful transition process still underway in Indonesia. Less dramatically, the difficulty of insulating the Japanese political process from powerful sectional interests or of ensuring genuine political turnover has contributed to policy deadlock there.

THE ROLE OF REFORM AND RECOVERY IN EAST ASIA

This brief consideration of the conceptual issues now permits more detailed answers to the three original questions.

The role of reform in recent macroeconomic performance

It is hard to argue that the recent recovery across the region reflects the impact of reforms already undertaken in the crisis economies. Reform programs are far from complete and the recovery in many economies is now well underway. In Korea, for instance, where recovery has been most rapid, the quantity of outstanding non-performing loans is still large and debt–equity ratios remain high.

   Although a large component of improved regional economic performance represents a cyclical recovery from the deep recessions of 1998, recent reforms have played an important role in *enabling* macroeconomic recovery. Some immediate action in the banking sector was a precondition for mitigating the problems of disintermediation and credit rationing that impeded the recovery in its early stages. But the influence of reform process has been broader. Although completion of the reforms themselves has not been necessary for recovery, some commitment to structural reforms and to credible economic management does appear to have been a prerequisite for a return of confidence and for the sharp rebound in domestic spending in the recovering economies. Those countries that have rebounded most sharply, Korea and Thailand, established that confidence swiftly, electing new governments that were firmly committed to structural change. In Japan too, recovery was preceded by a more vigorous government commitment to cleaning up the financial sector. By contrast, where the reform process has been less certain, as in Indonesia, foreign capital has been slower to return and the recovery has not yet appeared.

The notion that a credible reform commitment may play a role in current performance is consistent with forward-looking economic behaviour. The credible foreshadowing of reforms is sufficient to affect macroeconomic activity even before the impacts of the reforms themselves are felt. But the ability to reap benefits from announcing reforms suggests that there may be problems of time consistency in government commitments to reform. In Korea, in particular, the speed of recovery has raised concerns that the pressure for difficult reforms may ease. The false dawn' in Japan in 1996, when the economy recovered, only to stumble again, indicates that postponing the resolution of underlying problems is rarely costless and that governments that cannot deliver on reform are eventually punished.

The role of reforms in reducing vulnerability

The fact that macroeconomic recovery has been possible, largely independently of the completion of structural reforms, says much about the nature of the links between governance and economic performance. An important thrust of structural reform is concerned with reducing future vulnerability. It is possible, and well demonstrated by East Asian performance, to record strong economic performance even in the presence of severe structural weaknesses. Even where these weaknesses do not clearly affect performance in good times, they are likely to increase the economy's fragility to disturbances and to raise the cost of those disturbances when they occur. These problems were evident in East Asia, where economies that had histories of very strong macroeconomic performance did not prove robust to shocks. Those economies, like Singapore and Hong Kong, where financial sector weaknesses were less severe, generally found themselves less seriously affected by the crises, as Christopher Findlay, Cheng Yuk-shing and Chia Siow Yue (Chapter 11) point out.

Creating institutions that are robust under pressure is also important to how effectively economic management can tackle crises and recovery. In Indonesia, where governance was weakest, the system collapsed under stress. Initial government responses to the crisis were erratic and the lack of confidence in the political system's ability to deliver results was central to the scale of capital flight. The fragility of the political system in the face of a large downturn also explains why reform and recovery efforts have been slow and frustrating. It is no coincidence that it was here that economic problems turned into systemic crisis. Less dramatically, the Japanese decade of stagnation also indicates the problems of weak governance in responding to shocks. The asset price collapse of the early 1990s has had a much larger and more persistent impact on the Japanese economy than similar shocks in other economies, largely because of the difficulties of delivering the necessary adjustments through the existing system.

Regardless of its broader impact, there is little doubt that proposed reforms, particularly those related to the financial sector, should significantly reduce the vulnerability of affected economies to the kinds of deep crises that they have recently experienced. Dominic Wilson (Chapter 12) discusses a range of policy options to reduce future vulnerability to international capital flows. The pressure to address these vulnerabilities is one of the more important beneficial side effects of the crises. Identifying and tackling vulnerabilities in advance is problematic, since weaknesses are generally hidden in the booms that precede crises and pressure to address them when times are good is inevitably weaker. Given the different starting points, it is natural that details of the reform paths will differ across countries. In Thailand, for instance, the private sector and international banks have played a larger role in bank recapitalisation than elsewhere, as Bhanupong Nidhiprabha and Peter Warr (Chapter 5) note.

The impact of reforms on long-term performance

While short-term recovery has proceeded ahead of reforms, it is increasingly clear that long-term growth prospects are affected by structural weaknesses. There is now considerable empirical evidence linking the quality of institutions to economic performance. Cross-country regressions that examine the links between growth and measures of institutional quality (the quality of the bureaucracy, risk of expropriation and level of corruption) strongly support the notion that countries with stronger governance record higher long-term growth, all else being equal (Knack and Keefer 1995; Easterly and Levine 1997). This appears to be true not only because vulnerabilities can lead to deep crises, but also because trend growth appears to be adversely affected, particularly as economies exhaust potential for catch-up' growth.

There is no doubt that strong growth can also be achieved against a background of structural weakness. Even the extraordinary corruption of the Soeharto era did not prevent a long period of impressive growth. The constraints on growth posed by structural problems are weaker, the further an economy is from its technological frontier, when there is ample scope for productivity improvements despite structural inadequacies. But as returns on investment fall and the burden of growth shifts from accumulation to innovation, the constraints of institutional and policy weaknesses are likely to become more binding. Japan provides a clear example of how structural weaknesses can contribute to stagnant productivity performance. The Japanese case also indicates that the costs of delaying the reform process appear to rise with time. It is now widely accepted that increased competition and reform of the incentive structures facing firms and banks in Japan is a prerequisite to raising trend growth. By the same token, reforms elsewhere in the region should not only reduce vulnerability but improve future growth performance and prevent a sharp decline in growth rates as development continues.

PROBLEMS OF TRANSITION

Although the crisis presents new opportunities, the task of structural reform and the redefinition of the role of the state and economic enterprise in East Asia present considerable challenges for government policy.

At a general level, desirable directions for reform are relatively easy to identify. Financial sectors should be recapitalised, non-performing loans resolved and corporate sectors restructured. Competition policy should be strengthened and more effective systems of prudential regulation and risk management put in place. A move away from quantitative controls to market instruments in credit allocation and capital account restrictions, and the removal of obstacles to mergers and foreign participation in the financial and non-financial corporate sector are probably also desirable. In some countries, civil service reform and reform of the judicial system may be necessary if new regulations are to be effectively implemented and enforced. Even the Malaysian experiment, described by Prema-chandra Athukorala (Chapter 8), conforms to this broad pattern despite the flirtation with capital controls.

It is one thing to be able to list an ideal' set of regulations – it is quite another to design a path that can take a country to them. There is a tendency in recommending reforms to overlook the difficulties of transition that any reform process implies, particularly one that envisions a comprehensive overhaul of large sections of the economy. Particularly in the least developed economies, where problems are deeply entrenched and interconnected and where existing institutions are a long way from best practice, issues of sequencing and timing take on critical importance.

In China, for instance, Yiping Huang and Ligang Song (Chapter 10) identify the problems in existing relationships between unproductive state-owned enterprises and state-owned banks under pressure by government to continue lending to non-performing borrowers. It is relatively straightforward to sketch the features of a desired end-point: a system of tougher regulation, a banking system at arms length from the corporate sector, the resolution of non-performing loans successfully completed and state-owned enterprises either returned to solvency or closed down. It is much harder to be confident about how the government should move to improve the current situation. What should the government do first? How can the achievement of long-term goals be reconciled with short-term stability? How much control does the government actually have? What is politically feasible? These kind of questions need clear answers if a sensible reform process is to be implemented.

The reality is that governments in general have limited capacity and limited control over the reform process. The technical and institutional capacity needed to deliver effective government supervision must also be built – a process that will take considerable time. International institutions and foreign firms can play a useful supporting role, but building effective local capacity will be important over the longer term.

It is also true that separate reforms are interdependent, with the success of reform in one area often relying on accompanying reforms elsewhere. For that reason, the inappropriate sequencing of collectively desirable measures can create new problems. In many of the crisis economies, greater competition in the financial sector in the absence of adequate regulation reduced the franchise value of banks for instance and increased the willingness of financial institutions to take risks. The loss of bank business from the internationalisation of corporate bond markets in Japan may have encouraged more speculative bank financing. And while a more open capital account may be desirable in the long run, capital account liberalisation in China against the background of current financial sector weakness would be ill-advised.

Throughout the reform process, a wide range of groups and individuals must be persuaded to make adjustments and, in many cases, to take losses of one kind or another. Reform always generates resistance but is particularly difficult when the capacity of the government to deliver outcomes is itself at issue. Where the political process is dominated by interested parties, the very same institutional weaknesses that reforms must address may hamper the ability to carry out the reform process. The Japanese political system, for instance, has proved itself slow and resistant to reforming itself.

Resolving these transitional issues is not a peripheral problem, but the key to successful reform. The financial crises have inflicted a great deal of pain on the East Asian region. As other countries have learnt, the opportunities to take tough decisions in the wake of crises are often greater than at any other time. With many of the characteristics that supported East Asia's last high-growth period still in place (high savings, outward orientation and disciplined macroeconomic management), successful reforms undertaken now can play a large part in ensuring that the current recovery marks a return to sustained and stable growth throughout the region.

REFERENCES

Amsden, Alice (1989) *Asia's Next Giant: South Korea and late industrialization*, New York: Oxford University Press.

Easterly, William and Levine, Ross (1997) Africa's growth tragedy: Policies and ethnic divisions', *Quarterly Journal of Economics* 112 (November): 1203–50.

Knack, Stephen and Keefer, Philip (1995) Institutions and economic performance: Cross-country tests using alternative institutional measures', *Economics and Politics* 7(3): 207–27.

Krueger, Anne (1995) The East Asian experience and endogenous growth theory',
in Takatoshi Ito and Anne Krueger (eds) *Growth Theories in the Light of the East
Asian Experience,* Chicago: Chicago University Press.
Rodrik, Dani (1995) Getting interventions right: How South Korea and Taiwan
grew rich', *Economic Policy* 20: 53–97.
Wade, Robert (1990) *Governing the Market: Economic theory and the role of
government in East Asian industrialization,* Princeton: Princeton University Press.

2 East Asia after the financial crisis

Ross Garnaut

The financial crisis that attracted international notice with the devaluation of the Thai baht reached its greatest intensity in mid-1998. It pushed most Western Pacific economies into recession in 1998, several more deeply than ever before recorded in modern statistics.

The financial crisis began to lift in the third quarter of 1998, as swiftly as it had arrived. The recovery was reflected in financial markets, output and trade. Its effects were reinforced by interaction across regional economies, just as the earlier negative interaction had reinforced contractionary tendencies in each of the Western Pacific economies.

This chapter begins with a description of the recovery, referring to a series of charts on output, trade and financial markets. This is followed by discussion of the economic legacy of the crisis, including the legacy of ideas about economic policy and about the multilateral and regional economic infrastructure. A final section mentions a larger political legacy.

THE LEGACY

By the end of the third quarter of 1998, East Asian recovery was well established, with positive growth in every economy that experienced recession through or following the crisis.

It was a relatively strong recovery after a deep but short down-turn. The data are summarised in Figures 2.1 and 2.2, and the country detail in Figures 2.3 to 2.8. Within the general pattern of large declines in growth and quick and strong recovery, there were marked variations across countries.

Japan's growth on a year-to-quarter basis was negative in late 1997, and emerged into positive territory early in the first quarter of 1999. Japan was different from the developing East Asian economies, since recession during the East Asian crisis followed a long period of subdued growth in the 1990s. Japan's lower average growth in the 1990s reflected mainly the continuation of a long-term fall in growth potential, with the ageing of the population, beginnings of decline in the work-age population, reduced incentive to invest domestically with the lower growth trajectory and the internationalisation of investment opportunities. Lower growth potential was reinforced by the diminished opportunities for productivity growth that had been present in the manufacturing sector since Japanese industry had been operating at the international technological frontier. The decline in growth potential was obscured for a while by the boom in domestic demand in the late 1980s. The collapse of the resulting price bubble' in the early 1990s and the banking system's slow response to it pushed growth performance below trend for much of the decade, with some brief, stronger periods in the aftermath of several episodes of large-scale fiscal expansion. Output growth fell in the first half of 1997. This contributed to the weakness of the yen and to slow Japanese export growth which, in turn, helped to precipitate crises in East Asian economies with *de facto* or *de jure* dollar-connected currencies, including Thailand, Malaysia, Indonesia, Hong Kong and Korea. Japan was, in turn, affected by the contraction in output and imports in most other East Asian economies. This contributed to the exceptional depth of recession. Japan returned to year-to-quarter growth through 1999.

Few analysts now expect annual growth rates to return to the 4 per cent of the 1980s, but expectations have not yet adjusted fully down to the realities. Without major social change affecting labour force participation, the gradual decline in the labour force will depress potential economic growth. It is hard to imagine investment rising much above 25 per cent of GDP, which would cause the capital contribution to GDP growth to be no more than 0.9 per cent. Total factor productivity growth has been negative in the 1990s. The working through of the contractionary tendencies of the 1990s may be followed by a return to positive total factor productivity growth

Figure 2.1 East Asia annual growth rates, 1985–99

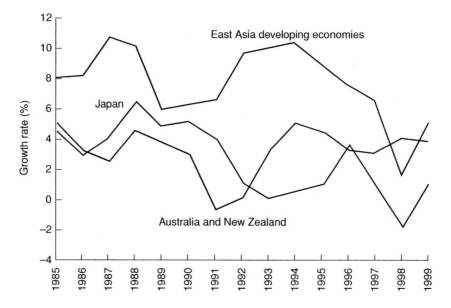

within the range of average levels of other OECD members – say, 0.6 per cent to 1 per cent. Putting these components together suggests long-term substantial growth a bit below 1.5 per cent. Above-trend growth can be expected only during the period of recovery from recession, in the absence of rather more radical reform of the low-productivity sectors than has seemed likely from the perspective of the late 1990s.

Japan has attempted to boost growth through the 1990s with unprecedentedly easy monetary policy and huge fiscal expansion. These policies are generally seen as having been ineffective, as reflected by the low average growth of the 1990s (1.7 per cent per annum 1991–7) and deep recession of 1998. If we take into account the reality of diminished growth potential, it is possible that domestic demand policies may have helped to lift average growth rates above the levels to which powerful tendencies to stagnation would otherwise have held them, although insufficiently, during the East Asian crisis. Low interest rates contributed to the weakness of the yen against the dollar in the lead-up to and the first year of the financial crisis, correcting during the East Asian recovery later in 1998.

Korea was a quarter or two later into recession than the Southeast Asian economies that had been damaged most in the crisis. When it arrived, the recession was remarkable for its severity and its brevity. Korean recovery was exceptional for its strength – the growth rate of the economy through the year from the depth of the recession in June 1998 was above the average for the decade preceding the crisis and it continued to rise through the second half of 1999.

Figure 2.2 GDP growth in East Asia, June 1996 – June 1999

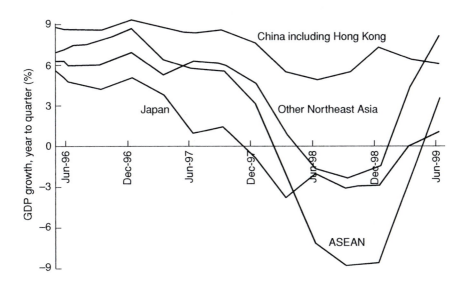

Thailand (Figure 2.4) was the first economy to move into financial crisis, the first into recession, and experienced greater loss of output than any economy except Indonesia. Recovery was weaker than in Korea, but still fairly strong. The Philippines, long thought of as a much weaker economy than any of the original Southeast Asian partners, experienced a mild downturn from which it has emerged through 1999.

Indonesia (Figure 2.5) received the greatest financial shock of the East Asian economies, and in 1999 experienced what was probably the largest loss of

Figure 2.3 Growth of Japan and Korea, June 1996 – June 1999

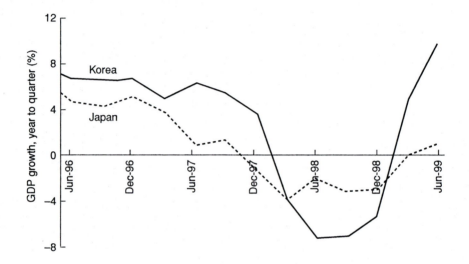

Figure 2.4 Growth of Thailand and the Philippines, June 1996 – June 1999

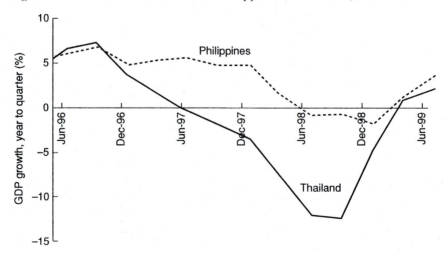

output in a year since the Second World War for a substantive market economy. (It is possible that China suffered a bigger loss in the Great Leap Forward, but the statistical evidence is not comparable.) Output stabilised and began to expand through 1999 from a desperately low base.

Malaysia was the third most deeply affected economy, stabilising and beginning to grow through 1999 on a similar trajectory to Indonesia. Unlike Thailand, Indonesia and Korea, it rejected any IMF recovery program. Its recovery strategy was distinguished by the fixing of the exchange rate, imposition of new exchange controls and fiscal expansion from the third quarter of 1998. But the rhetoric of policy was more distinctive than the reality, which was not so very far from the cautious approaches of the countries operating within IMF programs.

Australia in the mid-1990s was more closely oriented to East Asia than any other economy in the world in its export patterns, if China and Hong Kong are seen as a single entity. It is therefore remarkable that Australia was the only Western Pacific economy not to experience any economic downturn through the crisis (Figure 2.6). By contrast, New Zealand, despite its trade being buffered to some extent by its heavy reliance on the Australian market, went into recession in 1998. It has since recovered quickly and strongly.

The city economies of Hong Kong and Singapore are deeply integrated into regional markets for finance, goods and services. Hong Kong experienced deep and Singapore mild recession (Figure 2.7). Through 1999, output stabilised in Hong Kong and returned to growth in Singapore.

The Taiwan economy experienced lower growth but not recession through the crisis, and expanded at a rate near the average for the 1990s after mid-1998 (Figure 2.8).

Figure 2.5 Growth of Malaysia and Indonesia, June 1996 – June 1999

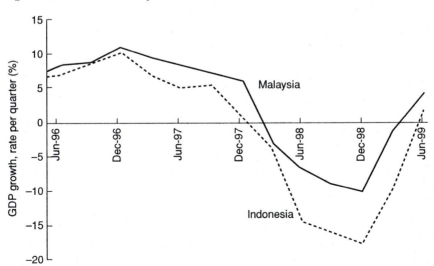

After Japan, China is the second largest economy in the Western Pacific, and the largest in purchasing power. Its policy response to the crisis was distinctive. The crisis came at a time when China's macroeconomic fundamentals were unusually robust: inflation low; exports growing strongly and supporting a large current account surplus. There had been high levels of capital inflow and, partly as a result of controls on short-term capital flows, almost entirely in the less volatile form of direct foreign investment.

Figure 2.6 Growth of Australia and New Zealand, June 1996 – June 1999

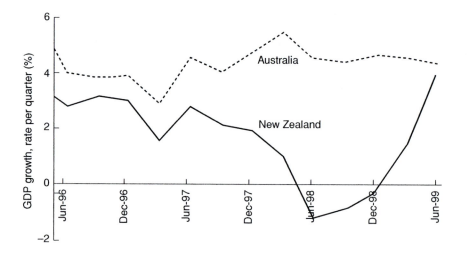

Figure 2.7 Growth of Hong Kong and Singapore, June 1996 – June 1999

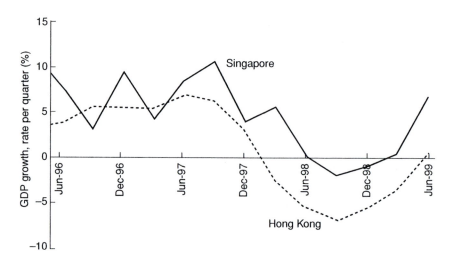

As a consequence of these factors, China had high and rapidly increasing foreign exchange reserves. China used these macroeconomic strengths to support the maintenance of a fixed exchange rate against the US dollar and a huge fiscal expansion. Growth sagged somewhat, although the fiscal expansion had a substantial moderating effect through the second half of 1998, when several East Asian economies were at the deepest points of recession (Figure 2.8).

One of the features of the long boom in East Asia that preceded the crisis was its association with rapid expansion of intra-regional trade. From the mid-1980s to the mid-1990s, over half of the huge increase in East Asian exports was to other East Asian countries. Rapid growth, trade and investment liberalisation and import expansion in each East Asian economy increased the export opportunities of other East Asian countries, fostering growth, trade liberalisation and import expansion in them. The growth in intra-regional trade went into negative in 1996. The decline in intra-regional trade growth preceded and helped to precipitate the crisis (Figure 2.9). The sharp contraction of East Asian imports from mid-1997 was an important cause of deepening economic recession throughout the region. The return to strong growth in intra-regional imports through 1999 was an indicator of and added impetus to recovery.

Figure 2.8 Growth of China and Taiwan, June 1996 – June 1999

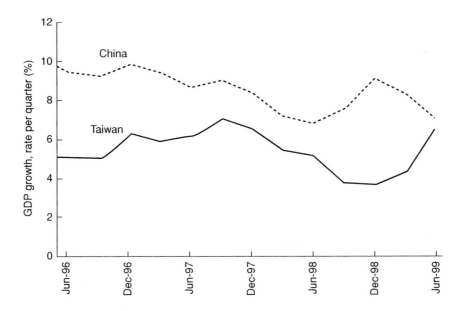

There was also strong recovery in East Asian financial markets from the September quarter of 1998. Table 2.1 describes changes in the value in US dollars of Asia Pacific stock market indexes from the eve of the crises (30 June 1997) to the depths of financial weakness (30 September 1998), and from then to the third quarter of 1999. Depreciating currencies and stock market collapses led to large falls in the international value indexes in the first five quarters of the crisis in all of the economies which experienced recession, with less extreme falls also in Taiwan and Australia. The declines were most severe in Southeast Asia and Korea, typically to one-quarter of their pre-crisis values, and to about one-tenth in Indonesia. The recovery from September 1998 had restored virtually all of the international value lost in the crisis in Northeast Asia, including Korea, and in Singapore, by the third quarter of 1999. By then, recovery had taken the international value indexes in the larger Southeast Asian economies back to about a half (Thailand, Malaysia, the Philippines) or a third (Indonesia) of their pre-crisis levels.

China's strategy of fiscal expansion and maintenance of the exchange rate peg against the US dollar could not have been sustained if the period of stagnation and weak financial markets in the rest of East Asia had exceeded more than a couple of years. The recovery in output growth, trade and currencies elsewhere in East Asia, and especially in Northeast Asia, validated the strategy. Appreciation of other East Asian currencies against the dollar had the effect of depreciating the real effective exchange rate of China (and Hong Kong), beyond the point where the appreciation in the first year of crisis had been reversed by the third quarter of 1999 (Figure 2.10). China's exports have grown at almost twice the rate of GDP since economic reform began in 1978, but declined with the contraction of intra-regional trade and

Figure 2.9 Intra-regional trade growth, June 1996 – June 1999

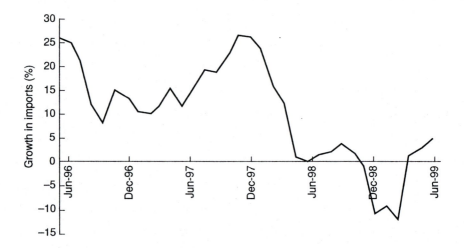

the strong renminbi in the first year of the crisis. The sharp decline in Chinese exports to East Asia reversed from about September 1998 (Figure 2.11), easing the pressure that the macroeconomic strategy was placing on the external sector of the economy.

THE ECONOMIC LEGACY OF CRISIS

With recession having been relatively short, the total loss of output associated with the crisis was much less than had been anticipated through 1998. Korean output was expanding at a rate above long-term sustainable levels by late 1999, and is in the process of recovering some of the output lost in the crisis. By the same time, there were signs that several other economies would also grow above trend rates for a while.

Earlier fears that East Asia, like Latin America after the debt crisis of the early 1980s, would experience low growth for a long period were not warranted by the reality.

Some economies, China more than others, emerged from the crisis with higher levels of public debt and financially weakened business sectors that have the potential to hold growth below trend for some years.

Indonesia provided a tragic extreme case of economic loss, mainly because the economic problems fed into dislocation of the political system to prolong low growth from a low base, with long-term consequences that still could not be readily foreseen in late 1999.

Table 2.1   Index of international capital stockmarket values, 30 June 1997 – 24 August 1999

Value of US$100 invested on the stock exchange on 30 September 1998			
Market	30-Jun-97	30-Sep-98	24-Aug-99
Northeast Asia			
Hong Kong	192	100	173
Seoul	385	100	348
Shanghai	100	100	133
Taipei	178	100	126
Tokyo	182	100	165
Southeast Asia			
Bangkok	357	100	180
Jakarta	1111	100	300
Kuala Lumpur	435	100	208
Manila	385	100	198
Singapore	250	100	226
Other Pacific			
Auckland	197	100	130
New York	98	100	144
Sydney	133	100	126
Toronto	127	100	130

The most important economic legacy of the crisis, more important than the loss of output in the crisis and in some countries slow recovery, was felt through ideas about economic policy and economic institutions. The legacy was complex, and varied a great deal across countries.

The crisis had macroeconomic origins, and left an important legacy of thought about macroeconomic policy. It reminded public policy managers and private investors of the speed limits of demand expansion. For some time, the settings of monetary policy were going to be more cautious than they became in the 1990s. In particular, there was greater awareness that the major Southeast Asian economies, with lower savings rates, a history of lower investment in education, and less structural flexibility, could not sustain growth at the high rates of the Northeast Asian economies in their periods of most rapid expansion.

Once crisis struck, there was a tendency for demand policies to be tightened excessively. The effects of the mutually reinforcing contractionary tendencies were underestimated and, except in China, Japan, Taiwan and Australia, exacerbated by demand policies. Such over-reaction is less likely in a future crisis as a result of the recent experience.

The fixed but adjustable exchange rates against the US dollar that were common prior to the crisis were unsuitable to the circumstances of the mid-1990s. Authorities moved towards floating rates (Thailand, Singapore, the Philippines, Indonesia, Korea, Taiwan), or committed themselves more firmly to a fixed rate (China and Malaysia). None was comfortable with the variability of floating rates, but all were weary of the risks of the old adjustable pegs. It is likely that the only exchange rate pegs that will survive for long periods

Figure 2.10   Real exchange rate, Greater China, August 1997 – August 1999

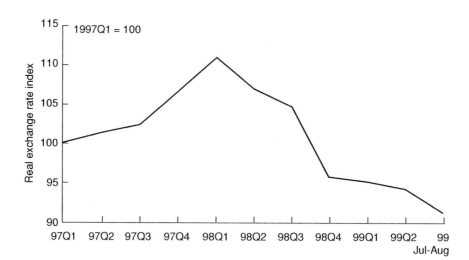

after the crisis would be supported by the non-discretionary monetary policies embodied in currency boards. Hong Kong remained firmly committed to its peg to the US dollar within a currency board system, but the depth of the Hong Kong recession was not persuasive to others after the crisis. The alternative was floating rates with more or less intervention from the authorities. The post-crisis trends in thought made floating rates rather than fixed rates with non-discretionary monetary policies the more likely destination of Malaysia and China.

It is of interest and importance that financial crisis and recession did not lead to retreat into trade protectionism. The powerful momentum of trade liberalisation that had accompanied the decade of economic expansion preceding the crisis was broken. What had been a steady stream of initiatives in almost all Western Pacific economies dried up, with the important exceptions of Taiwan and China, which tabled offers of major liberalisation as part of their negotiations to enter the World Trade Organisation. But there were few new protectionist initiatives, and programs of trade liberalisation that had been announced earlier (for example in Indonesia and the Philippines) continued to be implemented. This was a remarkable outcome in these circumstances, and different from the normal responses of developed and developing economies alike under such severe contractionary pressure. It underlines the extent of the region's commitment to open trade, and augurs well for the restoration of liberalisation momentum as confidence in growth is restored.

Figure 2.11   Growth of China's exports to East Asia, June 1996 – June 1999

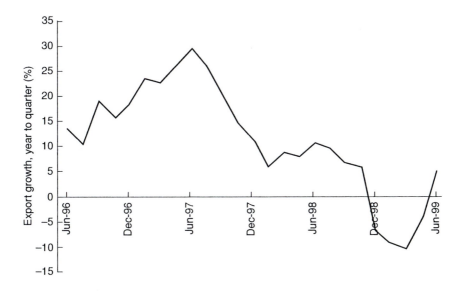

The most important protectionist responses to the East Asian crisis have been in developed countries outside the region, especially the United States. American protectionist moves have been in the form of proliferation of anti-dumping against East Asian exports that were rendered more competitive by exchange rate depreciation in the context of sharply higher East Asian trade surpluses with the United States. Continued strong growth and high employment dampened protectionist pressures in the United States, and the risks would increase if, as expected by many, US growth eased after 1999. The appreciation of most East Asian currencies against the US dollar from the third quarter of 1998 exerted some countervailing influence. The result of these conflicting pressures will have a large effect on the quality of East Asian recovery.

The legacy of thought about open capital accounts was more complex. The volatility of capital flows in economies with open capital accounts was recognised as a cause of the crisis. It was also recognised that direct foreign investment was less volatile through the crisis than bank and other lending, and portfolio flows more generally. The initial policy response in several countries was further to reduce barriers to direct foreign investment. This was a major feature of policy reforms within the IMF packages in Thailand, Indonesia and Korea, and was present to some extent elsewhere. The practical effect was to expand the role of direct foreign investment, most importantly in Korea. However, perceptions that foreigners were buying up potentially valuable assets at bargain basement' prices slowed development as recovery took hold.

The crisis left a legacy of greater legitimacy of controls on other capital flows in the developing economies of East Asia.

Malaysia in the third quarter of 1998 introduced new controls on conversion of the ringgit into foreign currencies and on the holding overseas of ringgit balances, as part of a package of measures that included fixing the (devalued) ringgit against the US dollar and new monetary expansion (Athukorala 1999). The recovery in Malaysian financial markets after the imposition of controls tended to validate the measures politically within Malaysia. There was some easing of controls – described at the time as temporary' – through 1999. Although the subject of much negative international comment at the time of their introduction, the controls do not seem to have had major positive or negative effects. Financial market and general economic recovery in Malaysia is well within the range of other East Asian experience. The main effect of the controls was heightened legitimacy for capital market interventions, in Malaysia and elsewhere, especially in Southeast Asia. Thailand re-introduced a range of controls that had been removed over the 1990s, but with much less public exclamation, and so far without large economic effects (Warr and Bhanupong 1999). Indonesia and the Philippines resisted domestic calls to move in this direction.

China and Vietnam entered the crisis with tight controls on capital movements. They were hosts to relatively low levels of potentially volatile international capital, and this insulated these economies against the regional financial contagion. The Chinese authorities became more cautious about further capital account liberalisation, and an earlier informal goal of capital account liberalisation by 2000 disappeared from public discussion.

But there was no lurch into substantially tighter and economically damaging controls on capital movements in East Asia. The legacy was of caution about further liberalisation and interest in modest interventions that seemed to have been helpful in reducing capital account volatility – such as Singapore's and Taiwan's restrictions on foreign lending by domestic banks.

The crisis left a legacy of heightened focus on improved transparency in corporate affairs and government–business relations, effective prudential regulation and generally on the importance of good corporate governance and competitive business sectors. Economies with institutionally weak business and, especially, financial sectors suffered much more damage in the crisis. The IMF programs in Thailand, Indonesia and Korea, and the old IMF program in the Philippines, placed a great deal of emphasis on these issues – excessive emphasis in the short term, given the urgency of macroeconomic adjustment. There has been heightened focus on institutional reform in the financial sector in other economies as well. Progress in reform was uneven and slow, but its elevation in the policy agenda seemed likely to lead to gradual improvements. This can be expected to make some contribution to reduced vulnerability to severe recession in the inevitable event of future financial crisis. It could also lead to some improvement in the efficiency with which capital is allocated, and so to some increase in total factor productivity and growth potential.

IMPLICATIONS FOR THE MULTILATERAL AND REGIONAL ECONOMIC ARCHITECTURE

The multilateral and regional economic institutions were called upon to play large roles in response to the crisis. The crisis led to considerable discussion of the adequacy of the international economic architecture'.

At the onset of the crisis, the International Monetary Fund was called in by the Thai, Indonesian and Korean governments to provide support in the form of foreign exchange and international policy blessing to enhance confidence. The IMF advice on policy responses was influential elsewhere, even to some extent in Malaysia where it was formally rejected. International liquidity was important to early stabilisation, especially to IMF stabilisation in Indonesia from early 1998.

The policy advice focused initially on fiscal and monetary contraction, as well as on a range (in the case of the Indonesia an extraordinary range) of structural reforms to improve the efficiency of the economy (Nellor 1998). Tight demand policy and structural reforms were advised partly on the grounds that they were necessary to the restoration of investor confidence in the troubled economies. The structural conditions' delayed the flow of liquidity, and in Indonesia's case, the high-profile failure of the government to meet them in January 1998 triggered the most damaging episode of low confidence and accelerating capital outflow. Throughout the region, by late 1999, there was a continuing legacy of structural reforms that had been influenced by the IMF and, as has been observed, these were bound to have long-term value for economic performance. But the structural reforms were not essential to recovery, and the excessive emphasis on them at the depth of the crisis was at best unhelpful and, in Indonesia, damaging. This was a view put to the IMF and the United States Treasury at the time by outside analysts, including from the Australian government and Reserve Bank. The episode seems to have left a legacy of clearer focus on economic priorities at times of crisis within the IMF.

Similarly, it is clear in retrospect that the international advice went too far on fiscal and monetary contraction early in the crisis – again, most damagingly in Indonesia. The misjudgement – by the national authorities in some economies as well as by the IMF – resulted from miscalculation of the extent of the recessionary pressures unleashed by the crisis. One source of miscalculation was the failure to take account of the mutually reinforcing effects of recession and the wide decline in imports across East Asia, at a time when more than half of developing East Asian economies' exports were to East Asia. The misjudgement had been corrected in IMF advice by mid-1998, and this met an important condition for regional recovery. The legacy was heightened awareness of the need for moderation in times of crisis, and greater awareness of the importance of economic interaction across East Asia.

There was some nationalist reaction to the IMF role in countries in which there have been IMF programs, and against IMF-style prescriptions in Malaysia. At times, these reactions were accompanied by a search for regional alternatives to the multilateral institutions as sources of funds and advice. This search has led to the development of regional activities that were complementary to the Fund, especially in the sharing of ideas about financial management, and technical assistance from advanced to developing financial systems. Principal amongst these were the Manila Framework' consultations amongst Western Pacific finance officials, which emerged from APEC Finance Ministers' meetings. Japan was the main source of emergency finance to troubled economies through the crisis. After some discussion of a separate Asia Fund', Japanese funding was provided principally in support of IMF programs where they existed, or directly through bilateral channels.

Asia Pacific Economic Cooperation (APEC) was not designed to provide crisis finance, and was criticised for being irrelevant to the largest economic issue facing the region through the crisis. In reality, APEC was a useful adjunct to multilateral institutions, through the Manila Framework', and in mobilising Asia Pacific governments' support for increased funding to troubled economies at the time of the 1998 Leaders' Meeting. Its main contribution, however, related to its core activities in supporting open trade: the high-level exchanges within APEC, and the shared commitments within APEC to long-term goals of open trade, were amongst the influences that helped to constrain protectionist pressures through the crisis. APEC was helpful in maintaining support for the World Trade Organisation through a period of stress in which that support could not have been taken for granted. The APEC support for the Millennial Round' of trade negotiations and for China and Taiwan membership of the WTO in 1999 were of particular significance, finally being effective in the aftermath of the Auckland meeting of APEC leaders.

There was considerable discussion of more far-reaching reform of the institutional financial architecture in the depths of the crisis in 1998. What remained one year into the recovery was a continuing interest within East Asia in sharing experience with modest interventions that held out the possibility of dampening volatility in the capital flows at low cost. There was also heightened interest in prudential management of financial systems.

A CONTINUING POLITICAL LEGACY

An economic shock of the dimension of the financial crisis in East Asia places huge strains on political systems, and has unpredictable economic effects through resulting political changes. The deep recession in Indonesia broke the back of the decades-old Soeharto administration, leading to a period of policy incoherence and political instability. The end point could be a form of democracy, or more incoherence. In Malaysia, the strains of crisis management contributed to an important split in the political leadership, raising important questions about leadership succession. Even in China, with economic performance less affected than in other countries, the slower growth contributed to some shift in the domestic political balance. It left a legacy of caution about some areas of reform that involved less employment in established state-owned enterprises, which could possibly have large implication for future economic stability. A complex political legacy of the crisis was bound to influence economic and other life in East Asia for some years into the future.

REFERENCES

Athukorala, Prema-chandra (1999) Capital mobility, crisis and adjustment: evidence and insights from Malaysia', paper presented at the conference on International Capital Mobility and Domestic Economic Stability hosted by the Reinventing Bretton Woods Committee, The World Bank and The Australian National University, 13–16 July 1999, Australian National University, Canberra.

Nellor, David (1998) The role of the International Monetary Fund', in R. McLeod and R. Garnaut, eds, *East Asia in Crisis: From being a miracle to needing one?*, London and New York: Routledge.

Warr, Peter and Bhanupong, Nidhiprabha (1999) What happened to Thailand?', *The World Economy*, vol. 22, July: 631–50.

3 Japan's bank crisis and the issue of governance[1]

Akiyoshi Horiuchi

INTRODUCTION

The Japanese banking sector has been struggling to find a way out of a morass of non-performing loans (NPLs) since the early 1990s. But the results have been disappointing. When the problem emerged in the early 1990s, both banks and government tried to conceal the fragility of the balance sheets. Their attitude was based on the optimistic expectation that the Japanese economy would soon recover from the aftermath of the burst of the bubble' at the beginning of the 1990s. They thought that economic recovery would quickly increase the prices of both shares and real estate, allowing them to manage the difficulties associated with NPLs in real estate and excessive investment on the part of borrower firms.

The rosy expectations of Japanese banks and the government were not realised. After a modest recovery in 1996, the Japanese economy fell into the long stagnation of negative GDP growth. The banking sector's NPL problem prevented banks from supplying credit to the industrial sector, aggravating the economic setback. In turn, economic deterioration worsened the business environment for borrower firms and increased the number of NPLs in the banking sector. Bank crisis and economic depression constitute a vicious circle from which Japan has yet to escape.

It is surprising that such a serious crisis has emerged in the Japanese banking sector, because conventional wisdom held that the Japanese financial system, centred on the banks, had worked efficiently to promote postwar industrial development. In particular, banks were considered to play an important role in the Japanese framework of corporate governance and in promoting industrial development. It was thought that they effectively monitored borrower firms via long-term relationships with them to prevent the agency problems associated with corporate finance (Aoki, Patrick and Sheard 1994). According to this view, it is a mystery why Japan's banking sector became so fragile over the last decade.

The purpose of this chapter is to provide an answer to this mystery from the perspective of corporate governance theory. Banks must play the essential role of monitor if efficient corporate governance is to be realised in a financial system centred on the banking sector. However, banks themselves are corporations to be monitored and disciplined. This is a case of Who monitors the monitor?'. The obvious answer to this question is that there should be a regulator to monitor bank management. The government has been assigned the task of regulating the banking industry, mainly to maintain the stability of the banking system.

The next question is Who monitors the regulator?'. If we fail to provide the regulators with effective incentives to monitor and discipline banks, the banking system is likely to be unstable, and to impose a heavy burden on taxpayers (Kane 1995). This chapter puts forward the hypothesis that Japan has not succeeded in resolving these issues. There is a vacuum of governance in bank management. This accounts for the fragility of the banking sector and, more importantly, the prolongation of Japan's NPL problem. The vacuum hypothesis helps us understand the implications of both the financial reforms led by both the big bang reformation plan' announced in November 1996 and the emergency policy the government has been implementing since 1998.

The chapter is organised as follows. The next section summarises the recent development of the NPL problem in Japan. The third section briefly explains the formation of the bank-centred financial system in postwar Japan. The fourth section, the core of this chapter, discusses governance in the Japanese financial system. This section takes up the disciplinary effects on bank management of market competition, the capital market, and supervision by the regulatory authority. These mechanisms have been prevented from working effectively mainly as a result of government policy. The fifth section explains how the vacuum of governance led to the serious crisis in the Japanese banking sector, and how the markets have responded to the crisis. The Japanese financial system has faced a crisis since late 1997. This crisis can be understood as a market attack on the vacuum of governance. The final section summarises the arguments and discusses how the financial reforms are expected to influence the Japanese economy in the context of the complicated nexus of corporate finance.

JAPAN'S BANK CRISIS

Table 3.1 summarises the disclosed data of NPLs in the banking sector. The Japanese banks began to disclose comprehensively defined figures of NPLs for the first time in March 1996. In March 1998 they further broadened the definition of NPLs to make the figures comparable to those of the United States. In addition, figures for problematic loans' have been reported since March 1998. Problematic loans' are loans that banks self-assess as more or less difficult to collect. The Financial Supervisory Agency has required the banks to provide this information in the process of bank examination.[2] Since there are at least three possible definitions of bad loans, and since the data only go back a few years, it is difficult to determine whether the worst is over. Both major banks and all banks decreased the amount of loan loss reserves substantially from March 1998 to March 1999. This indicates that banks wrote off a huge number of NPLs during this year. However, the number of NPLs in March 1999 scarcely changed from the number in March 1998. We can conclude from these facts that NPLs increased during the fiscal year of 1998, probably due to worsening of the macro-economy. Thus, the table warns us not to be optimistic about the current situation of the NPL problem.

Emergency policies

The huge number of non-performing loans is synonymous with a shortage of equity capital for banks. The major banks' self-assessed problematic loans amounted to 50 trillion in March 1998 (Table 3.1). If the major banks wrote off all problematic loans at once, they would have to inject a little more than 10 trillion to maintain the Bank of International Settlements (BIS) risk asset–capital ratio at the level of March 1998 (9.7 per cent).

Responding to this capital shortage in the bank sector, the government determined to inject public funds in order to help some banks strengthen their capital bases and to dispose of bank failures. At the beginning of 1998, the government prepared a special public account called the Account for Managing the Financial Crisis (AMFC) amounting to 13 trillion within the Deposit Insurance Corporation (DIC) following the enactment of the Emergency Law for Stabilising Financial Functions in February 1998. The AMFC was to be used to inject capital to solvent, but thinly capitalised banks'. In addition, another account of 17 trillion was instituted in the DIC to protect all depositors of failed banks. The government injected public funds of 1.8 trillion into twenty-one banks (eighteen major banks and three big regional banks). However, this emergency measure has not succeeded in calming the turmoil in financial markets since late 1997.

In October 1998, the Law on Emergency Measures to Revitalise the Functions of the Financial System and the Law on Emergency Measures to Promptly Restore the Functions of the Financial System were passed. The purpose of these emergency laws was to give financial authorities much wider authority to intervene in bank management to regain stability of the financial system. The laws also authorised the government to prepare public funds amounting to 43 trillion to dispose of failed banks and to recapitalise solvent' banks suffering from capital shortage.[3]

The package, based on the two laws on emergency measures of October 1998, has already been implemented to temporarily nationalise the two long-term credit banks that the Financial Supervisory Agency evaluated as having negative net wealth, the Long-term Credit Bank of Japan and the Nippon Credit Bank. The policy package also supplied capital of 7.5 trillion to fifteen major banks in March 1999 upon application by those banks, on condition they drastically restructure their management. Japanese banks accepted capital of more than 9 trillion in total from the government over the last two years. The capital injection in March 1999 increased the equity capital of those fifteen banks by 25.6 per cent, and pulled up their BIS capital ratio from a little lower than 9 to 11.3 per cent. The Financial Revitalisation Commission established by the Emergency Measures Law has reportedly been negotiating with other regional banks about injection of public funds since April 1999.

The injection of public funds has partly nationalised a core part of the Japanese financial sector, albeit temporarily. This policy, however, does not fully settle the issue of the fragility of the banks. The government

Table 3.1 Disclosed bad loans of Japanese banks, 1996–9 (100 billion)

	March 1996	*March 1997*	*March 1998*	*March 1999*
Major banks				
Narrowly defined[a]	218.7 (5.6)	164.4 (4.2)	145.2 (4.0)	
Broadly defined[b]			219.8 (6.0)	202.5 (6.3)
				203.7 (6.4)[d]
Self-assessed[c]			500.9 (11.9)	513.1 (12.6)[e]
Loan loss Reserve	103.5 (2.6)	93.9 (2.4)	130.0 (3.7)	92.6 (2.9)
All banks				
Narrowly defined[a]	285.0 (4.9)	217.9 (3.7)	195.3 (3.5)	
Broadly defined[b]			297.6 (5.4)	296.3 (5.8)
				302.9 (6.0)[d]
Self-assessed[c]			718.4 (13.0)	730.3 (12.2)[e]
Loan loss Reserve	132.9 (2.3)	123.3 (2.1)	178.2 (3.2)	148.0 (2.9)
Cooperative credit banks				
Narrowly defined[a]	63.0 (4.8)	61.1 (4.8)	54.5 (4.0)	
Broadly defined[b]				90.3 (6.7)
Self-assessed[c]			156.9 (11.6)	93.7 (6.9)
Loan loss Reserve	17.6 (1.3)	26.6 (2.1)	40.9 (3.0)	45.1 (3.3)

Notes: Major banks consist of city banks, long-term credit banks and trust banks. All banks includes major banks, regional banks and second-tier regional banks. (a) includes loans for failed borrowers, loans whose repayment has been suspended for 6 months or more, and loans with interest rates lowered below the BOJ discount rate at the time of the rate cut. (b) includes loans for failed borrowers, loans whose payment has been suspended for 3 months or more, and loans to enterprises undergoing creditor-assisted restructuring. (c) is the number of problematic loans' banks self-assessed following the supervisory classification, including loans that are non-collectable or of no value, loans where there are serious concerns about ultimate collection, and loans subject to specific management risk, which are not yet judged to be uncollectable but are deemed to require careful attention. (d) is broadly defined bad loans including bad loans of bank subsidiaries. (e) is the data for September 1998. It is not clear whether the amount of problematic loans' self-assessed by banks is underrated. For example, as the above table shows, the disclosed amount of problematic loans for major banks was 50 trillion as of March 1998. However, the special examination undertaken by the Financial Supervisory Agency (FSA) from July through November 1998 revealed that the amount of the problematic loans actually amounted to 57.4 trillion for major banks, nearly 15% more than the self-assessed amount. Furthermore, the FSA re-examined the problematic loans self-assessed by the regional banks as of March 1998 and the second-tier regional banks as of September 1998 and found that they under-rated the amount of problematic loans by 12% and 18%, respectively (Japanese Bankers Association, *Kinyu* 629 and *Nikkei Shimbun*, 3 September 1999).

will have to force those banks to restructure their management drastically to increase their market value. If the government fails to do so, it will incur capital losses on its stakes in the banking sector, and thereby increase the future burden on the budget. It will not be easy for the government to increase the productivity of the banks in the short term. And there remains the difficult task for the Japanese financial system of overcoming the current crisis.

PRECONDITIONS FOR THE BANK-CENTRED FINANCIAL SYSTEM

It is useful to overview the process of how Japan's bank credit centred financial system was formed, before investigating why it fell into crisis. During the so-called high growth era of the two decades from the early 1950s, bank credit was dominant in Japanese corporate finance. The dominance of bank credit was a rather new phenomenon. Table 3.2 presents changes in the composition of fund-raising by non-financial firms since the 1930s. The table shows that Japan's corporate finance has been dominated by bank credit since the 1940s.[4] In particular, during the high growth era, bank credit was the most important form of corporate finance. The conventional view that insists on the efficiency of relationships between banks and firms is based on evidence observed during the high growth period. This regime was produced by the policy of drastic restructuring of the banking sector in response to the severe bank crisis of the late 1920s, and by government policies to reconstruct the economic system immediately after the War. Now, the NPL problem since the early 1990s indicates that the regime has reached a dead end. The new bank crisis requires a drastic regime change in the Japanese financial system.

Restructuring in the prewar period

During the 1920s and 1930s, the Japanese banking sector underwent drastic structural changes after the bank panic of 1927. The Japanese government adopted a policy of reconstructing the banking sector by reducing the number of commercial banks. A new banking law instituted in 1927 prescribed a stringent minimum level of 1.0 million of required capital for banks. If banks could not satisfy the requirement within five years, they would be liquidated or merged with other banks.

After five years' grace, the Ministry of Finance continued its policy of reducing the number of banks with a view to increasing their scale. As a consequence, during the nineteen years from 1926 to 1945, the number of commercial banks was reduced from 1,420 to sixty-one. The drastic reduction in the number of banks was associated with substantial increases in bank size. The average size of regional banks increased thirty-seven times in terms of real deposits, and thirteen times in terms of real loans during the same nineteen years. This restructuring of the banking sector in the prewar period was an important precondition for the dominance of banks in postwar Japanese corporate finance.

Table 3.2 Composition of financing of Japanese non-financial firms (averages for periods, per cent)

	1931–40	1941–44	1946–55	1956–65	1966–75	1976–85
Retentions	37.0	28.8	37.0	41.1	43.8	58.8
Loans from private financial insts (bank credit)	27.3(21.1)	41.8(45.8)	45.4(31.7)	43.7(26.1)	45.8(23.8)	32.4(20.3)
Loans from government financial insts.	−0.9	1.2	6.8	4.3	4.9	4.4
Bonds	4.3	8.6	2.3	2.6	2.0	1.4
Stocks	31.0	19.5	8.7	8.3	3.4	3.1
Others	1.3	0.1	−0.2	0.0	0.1	−0.1
Total	100.0	100.0	100.0	100.0	100.0	100.0

Notes: The figures in retentions' are derived from the National Income Statistics, which is based on data sources prepared by the Economic Planning Agency. The data source of retentions is thus different from that of other figures estimated by the Bank of Japan. We need to treat these figures carefully. The BOJ stopped publishing this data in 1986.

Source: BOJ, *Economic Statistics Annual*, various issues.

Influence of the wartime controls

Some scholars emphasise that, for better or worse, the wartime controls implemented by the government formed the basis for the postwar financial system centred on the banking sector. The government started to restrict firms' ability to raise funds on the securities market, and to control the industrial allocation of bank credit in 1937. This restrictive policy weakened the function of securities markets in corporate finance. The government introduced the Designated Financial Institutions System in 1944. Under this system, each munitions company was assigned a major bank that catered for the firm's every financial need. The designated banks were to supply credit to the assigned munitions companies and to monitor their management.

Although it was abolished by order of the General Headquarters of the Allied Occupation (GHQ) in 1946, some scholars argue that this system was the origin of the main bank relationships that developed in the postwar period (Teranishi 1994; Hoshi, Kashyap and Loveman 1994). From the perspective of corporate governance, the validity of their argument is doubtful. It is widely recognised that the main bank relationship is important because banks can closely monitor their client firms based on long-term relationships (Horiuchi, Packer and Fukuda 1988; Aoki 1994). The Designated Financial Institutions System in itself, however, did not seem to enhance banks' monitoring abilities because the government insured bank credit to munitions companies, explicitly or implicitly. The designated banks did not need to worry about the creditworthiness of their major borrowers. The banking system was deprived of incentives to monitor borrowers under the designated system.[5]

There is some evidence that the deep involvement of banks in warfare weakened their abilities in financial intermediation. Suspension of government compensation for wartime expenses, amounting to 150 billion (17 per cent of GNP in 1946) in August 1946, was also damaging to banks. Table 3.3 shows the relative importance of bank loans compared with the amount of currency circulating in the economy. The latter is supposed to be a proxy for the level of nationwide financial activities. The ratio of bank loans to bank notes decreased during and immediately after the war, only recovering to the average level of the prewar period in 1955. This suggests how seriously the wartime controls damaged the banks' financial mediation capacity. Wartime controls did not directly contribute to constructing the bank-centred financial system but they did suppress the development of securities markets.

Postwar reconstruction of financial institutions

The Japanese government was very quick to reconstruct the banking sector immediately after the war. In particular, it is noteworthy from the corporate governance perspective that banks and financial institutions were excepted from the targets of the De-concentration Law of December 1947. This law was introduced under the guidance of GHQ to dissolve the organisations of *zaibatsu* and the monopolistic companies that had played important roles in the wartime economy.[6] In February 1948, the De-concentration Law identified more than 300 non-financial companies as targets for dissolution.

Table 3.3   Bank credit and currency in circulation

End of year	Bank credit (a)	Currency in Circulation (b)	Ratio (a)/(b)
1931	9,888	1,652	5.99
1932	9,578	1,727	5.55
1933	9,138	1,853	4.93
1934	8,800	1,938	4.54
1935	9,000	2,025	4.44
1936	9,500	2,193	4.33
1940	18,900	5,218	3.62
1945	97,600	56,600	1.72
1950	994,700	425,400	2.34
1955	3,195,800	694,900	4.60
1960	8,182,600	1,296,700	6.31
1965	19,217,900	2,697,600	7.12

Note: Bank credit is from accounts of all banks. Currency consists of the Bank of Japan notes, government notes and subsidiary coins.

Source: Research and Statistics Department, the Bank of Japan, *Economic Statistics Annual*, 1982.

The *zaibatsu* organisations were dissolved, as demanded by GHQ. The Holding Company Liquidation Commission, established in August 1947, designated eighty-three holding companies to be dissolved up to September 1947. Since the holding companies constituted the central nervous system of *zaibatsu* organisations, the dissolution greatly changed the governance structure of *zaibatsu* and other big companies, positioning major banks in the role of controllers of the corporate sector in postwar Japan (Miyajima 1994; Okazaki 1997). This process of reconstructing the Japanese economy promoted the formation of bank-centred corporate governance. As Table 3.2 shows, the reliance of non-financial companies on bank credit was particularly high during the high growth period.

Japanese banks are permitted to hold shares in their client firms up to a ceiling prescribed by the Anti-Monopoly Law. Thus, banks could mitigate the agency problem due to conflict of interest between debt-holders and shareholders by simultaneously taking on the roles of debt-holders and shareholders (Stiglitz 1985). Banks also played a leading role in the practice of mutual shareholding among firms and financial institutions.[7] This practice made it difficult for outsiders to threaten incumbent managers with hostile takeovers, thereby weakening the disciplinary mechanisms of the capital market. This does not necessarily mean there was no effective system of disciplining corporate management. Banks have been conventionally seen as monitoring and disciplining corporate managers in place of capital markets (Prowse 1992).

DEFECTS OF GOVERNANCE IN BANK MANAGEMENT

It has been argued that the postwar corporate governance structure based on bank credit worked efficiently to mitigate the agency problems associated with corporate finance (Hoshi, Kashyap and Scharfstein 1991; Aoki, Patrick and Sheard 1994). According to this view, banks discipline corporate managers in pursuit of efficient management in a considerably different way from the Anglo–American system where capital markets play dominant roles in corporate governance (Roe 1992). However, the NPL problem since the early 1990s reveals that banks are not always efficient in this role. The recent banking crisis has cast doubt on the conventional view that insists on efficiency of bank-centred financial systems (Weinstein and Yafeh 1998; Morck and Nakamura1998).

Corporate governance based on the bank-centred financial system does not work efficiently if banks are not effectively motivated to carry out their monitoring role. Japan has not succeeded in resolving the issue of how to motivate banks to be good monitors. The fundamental cause of the current bank crisis lies in this failure.

Generally speaking, bank management can be disciplined in the following ways:

(1) in the capital market where investors, including depositors, monitor performance of individual banks or the threat of hostile takeovers disciplines under-performing managers,

(2) competition in the banking industry that weeds out inefficient management, and
(3) supervision by regulatory authorities that prevents banks from taking excessive risks in the *ex ante* stages or forces managers of distressed banks to restructure their businesses in the *ex post* stages.

None of these disciplinary mechanisms has worked effectively in Japan. Deficiencies in managerial governance have led to inefficient management and, in particular, delayed responses to the management restructuring necessitated by growing NPLs since the beginning of the 1990s.

Lack of capital market discipline

The Anglo–American view of corporate governance stresses the importance of the disciplinary effect of the capital market on management. This did not work in Japanese banking, mainly because there was a wide-scope safety net that suppressed the incentives of investors to monitor bank management carefully. Another important factor is the practice of mutual shareholding involving major banks. The purpose of this traditional practice was to protect managers of corporations, including banks, from the pressures of capital markets. In this respect, the capital market was powerless to discipline bank managers in Japan.[8]

The mechanisms of the safety net in Japan

The financial safety net is a social system for dealing with distressed banks and distributing the social costs associated with bank failures among related parties. The safety net is widely recognised as indispensable to minimise the spillover effects of failures of banks and other financial institutions on the financial system as a whole (Diamond and Dybvig 1983). However, the operation of the safety net changes the *ex post* distribution of social costs associated with bank failures. This risk-sharing implication of the safety net decreases the monitoring incentives of depositors and other investors because they are either explicitly or implicitly protected from losses associated with bank failures (Black, Miller and Posner 1978). To maintain the viability of the safety net, appropriate incentive mechanisms are required to reinforce monitoring of bank management. The wider the scope of the financial safety net, the stronger the moral hazard incentives given to bank management, and thus, the more energetically the regulatory authorities must monitor banks to prevent excessive risk taking on behalf of depositors and investors.[9]

The Japanese financial system was covered by a wide-scope safety net implemented by the regulatory authorities. It was usual for the Ministry of Finance (MOF) to rescue or dispose of distressed financial institutions in close collaboration with the Bank of Japan (BOJ) and private financial institutions, particularly the major city banks and long-term credit banks. MOF's program protected depositors, investors in bank debts other than deposits, and even shareholders from the risk of bank failure.[10] MOF encouraged (or, more precisely, ordered) private banks to rescue their distressed peers. Japan did not have an explicit rule to provide public funds (taxpayers' money) to deal with bank failures. Major banks and financial institutions were required to bear the costs associated with the safety net. Needless to say, the burden was transferred to end-users of bank and financial services implicitly in the form of lower deposit interest rates, higher loan interest rates, and low quality financial services.

Probably the most important rescue program implemented by MOF before 1990 was the case of a merger between Sumitomo Bank and Heiwa-Sogo Bank in October 1986. Heiwa-Sogo got into difficulty during the first half of the 1980s. In 1985, MOF made a bailout plan to prevent the failure of Heiwa-Sogo from destabilising the Japanese banking industry as a whole. Finally, in 1986, MOF succeeded in persuading Sumitomo to absorb Heiwa-Sogo. Despite *de facto* bankruptcy, the closure of Heiwa-Sogo did not adversely affect depositors and holders of other debt issued by this bank. Sumitomo bore the cost of dealing with the distressed bank. On the other hand, Sumitomo was able to expand its branch network at once by absorbing Heiwa-Sogo's branches. This was beneficial for Sumitomo, which wanted to extend its branch network in the metropolitan area.

In other cases, MOF has placed its officers on the board of a distressed bank with a view to reorganising its management. Dispatching officials to a distressed bank may effectively be a signal to the public that the government has made a commitment to rescue the bank at any cost. This might have helped MOF persuade other banks to collaborate with the bail-out programs. This strategy is not always successful. A recent case was Hyogo Bank, to which the former chief of the MOF Banking Bureau was sent to conduct a management reorganisation. Despite the intervention, Hyogo went bankrupt in October 1995.

The BOJ has sometimes extended loans to distressed banks at the official discount rate, which is substantially lower than money market interest rates. After the rescue of Yamaichi in 1965, the BOJ used emergency loans (authorised by Article 25 of the BOJ Act) for the first time to support the Tokyo Kyodo Bank, established in 1995 to take over two failed credit cooperatives in the Tokyo metropolitan area. The amount of BOJ emergency loans increased abruptly during 1995 due to managerial crises in several small and medium scale banks (including Hyogo Bank), reportedly in excess of 1.0 trillion. [11]

Deposit insurance in Japan

At the end of the 1960s, some MOF officials were reportedly concerned that the coming deregulation in the financial service industry would increase the number of bank failures due to increased market competition. A system of deposit insurance was introduced in 1971 to maintain financial stability. However, the deposit insurance system was not actually used until 1992. MOF continued to implement the traditional safety net to avoid bankruptcy of banks and other depository financial institutions. MOF gave priority to the protection of weak (and therefore inefficient) banks over the promotion of competition in the Japanese financial industry, even after the introduction of deposit insurance. The Deposit Insurance Corporation (DIC) remained nominal for a long time. Its function, to pay off insured deposits in the case of bank failure, was limited compared with those of its US counterpart, the Federal Deposit Insurance Corporation (FDIC). In fact, the DIC has never resorted to pay-off. In 1986, the Law of Deposit Insurance was amended to strengthen the DIC. The amended law allows the DIC to support schemes to rescue or dispose of distressed banks by giving the necessary funds to the private agents involved. The DIC functioned for the first time in April 1992, when it supplied 8.0 billion to help Iyo Bank, a regional bank, absorb a small failed bank.

The DIC has been equipped with a means of paying off the insured deposits of failed banks from the time of its establishment. However, the government announced in December 1995 that they were not prepared to exercise it, although a quarter century had passed since the start of deposit insurance. In December 1997, the government declared that all investments into deposits and other bank debts such as bank debentures would be protected from bank failures.[12] The purpose of this policy is to calm people's growing concern over the danger of bank failures during the financial crisis following the bankruptcy of Hokkaido-Takushoku Bank and the failures of a few major securities companies, including Yamaichi at the end of 1997.

Of course, this commitment by the government is likely to produce further moral hazard on the part of bank management by weakening the incentives of depositors and investors to monitor bank management.[13] Even before the commitment, the long-standing wide-scope safety net had produced among depositors and other investors a perception that they would never be required to share the burden if their banks should go bankrupt. Because of this widespread perception, a government policy of paying off insured deposits without rescuing other bank debts would have resulted in an unexpected shock to the financial system, and exacerbated Japan's bank crisis. Thus, at the end of 1997, the Japanese government had no choice but to ensure that the traditional safety net was valid.

Limitation of the traditional safety net

Since the beginning of the 1990s, when the bubble' burst, it has become increasingly difficult for MOF to maintain the traditional method to bail out bank failures. This is reflected in the use since 1992 of the deposit insurance system to cope with the financial distress of individual banks, although the option of paying off insured deposits has never been exercised. The scale of the DIC is as yet limited, but its increasing use marks a significant change in the operation of the Japanese safety net. A reason for this shift is that, with structural changes in financial markets, the rent accumulated in the bank and other financial sectors decreased so that it became increasingly difficult to operate the safety net by depending on the rent. With financial deregulation, it has become difficult for the authorities to manipulate regulatory means to favour some financial institutions over others. For example, interest rate deregulation has reduced the meaning of branch offices for individual banks, making MOF's administration with respect to the branch network less important.[14]

As a result, the DIC began to play a significant role in dealing with troubled banks after more than twenty years' inaction. From April 1992 to May 1998, the DIC intervened in twenty-five cases of disposing of troubled banks and provided the banks participating in the bail-out schemes with subsidies of more than 2.4 trillion. In addition, the DIC is to be mobilised in thirty-five future cases of bank failure including Hokkaido-Takushoku. The traditional methods of dealing with bank failure have not yet disappeared, and many private banks still play an important role through collaboration with the regulators. However, the deposit insurance system will be more intensively utilised in future.

Disciplinary influence of market competition

As Nickell, Nicolitsas and Dryden (1997) show with regard to manufacturing industries, we can expect full-scale market competition to exert a strong disciplinary influence on corporate management by weeding out inefficiently managed firms. Regardless of its specific ownership or other financial governance structure, corporate management is disciplined by fierce market competition. It may be that Japanese manufacturing firms have achieved excellent performance not because they have been effectively disciplined via the bank-centred financial system, but because they have long faced fierce competition in the global market. Although this view remains a conjecture to be empirically tested, it is fairly well grounded. In contrast, Japanese financial services industries, including the banking sector, have been protected from full-scale competition by competition-restricting regulations. Thus, market competition has not worked to discipline management in these industries in Japan. This accounts for the current fragility of the Japanese financial system.

Role of competition-restricting regulations

Competition-restricting regulations, such as interest rate controls and restrictions on new entry into banking and other financial business through the system of compartmentalisation, conferred handsome rents on banks and other financial institutions. Although it has never been explicitly announced, the primary purpose of MOF's administrative guidance was to suppress full-scale competition in each of the compartmentalised financial businesses, thereby protecting the less competitive small-scale banks such as *sogo* banks, which converted to regional banks in 1989, *shinkin* banks and credit cooperatives. MOF's policy stance was often called the convoy administration'.[15]

Competition-restricting regulations are regarded as having contributed to the sustenance of the Japanese traditional financial regime in two ways. First, they produced the rent in the financial service industry that gave banks and other financial institutions incentives to refrain from excessive risk taking in order to continue enjoying handsome rents, even without effective prudential regulation (Hellman, Murdock and Stiglitz 1997). Thanks to the protection offered by competition-restricting regulations, even inefficient banks rarely went to the brink of managerial difficulty that is particularly likely to induce morally hazardous behaviour.[16] Second, the regulators were able to use the rents accumulated in the banking sector as a means of dealing with banks in financial distress. Specifically, the regulators relied on private banks' collaboration in implementing the safety net, and major banks faithfully bore a disproportionate share of the costs involved. This mechanism would not have worked had the major banks not enjoyed the rents stemming from the competition-restricting regulations. MOF also used the competition-restricting regulations to give private banks an incentive to accept its initiatives in the process of dealing with bank failures. MOF manipulated the regulatory means to do favours for those banks that toed the line and to penalise those that failed to heed their guidance. Specific administrative guidance based on competition-restricting regulations was an instrument for MOF to determine the distribution of rents among banks. Thus, competition-restricting regulations were strategically important for MOF to maintain the viability of the comprehensive safety net.[17]

Competition-restricting regulations were thus an ingredient in the Japanese traditional safety net. However, the regulation seems to be self-defeating. As has been pointed out, the rent could be an important incentive for prudent bank management. Nevertheless, but for a threat of elimination from the market, the incentive was ineffective. Competition-restricting regulations did not make good on the threat. Moreover, MOF's administration worked to keep the old-fashioned financial system intact in the face of rapidly developing financial services technologies. According to the terminology used by North (1990), competition-restricting regulations deprived the Japanese financial system of adaptive efficiency'.

Delayed deregulation in the financial markets

The Japanese government adopted a policy of gradually liberalising the financial system to prevent the unduly destabilising' impact of financial deregulation. In reality, this gradualism was synonymous with protecting vested interests in the financial industries. Gradualism suppressed the disciplinary effects financial deregulation was expected to exert on management in the financial industries, including banking.

Financial deregulation was promoted by pressures from abroad, particularly from the United States, rather than by government initiative. For example, the *ad hoc* yen/dollar agreement between the United States and Japan, which was realised under strong pressure from the Reagan administration in 1984, compelled the Japanese government to specify a timetable for liberalising financial markets.[18] Compared with international capital markets, Japanese financial markets have been slow to deregulate. The so-called big bang financial reform plan' proposed by former Prime Minister Ryutaro Hashimoto in November 1996 was the government's commitment to abandon the policy of gradualism. This sort of shock therapy' was needed to make up for lost time.

The impact of financial deregulation on domestic financial markets during the 1980s cannot be denied. In particular, major companies reduced their dependence on bank borrowing by issuing a large amount of corporate bonds on international markets. This internationalisation' of corporate finance induced the deregulation of the domestic corporate bond market from the mid-1980s (Horiuchi 1996). However, generally speaking, Japanese banks and other financial institutions were able to base their business on the huge amount of wealth accumulated by households. The gross amount of financial assets held by households reportedly amounted to 1,200 trillion as of the mid-1990s. The internationalisation of corporate finance exerted little influence on their business practices. Heavily protected in the domestic market, many Japanese banks surprised their foreign rivals by aggressive expansion of business in international markets during the 1980s. Since it sacrificed profitability, the aggressiveness undermined the soundness of bank management in Japan.

The role of regulators: another agency problem

Neither the capital market nor market competition were effective in disciplining bank management in Japan, mainly because the intervention of government (MOF) into the financial markets through the comprehensive safety net and control of deregulation process suppressed those disciplinary influences. This is a natural outcome of the current legal framework that assigns great authority and responsibility for monitoring bank management to MOF and the Financial Supervisory Agency (FSA) established in June 1998. The Banking Law authorises these regulators to intervene in the management of banks for the purpose of prudential regulation. The BOJ is also in charge of monitoring bank management, particularly from the viewpoint of money market adjustment.

Principal–agent problem with regard to regulators

As Black, Miller and Posner (1978) argue, the public delegates the task of supervising bank management to financial regulators. Ideally, these regulators maintain the safety net so as to impose the lowest social costs. Regulators do not automatically pursue this social obligation, however, because they tend to give priority to their own preferences over the policy objectives assigned by taxpayers through their legislators. If regulators fail to pursue their designated policy goals conscientiously, banks could aggressively extend their risk-taking activities, transfer this risk to taxpayers, and thereby undermine the viability of the safety net itself. Kane (1995) analyses how this aspect of the principal-agent problem between the regulator, banks, and tax-payers destabilises the financial system covered by the safety net.[19]

It is theoretically obvious that a bank's shareholders benefit when a safety net facilitates more aggressive risk taking by the bank. To limit this type of risk taking by banks at the expense of taxpayers, regulators are responsible for monitoring banks, using means such as requiring banks to keep their capital–asset ratios at sufficiently high levels. When asymmetric information hinders taxpayers' abilities to evaluate precisely regulators' behaviour, however, it is difficult for them to determine whether regulators collude with those they ostensibly regulate in pursuit of objectives quite different from those assigned by taxpayers.[20]

There is some evidence that regulators were ineffectively disciplined in Japan. For example, in 1954 MOF introduced the capital adequacy regulation, which required banks to increase broadly defined capital to more than 10 per cent of total deposits. However, MOF allowed banks to have capital substantially lower than the required levels. Consequently, banks, on average, decreased capital–deposits ratio from 6 per cent in 1970 to less than 4 per cent in the mid-1980s (Horiuchi 1999).

Horiuchi and Shimizu (2000) regard the prevailing *amakudari* practice in the Japanese banking industry of accepting ex-senior officials from the regulatory authorities (MOF and the BOJ) on bank managerial boards as a form of collusion in which banks provide regulators with job opportunities after retirement and, in turn, regulators assist banks to expand their business by increasing their leverage ratios. Since a higher leverage ratio implies a greater possibility of financial distress for banks and larger transfers of risk from banks to the safety net, the collusion manifest in *amakudari* ultimately undermines the viability of the safety net. Their empirical analysis based on data of more than 120 regional banks supports this hypothesis.

Disciplining the regulator

The principal–agent problem with regard to regulators also indicates the danger of forbearance policies. The regulator responsible for disciplining banks for sound management will want to conceal the existence of distressed banks and to postpone definite disposition of virtually failed banks. This forbearance policy induces those banks to undertake excessive risk taking, and increases the social costs of bailing them out to protect depositors and other investors.

National legislators could prevent collusion between regulators and banks from undermining the effectiveness of the safety net if they could precisely monitor the regulator or introduce incentives compatible with the policy objectives assigned to the regulatory agency. In reality, neither legislators nor taxpayers have access to all of the relevant information about regulators and their behaviour. Moreover, if those with access to relatively greater information are limited in number, they too can be seduced into a collusive relationship. In other words, we cannot neglect the principal-agent problem between legislator and taxpayers.

The Japanese people were not given incentives to monitor bank regulators until at least the beginning of the 1990s. And, although deposit insurance was introduced in 1971, it remained nominal until 1992. MOF dealt with the management problems of individual banks by forcing relatively sound banks (in most cases, large city banks) to merge with those on the brink of bankruptcy. Superficially, this policy did not create any obvious burden for taxpayers. In addition, the legal framework supporting deposit insurance did not include any explicit rules or procedures for injecting taxpayers' money into bailing out unsound banks. Until quite recently, the extent to which taxpayers were required to share the social costs of the safety net was obscured by regulatory practices. Because they were unaware of the actual costs of poorly managed banks, Japanese taxpayers were largely inattentive or indifferent towards monitoring bank regulators.

After the burst of the bubble' economy at the beginning of the 1990s, the growing number of NPLs in the banking sector and the clumsiness of MOF in dealing with distressed banks revealed the demerits of the safety net. As explained, the weakness of the safety net forced the Japanese government to prepare public funds to deal with the bank crisis. These developments made the Japanese people recognise the importance of monitoring the regulators' implementation of the safety net. As a result, in the late 1990s, the safety net in Japan has been revised considerably.

A VACUUM OF GOVERNANCE AND MARKET RESPONSES

This chapter has stressed the vacuum of governance in bank management. The hypothesis of managerial entrenchment was seen to be applicable to the Japanese banking industry. When they managed their firms independently from outsiders' control, corporate managers would (1) engage themselves in expansionism to display their managerial capability (Gorton and Rosen 1995), and (2) delay structural changes after their policy was found to fail (Boot 1992). These dangers of moral hazard on the part of bank management make the banking sector unsound. Were the dangers realised in Japan?

Was the 'bubble' a result of moral hazard?

If the hypothesis of a vacuum of governance is true, we must answer the question of why the defects of governance in bank management did not incur serious problems until the mid-1980s, and why they gave rise to the financial disorder of the bubble' economy in the late 1980s. It is a tough question. It would be too simplistic to explain the banks' excessive risk-taking only by the vacuum hypothesis. The policy error of continuing excessively easy monetary policy in spite of rapid increases in stock and land prices was particularly responsible for the financial bubble (Cargill, Hutchison and Ito 1997: 91–116). However, some structural changes in corporate finance seem to have caused banks to undertake morally hazardous behaviour in the late 1980s.

It is noteworthy that blue-chip companies substantially reduced their reliance on bank credit even during the high growth era. Table 3.4 shows structural changes in financing for major companies. Japanese blue-chip companies started to decrease borrowing from banks in the latter half of the 1970s. The relative importance of internal funds (depreciation plus retained profits) increased markedly.[21] This implies that Japanese big banks lost their lending business with their best client firms. Table 3.5 shows the big banks' lending to their main borrower firms' has steadily and rapidly decreased since the early 1960s. Lending to major firms, the best clients for banks, had already started declining as early as the mid-1970s.

However, a large amount of funds continued to flow into banks because the securities market was not sufficiently liberalised to provide ultimate savers (households) with investment instruments highly competitive with bank deposits. Thus, banks had an expanding supply of credit. Outlets for bank credit were the real estate industry and risky business related to property developments. Table 3.6 presents the movement of bank loans supplied by all banks relative to nominal GDP. According to this table, the relative importance of bank loans was quite stable from the mid-1960s to the early 1980s, staying in the 60 to 70 per cent range. However, the ratio began to rise abruptly in the mid-1980s, jumping up to almost 100 per cent at the end of the 1980s. The resurgence of bank credit seems to be an abnormal phenomenon representing the excessive expansionism of bank management. The abnormally high level of bank loans relative to GDP has been maintained since the beginning of the 1990s. Since the nominal value of bank loans includes the book value of NPLs, we need to discount the relative importance of bank loans during the 1990s. Nevertheless, the amount of bank credit is abnormally high, even at the end of the 1990s. This suggests that the Japanese banking sector will have to reduce further its scale of lending in the near future (Hoshi and Kashyap 1999).

Table 3.4 Composition of fund-raising by the Japanese major firms (average for periods, per cent)

	1960–4	1965–9	1970–4	1975–9	1980–4	1985–9	1990–4
Internal funds	22.9	37.5	35.1	45.8	55.3	45.2	87.3
Loans	33.8	36.9	41.6	26.5	16.4	6.4	5.2
Bonds	6.8	5.2	5.1	10.6	8.5	17.4	11.1
Stocks	10.8	3.8	3.2	8.0	10.4	15.8	4.6
Trade credit	16.2	22.7	21.9	17.7	9.6	5.0	-7.1
Others	9.5	-6.1	-6.9	-8.6	-0.2	10.2	-1.1
Total	100.0	100.0	100.0	100.0	100.0	100.0	100.0

Source: Bank of Japan.

Credit crunch?

The purpose of the emergency policies taken by the government since 1998 was not confined to stabilising the banking sector. The government was aware that restructuring bank management would decrease credit supply to enterprises, particularly to small businesses. So, the government injected funds into bank capital on the condition that the banks increase the supply of credit to small and medium-sized enterprises (SMEs) by at least prescribed rates. However, the banks into which the government injected capital have not accomplished the assigned targets of credit supply to SMEs. In this sense, the emergency policy has not been a great success.[22]

But should banks increase the credit supply? Not a few companies increased their leverage ratios during the bubble period' to support aggressive projects mainly related to real estate developments that were doomed to failure. After the bubble burst, those companies requested banks to continue to supply credit to survive the crisis. To rebuild an efficient industrial sector in Japan, the banks should not respond to the credit demands of such companies. Of course, there are genuine cases of enterprises that suffer from shortage of credit and they should be supported. However, it is difficult for banks to discern genuine applicant firms from hopeless ones. There is a danger that a substantial increase in bank credit will help the *de facto* failed companies survive, thereby postponing effective rationalisation in Japan's industrial sector. The conservative stance taken by banks is not necessarily to be criticised.

Delayed restructuring in bank management

As has been pointed out by Lindgren, Garcia and Saal (1996), the bank crisis is not peculiar to Japan. A surprisingly high number of countries have experienced bank crises since 1980.[23] However, Japan has taken too long to

Table 3.5 Importance of main borrowers for the big banks (per cent)

	Loans to own 'main firms' Per cent of total loans (a)	Loans to the big banks' 'main firms' Per cent of total loans (b)
1965	16.3	48.5
1970	11.7	42.4
1975	10.3	32.9
1980	7.4	26.3
1985	4.8	17.2
1990	3.0	10.4

Notes: A main firm' is one with which the bank maintains an intimate main bank relationship. The big banks in this table are the city banks and the long-term credit banks. The sample firms are those listed either in the first or the second section of Tokyo Stock Exchange.

Source: Keizai Chosa Kyokai

deal with this problem. The main reason for this failure has been the delayed response of bank management. More specifically, Japanese banks have hesitated to undertake the drastic restructuring necessary to deal with the difficulty of NPLs. The government was unable to take policy measures to force banks to reinforce their capital quickly in the face of increasing NPLs. Rather, it adopted a policy of forbearance to allow the *de facto* failed banks to continue operation. The forbearance policy induced *zombi* banks to undertake morally hazardous behaviour under the safety net, and thereby increased the social costs of disposing of bank failures. The peculiarity of

Table 3.6   Relative importance of bank credit

	Loans by all banks (¥1.0 billion)	GDP (¥1.0 billion)	Loan per GDP %
1960	9135	16681	54.8
1965	21860	33765	64.7
1968	32663	54947	59.4
1969	38178	65061	58.7
1970	44721	75299	59.4
1971	55250	82899	66.6
1972	69520	96486	72.1
1973	81428	116715	69.8
1974	90555	138451	65.4
1975	101314	152362	66.5
1976	112742	171293	65.8
1977	123901	190095	65.2
1978	137617	208602	66.0
1979	146950	225237	65.2
1980	157802	245547	64.3
1981	174727	260801	67.0
1982	193561	273322	70.8
1983	214439	285593	75.1
1984	238991	305144	78.3
1985	267759	324290	82.6
1986	300103	339363	88.4
1987	337686	355522	95.0
1988	372098	379657	98.0
1989	412344	406477	101.4
1990	439886	438816	100.2
1991	459147	463174	99.1
1992	470787	471882	99.8
1993	476863	476746	100.0
1994	477192	478841	99.7
1995	483466	489750	98.7
1996	485512	503787	96.4
1997	490434	504987	97.1

Note: The total loans supplied by city banks, long-term credit banks, trust banks, regional banks and second-tier regional banks.

Source: The Bank of Japan and the Economic Planning Agency.

Japan's bank crisis is not that banks suffered from so many NPLs, but that it took too long to deal with the problem.

Table 3.7 presents an international comparison of banking restructuring during the first half of the 1990s based on the BIS Annual Report (1996). This figure shows that, except for the United States, the profitability of commercial banks decreased in the first half of the 1990s compared with the latter half of the 1980s in all major industrial countries, including Japan. When we look at (1) the growth rate in the number of bank branches, (2) the growth rate in the total number of employees, and (3) changes in wage indexes, Japan was unique in the sense that none of these measures decreased during the 1990s against the latter half of the 1980s. Commercial banks in other major industrialised countries downsized or reduced their scale of business after recognising a fall in profitability during the 1990s. Table 3.7 shows that Japanese banks were hesitant to restructure their business in spite of decreasing profitability after 1990 in comparison with their rivals in most industrialised countries.[24]

How has the market responded to the crisis?

As long as financial markets investors believed in the government's ability to implement the safety net, the vulnerability of the banking sector fostered by the vacuum of management governance did not reveal itself. Although investors had recognised deteriorating bank performance due to rapid increases in NPLs, they trusted that the safety net would protect them from losses associated with ultimate bank failures. Thus, they did not need to differentiate good banks from bad ones in the capital markets.

However, as the NPL problem dragged on, the safety net apparently reached a dead end, incurring investors' distrust of the government's capability to bail out distressed banks. Major banks continued to be assigned by the government

Table 3.7 Restructuring in the banking industry international comparison, late 1980s to early 1990s

	Profit	*Branch*	*Employee*	*Wage*
Japan	−0.4	3.6	3.5	6
US	0.9	2.8	−4.4	−4
Germany	−0.2	−4.8	−6.0	−5
France	−0.5	−0.8	−4.3	0
Italy	−0.2	3.5	2.5	−4
UK	−0.3	−12.6	−13.4	−2

Notes: Profit (total profit per assets) is the difference between the average of 1986–8 and 1992–4. Branch is the growth rate of the number of branches from 1990 to 1995. Employee is the growth rate of the total number of employees from 1990 to 1994. Wage (the wage payment per total revenue) is the difference between the average of 1986–8 and of 1992–4.

Source: BIS, *66th Annual Report.*

the important role of bailing out weakened peers. However, the DIC has markedly increased its role in the framework of the Japanese safety net. This fact signals that the safety net, under which major banks bear the burden of bailing out distressed banks, is no longer functioning smoothly. It is at this point that the market starts to discipline bank management.

The Japan premium shows that Japanese banks pay a higher interest rate in the international inter-bank money markets. This premium reflects investors' evaluation of Japanese banks relative to their foreign rivals. The higher Japan premium suggests that investors are seriously concerned with capacity of Japanese banks to repay. Figure 3.1 presents movements of the Japan premium, defined by subtracting the London inter-bank offered rate (LIBOR) from the Tokyo inter-bank offered rate (TIBOR), with respect to the three-month dollar. The TIBOR is the average of inter-bank money market rates for sixteen Japanese and two foreign banks (Barclays and Citi) surveyed by the Federation of Bankers Associations of Japan, the two highest and the two lowest banks being excluded as outliers. Since the two foreign banks have enjoyed lower interest rates than Japanese banks during the last several years, the TIBOR can be regarded as the average offered rate for Japanese banks in Tokyo.

Figure 3.1 Japan premium (TIBOR–LIBOR) from the end of January 1997 to the beginning of October 1999

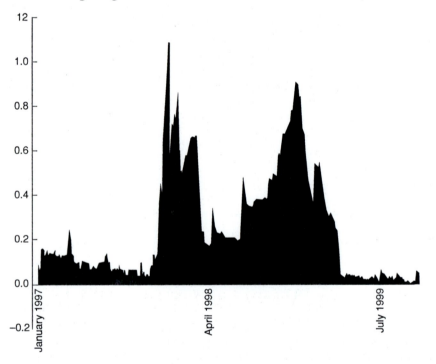

Sources: Bloomberg and Federation of Bankers Associations of Japan

On the other hand, the LIBOR is the average of London inter-bank money market rate for sixteen banks including three Japanese banks (Tokyo-Mitsubishi, Fuji, and Sumitomo Trust) cutting off the highest four and the lowest four from the average. Nowadays, the three Japanese banks are excluded from the LIBOR because the rates offered them are substantially higher than the rates for other banks in London. The difference between the TIBOR and LIBOR can be seen as a measure of the extent to which Japanese banks are negatively evaluated compared with their foreign rivals.[25]

The positive Japan premium was not observed until the end of September 1995. The Japan premium at 29 September was only 1.042 basis points. However, the premium jumped to 20.313 basis points on 2 October. This abrupt jump was caused by the announcement on 29 September that the US authority discovered Daiwa Bank's wrongdoing in New York. MOF badly mishandled the Daiwa case. This also contributed to market turbulence.[26] Associated with the increasing number of bank failures in the summer of 1995, this scandal triggered scepticism in the financial markets of the government's capability to stabilise the banking system by means of the traditional safety net. The abrupt jump in the Japan premium reflected the widespread scepticism among investors.

Investor scepticism about the safety net prompted the capital market to discipline bank management. Once investors lost confidence in the government's ability to implement the safety net, the capital market moved to fill the governance vacuum in bank management. To calm the capital market, the government should have quickly strengthened its monitoring and disciplining. Unfortunately, it did not recognise the developments in the capital market and failed to introduce effective measures to force banks to recapitalise. The disciplining mechanism of the capital market took place when most of the banks were overburdened with NPLs.

The financial turmoil triggered by the failures of Yamaichi and Hokkaido-Takushoku not only caused a resurgence of a significant Japan premium (Figure 3.1), but investors also started to differentiate among individual banks according to their respective performance. Table 3.8 compares the LIBOR (three-month US dollar) for Tokyo-Mitsubishi Bank with those for Sumitomo Trust Bank and Fuji Bank during the two time periods before and after November 1997. From 1 September 1995 to 31 October 1997, the market scarcely differentiated among these three Japanese banks. But from the beginning of November 1997, the inter-bank money market showed a stark differentiation. There was a significant divergence between the LIBOR for Tokyo-Mitsubishi and those for the other two banks, although there was no new information about Tokyo-Mitsubishi's superiority to the other two banks in the latter period. This change in the market attitude toward Japanese banks suggests that since late 1997 investors lost faith in the effectiveness of the safety net which used to make it unnecessary for them to evaluate the soundness of individual banks based on their respective performance.

It is not surprising that the disciplinary mechanism of the capital market was severe. Some criticise the capital market for its brutal way of dealing with distressed banks, even going so far as to argue for the suppression of the capital market to prevent its destructive impact on the banking system. However, they should note that the government has long neglected to fill the vacuum of governance in bank management, and that the capital market started to fill the vacuum at precisely the worst time. To avoid the destructive force of the capital market, the government should have taken action instead of leaving it to the capital market.

After jumping to a significantly positive level at the beginning of October 1995, the Japan premium remained positive until November 1997, when the Japanese banking sector faced a second attack, as shown in Figure 3.1. The government's policy of forbearance accounted for this Japan premium phenomenon. After the financial turmoil at the end of 1997, the government took emergency policy measures to regain financial stability. As explained above (Japan's Bank Crisis'), the government injected public funds' of 1.8 trillion into twenty-one major banks' capital in March 1998. Despite this emergency policy measure, the Japan premium did not disappear. Rather, it increased after the capital injection.[27]

The Japanese government apparently failed to bring about a positive response from the capital market. This was because the emergency policy measures from the beginning of 1998 did not convince investors that the government would truly abandon its forbearance policy, and fill the governance vacuum. The capital market required the Japanese banking system to be rationalised through drastic restructuring. However, from the investors' viewpoint, the emergency policy of injecting public funds into bank capital without properly considering individual banks' true performance was simply a policy to protect inefficiently managed banks.

In contrast to the first injection of public funds, the second, executed in March 1999 was persuasive to investors because the Financial Revitalisation Committee took a stringent line towards banks requesting funds. The market expected the regulator to abandon the notorious forbearance policy and

Table 3.8   Divergences of LIBOR (3-month US dollar) between Japanese major banks (per cent)

Period	SUMI-BOTM	FUJI-BOTM	JPN premium
1 September 95 –	0.00838	0.00446	0.10436
31 October 97	(0. 1985)	(0.01564)	(0.06733)
3 November 97 –	0.10000	0.10040	0.35279
6 October 98	(0.07342)	(0.07370)	(0.16539)

Notes: SUMI, FUJI, and BOTM are Sumitomo Trust Bank, Fuji Bank, and Bank of Tokyo-Mitsubishi respectively. JPN premium is the Japan premium defined by subtracting the LIBOR for Citi Bank from that for Bank of Tokyo-Mitsubishi. Figures in parentheses indicate standard deviations.

enforce drastic but essential restructuring on the banks. The Japan premium disappeared immediately after the second round of injection of public funds (Figure 3.1). Any proposed policy to cope with the current bank crisis will fail without a positive response from the capital market. The government and the capital market are struggling with each other to fill the governance vacuum in the bank management. If the government wins, the market will be calmed. If the government loses, the market will remain tough. This episode shows how the market can be an effective instrument not only for disciplining bank management, but also for disciplining the regulators in the financial system. The market mechanism could also be used to mitigate the principal-agent problem with respect to regulation.

CONCLUSION

This chapter is an overview of governance in the Japanese banking industry. Bank management has been independent from external control. Even the Ministry of Finance has not effectively monitored and disciplined bank management from the viewpoint of taxpayers. Thus, the question of Who monitors the monitor' in the Japanese financial system cannot be answered. There remains a vacuum of governance in bank management.

This is responsible for the delayed restructuring in the banking industry since the beginning of the 1990s when the problem of bad loans emerged. Only recently, in April 1998, the Japanese government introduced prompt corrective action rules. The government has also made public funds available to boost banks' capital on the condition that the banks submit an explicit time schedule for managerial restructuring. These policy measures seem to have at last induced hesitant banks to start restructuring their businesses. This fact in itself tells us that Japanese banks had no strong incentive to drastically reform their business practices on their own initiative.

To establish an efficient and robust financial system, the governance vacuum needs to be filled. There is no need for undue pessimism, because the process has already started. From the long-term perspective, the government has promoted full-scale financial deregulation. Responding to frustration with an inefficient financial system, the government announced the big bang' plan of financial reforms to promote market competition in the financial industry. This effort resulted in the important laws of financial reformation in 1998. Although there remains some uncertainty, these laws will push the Japanese financial industry nearer to the contestable market (Horiuchi 1999). It is noteworthy that non-financial firms have shown interest in entering into the financial service industry. Their entrance will make the industry more competitive. Further, the Japanese government made a commitment to pay off failed banks' deposits under the deposit insurance system in March 2001. This implies that the government will reduce the extent of the safety net. Large-scale depositors and other sophisticated investors will no longer be protected from bank failures. The capital market will be more active in monitoring bank management. As this chapter has explained, the financial markets have started to differentiate good banks from bad ones on the basis of their managerial performance.[28] Third, the Financial Supervisory Agency and the prompt corrective action rules that began in April 1998 signal a substantial change in government policy. The government acknowledges the importance of prudential regulation on banks and the corrective action rules will make government regulation more transparent and prevent the notorious policy of forbearance. The Financial Supervisory Agency is urging bank managers to reshape their ways of business as quickly as possible. This is a bitter pill for bank managers. But they will not be able to survive the current crisis without drastic restructuring.

Current policy is correctly directed towards filling the vacuum that has long existed in Japanese bank management. A well-balanced combination of market competition, a limited safety net, capital market pressures, and effective monitoring by the supervisory authority will regain stability in the Japanese financial system and promote efficiency in financial intermediation. The financial reforms are accompanied by substantial changes in corporate governance in general in Japan. Commercial banks, particularly big ones, have been forced to restructure their relationships with client firms to prepare for fierce competition. Big bank lending to blue-chip clients has decreased since the late 1970s. In addition, the recent turmoil in banking has forced big banks to reduce the stocks portfolios of their *keiretsu* firms. The banks cannot afford to continue holding a large amount of stock merely for the purpose of maintaining close relationships with client firms.[29] Some big banks have announced plans to merge with each other beyond the traditional *keiretsu* demarcations. Sumitomo Bank and Sakura Bank, which used to be core banks' of their respective *keiretsu,* will merge within a few years.

These changes on the part of financial institutions imply that corporate management will be exposed to stronger pressures from capital markets than before. It is not yet clear whether the change in corporate governance is substantial or merely superficial. For those who believe that traditional business relationships centred on banks produced an efficient business system in Japan, this change may seem destructive. However, as Tables 3.4 and 3.5 suggest, the *keiretsu* have become less influential in major companies' financing since the late 1970s. Thus, it may be safe to say that the eclipse of *keiretsu* in the financial system will not greatly affect the efficiency of Japanese industry.

NOTES

1   An earlier version of this chapter was presented at the International Conference, Reform and Recovery in East Asia: The Role of the State and Economic Enterprise on 21–2 September 1999 at the Australian National University, Canberra. The author has greatly benefited from joint research with Masaharu Hanazaki, Research Institute of Capital Formation, Japan Development Bank. Part of the earlier version was presented at the NBER Japan Project Meeting held on 17–18 April 1998, in Cambridge, Massachusetts, and the Econometrics Conference, Capital Market and Corporate Governance held on 9–11 July 1998, in Shiga, Japan. The author is grateful for the constructive comments of

Chris Becker, Patrick Bolton, Peter Drysdale, Michael Gibson, Shin-ichi Hirota, Anil Kashyap, Hugh Patrick, Eric Rosengren and Yoshiro Tsutsui. Financial support from the Japan Ministry of Education Scientific Research Grant is gratefully acknowledged.

2   The Ministry of Finance (MOF) classified bank loans into the following four categories: (1) loans expected to be collectable, (2) loans that the bank needed to manage carefully, (3) very difficult to collect loans, and (4) loans expected to be impossible to collect. The FSA has followed MOF's classification. Problematic loans' belong to the categories from (2) to (4). Problematic loans are identified by the business condition of each borrower. If a firm is regarded as being in financial distress, all the loans to the borrower are regarded as problematic. However, non-performing loans disclosed by banks are identified by the condition of each loan. Even if a borrower is in financial distress, the part of the loan to the firm that is covered by collateral is defined as performing. Due to these differences in definition, therefore, the number of problematic loans defined by FSA criteria tends to be considerably higher than disclosed non-performing loans.

3   The policy package of legislation passed in October 1998 provides for a public fund of 18 trillion for liquidating or temporarily nationalising failed banks, and a public fund of 25 trillion for recapitalising solvent but undercapitalised banks. (The AMFC, introduced at the beginning of 1998, was abolished by the October legislation, suggesting that the emergency policy of injecting 1.8 trillion into 21 banks at March 1998 failed to strengthen the Japanese banking sector.) In addition to these funds, the Deposit Insurance Corporation has been endowed by the government with funds of 17 trillion to be used to protect depositors of failed banks. Thus, the government has prepared public funds amounting to 60 trillion to deal with the bank crisis. Diet members were quite active in preparing the emergency policy package after the severe financial crisis in late 1997. They were mostly concerned with the credit crunch caused by the shortage of bank capital that would exacerbate the economic slowdown.

4   As Calder (1993: 29) puts it, in contrast to the post-World War II years, Japanese corporations in the 1920s and 1930s had relied heavily on bond finance. Even in 1931 bonds provided 29.9 percent of external corporate funding and bank loans only 13.6 percent.'

5   A recent theoretical analysis of bank–firm relationships predicts that asymmetric information between lenders and borrowers autonomously produces long-term relationships between banks and firms (Sharpe 1990, Rajan 1992). Thus, even if there had been no government enforcement like the Designated Financial Institutions System, the intimate long-term relationship would have formed between banks and firms. The system explains at most why a specific firm chose a specific bank as its main bank.

6   The Anti-Monopoly Law was instituted in April 1947 under pressure from GHQ. The purpose of this law was to prevent the emergence of monopolistic firms in the Japanese economy. But it was considered to be ineffective in preventing monopolistic behaviour in firms that had already established monopolistic status such as the large companies belonging to *zaibatsu* groups. The De-concentration Law was introduced to dissolve the *zaibatsu* organisations as a complement to the Anti-Monopoly Law.

7   The dissolution of *zaibatsu* forced disposal of large blocks of stock held by *zaibatsu*-related agents and caused diffusion of the stocks of *zaibatsu*-related companies among many small investors. This diffusion exposed those companies to hostile takeovers or greenmailing. In response, the companies instituted mutual shareholding to block external pressures on corporate management through the stock market (Sheard 1991).

8   From the viewpoint of the standard theory of corporate finance, the degree of concentrated ownership of firms is important as an effective device of capital market control of the corporate management (Prowse 1992). In reality, Japanese banks are more diffusely held than non-financial companies. According to Kim and Rhee (1997), the top six shareholders of banks hold on average 18.4% of total shares. In contrast, Prowse (1992) finds that the top five shareholders for the Japanese mining and manufacturing companies hold 33.1% of total shares. In this sense, the Japanese capital market is not so powerful in monitoring bank management.

We should also note that insurance companies have often occupied the status of largest shareholders of banks. The insurance companies were quite helpful to incumbent bank managers when they were required to strengthen their capital from the end of the 1980s. Specifically, Japanese banks issued a large amount of subordinate debt (or subordinate loans) to increase their equity capital following the BIS capital adequacy requirement. Insurance companies actively bought most of the debt to help bank management. The main objective for the insurance companies was not to monitor bank management, but to maintain business relationships with the banks. Insurance is the most heavily protected of Japan's financial industries. The government often tries to make use of the rent accumulated in the insurance industry for public purposes', and the insurance companies tend to obey government policy. For example, many market observers in the Tokyo Stock Exchange said that the Japanese government guided insurance companies and other institutional investors to keep their positions in the stock market in order to counterbalance the downward pressures on stock price levels. It was plausible that the government permitted banks to issue subordinate debts to increase their capital at the end of the 1980s immediately after the BIS capital adequacy regulation became effective, then ordered (or recommended?) insurance companies to support banks by buying most of the debts. If so, the insurance companies have been a far from reliable monitor of bank management.

9   Total abolition of the financial safety net would strengthen the incentives of depositors and investors to monitor and discipline bank management. However, most depositors are small-sized wealth-holders enjoying no economy of scale in collecting and analysing information about bank management. There is also a free rider' problem that hinders efficient information production. It would be unrealistic to depend totally on market discipline to maintain the stability of the banking system. As Dewatripont and Tirole (1994) argue, we need a financial safety net in order to protect small-sized investors in the banking sector.

10   We may regard the protection given to shareholders as compensation for their silence on bank management. In reality, the shareholders have been rather similar to debt-holders in the governance structure of bank management. This is evidenced by the fact that dividends on bank shares have been extremely stable regardless of bank performance. For example, the profits of city banks were either very small or negative during the five years from 1993 to 1997, mainly due to large loan loss provisions. Nevertheless, the city banks continued to pay almost constant amounts of dividends to their shareholders. Total profits for the city banks were less than 1.8 trillion for the five years. On the other hand, the total amount of dividends they paid was a little larger than 1.0 trillion for the same five years. If they had not paid the dividend, the total amount of capital would have been 10% larger for those banks than the actual amount in March 1998.

11   Strictly speaking, the government (more precisely, taxpayers) bears the bail-out costs indirectly. The interest rates on the BOJ's emergency loans were substantially lower than the distressed banks would have had to pay if they had raised them in the financial markets. Thus, the emergency loans are necessarily accompanied by subsidies. The subsidies decrease the BOJ's income, and thereby reduce the payment from the BOJ to the government. In this case, the seigniorage is partly a transfer from the government to the banks in distress.

12   The present framework of the Bankruptcy Law and the Corporate Rehabilitation Law requires time-consuming procedures when debt holders' stakes are reduced. It is impossible to operate the pay off within a few days under the current legal framework.

13   On 22 May 1999, the Financial Revitalisation Commission announced that Kohuku Bank, a regional bank located in Osaka, would be under the control of an official receiver appointed by the Commission. The chairman of the Commission accused the bank of borrowing the huge amount of money from inter-bank money markets with substantial premiums immediately after the Commission ordered the bank to take prompt corrective actions to strengthen its capital. This is typical of morally hazardous behaviour, and it is just the tip of the iceberg of the moral hazard prevailing under the wide-scope safety net.

14   With regard to branch administration implemented by MOF, see footnote 15 below.

15   MOF's administration of branch offices was another significant area of regulation. During the high growth period, when almost all deposit interest rates were under regulation, branch offices were an important means of non-price competition for banks and essentially the vehicle by which they competed for deposit funds. Under MOF's administration,

banks were not free to expand or change the location of their branch networks. In permitting new branches, MOF reportedly gave preferential treatment to small banks. The number of branches of small-scale banks increased more rapidly than did city banks, both during and after the high growth period (Horiuchi 1984). MOF partially abandoned branch administration by allowing regional banks and *shinkin* banks to freely increase the number of branch offices in May 1993. At that time, MOF announced that the branch regulation for city banks would be gradually liberalised while taking into account the influence on small and medium-sized financial institutions. In May 1995, MOF totally liberalised the regulation regarding the number of branch offices for all banks.

16   Aoki (1994) argues that by assuming asymmetric information about banks' monitoring activities, the rent was necessary to motivate private banks to faithfully and efficiently monitor their borrowers. He suggests that the long-term relationship between major banks and borrower firms, the main bank relationship', was crucially dependent on competition-restricting regulations. However, restricting full-scale competition was not always necessary to motivate banks to supply a high quality' level of monitoring. The *laissez-faire* market would be able to motivate banks to conduct good monitoring. See Klein and Leffler (1981).

17   Even now, MOF manipulates its administrative guidance with a view to induce private banks to collaborate with its rescue program. In 1994, for example, Mitsubishi Bank obtained preferential treatment from MOF in exchange for rescuing Nippon Trust Bank, which had been seriously damaged by the accumulation of a huge amount of bad loans since the early 1990s. Mitsubishi Bank was rewarded' by being allowed to pursue a full complement of trust banking business through Nippon Trust, which is now its subsidiary. Other banks are prohibited by MOF from engaging in full-line trust banking business through their trust bank subsidiaries. The same is true of the case in which Daiwa Bank financially supported Cosmo Securities Company, which was seriously damaged by the depression in the securities market after the bubble' burst at the beginning of the 1990s. Cosmo has been a subsidiary of Daiwa Bank. However, Cosmo retained its stock brokerage business, which has not yet been permitted to the securities subsidiaries of other banks.

18   Frankel (1984) explains the process of the yen/dollar agreement. Takeda and Turner (1992) discuss the relationship between the internationalisation of Japanese financial markets and domestic financial deregulation in great detail.

19   Kane (1995) warns against carelessly assuming that regulators are fully trustworthy or automatically pursue the social role assigned to them. As he argues, the faithful agent presumption focused economists' attention on evaluating pricing and regulatory structures rather than on analyzing the web of incentives facing the officials responsible for designing and enforcing these structures'.

20   At this point one must address Kane's (1995: 441) suggestion that the manager–stockholder conflict poses a counterincentive to pressures for deposit-institution risk-taking'. That is, if managers dominate bank decision making, the safety net will not necessarily motivate banks to expand risk taking because this activity exposes the manager's human capital to career damage that is hard to diversify'. This argument is relevant here because conventional wisdom holds that Japanese corporations, including banks, are organised and monitored in ways that bear little resemblance to the commonly assumed shareholder-oriented agency model of corporate management (Prowse 1992: 1122 and Milhaupt 1996). In addition, the practice of long-term employment in Japan makes human capital more specific so that career damage becomes a more serious issue. Even if managers dominate decision making, regulators can mitigate the threat greater bank risk poses to human resources for bank managers if they adopt a policy of forbearance towards those banks with which they collude. To the extent this regulatory approach limits career damage, it also reduce the effectiveness of the counter-incentive mechanism identified by Kane (1995). More specifically, if bank managers can collude with regulators through *amakudari* to reduce the likelihood of a human capital crisis for managers, the practice of *amakudari* is likely to be associated with more aggressive risk-taking on the side of bank management than would otherwise be the case.

21   From the perspective of corporate governance theory, the reduction in firms' dependence on borrowing and the increase in retention would give rise to the emergence of managerial

entrenchment associated with inefficient management (Jensen 1989). However, Japan's major companies seemed to maintain managerial efficiency despite the substantial reduction in borrowing since the 1970s. This may suggest that the bank–firm relationship was not so important in the corporate governance framework as has been widely believed. The fierce international competition most major companies have faced since the 1960s may have exerted strong disciplinary influence on their management.

22   According to interim reports submitted in July 1999 by 15 banks that received public funds in their capital, the total amount of outstanding loans to SMEs as of March 1999 was 113.4 trillion, a little lower than the target they had been assigned (114.1 trillion).

23   Lindgren *et al.* (1996: 20) says that [a] review of the experience since 1980 of the 181 current Fund member countries reveals that 133 have experienced significant banking sector problem at some stage during the past fifteen years'.

24   Peek and Rosengren (1998a) point out that some Japanese big banks restructure their business inefficiently. According to their analysis, Japanese banks increased their lending to the US real estate sector in the early 1990s. At the peak in 1992, their US subsidiaries held around 20% of all commercial real estate loans in the US banking sector. However, they cut back their lending in the US in response to a sharp decline in real estate prices in Japan even though US real estate prices were rising. At the same time, Japanese banks expanded their lending to the domestic market where prices were plummeting. Thus, they transferred their loans from more profitable sections to less profitable, and much riskier sections.

25   Neither LIBOR nor TIBOR show the offered rates for individual banks. But apparently Japanese banks are not greatly differentiated from each other. For example, on 22 June 1998, the Japan premium defined by TIBOR–LIBOR was 20.834 basis points. On the same day, the inter-bank offered rate was 5.875% for Tokyo-Mitsubishi, and 5.9375% for both Fuji and Sumitomo Trust respectively in London. The difference was only 6.22 basis points between Tokyo-Mitsubishi and the other two banks. Meanwhile, the offered rate for all the foreign banks was the same at 5.687% on 22 June 1998.

26   On 16 October 1995, the public hearing with regard to Japan's financial system was held at the House of Representative in Washington, DC. This public hearing seemed to promote market scepticism about the abilities of Japanese financial authorities. The Japan premium went up further immediately after the public hearing, reaching the unprecedented high of 52.605 basis points on 25 October.

27   Interestingly, from 13 March to 2 April 1998, the LIBOR divergences between Tokyo-Mitsubishi and the other two banks disappeared while the Japan premium remained significantly positive. This suggests that the inter-bank money market regarded the capital injection in March 1998 as a partial revival of the traditional safety net. The financial market thought that the traditional safety net no longer worked to resolve the banking problem in Japan.

28   Until the end of 1999, the Council of Finance (*Kinyu Shingikai*) organised by MOF will prepare a report insisting the importance of starting the pay-off' in April 2001 as the government promised. Nevertheless, there is great uncertainty whether it will really start, because some congressmen are strongly arguing against it. They are worried about the adverse influence on small-scale banks and cooperative credit banks that the start of the pay-off' is expected to exert.

29   This is also true of life insurance companies. Life insurance companies not only suffer from extremely low rate of returns on their securities portfolios, but also face an ageing society that will require them to take more consumer-oriented strategies. They are no longer allowed to be stakeholders in client firms merely for the reason of maintaining relationships.

REFERENCES

Aoki, Masahiko (1994) Monitoring characteristics of the main bank system: An analytical and developmental view', in Aoki and Patrick: 109–41.

Aoki, Masahiko and Patrick, Hugh (eds) (1994) *The Japanese Main Bank System: Its relevance for developing and transforming economies*, New York: Oxford University Press.

Aoki, Masahiko, Patrick, Hugh and Sheard, Paul (1994) The Japanese main bank system: An introductory overview', in Aoki and Patrick: 3–50.

Bank for International Settlements (1996) *66th Annual Report.*

Black, Fisher, Miller, Merton H. and Posner, Richard A. (1978) An approach to the regulation of bank holding companies' *Journal of Business* 51: 379–412.

Boot, Arnoud W.A. (1992) Why hang on to losers? Divestitures and takeovers', *Journal of Finance* 47: 1401–23.

Calder, Kent (1993) *Strategic Capitalism: Private business and public purpose in Japanese industrial finance*, Princeton University Press.

Cargill, Thomas F., Hutchison, Michael M. and Ito, Takatoshi (1997) *The Political Economy of Japanese Monetary Policy*, The MIT Press.

Dewatripont, Mathias and Tirole, Jean (1994) *The Prudential Regulation of Banks*, Cambridge: MIT Press.

Diamond, Douglas W. and Dybvig, Phillip H. (1983) Bank runs, deposit insurance, and liquidity', *Journal of Political Economy* 91: 401–19.

Frankel, Jeffry A. (1984) *The Yen-Dollar Agreement: Liberalizing Japanese capital markets*, Policy Analyses in International Economics 9, Washington, DC: Institute for International Economics.

Gorton, Gary and Rosen, Richard (1995) Corporate control, portfolio choice, and the decline of Banking', *Journal of Finance* 50: 1377–420.

Hellman, Thomas, Murdock, Kevin and Stiglitz, Joseph E. (1997) Financial restraint: Toward a new paradigm', in Masahiko Aoki, Hyung-Ki Kim and Masahiro Okuno-Fujiwara (eds) *The Role of Government in East Asian Economic Development: Comparative institutional analysis*, New York: Oxford University Press, 163–207.

Horiuchi, Akiyoshi (1984) Economic growth and financial allocation in postwar Japan', Brooking Discussion Papers in International Economics 18.

, Packer, Frank and Fukuda, Shin'ichi (1988) What role has the main bank played in Japan?', *Journal of the Japanese and International Economies* 2: 159–80.

(1996) An Evaluation of Japanese financial liberalization: A case study of corporate bond markets', in Takatoshi Ito and Anne O. Krueger (eds) *Financial Deregulation and Integration in East Asia*, Chicago: University of Chicago Press: 167–91.

(1999) Financial fragility and recent developments in the Japanese safety net', *Social Science Japan Journal* 2: 23–44.

and Shimizu, Katsutoshi (2000) Did *amakudari* undermine the effectiveness of regulatory monitoring in Japan?', *Journal of Banking and Finance*, forthcoming.

Hoshi, Takeo, Kashyap, Anil and Scharfstein, David (1991) Corporate structure, liquidity, and investment: Evidence from Japanese industrial groups', *Quarterly Journal of Economics* 106: 33–60.

, Kashyap, Anil and Loveman, Gary (1994) Financial system reform in Poland: Lessons from Japan's main bank system', in Aoki and Patrick: 592–633.

, and Kashyap, Anil (1999) The Japanese banking crisis: Where did it come from and how will it end?', forthcoming in the *NBER Macroeconomic Annual 1999.*

Jensen, Michael C. (1989) The eclipse of the public corporation', *Harvard Business Review* 67: 61–74.

Kane, Edward J. (1995) Three paradigms for the role of capitalization requirements in insured financial institutions', *Journal of Banking and Finance* 19: 431–59.

Kim, K.A. and Rhee, S.G. (1997) Large shareholders of banks: Shareholder activism and the impact of the regulatory environment', unpublished manuscript.

Klein, Benjamin and Leffler, Keith B. (1981) The role of market forces in assuring contractual performance', *Journal of Political Economy* 89: 615–41.

Lindgren, Carl-Johan, Garcia, Gillian and Saal, Matthew I. (1996) *Bank Soundness and Macroeconomic Policy*, Washington, DC: International Monetary Fund.

Miyajima, Hideaki (1994) The privatization of ex-zaibatsu holding stocks and the emergence of bank-centered corporate groups in Japan', EDI Working Papers no. 94-52.

Milhaupt, Curtis J. (1996) A relational theory of Japanese corporate governance: Contract, culture, and the rule of law', *Harvard International Law Journal* 37: 3–64.

Morck, Randall and Nakamura, Masao (1998) Banks and corporate control in Japan', *Journal of Finance* 54: 319–39.

Nickell, S., Nicolitsas, D. and Dryden, N. (1997) What makes firms perform well?', *European Economic Review* 41: 783–96.

North, Douglas C. (1990) *Institutions, Institutional Change and Economic Performance*, Cambridge University Press.

Okazaki, Tetsuji (1997) The government–firm relationship in postwar Japanese economic recovery: Resolving the coordination failure by coordination in industrial rationalization', in Aoki Masahiko, Hyung-Ki Kim and Masahiro Okuno-Fujiwara (eds) *The Role of Government in East Asian Economic Development: Comparative Institutional Analysis*, Oxford University Press,74–100.

Peek, Joe, and Rosengren, Eric (1998a) The international transmission of financial shocks: The case of Japan', *American Economic Review* 87: 495–505.

—— (1998b) Determinations of the Japan premium: Actions speaks louder than words', unpublished manuscript, Federal Reserve Bank of Boston.

Prowse, Stephen D. (1992) The structure of corporate ownership in Japan',*Journal of Finance* 47: 1121–40.

Rajan, Raghuram (1992) Insiders and outsiders: The choice between informed and arm's length debt', *Journal of Finance* 47: 1367–400.

Roe, Mark (1992) Corporate governance in Germany, Japan, and America', Columbia Law School Working Paper.

Sheard, Paul (1991) The economics of interlocking shareholding in Japan', *Richerche Economiche* 45: 421–48.

Sharpe, Steven A. (1990) Asymmetric information, bank lending, and implicit contracts: A stylized model of customer relationship', *Journal of Finance* 45: 1069–87.

Stiglitz, Joseph E. (1985) Credit markets and the control of capital', *Journal of Money, Credit and Banking* 17: 133–52.

Takeda, Masahiko and Turner, Phillip (1992) The liberalization of Japan's financial markets: Some major themes', *BIS Economic Papers* 34.

Teranishi, Juro (1994) Emergence of loan syndication in wartime Japan: An investigation into the historical origin of the main bank system', in Aoki and Patrick: 51–88.

Weinstein, David E. and Yafeh, Yishay (1998) On the costs of a bank-centered financial system: Evidence from the changing main bank relations in Japan', *Journal of Finance* 53: 635–72.

4 The state, banking and corporate relationships in Korea and Taiwan[1]

Heather Smith

Prior to the Asia crisis these two economies were often cited as examples of identical economic phenomena, characterised by high and sustained economic growth and export-led industrialisation. But while Taiwan and Korea have always been broadly similar in economic structure, performance and policies, there have also been important differences in the means by which development was achieved. State intervention has always been more overt in Korea than in Taiwan. The Taiwan government did not promote private industrial conglomerates. Nor did it attempt the intense drive into heavy industry that Korea embarked on in the 1970s.

For Korea and Taiwan, the 1980s was a particularly crucial decade. Both undertook substantial market-oriented reform, although the pace and degree of liberalisation varied, reflecting, in the Korean case, constraints from earlier interventions. Economic liberalisation was also accompanied by a broader process of political liberalisation, with both Korea and Taiwan in the mid- to late 1980s evolving into democratic states. However, by the first half of the 1990s there were evident differences between the two as regards the efficiency of the financial sector, the industrial structure, and the nature of government–business relations. Taiwan, having adapted to the changes in the domestic and international environment, looked increasingly resilient. Korea, lacking the flexibility to internalise changes in global competitive conditions, looked increasingly fragile.

This chapter seeks to explore these similarities and differences in greater detail. The first section provides a brief overview of the development experience of Korea and Taiwan. The second section compares the pre-crisis banking and corporate-sector relationships in the two economies. The third section provides a reassessment of the government-led model of East Asian development in the wake of the crisis, highlighting lessons from the relative experience of Korea and Taiwan for other developing economies in their industrial upgrading. Finally, the fourth and fifth sections focus on the key institutional challenges facing the two economies in managing their transition to later stage development. In the case of Korea, deficiencies in corporate governance structures are discussed, while in the case of Taiwan, weaknesses in its financial system are highlighted. The chapter concludes by noting two features that seem likely to hold, at least in the short to medium term, in the case of Korea. The first is that it would seem premature to expect the increased market orientation of Korea's business environment to lead to a convergence of its corporate organisation with that of Western' firms. The second is that the state will continue to play a role in the economy. However, reducing the government's role in the economy and replacing it by the working of the market under fair and transparent rules of competition will be critical to Korea's longer-term performance. Failure to do so would not only see a continuation of the inherent inefficiencies that contributed to Korea's crisis, but would also entail serious implications for Korea's future growth prospects.

OVERVIEW OF DEVELOPMENT MECHANISMS[2]

Korea's and Taiwan's rapid growth during the past four decades have been cited as models of successful economic development. Between 1965 and 1990, growth rates of per capita GNP in the two economies averaged 7.1 per cent. This trend continued into the 1990s, with growth rates of per capita GNP averaging 7.3 per cent between 1991 and 1997. The major thrust for economic take-off was the adoption of an outward-looking development strategy based on export promotion, in the early 1960s in the case of Taiwan and in the mid-1960s in the case of Korea. This development strategy led to increases in employment, income and savings, by enabling both economies to benefit from economies of scale in production and technology transfer.

From the early 1970s, however, the development mechanism of the two economies diverged. Despite economic growth of 8.7 per cent, and average export growth of 39 per cent between 1962 and 1971, Korea in 1972 shifted from general export promotion to the targeting of heavy and chemical industries. Under the heavy and chemical industry drive (1973–9), industry-neutral incentives for exports were replaced by industry-specific and, in some cases, firm-specific measures. Industries designated as strategic' included steel, shipbuilding, heavy machinery, petrochemical, industrial electronics and non-ferrous metal industries. The main tool of promotion was preferential access to bank credit. Over the course of the plan, almost 60 per cent of total bank loans and more than 75 per cent of total manufacturing investment went to these sectors, stifling the flow of funds available to light manufacturing industries. Investment, in turn, was funded predominantly by external borrowings, resulting in a rapid rise in foreign debt from 25 per cent of GNP in 1970 to 49 per cent by 1980.

While the industrial conglomerates (*chaebol*) had already begun to play a major role in Korea's economic development, their period of most rapid growth was during the heavy and chemical industry drive. Good performers were rewarded with licences to expand into more lucrative sectors, thus leading them to further diversification. On any indicator, the rapid growth and diversification of the *chaebol* during the 1970s radically transformed the industrial structure and market concentration in Korea. By 1977, 93 per cent of all commodities were produced under monopoly, duopoly or oligopoly conditions in which the top three producers accounted for more than 60 per cent of market share. Between 1973 and 1982, the share of manufacturing output of the twenty largest groups increased from 7 per cent to 29 per cent (OECD 1994: 60). By 1980, the ten largest *chaebol* accounted for 48 per cent of GNP (Kim 1997).

The socialisation of bankruptcy risk that accompanied the plan, combined with the low interest rate ceilings, made the cost of debt financing very cheap for firms in targeted sectors, encouraging firms to take on excessively high levels of debt and to increase market share rather than profitability and shareholder value (Huh and Kim 1994: 26). Between 1963 and 1971, the debt–equity ratio of the manufacturing sector increased more than fourfold, from 92 per cent to 394 per cent, increasing further to 488 per cent by the end of the heavy and chemical industry drive in 1980. The ratio fell over the 1980s and by 1990 was 285 per cent. By 1996, the debt–equity ratio of the manufacturing sector was 336 per cent and that of the top thirty *chaebol* was 389 per cent.

By the early 1980s the Korean economy was experiencing severe structural difficulties. The massive investment in heavy and chemical industries ended at the outset of the global and domestic economic downturn, leaving many of the heavily targeted industries of the 1970s with severe over-capacity problems. The international competitiveness of Korean exports was also weakened as a result of high wage increases in the late 1970s, overvaluation of the Korean currency, and under-investment in the development of technology and training of skilled manpower by both the government and private sector (Koo 1986: 19). This, combined with the second oil shock, a bad agricultural harvest and the political instability following the assassination of President Park, saw Korea in economic crisis in 1979–80. These circumstances led the Korean government to examine critically its role in the nation's overall economic development.

In response to the economic crisis in 1979–80, the Korean government once again set out on a major policy shift. A macroeconomic stabilisation plan was accompanied by a liberalisation of structural policies. In contrast to the 1970s, Korea's shift to technology-intensive industries in the 1980s was largely designed around more functional policies supportive of industrial upgrading. From the mid-1980s, increasing foreign government pressure to eliminate unfair trade practices also played an important part in continuing to bring about significant changes in policy. The government wound back its use of direct production subsidies and ceased employing export subsidies. Trade barriers were reduced by the 1984 five-year tariff reduction plan. Rather than directing resources to industries considered strategic', the government's industrial initiatives instead focused on the restructuring of declining industries and measures to promote a greater role for small-scale enterprises (Smith 1994).

Government policy towards the *chaebol* shifted from one of promotion in the 1960s and 1970s to regulation of their growth in the 1980s. The introduction of the Fair Trade Act of 1980 included the prohibition of cartel practices and cross-investment among affiliated companies, a ceiling on credit to the larger *chaebol*, and restrictions on their vertical and horizontal integration. The government also directed the thirty largest *chaebol* to restructure their businesses around three or fewer core sectors (Kim 1997: 34). Still, a significant gap existed between policy pronouncements and implementation, as the *chaebol* continued to grow.

Steps were also taken in the early 1980s to liberalise the financial sector. These included the privatisation of commercial banks, relaxation of entry barriers to non-bank financial markets, and the gradual opening of the financial sector to foreign investment. But it was not until the early 1990s that a more comprehensive plan for liberalisation of the financial sector was undertaken. The so-called 1993–7 Financial Sector Reform Plan' was designed to overcome the inefficiencies introduced by the non-price allocation of credit in the economy, by opening the financial sector to foreign participation and gradually removing controls on long and then short-term international capital movements. Some factors did not change. Government policies continued to invite excesses. The government continued to view economies of scale as important, and favoured the intensive use of funds raised at home and abroad (Abe, Sato and Nagano 1999: 3). Within that framework, the bulk of the risk continued to be borne by the government. As labour-intensive industries lost their competitiveness amid rising real wages in the latter half of the 1980s, the *chaebol* placed an increasingly disproportionate emphasis on capital-intensive industries, using their abilities to raise funds as the main source of their competitiveness.

While the financial system underwent significant liberalisation, it still remained credit-based and subject to government influence. The Korean government's aggressive industrial policy in the 1970s tended to retard the development of private institutions that share in industrial decision making and risk bearing. Equity markets remained small and the financial decision-making experience of commercial banks thin. The government remained closely involved in credit policy which, in turn, forced it to become involved in many additional *ad hoc* regulations. The major constraint on financial liberalisation continued to be the legacy imposed by interventions in the 1970s that had led to an accumulation of non-performing loans. As Park (1994: 161) points out, rather than undertaking a course of adjustment that might have been effective but [was] definitely bound to be painful, the government instead bailed out an increasing number of troubled firms by forcing the banks to assume their debt'.

Despite rapid export expansion in the 1960s and 1970s, by the early 1980s the Taiwan economy was also facing a number of structural pressures. A shortage of labour became gradually apparent in the manufacturing sector from the late 1970s, and more so after the mid-1980s, resulting in firms relocating industrial activities offshore to mainland China and Southeast Asia. Labour costs rose as a result of this labour shortage, and the average monthly wage increased in real annual terms by 6.5 per cent during 1981–6, and by 11.4 per cent between 1986 and 1990 (Smith 1997).

Persistent trade surpluses were placing heavy upward pressure on the exchange value of the New Taiwan (NT) dollar and intensifying trade friction with the United States.[3] Taiwan's trade surpluses also created pressures to liberalise quite separately from US pressure. Haggard (1988) notes that the surpluses gave new impetus to liberalisation on purely economic grounds and that Taiwan became a target of US attention precisely as a result of domestic policies that contributed to external imbalance. Hence, the adjustment process demanded went beyond exchange rate adjustments to encompass broader domestic reforms.

The NT dollar, which had remained quite stable during 1979–85, appreciated by 40 per cent against the US dollar over the 1986–8 period. During this period the government had undertaken a policy of partial liberalisation' of the foreign exchange market, with the central bank intervening to ensure that the NT dollar appreciated only gradually. This partial liberalisation, in giving rise to an expectation of further appreciation, induced large speculative capital inflows and fuelled the problem created by the trade surplus. The overall imbalance in the balance of payments generated the interrelated problems of a rapid build-up of foreign currency reserves, a dramatic increase in the money supply, and rising asset prices in the stock and real estate market (Liu 1992: 128–32).

In recognising that structural adjustment of the economy required a more liberal environment, the Taiwan government in 1984 announced its intention to promote a strategy of economic liberalisation and internationalisation of the economy. A trade surplus reduction program was announced that included the relaxation of foreign exchange and interest rate controls, the lifting of foreign investment restrictions and tariff reductions. These measures were aimed at ensuring that domestic demand, rather than foreign demand, became the driving force behind future industrial development (Smith 1997).

Liberalisation of the financial sector was also accelerated in response to both structural and crisis-driven factors. In 1985, Taiwan suffered a minor financial crisis when a major credit cooperative was declared insolvent and two trust companies ran into difficulties after pursuing imprudent lending policies.[4] Forces for liberalisation also came from economists pushing for financial deregulation; from foreign banks demanding national treatment; and from domestic business requesting the divestment of state-owned banks and the establishment of new private banks. However, according to Cheng (1993: 86), the fundamental reason for the liberalisation had less to do with these actors' advocacies than with the volatile pressures that had built in the financial markets after the large-scale currency appreciation that exposed the weakness of the overly controlled financial institutions.

Importantly, the process of gradual liberalisation continued, and in some cases even accelerated, during economic downturns (Ranis and Mahmood 1992: 129). By the 1990s, the economic agenda in Taiwan came to be increasingly dominated by debates over privatisation and social welfare issues (Noble and Ravenhill 2000), whilst in Korea, policy makers continued to be divided as to the costs and benefits of the *chaebol* system of business organisation – whether it should be regulated to prevent excessive diversification or deregulated to cope with globalisation.

Commonalities and contrasts

The most striking difference between Korea and Taiwan lay in the size and structure of their business groups. The origins of the family unit in Taiwan's industrial structure differed significantly from those in Korea, in part because of Chinese inheritance practices and in part because of government policy. Taiwan firms were characterised by flexibility, paternalistic leadership, high levels of internal operating efficiency and low levels of organisational complexity. From the early days of Korean economic development when firms were largely financed by bank loans under government influence, a relationship-based system developed among firms, their banks and the government, through ownership, family ties and political deal making (Dobson 1998).

Reflecting these differences in their industrial structures and social networks, Korea's trade came to be structured around exports by industries that enjoyed economies of scale, and the concentration rate of export items became relatively high. Taiwan's exports on the other hand became increasingly diversified, targeting high value-added niche markets, rather than scale-intensive production. Related to this was the fact that Taiwan's firms, unlike their Korean counterparts, could not find a source of competitiveness in massive funding power. As they had to shoulder most of the risks themselves, they acquired a sharp sense of risk and grew cautious about borrowing (Abe, Sato and Nagano 1999).

A feature common to both economies by the early 1980s was the pressure to upgrade and restructure industry from labour- and capital-intensive to technology-intensive industries, thereby reducing its dependence on Japan for intermediate goods. Compared with Korea, Taiwan appears to have adopted a more comprehensive approach in addressing this challenge. Market-oriented reform and the government's creation of a policy environment conducive to industrial upgrading were important factors in this process. The government's support for the building up of science and technology infrastructure for future growth also had a significant influence, shaping the process of technology upgrading.[5] The latter policy in particular reflected the domination of Taiwan's industrial structure by small and medium-sized enterprises (SMEs) that lack the capacity to undertake intensive research and development.

Common to both economies was the declining contribution of manufacturing to growth and the continuous rise of the services sector. The contribution of manufacturing to GDP of both economies reached their peaks of 33 per cent in 1988 in Korea and 40 per cent in 1986 in Taiwan (Hattori and Sato 1997: 343). In terms of the expanding shares of financial and other services sectors, Taiwan was ahead of Korea by a combined gap of over 10 percentage points by 1997. Meanwhile, Korea's construction industry grew rapidly in the 1990s, with Korea over ten points ahead (as a share of GDP) of Taiwan in this sector in 1997 (Abe, Sato and Nagano 1999: 13).

There were also clear differences in their respective economic fundamentals. Taiwan displayed diminishing fluctuations both in its growth and external accounts, whereas Korea continued to experience more erratic gyrations (Figures 4.1–4.4). With the exception of a few years during the late 1980s, Korea experienced current account deficits as investment exceeded savings, while Taiwan after 1971 continued to experience surpluses. In terms of the factors that have been associated with the crisis, Taiwan lagged behind Korea in the deregulation of the capital account, preventing the inflow of short-term capital in large amounts. From the mid-1980s, Taiwan rapidly accumulated foreign exchange reserves (US$83 billion by the end of 1997), thus providing little room for speculators to mount an attack on the currency (Abe, Sato and Nagano 1999: 2). Taiwan's external debt has always been negligible. At the end of 1997, Taiwan's external liabilities stood at $30 billion, compared with $158 billion in the case of Korea (see Figure 4.2).

Unlike Korea, Taiwan experienced no major corporate failure or major instability of the financial system until late 1998. While lending to the manufacturing sector in both economies grew at an annual rate of around 20 per cent during the late 1980s and early 1990s, the rate of increase slowed from 1993 onward in Taiwan due to the decline in asset prices. As Abe, Sato and Nagano (1999: 71) point out, curbs on real estate lending,

Figure 4.1 Growth rate (%) of GDP, Taiwan and Korea, 1980–98

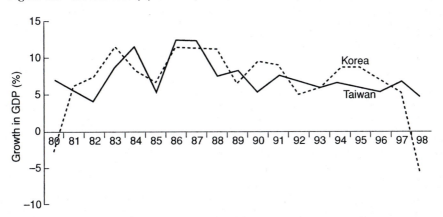

Source: Taiwan Statistical Data Book, Council for Economic Planning and Development (various years) and Bank of Korea. Available at http://www.bok.or.kr

restrictions on per-borrower large loans, and commercial banks' strict collateral assessment generally kept the decline in asset prices from destabilising Taiwan's financial system.

BANKING AND CORPORATE RELATIONSHIPS

Despite the significant liberalisation carried out in both economies in the 1980s, there were clear differences between the two as regards the motivation and the degree of liberalisation undertaken in the financial sector, in the structure of bank ownership, and in the relationship between financial and industrial capital.

Figure 4.2 Current account balance, Taiwan and Korea, 1981–98

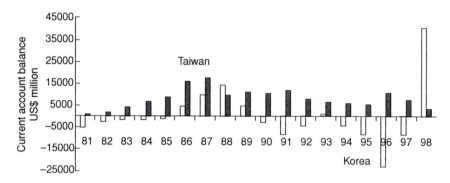

Source: See Figure 4.1.

Figure 4.3 Terms of trade index, Korea, June 1988 – December 1998

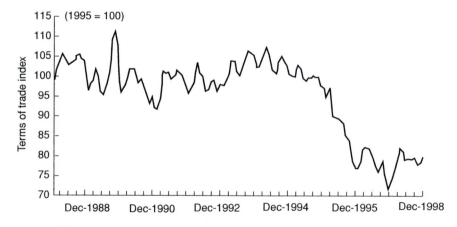

Source: CEIC Asia Database, dX Econ Data Pty Ltd.

Inefficiencies in Taiwan's financial sector were especially pronounced in the mid-1980s under conditions of excess liquidity which, in turn, was a direct result of the build-up of large trade surpluses. In order to prevent a serious financial crisis, the government designed a series of economic and financial measures that aimed to address these problems, but in retrospect also formed a systematic package of restructuring and liberalisation (Kuo and Liu 1998: 180–1). Importantly, reform of the banking sector and partial liberalisation of capital markets all took place within the context of a sound banking sector and the strengthening of prudential controls and standards.

The reform measures took the form of the approval of three key financial laws in the final years of the 1980s, involving the foreign exchange, banking and securities sectors. These included the 1987 Statute for the Administration of Foreign Exchange, the Securities and Exchange Law of 1988 and the New Banking Law of 1989. Foreign exchange controls were lifted on trade-related transactions and residents were allowed to hold and use foreign currencies after July 1987 (although remittances of foreign exchange were still subject to quantitative limitations). Interest rates were decontrolled and a new Banking Law enacted in 1989–90 removed all interest rate restrictions on both the lending and deposit side.[6] The implementation process was largely complete by 1991–2 when sixteen new private bank licences were granted.

Formed with the aim of providing stable competition to state banks, the new banking law placed tough criteria on the establishment of the new banks. New private banks were required to provide start-up capital of NT$10 billion (which was the equivalent of US$370 million based on the exchange rate at the end of 1990), a figure much higher than that required in the establishment of a new bank in the United States. The share of each stockholder of a new bank could not exceed 5 per cent of the total shares, and the share of a group of relevant stockholders could not exceed 15 per cent.

Figure 4.4 Terms of trade index, Taiwan, June 1988 – December 1998

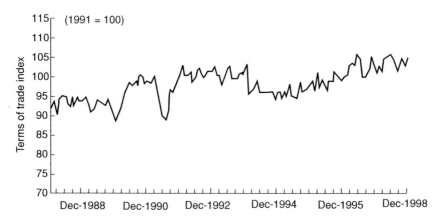

Source: See Figure 4.3.

In tandem with the financial deregulation, the ceiling of 5 per cent was also imposed on a business group's ownership of commercial banks. Although newly established banks did have connections with certain business groups, government regulations placed limitations on the total loans that could be lent to affiliated business groups. Nonetheless, the subsequent increase in the concentration of bank ownership in the hands of large business groups by the mid-1990s was in clear violation of the original intention of the New Banking Law, with the private banks emerging as the weak link in Taiwan's financial sector in the wake of the Asian crisis.

In Korea, social concerns about the strong economic influence of the *chaebol* translated into strict restrictions on the bank ownership structure. In 1982, when the privatisation of the banking sector was commenced, a ceiling of 8 per cent was imposed on individual ownership of commercial banks, in order to prevent any single shareholder from exerting excessive influence and control over a bank's management. This restriction was further strengthened with the lowering of the ceiling to 4 per cent in 1994 (Nam, Kang and Kim 1999: 28). Despite financial deregulation, government control of the banking sector persisted. The asset portfolios of banks were still constrained by limits on lending and, although the banking sector had been largely privately owned since the mid-1980s, the government did not allow it to have full managerial autonomy (Smith 1998a).

In contrast to the commercial banks, Korea's non-bank financial institutions have been more loosely regulated and were allowed greater freedom in their management of asset and liabilities. As a result, many non-banks are currently owned or actually controlled by the *chaebol*. As of 1997, the seventy largest *chaebol* owned a total of 109 financial affiliates concentrated among securities firms, merchant banks and non-life insurance firms (Nam, Kang and Kim 1999: 28).

While Taiwan's financial liberalisation after the mid-1980s primarily dealt with the deregulation of domestic financial institutions, Korea's measures took the form of the liberalising of fund-raising overseas. In Taiwan, the increased number of retail branches expanded the delivery channels of financial services, resulting in greater benefits for consumers (Abe, Sato and Nagano 1999: 70). In Korea, the inflow of short-term capital after 1992 was followed by failures of merchant banks, with ripple effects spreading to the corporate sector and commercial banks, considerably destabilising the entire financial system (Abe, Sato and Nagano 1999: 70).

In Korea, the government in 1993 relaxed restrictions on the usage for long-term foreign currency denominated loans, while maintaining restrictions on long-term borrowing, so as to limit total capital inflows in the face of liberalised short-term borrowing. In addition, the deregulation of foreign exchange transactions saw the number of financial institutions licensed for foreign exchange business jump from 1994. During 1994–6, Korean banks opened twenty-eight foreign branches, while finance companies were allowed to conduct foreign exchange businesses upon their conversion into merchant banking corporations.[7] These institutional changes in the midst of a strong investment boom during 1994–5 triggered the dramatic increase in short-term foreign debt of financial institutions and severe maturity mismatch problems (Nam *et al.* 1999: 9).

An unwillingness to use credit as a principal instrument of industrial policy distinguishes Taiwan from Korea. While Korean banks extended credit to favoured borrowers on the basis of directives from the government, the Taiwan government has generally taken a hands-off policy on bank lending. This does not imply that the Taiwan government did not at various times adopt credit rationing policies to accommodate the financing needs of some specific industries, economic activities or borrower groups, in order to promote economic growth or to equalise to some extent the availability of bank loans among borrower groups (Yang 1990: 19).[8] However, real lending rates in Taiwan were never as severely repressed as in Korea, with policy loans broadly targeted to support exports and industry-specific loans rare (Cheng 1993).[9] Although state-controlled, most of Taiwan's banks were generally free to lend on commercial criteria, rather than government policy-lending fiat or cronyism.[10] A conservatively managed banking system has also prevented excessive lending. With risk-averse state bankers, Taiwan's financial sector has remained largely immune from the problem of non-performing loans seen in Korea (Cheng 1993).

After increasing in the first half of the 1980s to average 4.5 per cent for state banks (and 5.3 per cent for private banks), non-performing loans of Taiwan banks then fell, in response to reforms in the financial sector in the wake of the financial scandals in the mid-1980s and the excess liquidity in the financial sector following the currency appreciation of the second half of the 1980s (Table 4.1). By 1995, the ratio of non-performing loans for all domestic banks in Taiwan was 2.7 per cent, rising to an average of 3.8 per cent by the end of 1997. The Bank of International Settlements required capital adequacy ratio of 8 per cent included in the Banking Law in 1989 saw banks undertake recapitalisation early in the 1990s, implement tighter auditing procedures and replace personnel. At the end of 1997, the capital adequacy ratios of domestic long-established banks and new banks were 11.3 per cent and 12.3 per cent, respectively (Kuo and Liu 1998).[11] Only one of Taiwan's forty-seven banks failed to meet the 8 per cent threshold; thirty-six banks had ratios in excess of 10 per cent.

The Taiwan case was in dramatic contrast to that of Korea. At the end of 1984, the Bank of Korea estimated that non-performing loans in total credit at commercial banks were close to 11 per cent of their total loans and 2.6 times their net worth. The share of non-performing loans had begun to rise from the late 1970s, and emerged as a serious threat to the soundness of Korea's commercial banks in 1981, when the ratio rose to 7.3 per cent of their total credit, and then averaged 10.5 per cent during 1984–6. In fact, Park and Kim (1994: 209) argue that if international criteria for a sound bank were applied, most of the commercial banks in the early 1980s were insolvent. After restructuring associated with industry rationalisation began in 1986, the ratio came down substantially, falling to 5.9 per cent by 1989. But the data show that the government kept supporting troubled firms for more than five years after their problems became obvious, thereby postponing restructuring (Park and Kim 1994: 212–13). In this sense, they argue, the authorities were lucky. Beginning in 1986, the economy entered an upward swing, with growth averaging more than 12 per cent for the three years 1986–8. Corporate bankruptcies during 1997 immediately translated into a dramatic increase in non-performing loans of financial institutions, with the proportion of non-performing loans in the banking system estimated to be 15–18 per cent at the end of 1997, or 7.5 per cent (Smith 1998a).

Table 4.1   Non-performing loans as a percentage of total loans, Korea and Taiwan, 1977–90

Year	Korea Commercial banks	Local banks	Taiwan Govern- ment banks	Private banks	Specialised government banks
1977	1.67	1.35	5.38	6.85	6.55
1978	1.08	1.43	4.52	3.10	5.47
1979	3.43	4.63	4.81	3.80	6.42
1980	2.74	8.89	4.39	3.47	5.96
1981	7.25	6.85	3.91	3.83	5.12
1982	6.95	5.51	4.42	4.07	4.03
1983	8.57	6.90	4.60	5.00	3.86
1984	10.85	8.47	4.42	6.50	3.53
1985	10.22	8.18	5.02	6.93	3.85
1986	10.53	8.54	4.45	5.59	4.32
1987	8.42	7.36	3.99	5.31	3.67
1988	7.44	6.16	2.95	3.20	2.86
1989	5.86	4.11	2.33	2.57	2.13
1990	n.a.	n.a.	2.18	2.52	2.16

Note: In the case of Taiwan, bad loans, called accounts and overdue loans are collectively called non-performing loans. Overdue loans' are those late in being paid, called accounts' are overdue loans which are either 6 months overdue or less than 6 months overdue but the loan's collateral is claimed by creditors. Overdue loans and called accounts are deemed bad loans' if the loan cannot be paid back, the loan is two years overdue, having been called but not paid, and the value of the collateral is not enough to cover the balance remaining on the loan. In Korea, non-performing loans include those classified as substandard, doubtful and estimated loss. Substandard loans' are total credit, covered by collateral, for customers with an unfavourable transactions record and for whom a definite schedule must be agreed to collect or control debt; doubtful loans' include that portion of credit not covered by collateral which is lent to substandard' customers and which is expected to result in a loss when realised; and estimated loss', that portion of credit not covered by collateral which is lent to substandard' customers and for which collection is not possible in a foreseeable period.

Sources: For data on Korea, Table 5.15, Park and Kim (1994: 215). For Taiwan, Tables 7.17–7.18, Yang (1994: 312–13).

Industrial characteristics

Korea's industrial structure has always been characterised by a relatively high level of internal ownership, reflecting the desire of owner-managers to maintain control and their reliance on debt finance (OECD 1998). Although by conventional measures the degree of concentration was not particularly high relative to industrialised economies, this ignores the extent of cross-affiliation within groups and the extent of family ownership. In 1994, families of the *chaebol* founders held 10 per cent of the publicly quoted shares of the company in the thirty largest groups, compared with 17 per cent in 1983. Inter-group shareholding accounted for another 34 per cent of the shares of the top thirty *chaebol* in 1997, having fallen from 40 per cent in 1983 (Yoo 1995; OECD 1998: 94; Nam *et al.* 1999).[12]

In terms of output, the *chaebol*'s share has fluctuated between 35 and 40 per cent since the late 1970s (Table 4.2). The top five, in particular, have steadily increased their share of output and currently account for around one quarter of the total in the mining and manufacturing sector. The *chaebol* are less important in the service sector, with the shares in GDP accounted for by the thirty largest and the five largest *chaebol* estimated at 16 per cent and 9 per cent, respectively, in 1995 (OECD 1998: 90).

In addition, there is a considerable gap between the size of the largest groups and the other *chaebol*. The combined sales of the five largest *chaebol* as a percentage of GDP increased from 12.8 per cent in 1975 to 52.4 per cent in 1984, decreasing slightly to 49 per cent by 1994. Table 4.3 shows that the ratio of total sales for the top business groups was strikingly different between Korea and Taiwan, particularly that of the top five groups (Abe and Kawakami 1997). Although increasing in the first half of the 1990s, the *chaebol*'s overall role in employment has declined over time, with SMEs accounting for an increasing majority of employment.

The tapering off of the *chaebol*'s growth around the mid-1980s reflects a shift in the government's policy towards the *chaebol*, from one of promotion in the 1960s and 1970s to regulation of their growth in the 1980s. The introduction of the Monopoly Regulation and Fair Trade Act of 1980 was designed to strengthen the system of credit supervision for

Table 4.2 *Chaebol* concentration ratio, 30 largest mining and manufacturing firms, 1977–94 (per cent)

	1977	1982	1984	1986	1988	1990	1992	1994
Output	32.0	40.7	40.3	37.7	35.7	35.0	39.7	39.6
Value added	29.1	33.2	33.5	32.4	30.4	30.0	35.9	36.9
Fixed assets	–	37.2	40.3	39.1	37.3	32.2	44.5	45.0
Employment	20.5	18.6	18.1	17.2	16.9	16.0	17.5	17.7

Sources: Yoo (1995); EAAU (1999).

large *chaebol*, to undertake ongoing amendments to prevent cross-equity investment of the *chaebol*, and to limit *chaebol*'s total equity investment in their group firms. The latter measure, in particular, was intended to prevent *chaebol* from inflating their group firms' capital base and establishing new group firms without actually increasing their overall equity capital base (SaKong 1993: 63). With the introduction of this measure, the cross-equity investment of the top thirty *chaebol* fell from 43.9 per cent when a 40 per cent limit was introduced in 1987, to 26.8 per cent in 1994. Exemptions to the ceiling were allowed, such as in cases where the investment was part of a rationalisation plan for a declining industry or when it involved social overhead capital considered important for national competitiveness (OECD 1996: 115–16).

In funding their activities, Taiwan firms have tended to rely on a combination of bank finance, retained earnings, the informal curb market and *guanxi* (Dobson 1998). Table 4.4 shows that within the private sector, both SMEs and large enterprises relied on external finance for around a half to two-thirds of their financial needs during the period 1985–95, with the rest being financed from internal sources. SMEs, in particular, have relied on the curb market for around 30–40 per cent of their external financing, with this share remaining relatively constant over the period 1985–95. Large enterprises, on the other hand, have relied almost exclusively (around 90 per cent) on the regulated finance sector.

Korean firms, by contrast, have relied almost exclusively on external finance, with banks serving as the major channel through which policy-directed loans were distributed (Park and Kim 1994: 195). Despite the intention of phasing out policy-directed' loans, they still remained and their share, either in terms of total loans or assets, had changed little by the early 1990s. By 1990–1, policy-directed loans as a percentage of total deposit money bank loans (commercial bank and specialised banks) were still around 31 per cent, compared with 35 per cent in 1985–9, and 41 per cent during the height of the heavy and chemical industry drive in 1975–9 (Park 1994). State influence over the banking sector began to wane along with the progress in financial liberalisation, particularly following the privatisation of commercial banks. During the 1990s, firms came to rely increasingly on non-bank sources of funding. A key feature in 1997 was the marked rise (from 9 per cent to 28 per cent) in financing coming from non-banks (especially merchant banks), reflecting weak bond and equity markets, as well as the reluctance of banks to increase their lending activities (OECD 1998: 26).

Corporate sector performance

Prior to the crisis there were striking differences in the financial health of Korean and Taiwan firms. Korea's corporate sector was characterised by thin business margins and poor shareholder returns; very low shareholder equity, which fell by a third in the course of 1997; and high and rising debt service as a proportion of corporate cashflow, with financial costs at 15 per

Table 4.3 Total sales of top business groups as a percentage of GDP, Korea and Taiwan, 1994

	Korea	*Taiwan*
Top 5 groups	49.0	12.3
Top 10 groups	60.4	19.7
Top 30 groups	73.7	31.3

Source: Table V, Abe and Kawakami (1997: 395).

Table 4.4 Sources of finance of SMEs and large enterprises, Taiwan, 1985–95

		External finance	*Internal finance*	*External financing from curb market*	*External finance from the formal financial sector*
1985	SMEs	58.7	41.3	36.4	63.6
	Large enterprises	61.1	38.9	7.3	92.7
1987	SMEs	62.4	39.1	33.0	67.0
	Large enterprises	58.6	41.4	8.0	92.0
1989	SMEs	58.2	41.8	21.5	78.5
	Large enterprises	56.7	43.3	6.7	93.3
1991	SMEs	59.3	40.7	37.5	62.5
	Large enterprises	54.3	45.7	13.4	86.6
1993	SMEs	60.7	39.3	38.5	61.5
	Large enterprises	55.0	45.0	10.8	89.2
1995	SMEs	65.8	34.2	37.1	62.9
	Large enterprises	53.3	46.7	9.0	91.0

Source: Smith (2000). Taken from *Survey of Financial Conditions of Public and Private Enterprises in Taiwan,* Central Bank of China, Republic of China (various years).

cent of total business costs in 1996, three times higher than in the United States, Japan and Taiwan (OECD 1998: 26).[13]

By 1995, Korea's debt–equity ratio was the highest among East Asian countries, and around three times higher than that of Taiwan (Figure 4.5). The low debt–equity ratio of Taiwan firms was largely a result of conservative financing by financial institutions, especially under the system where the major members were publicly owned banks before 1990. Despite the banks' more aggressive financing under the liberalisation of the 1990s, debt–equity ratios remained low, indicating that firms themselves have cautious attitudes toward borrowing.

By 1996, both Korean and Thai firms had the lowest interest payment coverage ratios,[14] around 2.1 and 2.7, respectively. Taiwan firms had the highest interest payment coverage ratio (exceeding 6.0), due to their low financial leverage and strong profitability performance (Nam, Kang and Kim 1999: 32). With such high financial leverage and non-liquid asset liability structure, Korea's corporate sector was faced with high default risk over the business cycle. This inherent vulnerability came to the fore following the large negative terms of trade shocks in 1995 and 1996.

Competitiveness

Despite Korea's industrial success, a major obstacle to ongoing restructuring has been the lack of technological capability in Korean industry necessary to upgrade to higher value-added activity. The closed and concentrated nature of Korean markets has meant that Korean enterprises lacked incentives to acquire or develop leading-edge technology (Graham 1996). Compared with Taiwan, Korea made little use of foreign direct investment (FDI) as a source of technology transfer in the early stages of its industrialisation, relying more heavily on external borrowing, technology licensing and the importation of capital goods. In fact, imports of capital goods, and the transferral of new foreign technologies embodied in them, far surpassed other means of technology transfers in terms of value. The size of FDI and its proportion to total external borrowing were significantly lower in Korea than in other newly industrialising economies (NIEs). For example, Korea's stock of FDI in 1983 was only 23 per cent that of Singapore, and less than half that of Taiwan and Hong Kong, while the proportion of FDI to total external borrowing was only 6.1 per cent in Korea compared with 91.9 per cent in Singapore and 45 per cent in Taiwan (Kim 1997: 42).

Figure 4.5 Debt–equity ratios, Korea, Taiwan and the United States, 1980–97

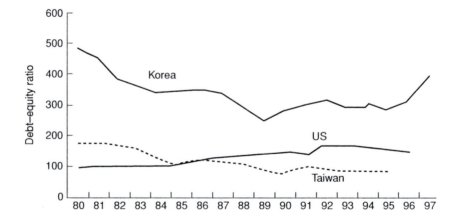

In entering newer industrial areas, the Taiwan government did not encourage the growth of large-scale firms. Taiwan firms increasingly competed at the early phase of the product life cycle, introducing new improved designs in anticipation of market needs. In the 1970s, a network of SMEs that had begun producing household electronic items then expanded into personal computer production. The flexibility and quick responses of this SME network was ideally suited to the short commodity cycle of computer manufacturing (Hattori and Sato 1997: 351). In Korea, the *chaebol* formed by the government's industrial policy used its financial power to begin DRAM production.

Taiwan's government utilised technology diffusion institutions (such as the Industrial Technology Research Institute) to introduce new technologies, develop new products and processes, diffuse knowledge, and scan international markets for both products and processes. Moreover, the ability to attract back Taiwan nationals or to utilise the knowledge of those who remained abroad has been critical since the 1980s (Pack 1992).[15] In fact Lin (1998: 190) cites the contribution of such expatriate scholars to technological development in Taiwan as a factor unmatched in most other developing countries. Many of Taiwan's high technology start-ups entered the late 1970s and early 1980s with product innovation often achieved by individuals with overseas experience in US firms or universities. Relative to both Japan and Taiwan, Korea was late in developing an institutional framework for technology diffusion to SMEs. Only in 1979 did the government begin establishing several important institutions as a way to support SMEs in developing technological capability and promoting their exports (Kim 1997).

Korea's form of industrial structure tended to invite current account deficits and excess capacity. The pursuit of economies of scale tended to lead to excessive investment competition into plant and equipment among enterprises. Equipment investment, in turn, encouraged burgeoning imports. Korea's leading industries also continued to operate precisely in areas where their Japanese counterparts were still very much competitive. Some of these leading industries' products were susceptible to price fluctuations (Abe, Sato and Nagano 1999: 25). The rise in the yen from 1993 coincided with Korea's transition from 4-megabyte to 16-megabyte DRAM chips. As Korean manufactures had introduced 16-megabyte chip mass-production lines earlier than their foreign competitors, they were able to capture a large market share (Abe, Sato and Nagano 1999). A depreciating yen after June 1995, combined with the more than 70 per cent fall in the unit export price of semiconductors during 1996, saw Korea's terms of trade deteriorate by 20 per cent in 1996, the largest drop since the first oil shock of 1974 (Nam *et al.* 1999: 5). Merchandise export growth slowed sharply to 5 per cent in 1996 from 32 per cent in 1995, significantly constraining the cash flow of *chaebol*. Possessing similar export structures, Korea's competitors also suffered a slowing down of export growth, but none of the associated flow-on effects. Export growth in Taiwan slowed from 21 per cent in 1995 to 4.7 per cent in

1996; in the case of Japan from 11.2 per cent to 8.7 per cent; and from 21.5 per cent to 2.9 per cent in the case of Singapore (Smith 2000).

GOVERNANCE AND LATECOMER INDUSTRIALISATION

Considerable scholarly effort has been directed towards debating the role of state intervention in the growth experience of East Asia. The market-led explanations, identified with such authors as Bhagwati, Krueger, Ranis and Fei, and Balassa, sought to describe the way a developing country changes its structure as it moves into modern growth. The common feature of most of these approaches resides in the recognition that organisational and policy choices were basic to the explanation of development success and failure. In particular, increased openness and reduced government intervention are generally associated with improved development performance (Ranis and Fei 1988: 102).

In characterising the experience of Korea and Taiwan, the neoclassical approach has been to argue that while relying on protection at varying stages, both countries ensured their trade regimes were more neutral than most economies between import substitution and export activities, still enabling specialisation on the basis of comparative advantage. Great importance is attached to the ongoing process of trade liberalisation and strengthening of the market mechanism in maintaining the growth momentum. Government interventions are not the *sine qua non*, with the statist explanations considered to have over-estimated the importance of government intervention and distortion of the market mechanism in explaining growth. Instead, macroeconomic stability in particular is emphasised as the cornerstone on which East Asia's export success was built (Smith 2000). High rates of savings and investment, including rapid accumulation of human capital, were the principal engines of growth. Integration with the world market provided an indispensable advantage for rapid economic growth, with the gains from progressive interaction increasing over time (Yoo 1996).

The government-led view, on the other hand, has countered that state interventions have made a significant contribution to the growth of these economies. In particular, the policy regime is thought to have been designed to promote industries with an emerging comparative advantage. Interventions, it is argued, have been correcting for market failures associated with externalities. Technological change is seen as having been the focus of selective intervention (Wade 1990). Close cooperation between government and business is considered to have been an essential component of an industry policy strategy. A great deal of this literature has been directed towards documentation of government interventions and their apparent success; less effort has been directed towards establishing the effectiveness of these interventions and the costs of discriminatory policies.

In particular, much was made of the political relationship between the government and the private sector, and how the relationship contributed to coherent and credible policy. Incentives were considered to have been dynamically efficient because of the capacity of the state to discipline' business use of them. Wade (1990) and Amsden (1989), in particular, stressed the importance of corporatism' in controlling business demands in Taiwan and Korea, assuming that these governments have been capable of solving the coordination problems that might have blocked the transition from a low growth to a high growth trajectory (Haggard and Kim 1997: 60–1).

In retrospect, this institutional structure would seem to have had both advantages and disadvantages. The centralisation of power permitted a high degree of flexibility in the formulation and implementation of policy, especially in the early stages of development (Haggard, Cooper and Collins 1994). In Korea, the government's continuous communication with business leaders and close monitoring of firms through various channels helped reduce the risk of government failure (Cho 1997: 226). Export orientation also imposed a strict discipline on both industry and governments. Also, with little interference from interest groups, the leadership could respond swiftly to events. Compared with other developing countries, Korea is most striking for the vigour with which macroeconomic policy adjustments were undertaken, especially following the two oil shocks (Haggard and Collins 1994: 78–9).

Over time the absence of a system of checks and balances in the political and economic decision-making process became the major obstacle towards structural adjustment. In Korea, the government–business–banking triad continued to thrive, and corruption and moral hazard became endemic. Economic rent seeking associated with credit allocation remained substantial, and distribution of credits on favourable terms continued to constitute the major government tool for corporate governance and industrial policy (Cho 1997: 220). Although the provision of credit began with the benign objective of overcoming imperfections of the capital market, debt-based industrial development itself created an obstacle to financial liberalisation, as the major beneficiaries developed a vested interest in maintaining the status quo. The role of state agencies in directing development, combined with lack of financial transparency, led to excessive cronyism and corruption, as revealed by the case of Hanbo Steel in early 1997 (Mathews 1998). A rigid bureaucracy inhibited the economy from responding creatively to the rapidly changing market environment.

Rather than the crisis having settled the debate over the efficacy of state intervention in East Asia, it has once again rekindled its discussion. A central tenet of the government-led model has always been the controversial point that financial repression has facilitated rapid economic growth in Japan, Korea and Taiwan (Zysman 1983; Wade 1988, 1990). Wade, for example, argued that Taiwan's industrial experience reflected the importance of promoting a bank-based financial system under close government control.[16] Control over the financial system could be used to build up coalitions needed to support the government's objectives, thus helping to implement the industrial strategy. State-controlled credit-based systems are also alleged to produce rapid growth by permitting a faster rate of investment, be less prone to speculative attacks, and avoid the bias towards short-term profitability associated with stock markets. Achieving this requires a cleavage between the domestic economy and the international economy with respect to financial flows. Without this, the government's control over the money supply and cost of capital is weakened, as is its ability to guide sectoral allocation (Wade 1990: 364–8).

More recently, Wade and Veneroso (1998: 7) have argued that, in spite of the crisis, there are still powerful developmental advantages to the bank-based high debt model'. This, they argue, is especially the case for firms that aim to make an assault on major world industries, which they can only do by borrowing. Neither equity markets nor corporate retained earnings are feasible alternatives for mobilising resources on the scale required to compete in these export markets and continually upgrade.'

High levels of debt can be sustained, it is argued, provided that banks and firms have mutual understandings about refinancing of the debt, and provided the government supports them. Restrictions on the freedom of firms and banks to borrow abroad, and coordination of foreign borrowing by government, still remain a necessary part of this system in order to buffer highly leveraged corporate sectors from systemic shocks. This, says Wade (1998a), is the economic rationale for the pattern of alliance capitalism', derogatorily called crony capitalism'. Rather than leading to a reassessment of the efficacy of the development state model, the decline of the monitoring role of the state in the 1990s is considered to have fundamentally contributed to the crisis.[17] Implicit in this model is the rejection of the notion that governments should become less dirigiste as industrialisation advances. Also implicit is a rejection of concerns about the risks of government failure.

While an alliance-based system may perform the task of resource allocation relatively well when legal and contractual infrastructures are not well developed and price signals are not informative, over time, resource misallocation can be significant under such a system that lacks monitoring and discipline from the market. It would also seem to entail serious growth implications.

The crisis has clearly demonstrated that healthy macro fundamentals are not the only decisive factors in determining sustained growth. Sound institutional arrangements are also essential and by their very nature their development is a long-term and complex process. Nam, Kang and Kim (1999: 11–12) advance several reasons as to why market institutions can remain underdeveloped as development proceeds. Part of this failure would seem to be a reflection of a country's relative history of market capitalism. Institutional arrangements can also be kept from evolving into ones that correspond to the economic conditions due to the influence of the elite in political and business spheres. The more important source of the failure in governance can be found in governments' interventionist industrial policies.

Governments' direct control on the allocation of financial resources can distort the incentives of financial institutions, creating severe moral hazard, and impede the development of necessary corporate governance mechanisms.

In the Korean context, the bank-based high debt model' has clearly impeded the development of institutional structures. As governments provided subsidised credit to firms in the targeted industrial sector, and implicitly shared their investment risk, those firms, and more importantly the dominant shareholders of those firms, were excessively protected from market competition and discipline. As Nam *et al.* (1999: 65) point out, the heavy dependence on bank loans for corporate financing and the relationship-based system set in motion a vicious cycle for the insolvency regime. Both the banks and a troubled firm had large incentives to reschedule the firm's debt without going through the court procedure, especially when they are closely tied by ownership or by government policy. In turn, the government often bypassed the formal procedure by bailing out the large corporations.[18] As a result, the insolvency laws and the court system were given insufficient opportunity to develop as the economy's size and complexity grew. Not only did this hamper development of the capital market, because potential investors were not confident that their claims would be properly repaid in case of bankruptcy, and many chose to stay out, but it also reinforced firms' reliance on loans from banks and other financial institutions. The lack of disciplinary function from the insolvency law regime in turn contributed to a concentrated ownership structure and weak corporate governance in the corporate sector. Inadequate accounting standards and rules also helped grant a free rein to corporate insiders at the expense of outside shareholders.

Also pointed to are the effects of financial repression on the sociopolitical system where finance is used to support the political apparatus in power, to finance elections and to reward supporters. The power to allocate credit on preferential terms and to determine who receives the rents creates a clear potential for abuse. It can be significant at both individual and systemic levels, although individual instances of such misuse of power, while important, are not the main issue. Rather, it is the costs imposed by rent-seeking corporations and public officials and the corrosive effects this has on the political economy (Patrick 1994: 337–8). The efficiency costs of financial repression probably have been more in the form of less rapid improvements in welfare – less housing and consumption – than in measured GNP performance (Patrick 1994).

While Korea has clearly achieved a high level of industrial success, the Korean experience, for several reasons, would seem to offer little in the way of positive lessons for developing countries (Smith 2000).[19] First, the sustainability of intervention seems highly questionable as an economy becomes increasingly complex. The government's control of credit allocation fuelled rapid industrialisation in the 1960s and 1970s, but it also inhibited the development of an efficient banking system and fostered economic concentration. While the *chaebol* have been an important asset in Korea's industrialisation, the absence of a healthy small and medium-sized business sector has been one of the weakest links in Korea's overall industrial structure, and has been in sharp contrast to economies such as Japan and Taiwan.

Second, as industrial development proceeds, governments need to reassess their role with a view towards a greater reliance on the market mechanism. In this regard, Korean policy makers took a gambler's approach to industrial upgrading by attempting to grow out of the problems created by earlier interventions. Third, the cost of an industrialisation strategy based on pervasive industry policy interventions can be substantial and these costs are exacerbated as economic development advances. A fourth lesson, dramatically underscored by Korea's crisis, is the importance of financial liberalisation being paced with improvements in the regulatory and supervision standards of domestic financial institutions.

Finally, for developing countries looking for a development model against which to benchmark', the Korean experience would appear to offer little in the way of positive lessons for developing countries. Taiwan's experience, on the other hand, would suggest that state intervention need not be a prerequisite for industrial upgrading and the maintenance of strong and sustained industrial growth (Smith 2000). While it is impossible to test the counterfactual, the experience of Korea and Taiwan comes very close to a controlled experiment, given the two economies' similar characteristics, except in one important respect – the degree of government intervention. If government interventionism was really the reason behind Korea's industrial success, then Korea should be ahead of Taiwan in economic performance (Yoo 1996).

POST-CRISIS ISSUES: KOREA

In the wake of the crisis, the Korean government is now seeking to create a new economic paradigm'. The goal of the current reform process is to transform fundamentally an economy long based on economic dirigism into a modern, free market economy. The core features are to create a legal and institutional framework necessary for rational incentives structures to govern economic behaviour. Essentially, this entails exposing the economy more fully to competition and introducing governance structures into banks and corporations (OECD 1998: 54).

Nam, Kang and Kim (1999: 6) identify three interrelated policy issues that need to be at the forefront of this process in order to sustain long-term growth. First, market liberalisation will continue to be important. As long as exports still remain an important component of economic growth, the domestic market and production processes need to be ever more deeply integrated with the global economy. Second, provision of low-cost long-term financing to the corporate sector will be crucial. In this regard, the healthy growth of the capital market along with a prudent banking sector will be essential. Third, better investment decisions and a mechanism to induce such decisions will be needed. This points to the importance of the signalling function of market prices, and to an increased effectiveness and transparency in corporate governance systems.

Korea's crisis management over the past two years has broadly followed three stages. The policy priority in the first stage (from the onset of the crisis to April 1998) was to overcome the immediate liquidity crisis and stabilise the currency. During the second stage (April–October 1998), non-viable financial institutions were either closed or suspended, while corporate work-out programs were applied to medium-sized *chaebol* that ranked sixth and below. During this period, ninety-four financial institutions had their operations suspended or were closed down. In the restructuring process, the government provided fiscal support of 10 per cent of GDP for the disposal of non-performing loans, recapitalisation of banks, and depositor protection. As a result, most Korean banks have obtained Bank of International Settlements capital adequacy ratios of 10–13 per cent (Nam *et al.* 1999: 12). The second stage also witnessed a dramatic liberalisation of the capital market. Restrictions on foreign equity ownership and foreign portfolio investment in the short-term money market were eliminated, while mergers and acquisitions were fully liberalised. Legal standards related to corporate governance were strengthened to ensure transparency and accountability in corporate management.[20] The third stage, which began in late 1998, has seen corporate sector restructuring focus on the five largest *chaebol*.

Notwithstanding the significant reforms undertaken since the onset of the crisis, several fundamental issues remain to be addressed.

The role of financial institutions

Financial institutions will clearly need to play a more active monitoring role commensurate with their increasing weight in corporate finance. Although banks prior to the crisis held almost 10 per cent of shares in terms of value, they have remained passive in exercising their voting rights and monitoring management. The behaviour of these large shareholders has been attributed in large part to government intervention in bank management. A bank's role as a shareholder was also constrained by regulations mandating shadow voting', whereby financial intermediaries were obliged to vote with the management, which was usually the major shareholder in the firm (Nam, Kang and Kim 1999: 28). In 1998, the ceiling was relaxed to 15 per cent to allow commercial banks to increase their shareholdings of non-financial firms in their asset portfolios. To date, the underlying motivation for banks to increase their shareholdings in non-financial businesses seems to have been capital gains rather than management control or influence.

Further measures also need to be undertaken to improve the financial sector's own internal governance structures. The Financial Supervisory Commission (FSC) has been given considerable powers to impose civil and criminal liabilities on directors of financial institutions. It can also impose sanctions on external auditors and examiners of supervisory authorities for neglect of duties (Nam *et al.* 1999: 54).

Increased foreign and domestic competition should also improve the governance of financial institutions, while putting pressure on firms to adopt more effective corporate governance practices. Since early 1998, foreign banks and securities companies have been able to establish subsidiaries and to purchase domestic financial institutions, albeit still subject to cumbersome approval procedures and important discretionary elements in allowing foreign takeovers.

Deregulation of financial markets will also need to be accompanied by a substantial upgrading of prudential regulation. In the wake of the crisis, rules for bank ownership were eased, in order for investors to acquire stakes in financial institutions. As large owners reach the threshold of 10 per cent, 25 per cent and 35 per cent of total equity, the FSC has indicated that they will be subject to increasingly stringent review (Nam *et al.* 1999: 54). Given the central role of the *chaebol*-affiliated merchant banks in the crisis, it is essential to monitor closely the relationship between financial institutions and the large business groups. Indeed, past abuse of these relations justifies a more stringent restriction on related lending (OECD 1998).

Prior to the crisis, non-banks, with the exception of life insurance companies and investment trust companies, were free of ownership restrictions. As a result, many non-banks are currently owned by the *chaebol*. These close links have created scope for conflicts of interest, with the *chaebol* having relied on their affiliated non-banks to finance the activities of other subsidiaries within their group. Worse still, the financial resources with which the *chaebol* may now move to purchase equity of banks may mostly be derived from the funds that firms under their control have borrowed from financial institutions.

A worrying trend in the post-crisis environment has been the intensification of the top five *chaebol*'s overall domination of the non-banking sector. According to the Korea Institute of Finance, the top five *chaebol*'s market domination in the non-bank sector, measured in terms of assets, rose from 22.5 per cent to 35 per cent between March 1997 and March 1999. In terms of deposits, their market share has doubled from 18.6 per cent to 34 per cent. There are particular concerns over the *chaebol*'s dominance of investment trust funds created by their financial affiliates.[21] Between May 1998 and April 1999, an estimated 140 trillion won flowed into investment trust funds, with the bulk of the funds believed to have been used to shore up financially weak affiliates. The need to lower debt–equity ratios may also have prompted *chaebol*-run funds to buy affiliates' shares to help boost their stock prices and thus facilitate rights issues. Backing up the suspicion that the *chaebol* are engaging in cross-buying, the number of top ten *chaebol*'s equity holdings in non-affiliated listed firms grew 71 per cent to 294 million shares between December 1998 and May 1999 (*Newsreview* 1999: 30–1).

Despite government pressure to rationalise its operations, it is clear that some of the *chaebol* continued to expand. Already a highly leverage company, Daewoo's debt grew by 17 trillion won in 1998. By mid-July 1999, the group's debt had risen to around 57 trillion won, nearly 3.5 times its equity. What nearly pushed Daewoo to bankruptcy around mid-1999 was 7 trillion won in maturing debt due in July 1999, most of it held by investment trust companies. Creditor banks agreed to extend fresh loans of 4 trillion won (US$3.37 billion) and roll over short-term debts of over 10 trillion won (US$8.5 billion) for six months. In return, Daewoo will offer 10.1 trillion won (US$8.42 billion) of stock as collateral, including the personal stock of its chairman. The company has six months to restructure, by mergers and sales to foreign investors, to avoid being dismantled by its creditor banks. In order to prevent investment trust companies, which held most of Daewoo's short-term debt, from facing a liquidity crisis, the government asked investors to refrain from redeeming their deposits. If financial institutions, especially the investment trust firms, face liquidity shortages, the Bank of Korea indicated it would provide emergency funds.

Daewoo's recent near-failure not only underlines how much needs to be done in the area of corporate reform, but also indicates how vulnerable Korea's financial system remains to the risk of large *chaebol* bankruptcies, despite real progress in financial sector reform. The too-big-to-fail' dilemma is particularly relevant in the case of Daewoo, given its vertically integrated industrial structure and contribution to economic output (around 5 per cent of GDP).

Improving exit mechanisms

Much remains to be done if Korea is to have a modern insolvency framework on which domestic and foreign investors can rely with sufficient confidence. While more than 17,000 cases of insolvency were reported in 1997 by the Bank of Korea, only 490 were filed before the courts. Nation-wide, only forty-one judges handle bankruptcy cases. Lengthy proceedings, often lasting several years, make insolvency an unattractive course of action to creditors (OECD 1998: 112).

Two types of formal insolvency procedure have operated in the past. One is liquidation (administered under the Bankruptcy Act) or winding up. The other is reorganisation (or rescue) under the Company Reorganisation Act, which may be initiated by the debtor firm, its creditors and shareholders. The Company Reorganisation Act provides for the continuation of an insolvent debtor with restructuring of the financial claims of its creditors and shareholders, but entails a change in the management and ownership structure. A variant on the reorganisation procedure is the Composition procedure, which differs from the Corporate Reorganisation Act in three important ways. First, the Composite procedure can only be initiated by the debtor firm, and its management remains in charge of its operation during the process. Second, a Composition plan can only be proposed by the debtor firm. Third, the Composition plan can only reschedule or modify the terms of the existing unsecured debts (Nam *et al.* 1999: 62–3).

In the past these formal procedures have rarely been drawn upon. Between 1990 and 1997, there were only 172 cases under the Bankruptcy Act and around 400 cases under the Corporate Reorganisation Act. The Composition procedure has been invoked even less often. Since its introduction in 1962, there have been only twenty-six petitions, although over 300 firms filed for the Composition procedure in 1997. In addition, formal procedures have not been very effective in restructuring and rehabilitating debtor firms in trouble. For example, under the Reorganisation procedure, only slightly over 20 per cent of the firms that had filed emerged successfully out of the process (Nam *et al.* 1999: 63). Under-utilisation of formal insolvency procedures largely reflects the fact that legal proceedings tend to be time-consuming and expensive. It is also a reflection of the level of development of legal infrastructure in general, and a lack of expertise and professional assistance within the court in particular, since a separate bankruptcy court did not exist. There were also cases where the rules were not specific, leaving room for much discretion by judges and abuse by debtor firms.

The government took the first step towards addressing these issues by amending the bankruptcy law in February 1998. From a procedural point of view, the legal changes made it easier for a court to accept and to hear cases, by allowing the consolidation of related cases, such as when a case concerns different companies belonging to the same *chaebol*. In the wake of the crisis, the Korean government also adopted the Corporate Restructuring Agreement', to which all financial institutions were required to be signatories. This informal procedure arose in response to the mounting cases of financially distressed firms, and with the courts and the formal procedures thought to be unable to handle them in an efficient manner. The process can be initiated by the lending financial institution of a debtor firm, which then proposes a debt-restructuring plan. If the creditors representing more than 75 per cent of the firm's debt vote for the plan, it becomes binding to all the institutions. If creditors cannot reach an agreement after two attempts, the case is referred to the Corporate Restructuring Coordinating Committee, whose decision becomes binding (Nam *et al.* 1999: 65).

Not surprisingly, the most popular bankruptcy route, chosen by more than 80 per cent of firms that filed for court protection in 1998, has been the Composite procedure that essentially leaves the existing management in place. It also allows firms to defer their existing debts and interest payments, and to take out new loans, without relinquishing day-to-day control. The most stunning example in this regard is Hanbo Steel, the first *chaebol* to go bankrupt in early 1997. Under the past two and a half years of court protection, it has continued to produce steel. A much smaller number of firms (seventy-nine firms to date) have undergone restructuring under the Corporate Reorganisation Agreement. These firms are given preferential treatment by the banks, including debt-for-equity swaps, lower interest rates, and access to a pool of 2 trillion won in new loans and trade financing (*Economist*, 17 July 1999).

To the extent that a systematic bankruptcy of the corporate sector should be avoided and that the existing formal insolvency procedures are neither well developed nor efficient, informal workout procedures can be thought of as appropriate policy responses. As Nam and his colleagues point out, there is no guarantee that they will achieve the following three important tasks of an insolvency mechanism: preventing bankruptcy of economically viable, though heavily indebted, firms; preventing banks and other financial institutions from being unfairly expropriated to save' the corporate sector; and disciplining incompetent management and controlling shareholders. Related to these are concerns as to the ineffectiveness of the existing formal procedure as a threat to the creditors and the debtor firm, in case of failure of the informal one, and the lack of effective corporate governance within the financial institutions involved in the workout procedures (Nam *et al.* 1999: 65–6).

Promoting the restructuring of business groups

Though financial institutions are supposed to play the role of mediators, in practice the government has led the process by applying strong pressure on the top five *chaebol* to accelerate their business line swaps. The Big Deals' policy, adopted by the government in late 1998, aims to consolidate the top *chaebol*'s duplicative investments to gain economies of scale. The rationale for the policy is that the *chaebol* are unlikely to undertake restructuring voluntarily.

The policy however bears many similarities to the government-led investment realignment in heavy and chemical industries in the early 1980s. The *chaebol* came into existence largely because the government limited the number of entrants to various industries. This policy could be creating a similar scenario: increasing the dominance of the *chaebol* but reducing the number of players in certain sectors and doing little to reduce capacity. The Big Deals policy can also be criticised on other grounds. Such an approach would seem to be an ineffective means of strengthening international competitiveness, given that the companies involved are being pressured by the government as well as labour unions to minimise lay-offs, and that, at least in the nine designated industries, mergers or strategic alliances with foreign multinationals have been precluded. The policy also appears to be at least partially politically driven, to demonstrate to the public that the top *chaebol* are sharing the restructuring burden while attempting to maintain social stability through artificially guaranteeing employment, as well as support for related suppliers and distributors (Jung 1999: 86–8).

Although some deals have been struck, notably that between Hyundai Electronics and LG Semicom in May 1999, others have come to nothing or have seen very slow progress. The most high-profile failure to date was the deal in December 1998 whereby the government coerced Samsung and

Daewoo to swap their vehicle and electronics businesses in an attempt to consolidate the overbuilt car industry. But the asset swap fell through over disagreements over how to deal with Samsung Motor's 4.3 trillion won (US$3.6 billion) debt. Samsung then announced at the end of June 1999 that it would seek court protection from creditors as it moved to close the company. Then, in the wake of government pressure, the owner of Samsung pledged to repay 2.8 trillion won of the debt by selling 4 million of his own shares in Samsung Life insurance, Korea's largest privately held life insurance company. The FSC subsequently agreed to allow the company to be listed on the stock exchange from the year 2000. With the owner of the *chaebol* and his family believed to own much more than the 4 million shares in the life insurance subsidiary, the company's shares would be worth many more time their face value if they were publicly traded.[22]

The direction of *chaebol* restructuring will increasingly need to shift from a government-driven process to one allowing the operation of more market-based solutions. In many ways, corporate reforms removing debt guarantees, improving financial structures, increasing corporate transparency and enhancing shareholder rights are more important, and combined with increased competition from foreign investors and financial sector reform, are likely to prove more effective mechanisms to significantly affect *chaebol* governance (EAAU 1999; Yoo 1998). Similarly, intra-group transactions among *chaebol* subsidiaries should eventually be addressed not by the government but by shareholders and creditors under more transparent corporate accounts.

Further strengthening of corporate governance-related regulations and relevant legislation, including bankruptcy procedures, will also be essential in order to render current policies workable and credible. Korea's Fair Trade Commission will also need to play a more pro-active role in overcoming excessive *chaebol* power, through enhanced monitoring and by upgrading the regulatory framework and legal enforcement of competition policy. This in turn will require strong political support.

Competition policy

Competition policies were introduced in Korea in the 1980s, but implementation has clearly lagged behind the nominal powers of the enforcement agency, the Korean Fair Trade Commission (KFTC). The law, which had been amended several times prior to the crisis, restricts monopolies and cartels, prohibits price fixing and activities that restrict members' business activities, and requires review of mergers. While meant to be concentrating on the *chaebol*, its enforcement has been subordinated to industrial and trade policy goals and has displayed ambivalence about the activities of the *chaebol*. Only in 1995 did KFTC become an independent agency charged with policy responsibilities for competition and for enforcing anti-monopoly activities (Graham 1996). During 1995–6 the KFTC took almost 2,000 actions, a significant increase from the annual average of around 600 a year between 1981 and 1994 (Table 4.5). The majority of the cases concerned unfair trade practices. Around three-quarters of the cases resulted in warnings or recommendations for correction, while surcharges were imposed in seventy-three cases (OECD 1998: 151).

It is widely suspected that *chaebol* companies are still able to transfer financial resources to and from one another in order to keep ailing firms under their control. Many of these transactions could be found to be acts of breach of trust if they are brought to court. The KFTC has been the main regulator of self-dealings by *chaebol* families. In 1998, the KFTC twice investigated the top five *chaebol* and found illegal self-dealings that entailed transactions amounting to more than 5.5 trillion won, and subsequently handed down administrative fines amounting to 93 billion won to the companies involved. The move by the KFTC was widely interpreted as a response by the government to the efforts of *chaebol* families to keep under control the firms that should have been declared bankrupt. There are still few cases of breach of trust involving large listed companies transferring financial resources to and from one another as the needs for such transfers arise, even though self-dealings among the companies controlled by the same *chaebol* family have clearly been prevailing (Nam *et al.* 1999: 29–30).

While KFTC regulation on self-dealings between *chaebol* companies seems to be the only working mechanism that could check self-dealings by *chaebol* families, it has several shortcomings. First, the logic of the relevant Article of the KFTC Act is essentially a predation argument, and is not *per se* related to expropriation of minority shareholders. Second, from the perspective of corporate governance, the current regulation may be pointing the finger at the wrong parties. Currently it is the firm rather than members of the *chaebol* families that pays the fine. However, the firm and minority shareholders not only suffer from self-dealings that are detrimental to them in the first place, but also from fines that further aggravate their interests (Nam *et al.* 1999: 32).

While the strengthening of competition laws is an important part of the government's reform agenda, the stance of the KFTC has been not to challenge anti-trust cases. This is in spite of the fact that the Big Deal policy is actually

Table 4.5 Actions taken by the Korea Fair Trade Commission, 1981–96

Type of case	1981–92	1993–94	1995–96	Total
Abuse of market-dominating position	17	3	4	24
Mergers	346	37	59	442
Concentration of economic power	100	17	17	134
Collusive activities	94	36	62	192
Trade association activities	255	102	106	463
Unfair trade practices	3 568	1 270	1 210	6 048
Unfair international contracts	2 141	120	534	2 795
Total	6 532	1 702	1 992	10 226

Source: OECD (1998).

making enforcement looser. For example, the merging of LG Semicon's and Hyundai's semiconductor operations is in violation of Article 7 of the Fair Trade Law that prohibits competition-restricting corporate consolidations.

The history of Taiwan's enforcement of its Fair Trade Law is much shorter compared with the twenty years of Korea. First implemented in 1992, the Law requires that monopolies be monitored and, as specific tests of such behaviour, it prohibits abuse of monopolistic positions, regulates mergers and prohibits cartels. While Taiwan's FTC has not developed a comprehensive set of specific policies or guidelines, it does display a general sympathy towards SMEs. Four major economic objectives seem to underlie the Fair Trade Law: how to prevent large firms from abusing SMEs (via their dominant position); how to prevent excess competition among SMEs; how to allow SMEs to collaborate in order to compete against large firms; and how to make (financial) resources accessible to SMEs (Smith 1998b). Although the FTC has produced a body of decisions (see Table 4.6), implementation is largely by moral suasion (Graham 1996).

POST-CRISIS ISSUES: TAIWAN

Although Taiwan's financial sector has remained in far better shape than the crisis economies, as economic activity began to slow in 1998 weaknesses in the financial sector were exposed as credit quality among some financial institutions began to deteriorate and bankruptcies of financial institutions and business groups began to emerge.[23] In particular, the crisis had the effect of exposing prudential weaknesses in the financial system that had built up in the wake of financial deregulation. The establishment of new

Table 4.6 Actions taken by the Taiwan Fair Trade Commission, 1992–9

Type of case	1992–93	1994–95	1996–97	1998–99[1]	Total
Restriction on competition	33	33	45	29	140
Combination	1	1	6	3	11
Concerted action	4	7	15	14	40
Restriction on resale price	13	3 ·	6	2	24
Impediment to fair competition	15	21	20	10	65
Unfair competition	112	274	350	255	991
Counterfeiting	1	0	4	9	14
False, untrue or misleading articles	97	174	213	135	619
Damage to business reputation	0	4	4	2	10
Deceptive/obvious unfair acts	14	93	· 130	111	348
Unlawful multi-level sales	15	29	25	31	100
Other	6	15	19	24	64
Total	151	322	414	308	1195

Note: End June 1999.

Source: Taiwan Fair Trade Commission. Available at http://www.apeccp.org.tw/doc/Taipei/statistics/stat862.html

financial institutions saw the number of banks increase from sixteen at end 1989 to forty by June 1998, with the number of branches rising to 1,902 from only 692 as of December 1989. The easing of regulation on bills-finance companies at the end of 1994 saw their numbers rising from three to sixteen by August 1998.

As Abe, Sato and Nagano (1999: 39–40) have argued, these changes gave rise to two negative impacts. First, they enabled business groups to establish their own financial arms. Prior to liberalisation, private business groups were prohibited from entering the banking business. As Abe, Sato and Nagano (1999: 40) point out, the number of bills-finance companies increased precisely because business groups aggressively entered the financial business. Most of the new banks and new bills-finance companies were thus creations of a single business group or more than one group working together. Of the four financial institutions that failed in 1998, three had been established in this manner. Second, banks became more aggressive in their lending operations as competition intensified as more financial institutions joined the market. While Taiwan banks, including the new ones, still retained their conservative character, sharper competition led banks to lend to riskier projects than before.

In the first quarter of 1998, non-performing loans of commercial banks rose from 3.8 per cent to 4.2 per cent. By April 1999, the Central Bank of China estimated non-performing loans in the banking sector at NT$350 billion (US$10.6 billion), representing a record 5.2 per cent of total outstanding loans.[24] Meanwhile, non-performing loans of the loosely regulated farmers' associations and credit cooperatives (which account for only 2 per cent of all lending)[25] were estimated by the government to have risen to 11.7 per cent and 7.8 per cent, respectively, by the end of 1998, with some individual institutions reporting levels of above 20 per cent.

The deterioration in loan quality largely reflected both imprudent lending by banks and imprudent business practices by several business groups. Several business groups became insolvent in 1998 after exhausting their funds in an attempt to buy member firms' stock shares in order to shore up the prices of these shares (Abe, Sato and Nagano 1999: 36). This practice, known as creating shell companies', was particularly used by construction companies from the mid-1990s. Under the practice, a business group identifies a company whose listed stock price is low, buys the company's shares and takes over its management. The group then shifts a profitable operation to the company, raising the firm's share price. The purchasing group then borrows money from financial institutions using the company's shares as security. These funds are then recycled into the stock market, pushing up stock prices further, in turn making it possible for the borrowers to borrow more to buy more stocks. It was not uncommon for the same shares to be used as security for loans from more than one bank. For some business groups, a short-cut to this was to have its own financial institution. The slowdown of the economy disturbed the operation of this mechanism. Firms that had heavily borrowed against rising stock prices failed, bringing down related financial institutions (Abe, Sato and Nagano 1999: 36–9).

In the wake of these events, government policy has focused on three areas. The first has involved measures to deal with the failing companies and financial institutions. These have included moratoriums on debt repayments for a maximum of six months for debt-saddled companies, and new regulations compelling credit unions and cooperatives to merge or to close if they are unable to achieve capital adequacy ratios of more than 8 per cent within three years. Meanwhile, banks are required to achieve a non-performing loan ratio of 2.5 per cent by 2003.

Second, government funds were extensively employed during 1998 to support stock prices. Further, in July this year the government announced a US$15.2 billion stabilisation fund would be established to guard against stock market instability following an increase in China–Taiwan tensions.[26] The plan requires four government-supervised funds (labour pension fund, labour insurance fund, public servants pension fund, and postal savings deposits) to buy blue-chip stocks and shares of mutual funds for the purpose of insulating the stock market from irregularities. The government has also said that a similar scheme will be in operation to manage capital flows, when (and if) short-term capital flows are fully liberalised.

Third, several measures have been used to stimulate the real economy. During 1999, Taiwan has followed a steady course of currency intervention and frequent manipulation of the credit environment, with the aim of keeping exports competitive while boosting domestic liquidity (EIU 1999). Several measures introduced in the first quarter of 1999 are designed to free up liquidity in the banking sector, enabling banks to write off non-performing loans while simultaneously stimulating domestic demand. These have included cutting the reserve requirement over several months, reducing corporate banking tax, removing some taxes on bank transactions, and pressuring banks to apply looser credit requirements for SMEs.

Despite government pronouncements to the contrary, the crisis is likely to put on hold any plans to completely liberalise capital flows. Prior to the crisis, Taiwan still retained a number of controls on international capital flows, although these were in the process of being gradually relaxed. The most significant are the requirement that both inward and outward direct investments be approved by the Ministry of Economic Affairs, and limitations on foreign investment in Taiwan-listed stocks.[27] Plans were put in place to remove restrictions on foreign share ownership by end of 2000, but have now been put back until 2001.

FUTURE CHALLENGES

Korea has made visible and indeed impressive progress in financial sector restructuring and in reform of corporate governance systems over the past two years, particularly given the severity of the problems in the financial and corporate sectors. On the presumption that the improved regulations, standards and financial supervision are properly enforced to ensure the compliance of both financial and non-financial corporations, these reforms will have had a significant effect not only on governance structures but on the entire economy as well.

Several fundamental reforms remain at issue. In particular:

The fragility of the legal and institutional framework and the lack of credible enforcement with regard to corporate governance systems remain a concern (Nam, Kang and Kim 1999: 40).

The modality of financial and corporate-sector restructuring will need to become increasingly consistent with clear market principles. The reorientation of the role of financial institutions and the normalisation of prudential regulation will be affected by the privatisation of the recapitalised banks and the post-privatisation governance structure. The success of corporate governance reform will be seriously jeopardised if the privatisation process is delayed or ill-managed, or a small number of *chaebol* families continue to exercise dominant control in both corporate and financial sectors (Nam, Kang and Kim 1999: 42).

There remains the increasing danger that the dominant *chaebol* will come to monopolise financial resources in the non-bank sector. Under such circumstances, it is hard to expect sound corporate governance structures to be developed. Regulatory reforms in this area are still at an early stage and will require ongoing monitoring.

Interventionist industrial policies, which had constituted grounds for governance failures in the corporate and financial sectors, as well as in insolvency proceedings, may continue to stand in the way of corporate governance reform. This is because capital markets, particularly long-term financing facilities, along with internal governance structures in both the financial and non-financial sectors, will take time to develop. In the meantime, the possibility of continued industrial policy cannot be ruled out (Nam, Kang and Kim 1999: 43).

Korea has yet to make satisfactory progress in the area of market for foreign takeover. Although some firms and banks were sold to foreign investors in the course of corporate and financial sector restructuring, Korea's rapid recovery may see the momentum for restructuring ease as firms and the government lose their enthusiasm for selling assets to foreign investors.

As Nam, Kang and Kim (1999: 41) point out, there is no instantaneous fix for these problems. Rather, the government must continue to improve the legal and institutional framework for corporate governance, and strengthen their enforcement by biting the bullet'. This requires government scrutiny of the regulatory framework and legal institutions, careful analysis of the incentive structure embodied in the framework, and the elimination of any unclear provisions in laws and regulations. It also requires the establishment of an appropriate incentive structure for regulators in order to ensure credible enforcement.

Institutional frameworks supportive of growth cannot be simply established, but in reality must be learnt over time by all the parties involved. In this respect, the most difficult hurdle for Korea lies in moving away from the past managerialist' approach to development, whereby the government manages the economy as if it were a household or a firm, to one whereby market forces take the lead. The role of government is then to set right the rules of the game' under which economic agents interact with each other in the areas of private property, contract, exchange, trade and competition (Yoo 1996: 40–3).

Compared with Korea, the challenges facing Taiwan in the post-crisis environment look considerably less daunting. Before the crisis, Taiwan's industrial structure was probably one of the best prepared in East Asia for the challenges of the twenty-first century. However, in approaching industrial maturity, Taiwan will also need to accelerate its own restructuring and enhance competitiveness, as other Asian economies re-emerge from the East Asian crisis. Part of this strategy requires stable cross-Strait relations and closer economic linkages with mainland China if Taiwan is to successfully transform its economy into a service-oriented one and attract US and European multinationals as a gateway to East Asian markets. Encouraging inward foreign investment in larger scale enterprises with the capacity to undertake significant research and development, and the fostering of production links to Southeast Asia and China will continue to be important.

A related challenge is liberalisation of capital markets, although the events of 1997–8 are likely to see a delay in the opening up of Taiwan's capital markets, with the government seeing Taiwan's curbs on capital flows and foreign exchange trading as having insulated Taiwan from regional turmoil (Smith 2000). More significantly, ongoing uncertainty in China–Taiwan relations is likely to dictate the pace of opening.

Evolutionary issues

The most obvious evolution in Korea's business environment will be its increasing market orientation in the wake of deregulation, privatisation, greater foreign business presence and international capital inflows. Under this scenario, profound changes should occur in the way business is conducted and the structure of corporate governance. Businesses will become more concerned with profits and cash flow than with sales and asset growth. Their investment behaviour will change as they rely more on equity financing than on debt. Group structures will be loosened with the elimination of loan guarantees between affiliate companies of the same group, empowerment of minority shareholders, liberalised regulations on mergers and acquisitions of listed companies, and the preparation of consolidated financial statements (Jung 1999: 90). Increased competition in the domestic market will create incentives for firms to learn and innovate.

Exogenous forces will also be working for change. As international market forces play a freer role, there will also be pressures to adopt international rules with respect to market access for foreign producers and foreign capital. Western firms will push for greater transparency in regulation and for a legal framework to settle disputes and protect property rights.

But while the domestic business environment will become more market oriented, it would be premature to conclude that this will create incentives for convergence of the internal organisation of Korean firms with that of Western' firms. It does not necessarily follow, for example, that an increase in competitive forces and organisational learning will undermine established relationships, either because established cultural values do not change, or because vested interests have been built up, both in business and the bureaucracy. These features are likely to slow or block changes in rules that would bring about changes in internal organisation (Dobson 1998).

Given this, two trends seem likely in the short to medium term. The first is that the state will continue to play an important role in the economy. One obvious irony of the crisis has been the increasing influence of the government in the economy through increased bank ownership and direct intervention in the *chaebol* restructuring, despite the policy failures for which the government itself was primarily responsible. How successfully the government can reduce its role and allow the market to operate under fair and transparent rules of the game will be critical in determining long-term competitiveness. The second trend is that family-centred business could remain a primary management style in Korea for some time. A professional management system based on separation of ownership and management will evolve only gradually as performance evaluation takes root and as a cadre of professional managers is groomed (Jung 1999: 90). Fundamental change in corporate organisation and governance requires above all else a change in the attitudes of the different players, whereby management begins to focus on increasing all shareholders' value and shareholders learn to exercise their rights and to actively monitor the way management runs corporations.

In some ways, though, the business systems of Taiwan and Korea may undergo convergence. The current Korean reform process is clearly designed to provide for a more balanced industrial structure through a greater role for innovative and vibrant small and medium-sized firms and for greater foreign participation. The *chaebol,* in continuing to be the engine of growth into the twenty-first century, are also being encouraged to become more closely-knit industrial groups.

How quickly this transformation takes place depends largely on the success with which the current agenda of reforms is carried out. Reform' in this sense means the replacement of the government's will and judgment in resource allocation by market rules and institutions. Establishing this is one of the most difficult challenges in development and will be the crucial factor in determining Korea's long-term economic performance.

NOTES

1   Comments and suggestions from Jungho Yoo are gratefully acknowledged.
2   This section draws on Smith (1999; 2000).
3   Both Korea and Taiwan share similar trading partners. At the peak years during the 1980s, both economies relied on the US to consume 40% or more of their exports, while over 30% of the goods and services imported into the two economies came from Japan (Hattori and Sato 1997: 344).
4   The three 1985 cases involved the Tenth Credit Cooperative Association, Cathay Investment and Trust Company, and the Overseas Investment and Trust Company. In all cases the government provided support and had the institutions taken over by others. See Yang (1994: 314) for a comprehensive discussion of these cases.
5   One component of this policy was the government's adoption in 1982 of sectoral policy of identifying strategic' high technology industries, although the amount in subsidy terms was quite small. Empirical investigation into this policy, however, shows that the beneficiaries of these policies were not strategic industries. Rather, the major recipients of subsidies were in fact those industries with a declining comparative advantage (Smith 2000).
6   Ceiling and floor rates for lending, and floor rates for deposits were abolished in 1985–6. For a comprehensive discussion of financial reform see Cheng (1993), Yang (1994) and Shea (1994).
7   As of the end of June 1989, there were 6 merchant banks as joint ventures with foreign-affiliated firms. The number rose to 30 as all 24 investment and finance companies converted themselves into merchant banks. As a result, merchant banks became involved in a broad range of corporate finance activities, in particular, using funds raised overseas to provide short-term business loans to *chaebol* groups.
8   Preferential credit has largely been directed towards state and party-run enterprises.
9   As McKinnon (1991: 37) notes, although some financial repression existed in the form of preferential interest rates for exporters, these rates were generally kept positive and substantial in real terms; nor was this commitment to finance exporters sufficient to undermine the central bank's control over the monetary base.
10 Although, as Cole and Patrick (1986) point out, inefficiencies of financial repression may not always manifest themselves, because of the behaviour of the informal credit market. Thus, when formal financial institutions are regulated, informal credit markets expand.
11   Long-established' banks are banks existing for more than 50 years; new' banks are banks established from 1992.
12 For example, the dominant shareholder of Samsung group controls more than 46% of the shares of the companies, even though his personal shares are only 4 per cent (Nam *et al.* 1999: 19).
13 From 1987 to 1995, pre-tax rates of return on capital in industrial companies were below pre-tax cost of debt. Only the steel industry realised profits in excess of debt charges, from 1993 to 1995 (OECD 1998: 162; McKinsey 1998).
14 The interest payment coverage ratio is calculated as operating earnings over interest expenses. Those firms whose interest payment coverage ratios are below 1 are likely to go bankrupt (Nam, Kang and Kim 1999: 32).
15 During the 1980s thousands of Taiwan nationals went abroad to study and to work for foreign corporations, mostly in the US and Japan. From the mid-1980s, returning locals trained in foreign multinational companies became a direct source of technology and new skills. The ratio of returnees from abroad

to students abroad increased from 15.6% during 1971–81 to 21.6% during 1982–93. In particular, returnees with science and engineering degrees totalled 6,172 in 1993, almost 5.6 times the number returning in 1982. In contrast, of the 15,000 Koreans who have earned science and engineering PhD degrees abroad, only about 1,200 are believed to have returned to Korea (OECD 1996: 109).

16 The empirical validity of the bank-based high debt model' to Taiwan is highly questionable in light of the other analyses offered by Cheng (1986), Yang (1990), Shea and Yang (1990) and Smith (2000).

17 For example, Wade (1998a) contends that in Korea the marginalisation and abolishment of the Economic Planning Board's traditional role of coordinating investment in large-scale industries made it easier for market failure to manifest itself in excess capacity in the auto, shipbuilding, petrochemical and semiconductor industries.

18 The Korean government was involved in massive bailouts on numerous occasions, including the emergency debt-freeze in 1972, industrial restructuring of major HCIs in the early 1980s, and industrial rationalisation measures in overseas construction and shipping during the mid-1980s (Nam, Kang and Kim 1999: 27).

19 See Yoo (1990) for a discussion of why it remains difficult to conclude that the export growth in the 1980s of products of the heavy industries promoted during the 1970s was the result of successful government intervention.

20 The *chaebol* were required to submit combined financial statements, which show transactions between affiliated firms, starting from the 1999 fiscal year. They were also required to reduce their debts to 200% of their equity or below by the end of 1999. The *chaebol*, however, will find it difficult to meet the year-end deadline. By mid-1999, the top 30 business groups still needed to raise 180 trillion won, double the amount of the national budget, to get their debt levels below 200%.

21 Investment trust companies serve as fund managers, beneficiary certificate sellers, and investment advisers.

22 Political factors have also played a role. Samsung Motors is located in Pusan, the power base of former president Kim Young-sam, who approved the project. With national assembly elections due in April 2000, the government may shrink from shutting the plant for fear of job losses.

23 In the second half of 1998, two bills-finance companies (whose major business is as short-term debt underwriters), two banks and several firms ran into financial difficulties.

24 Some private sector estimates put non-performing loans of the new banks at around 7–8% in 1998.

25 Returns on assets for the 400 credit unions and cooperatives average well under 1% and average profit margins are only 2.5%.

26 Taiwan's stock market remains one of the most underdeveloped in East Asia. This in part reflects the low proportion of institutional investors (around 8% in 1997), and the concern over short-term capital flight when relations with the mainland deteriorate. For example, the increase in tensions between China and Taiwan in the period from July 1995 to March 1996, following Taiwan's president Lee Teng-hui's visit to the United States, resulted in considerable outflow (US$14.1 billion) of short-term capital.

27 Foreign individuals were only granted access to the stock market in March 1996. Until recently the cap on aggregate foreign ownership of shares had been raised only gradually. In early 1999 the cap was raised to 50% from 30%, while the ceiling on foreign ownership of individual stocks has been lifted to 50 per cent from 19%. Until July 1997, Taiwan's companies were not allowed to issue shares abroad. Securities firms were also required to limit overseas investments to 20% of net assets.

REFERENCES

Abe, M., Sato, Y. and Nagano, M. (1999) *Economic Crisis and Korea/Taiwan*, Institute of Developing Economies, Tokyo.

Abe, M. and Kawakami, M. (1997) A distributive comparison of enterprise size in Korea and Taiwan', *The Developing Economies* 35(4): 383–400.

Amsden, A. (1989) *Asia's Next Giant: South Korea and late industrialisation*, New York: Oxford University Press.

Cheng, Hang-Sheng (ed.) (1986) Financial policy and reform in Taiwan, China', *Financial Reform in Pacific Basin Countries*, Lexington, Mass.: Lexington Books.

Cheng, Tun-jen (1993) Guarding the commanding heights: The state as banker in Taiwan', in S. Haggard, C.H. Lee and S. Maxfield (eds) *The Politics of Finance in Developing Countries*, Ithaca and London: Cornell University Press.

Cho, Yoon Je (1997) Government intervention, rent distribution, and economic development in Korea', in M. Aoki, H. Kim and M. Okuno-Fujiwara (eds) *The Role of Government in East Asian Economics Development*, Oxford: Clarendon Press.

Cole, D.C. and Patrick, H.T. (1986) Financial development in the Pacific Basin market economies', in A.H.H. Tan and B. Kapur (eds) *Pacific Growth and Financial Interdependence*, Sydney: Allen and Unwin.

Dobson, W. (1998) Business networks in East Asia', in Rong-I Wu and Yun-Peng Chu (eds) *Business, Markets and Government in the Asia Pacific*, London and New York: Routledge.

Economist (1999) Death, where is thy sting?, 17 July: 61

Economist Intelligence Unit (EIU) (1999) *Country Report – Taiwan* (2nd quarter), United Kingdom: EIU.

East Asia Analytical Unit (EAAU) (1999) *Korea Rebuilds: From crisis to opportunity*, Canberra: AGPS.

Graham, E.M. (1996) Competition policies in the dynamic industrialising economies', *APEC Working Paper Series* 96–9, Washington DC: Institute for International Economics.

Haggard, S. (1988) Policy, politics and structural adjustment: The U.S. and the East Asian NICs', paper presented at Conference on Economic Development Experience of Taiwan and its Role in an Emerging Asia–Pacific Area, vol. II, Taipei: Academia Sinica.

and Collins, S. (1994) The political economy of adjustment in the 1980s', in S. Haggard, R. Cooper, S. Collins, Choongsoo Kim and Sung-Tae Ro (eds) *Macroeconomic Policy and Adjustment in Korea, 1970–1990*, Cambridge, MA: Harvard University Press.

and Kim, Euysung (1997) The sources of East Asia's economic growth', *Access Asia Review* 1(1): 31–63.

, Cooper, R.N. and Collins, S. (1994) Understanding Korea's macroeconomic policy', in S. Haggard, R. Cooper, S. Collins, Choongsoo Kim and Sung-Tae Ro (eds) *Macroeconomic Policy and Adjustment in Korea, 1970–1990*, Cambridge, MA: Harvard University Press.

Hattori, T. and Sato, Y. (1997) A comparative study of development mechanisms in Korea and Taiwan: introductory analysis', *The Developing Economies*, 35(4): 341–57.

Hobday, M. (1995) *Innovation in East Asia*, United Kingdom: Edward Elgar.

Hughes, H. (1993) Is there an East Asian model?', *Economic Division Working Papers* no.4, Canberra: Research School of Pacific Studies, The Australian National University.

Huh, Chan and Sun Bae Kim (1994) Financial regulation and banking sector performance: A comparison of bad loan problems in Japan and Korea', *Economic Review* (Federal Reserve Bank of San Francisco) 2: 18–29.

Jung, Ku-Hyun (1999) Asian economic crisis and corporate restructuring', *Korea Focus* 7(3): 77–90.

Kim, Linsu (1997) *Imitation to Innovation,* Harvard, Mass.: Harvard Business School Press.

Koo, Bohn-Young (1986) The role of government in Korea's industrial development' in Kyu-Uck Lee (ed.) *Industrial Development Policies and Issues,* Seoul: Korea Development Institute.

Kuo, S.W.Y. and Liu, C.Y. (1998) Taiwan', in R. Garnaut and R. McLeod (eds) *East Asia in Crisis: From being a miracle to needing one?* London: Routledge.

Lin, O.C.C. (1998) Science and technology policy and its influence on economic development in Taiwan', in H.S. Rowan (ed.) *Behind East Asian Growth: The political and social foundations of prosperity,* London: Routledge.

Liu, C.Y. (1992) Liberalisation and globalisation of the financial market', in N.T. Wang (ed.) *Taiwan's Enterprises in Global Perspective,* New York: M.E. Sharpe.

Mathews, J.A. (1998) Fashioning a New Korean Model Out of the Crisis', *Japan Policy Research Institute Working Paper* no. 46.

McKinnon, R.I. (1991) *The Order of Economic Liberalisation,* Baltimore: Johns Hopkins University Press.

McKinsey Global Institute (1998) *Productivity-led Growth for Korea,* Seoul: McKinsey and Company Inc.

Nam, Il Chong, Kim, Joon-Kyung, Kang, Yeongjae, Joh, Sung Wook and Kim, Jun-Il (1999) Corporate governance in Korea', paper presented at the OECD/KDI conference on Corporate Governance in Asia: A Comparative Perspective, Seoul, 3–5 March. Available at http://www.oecd.org

Nam, Il Chong, Kang Yeongjae and Kim Joon-Kyung (1999) Comparative corporate governance trends in Asia', paper presented at the OECD/KDI conference on Corporate Governance in Asia: A Comparative Perspective, Seoul, 3–5 March. Available at http://www.oecd.org

Newsreview (Korea Herald) (1999) Big brother is getting fatter', 10 July: 30–1.

Noble, G.W. and Ravenhill, J. (2000) The good, the bad and the ugly?', in G.W. Noble and J. Ravenhill (eds) *The Asian Financial Crisis and the Reform of the Global Financial Architecture,* United Kingdon: Cambridge University Press (forthcoming).

Organisation for Economic Cooperation and Development (OECD) (1994) *OECD Economic Survey – Korea,* Paris.

   (1996)   *OECD Economic Survey – Korea,* Paris.

   (1998)   *OECD Economic Survey – Korea,* Paris: OECD.

Pack, H. (1992) New perspectives on industrial growth in Taiwan', in G. Ranis, *Taiwan: from developing to mature economy,* Boulder: Westview Press.

Park, Yung Chul (1994) Korea: development and structural change of the financial system', in H.T. Patrick and Y.C. Park (eds) *The Financial Development of Japan, Korea and Taiwan: Growth, repression, and liberalisation,* New York and Oxford: Oxford University Press.

   and Dong Won Kim (1994) Korea: development and structural change of the banking system ', in H.T. Patrick, and Y.C. Park (eds) *The Financial Development of Japan, Korea, and Taiwan: Growth, repression, and liberalisation,* New York and Oxford: Oxford University Press.

Patrick, H. (1994) Comparisons, contrasts and implications' in H. Patrick and Y.C. Park (eds) *The Financial Development of Japan, Korea and Taiwan: Growth, repression, and liberalisation,* New York and Oxford: Oxford University Press.

Ranis, G. and Fei, J.C. (1988) Development economics: What next?', in G. Ranis and T. P. Schultz (eds) *The State of Development Economics,* Oxford: Blackwell.

Ranis, G. and Mahmood, S.A. (1992) *The Political Economy of Development Policy Change,* Oxford: Blackwell.

SaKong, Il (1993) *Korea in the World Economy*, Washington, DC: Institute for International Economics.

Shea, J.D. and Yang, Y.H. (1990) *Financial System and the Allocation of Investment Funds*, Taipei: Chung-Hua Institution for Economic Research.

Shea, J.D. (1994) Taiwan: development and structural change of the financial system', in H.T. Patrick and Y.C. Park (eds) *The Financial Development of Japan, Korea and Taiwan*, New York and Oxford: Oxford University Press.

Smith, H. (1994) Korea's industry policy in the 1980s', *Pacific Economic Papers* no. 229.

—— (1997) Taiwan's industry policy in the 1980s: an appraisal',   *ASEAN Economic Journal* 11(1): 1–33.

—— (1998a) Korea', in R. Garnaut and R. McLeod (eds)   *East Asia in Crisis: From being a miracle to needing one?*, London: Routledge.

—— (1998b) Summary of discussion', in Rong-I Wu and Yun-Peng Chu (eds) *Business, Markets and Government in the Asia Pacific*, London and New York: Routledge.

—— (1999) The failure of Korea Inc.',   *Agenda* 6(2): 153–66.

—— (2000)   *Industry Policy in Taiwan and Korea: Winning with the market in the 1980s*, United Kingdom: Edward Elgar.

Wade, R. (1990) *Governing the Market: Economic theory and the role of government in East Asian industrialisation*, Princeton: Princeton University Press.

—— and Veneroso, F. (1998) The Asian crisis: The high debt model   *vs.* the Wall Street Treasury–IMF complex', *New Left Review*, March–April, no. 228, 3–220.

—— (1998a)   The Asian debt and development crisis of 1997–?: Causes and consequences', *World Development*, August.

—— (1998b) From miracle to meltdown: vulnerabilities, moral hazard, panic and debt deflation in the Asian crisis', manuscript. Available from wade@rsage.org

Wu, Rong-I and Chu, Yun-Peng (eds) (1998) *Business, Markets and Government in the Asia Pacific*, London and New York: Routledge.

Yang, Ya-Hwei (1990) The influence of preferential policies on strategic industries: An empirical study of Taiwan', Taipei: Chung-Hua Institution for Economic Research, Discussion Paper no. 9003.

—— (1994) Taiwan: development and structural change of the banking system', in H.T. Patrick and Y.C. Park (eds) *The Financial Development of Japan, Korea and Taiwan*, New York and Oxford: Oxford University Press.

Yoo, Jungho (1990) The industrial policy of the 1970s and the evolution of the manufacturing sector in Korea', *Korea Development Institute Working Paper* no. 9017. Seoul: Korea Development Institute.

—— (1996) Challenges to the newly industrialised countries: A reinterpretation of Korea's growth experience', KDI Working Paper no. 9608.

—— (1997) The influence of the world market size on the pace of industrialisation', *The KDI Journal of Economic Policy* 19(2) [Korean].

Yoo, Seong Min (1995) Chaebol in Korea: Misconceptions, realities, and policies', *Korea Development Institute Working Paper* no. 9507, Seoul: Korea Development Institute.

—— (1998) Corporate restructuring in Korea: Policy issues before and during the crisis', paper presented at conference on Financial Reform and Macroeconomic Management in Korea, Australian National University, 3 November.

Zysman, J. (1983) *Government, Markets and Growth: Financial systems and the politics of industrial change*, Ithaca, New York: Cornell University Press.

5 Thailand's experience with reform in the financial sector[1]

Bhanupong Nidhiprabha and Peter G. Warr

INTRODUCTION

The magnitude of Thailand's recent crisis may be gauged roughly by its effect on GDP. After a decade of growth of real GDP in excess of 9 per cent, in 1997 real GDP declined slightly (around 1 per cent) and in 1998 it declined by around 9 per cent. Recovery has been slower than was hoped, but positive though small GDP growth was recorded for the first two quarters of 1999. For calendar 1999 growth should be around 3 per cent. The sustainability of this recovery depends on the success of its reform program, especially that involving the financial sector. This reform program is the focus of the chapter.

Thailand's economic crisis began with a currency crisis. It derived from a loss of confidence in the capacity of the central bank, the Bank of Thailand, to maintain its fixed exchange rate policy in the face of a capital outflow. The outflow had itself been precipitated by a slump in exports in 1996 during a time of large current account deficits, averaging around 8 per cent of GDP in the mid-1990s. In the 1980s the Bank of Thailand had twice shown its willingness to devalue the currency, significantly and without warning, in such circumstances. Fearing such a devaluation, holders of internationally mobile capital attempted to flee from baht-denominated assets.

What should have been a minor adjustment problem became much more serious because of the very large volume of internationally mobile capital present in Thailand at the time relative to the level of the Bank of Thailand's international reserves.[2] This situation meant that unless the Bank of Thailand was able to bolster its reserves by borrowing massive volumes of funds internationally at short notice, it would be unable to defend the currency in the face of a capital outflow. No such source of funding was readily available and, as the very large magnitude of the capital outflow became apparent to market participants, a large devaluation, rather than a small one, became increasingly probable.

The crisis-vulnerability of economies like Thailand's was not adequately appreciated in the lead-up to the crisis and understanding this phenomenon is therefore a prerequisite for drawing appropriate lessons for averting future crises of this kind. Vulnerability does not mean a state in which things necessarily *will* go wrong; that requires a trigger, in this case the 1996 export slowdown. What it means is that if things go wrong, then suddenly a lot goes wrong' (Dornbusch 1997).

The large volume of internationally mobile capital in Thailand was the result of accumulation through the decade of economic boom which preceded the crisis. Several factors contributed to the massive inflow of volatile foreign capital during this period. Large returns were being made from investing in Thailand and this situation had been sustained over several years. Euphoria induced by almost a decade of high growth produced over-confidence on the part of both borrowers and lenders. In addition, the government was assuring the public that reserves were adequate to maintain the fixed exchange rate and the International Monetary Fund (IMF) also seemed satisfied, judging from its public statements. Investing in Thailand seemed both safe and profitable. Not to participate was to miss out.

Through the first half of the 1990s, investment in real estate and commercial office space soared. The rate of inflow was so rapid that the quality of the investment inevitably declined, much of it proving to be financially non-performing, destroying the companies that had financed it. But why had investors acted so imprudently? Over-confidence was an important part of the story, but the underlying real appreciation was another. The classic bubble economy is one in which real estate prices continue to rise well beyond levels justified by the productivity of the assets, but so long as the prices continue to rise, existing investors are rewarded and collateral is created for new loans to finance further investment, and so on – until the inevitable crash.

Unrealistic expectations of continued boom are the underlying fuel for this process. These expectations are generally possible only after several years of sustained boom. The boom therefore generates the mechanism for a crash. This is why economic booms almost never peter out gradually. They collapse. In these respects, Thailand's financial panic was similar to many previous examples around the world, including the Mexican crash of 1994 (Edwards 1998).

In the Thai case, there were four other, less well understood causes for over-investment and over-reliance on short-term debt financing, each of which was policy-induced. First, as described above, the Bank of Thailand was attempting to sterilise the monetary consequences of capital inflows, despite its own relaxation of capital controls. Increasing domestic interest rates encouraged further short-term capital inflows.

Second, beginning in 1993 the Thai government encouraged banks to borrow short term through its establishment of the Bangkok International Banking Facility (BIBF), again with the apparent approval of the IMF. This development made short-term borrowing from abroad easier and more attractive for domestic banks and, from the point of view of the foreign lender, these loans were protected by implicit guarantees from the Bank of Thailand. The dramatic increase in short-term bank loans began at this time. In addition to new short-term loans, significant substitution of short-term loans for longer-term loans also occurred. Beginning in 1993, the stock of long-term loans actually declined for around two years while short-term loans accelerated.

Third, Thailand's corporate tax policy contributes to the preference for debt financing over equity financing which pervades Thailand's corporate and financial sector. Family-owned enterprises, which dominate among both small and large-scale firms in Thailand, strongly prefer retention of ownership and management control within the family unit. Thailand's tax regime reinforces this preference because interest payments are deductible expenses for the purposes of corporate income taxes, whereas dividend payments are not.

Fourth, the Bank of Thailand also indirectly encouraged short-term borrowing by non-bank financial institutions. For many years prior to the crisis, banking licences in Thailand had been highly profitable. The issuance of new licences is tightly controlled by the Bank of Thailand but it had become known that the number of licences was to be increased significantly. Thai finance companies immediately began competing with one another to be among the lucky recipients. To project themselves as significant players in the domestic financial market, many companies were willing to borrow large sums abroad and lend domestically at low margins, thereby taking risks they would not ordinarily contemplate. With lenders eager to lend vast sums, real estate was a favoured investment because purchase of real estate requires almost no specialist expertise, only the willingness to accept risk.

The effect of the currency crisis on the real economy operated through a contraction of aggregate demand.[3] Following the float, the plummeting value of the baht was identified as the major policy concern. The Bank of Thailand gave first priority to arresting the rate of depreciation as a precondition for restoring confidence. Monetary policy was tight and interest rates rose through the second half of 1997 (see Figure 5.1). Investment declined dramatically. Government spending also contracted, along with public sector revenues. Fiscal contraction was a temporary objective. A fiscal *surplus* was initially required by the IMF, despite the impending recession, but large deficits were later agreed to. It is now accepted within Thailand and international institutions such as the IMF and the World Bank, that a Keynesian fiscal stimulus is required. A fiscal deficit of 7 per cent was recorded for 1999, but recovery cannot depend on this source of demand alone.

In Thailand, as in other crisis-affected economies, public sector debt is projected to become a serious problem (Table 5.1). Expanded public spending therefore cannot be the principal source of demand-led recovery. A recovery of private investment is central to a sustainable recovery. However, availability of credit has been a serious constraint on private sector recovery. Considerable damage was done to the financial system during the course of the crisis and recovery requires that these problems be now addressed through appropriate reforms. Accordingly, this chapter charts the course of Thailand's financial sector reforms.

Figure 5.1 Exchange rates and inter-bank interest rates, Thailand, 1997–9

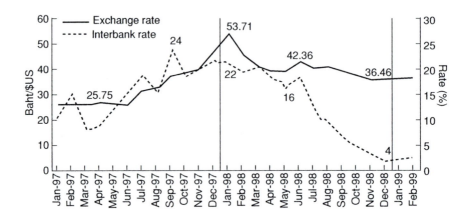

THE FINANCIAL SECTOR BEFORE THE CRISIS

Two types of institution dominate Thailand's financial system: private commercial banks and finance companies. Between 1990 and 1997 these two institutions represented 85 per cent of all household savings intermediated by financial institutions and 90 per cent of all credit extended. This implies a relatively small role for all other types of private financial institution – life insurance companies, agricultural cooperatives, savings cooperatives, pawnshops and mutual fund management companies, as well as specialised public sector institutions – Government Savings Bank, Bank for Agriculture and Agricultural Cooperatives, Industrial Finance Corporation of Thailand, Government Housing Bank, Small Industry Finance Corporation and the Export–Import Bank of Thailand (Vichyanond 1999).

A series of liberalisations through the early 1990s made possible a considerable expansion in the scope of activities undertaken by the commercial banks and finance companies, especially as it related to foreign transactions. Prior to this, exchange controls were in place which intentionally restricted capital movements into and out of Thailand. Because international transactions played such an important role in the crisis and the lead-up to it, a review of the changes to the policy environment relating to these transactions is important.

Capital controls before 1990

Over the two decades ending in 1990, four forms of capital control were important: interest rate ceilings, direct capital controls, controls on the foreign exchange positions of commercial banks, and the withholding tax on foreign borrowing.

Table 5.1 Government debt in crisis-affected East Asia

	% of GDP 1996	1999p	2000p
Thailand	11.0	55.4	52.7
Domestic	2.0	26.4	24.7
Foreign	9.0	29.0	28.0
Malaysia	47.7	59.5	63.3
Domestic	31.7	36.5	39.3
Foreign	16.0	23.0	24.0
Korea	28.2	41.3	40.7
Domestic	19.2	25.3	24.7
Foreign	9.0	16.0	16.0
Indonesia	51.1	93.0	98.3
Domestic	25.1	57.0	64.3
Foreign	26.0	36.0	34.0

Note: p = projected
Source: World Bank, *Recovery in East Asia*, 1998.

1 *Interest rate ceilings.* Regulatory ceilings on domestic interest rates – both lending and borrowing rates – prevented the domestic interest rate increases that would otherwise have induced capital inflows when the domestic money supply was contracted. These interest rate ceilings were adjusted only slightly during shocks. Their impact on domestic interest rates seems clear. For example, from 1970 to 1981, commercial banks' deposits rates were equal to the ceiling rates, and from 1982 to 1985, the actual time deposit rates of interest paid by commercial banks remained 0.5 per cent below the ceiling.

2 *Direct capital controls.* Bank of Thailand permission was required to move capital out of Thailand and this policy was policed vigorously. During periods of monetary expansion this arm of policy enabled the monetary authorities to prevent the outward flow of capital which would otherwise deprive them of the capacity to expand the domestic money supply when desired. All outgoing payments were subject to approval. Until 1990, exporters were required to submit foreign exchange currency to banks within seven days of receiving payments from abroad.[4]

Until 1990 holdings of foreign exchange deposits by Thai citizens were not permitted. Thais could not purchase foreign currencies for investment overseas and were thus greatly restricted in taking advantage of differentials between domestic and foreign rates of interest. Individuals were not permitted to take out of Thailand domestic currency exceeding 500 baht (around US$20) or foreign currency exceeding US$1,000. In 1993 these limits were 50,000 baht (around US$2,000) and US$10,000 of foreign currency. The degree of substitution between domestic and foreign assets was far from perfect; similarly, foreign liabilities were imperfect substitutes for loans obtained from domestic banks, since domestic deficit units could not access foreign capital markets. The government also imposed a limit on the volume of foreign debt of public enterprises.

3 *Controls on foreign exchange positions of commercial banks.* In addition to the above instruments, the net foreign exchange positions of commercial banks was subject to regulation since 1984. Following the 1984 devaluation, the net future and current position of each commercial bank – whether positive or negative – could not exceed US$5 million in either direction or 20 per cent of the net worth of the bank, whichever was smaller. In April 1990, the ceiling on the net position of commercial banks was raised to 25 per cent of capital funds.

4 *Withholding tax on foreign borrowing.* A withholding tax was applied to foreign borrowing at rates which were varied by the Minister of Finance either to encourage or discourage foreign capital inflows. This instrument created a tax wedge between the domestic and foreign costs of capital. The withholding tax rate was usually imposed at 10 per cent of the interest payments when the government wanted to reduce the capital inflows. It was exempted whenever the government considered that the domestic money market was too tight. Exemption was sometimes granted for loans with long maturity periods, such as one to three years, to attract long-term capital funds. The withholding tax rate was varied significantly from time to time. The adjustments were directed at influencing capital flows for stabilisation purposes.

Did the controls work?

The exchange controls were justified by the need to regulate speculative and destabilising capital movements. The paradox is that during most of the period prior to 1990 when the controls were operative large capital movements were not occurring. Large capital inflows did not begin until around 1987. But during the brief period before they were abolished, the controls were indeed inhibiting capital movements and this was a major reason for their removal. The controls were dismissed as anachronistic and unnecessary. Moreover, the forthcoming restoration of Chinese authority in Hong Kong led many to believe that if Thailand's capital markets were liberalised, Bangkok could become a major regional financial centre.

Given the current controversy over the efficacy of capital controls, the question arises as to whether the dismantling of Thailand's capital controls played a significant role in causing the crisis. We shall first review the capital controls Thailand in fact had in place prior to 1990. The effectiveness of the controls in controlling short-term capital may be assessed by the behaviour of Thai interest rates. Over the period from 1970 to around 1990, during periods in which the Bank of Thailand had pre-announced its intention to induce a monetary contraction, Thai interest rates rose, and the spread between Thai interest rates and LIBOR (London inter-bank offered rate) increased. The reverse occurred during periods of monetary relaxation (Warr and Nidhiprabha 1996). The point is that this occurred in spite of Thailand's fixed exchange rate.[5] If capital mobility was unrestrained, such an outcome would be impossible because short-term capital flows into or out of the country would defeat the efforts of the Bank of Thailand to influence domestic interest rates.

The impact was small, and short-lived. Regulated bank interest rates were clearly affected by the controls.[6] However, the medium-term elasticity of short-term capital flows with respect to domestic interest was large (Warr and Nidhiprabha 1996) and although short-run deviations of domestic interest rates from international rates was made possible by the controls, over longer time periods Thai interest rates followed international rates very closely.[7] The evidence suggests that capital controls were effective in slowing down the capital flows that lead to interest rate convergence, but that they did not prevent these flows.

Financial liberalisation after 1990

In May 1990 Thailand accepted the IMF's Article VIII, removing controls on foreign exchange for current account transactions. Several further measures followed. In April 1991 most restrictions on capital account transactions were lifted. In March 1993 the Bangkok International Banking Facility was established. The intention was to develop Bangkok as an international financial centre. To enhance its competitive position in relation to other such financial ventures, transactions occurring through the BIBF were granted tax concessions including reduction of corporate income tax, exemption from some other taxes including special business tax and the withholding tax on interest income. In February 1994 all foreign exchange restrictions related to outward direct investment and travel expenditures were removed. Finally, in January 1995 the government permitted the BIBF to open branches outside Bangkok.

A series of measures removed the interest rate ceilings described above. The purpose was to encourage private savings and improve the responsiveness of the financial system. Interest rate ceilings on long-term time deposits were removed in June 1989. The ceilings on savings and short-term time deposits followed in January 1992 and loan rate ceilings were abolished in June 1992.

The requirement that commercial banks hold a specified quantity of government bonds as a condition for opening new branches was gradually lifted, beginning in 1992, to encourage commercial banks to compete at the local level more aggressively. At the same time, requirements that commercial banks extend credits to rural borrowers were relaxed by widening the definition of rural' to include more geographical areas and some occupational groups unrelated to rural activities. Finally, commercial banks, finance companies and securities companies were permitted to undertake new commercial activities not directly related to their core businesses, such as financial consulting services, feasibility studies, selling government bonds, management of mutual funds and so forth.

In May 1992 the Securities and Exchange Act was introduced, giving qualified limited companies access to equity finance by issuing common stocks and debt instruments. The Securities and Exchange Commission was established by the Act with the task of supervising capital market activities involving equities, bonds and derivatives.

The purpose of the above liberalisation was to improve the competitive position of Thailand's financial system within the region with the hope of making Bangkok a regional financial centre and to introduce more competition into the domestic financial system. It is noticeable that the number of commercial bank licences was not expanded. No new licences have been issued since 1965.

Partial reintroduction of controls after 1995

Thailand's capital account liberalisation that began in the early 1990s was interrupted by the reintroduction of barriers to capital inflows to curb surges in capital flows. In mid-1995, the Bank of Thailand imposed capital control measures to restrict short-term capital inflows. A maximum credit to deposit ratio was also introduced to restrict banks from extending loans requiring foreign borrowing. In addition, a ceiling on loan growth rate was set at 24 per cent in 1995 and subsequently at 21 per cent in 1996. The capital control measures also included reserves for out–in activities of the BIBF's borrowing, increasing the cash reserve requirement from 2 to 7 per cent for non-resident baht accounts, and the minimum reserve requirement of loans was raised from 500,000 baht to 2 million baht.

These measures were not quantity restrictions. They simply imposed higher costs on foreign borrowing. But these policy responses to capital inflows were too lenient and too late to stop huge inflows to the private sector. Both banks and non-bank corporations were already highly leveraged with unhedged short-term foreign liabilities.

THE FINANCIAL SECTOR AFTER THE CRISIS

The exposure of the financial sector at the time of the crisis is summarised in Figure 5.2. First, the increased level of banks' foreign indebtedness relative to their lending base increased their exposure to exchange rate risk. Second, the increased level of bank credit to GDP increased their exposure to a domestic contraction.[8] Both on their revenue side (repayment of domestic loans they had advanced) and on their cost side (repayment of their own debts to foreign creditors), Thai financial institutions were negatively affected by the aftermath of the crisis.

Non-performing loans (NPLs) became a growing problem as asset prices fell and economic activity contracted. At the time of the currency float, in mid-1997, NPLs constituted around 8 per cent of total credit outstanding. By the end of 1997 this had risen to 20 per cent and by December 1998 the proportion was 45 per cent of credit outstanding, around 2.7 trillion baht, equivalent to US$75 billion or 56 per cent of GDP. Not all of this was a reflection of genuine inability to pay on the part of debtors. The problem of NPLs was so vast that many borrowers saw the opportunity to default on loans. Strategic or fake' NPLs have been estimated at around one-third of total reported NPLs.

Table 5.2 summarises the structure of the Thai financial system as of December 1998 in terms of the volume of credit outstanding and the magnitude of NPLs. It includes the eight surviving private Thai commercial banks, the state-run commercial banks (which, in this table, includes private banks taken over following the crisis), the foreign commercial banks and the thirty-five surviving finance companies. As the table makes clear, private commercial banks dominate the financial sector with 51 per cent of credit outstanding. The thirty-five finance companies that survived to December 1998, out of ninety-one two years earlier, represented only 8 per cent of total credit outstanding but 12 per cent of all NPLs. The state commercial banks show a higher share of NPLs than credit outstanding, but this is largely due to their take-over of some ailing commercial banks. The problems of the finance companies have dominated much public discussion of Thailand's financial sector problems, but as the table reveals, the problems of the private commercial banks are much more important.

Figure 5.2 Bank exposure, Thailand, 1988–98

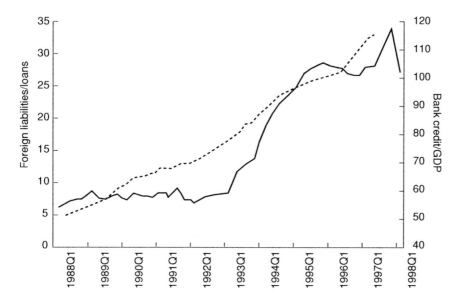

Table 5.2   Credit outstanding and non-performing loans, Thailand, December
1998 (billion baht)

Institution	Credit out-standing (1)	% share of (1) (2)	NPLs (3)	% share of (3) (4)	NPLs/ credit [(3)/(1)] (5)
Private commercial banks	3,063	51	1,293	47	42
State commercial banks[a]	1,660	28	1,037	38	62
Foreign commercial banks	756	13	75	3	10
All commercial banks	5,479	92	2,405	88	44
35 finance companies	461	8	322	12	70
Total	5,940	100	2,727	100	46

Note: a Including private commercial banks nationalised following the financial crisis.
Source: Bank of Thailand and Vichyanond (1999).

THE REFORM PROGRAM

Capital controls

It has often been said that a clear difference between the post-crisis reform
programs pursued by Malaysia and Thailand has been that Malaysia resorted
to capital controls whereas Thailand did not. This characterisation is not
strictly correct. Although the emphasis on capital controls was certainly
greater in Malaysia, Thailand had reintroduced some capital controls even
prior to the crisis, as noted above, and controls remain a feature of the
reform process today. Shortly after the currency crisis, the Bank of Thailand
introduced strict controls on all transactions of commercial banks' sales of
foreign exchange, requiring supporting documents to make sure that all
private transfers were genuine and unrelated to speculation or capital flight.

In January 1998, the Bank of Thailand put a limit on the amount of credit
denominated in baht which each institution could provide to non-residents.
The measure was introduced when the baht depreciated to a record low level
in early 1998. Nevertheless, there were some loopholes in this regulation since
each branch of a foreign bank could still borrow up to 50 million baht. In effect,
a foreign bank with five branches could borrow up to 250 million baht. These
loopholes permitted foreign banks to dump the baht through forward sales.
The Bank of Thailand (BOT) considered that in the absence of currency
speculation the exchange rate would not have fallen below 40 baht to the
dollar. In October 1999 alone the BOT spent 70 billion baht in intervention in
the foreign exchange market to prevent further currency depreciation.

On 5 October 1999 the Bank of Thailand imposed a maximum amount of 50
million baht that foreign investors could borrow in total, unless backed by
genuine trade and investment in Thailand. This was additional to the measure
taken earlier in January 1998 to limit the amount of baht credit each financial

institution could provide to non-residents. Under the new regulation, the 50 million baht ceiling applied to the total of all transactions of all branches and the head office. Apparently as a result of the new capital control, the baht rebounded strongly immediately after the limit was set. The Bank of Thailand also prohibits lending to non-residents without collateral.

Banking reform

During the boom years, the number of finance and securities companies rose rapidly, but the number of banks remained constant. The government had considered opening three new banks just before the crisis developed. After July 1997, some banks and finance companies experienced severe liquidity problems. In December 1997, six months after the currency crisis, the Bank of Thailand closed fifty-six finance companies and nationalised six commercial banks. These were: Bangkok Metropolitan Bank, Siam City Bank, First Bangkok City Bank, Laem Thong Bank, Union Bank of Bangkok and Nakornthon Bank. The Bangkok Bank of Commerce had been nationalised earlier and was finally closed. The Union Bank of Bangkok, Krung Thai Tanakit, a finance company owned by the government-owned Krung Thai Bank (KTB), and twelve other finance companies were merged to form a new bank, Bank Thai. Krung Thai Bank itself accepted assets and liabilities from First Bangkok City Bank (FBCB). It has to continue to pay off depositors of FBCB and suffers a substantial loss from loans transferred from FBCB, most of which are NPLs.

Stringent banking rules have been imposed. Banks have been ordered to comply with higher capital adequacy ratios and to recapitalise after capital write-downs of bad debt. A new definition of non-performing loans has been imposed to include any loans in arrears longer than three months. Before the crisis, only loans whose borrowers failed to service the debt for more than one year were classified as non-performing. Higher loan loss provisions were imposed on banks and finance companies. Although these new requirements are precautionary measures for a sound financial system, they were so severe that extreme liquidity shortage resulted. These strict prudential regulations had a negative impact on loan expansion, which is badly needed during the early phase of economic recovery. The lack of liquidity and working capital can prolong recession and preclude sustained recovery.

After successful bank recapitalisation, either by injection of public funds or by selling a majority of bank shares to foreign banks, debt restructuring is the next important step. For banks to resume normal lending, they must reduce their NPLs, which were expected to decline following the trend of interest rates. Since the overall volume of NPLs for the whole banking sector is close to 50 per cent of total loans, it would take several years of strong economic growth to generate business profit before a significant fall in the level of non-performing loans could be observed. Despite the fact that new bankruptcy foreclosure laws came into effect in 1999, there has been no significant improvement in the debt restructuring process.

On 14 August 1998, the government established a 300 billion baht (US$8.6 billion) fund to restructure financial institutions. The plan attempts to accelerate consolidation of bank and finance companies, to encourage private investment in the banking sector, to provide public funds to recapitalise financial institutions, and to develop private asset-management companies. The capital support schemes provide funds to recapitalise viable financial institutions so that they can resume normal lending. To qualify for the funds, the financial institutions must have positive equity.

Under the tier-one program, banks and finance companies can issue preferred shares in exchange for ten-year government bonds, on the condition that applicants must make full provision for loan losses, implement restructuring programs and accept management changes ordered by the Bank of Thailand. Under the tier-two program, applicants can issue subordinated debentures in exchange for government bonds. The amount of capital to be allocated to these ailing financial institutions varies according to the level of new lending and debt restructuring progress. The stringent conditions led to a low disbursement rate and a delay in rehabilitating the ailing financial institutions. By November 1999, the disbursement of the fund was less than 50 billion baht (US$1.4 billion).

The market structure of the Thai banking industry has changed drastically since the crisis. The five smallest banks suffered severely from the crisis. The Financial Institution Development Fund (FIDF) of the Bank of Thailand injected public money into these troubled banks. When their situation did not improve, their capital was written down. Thailand's small banks are mainly family-owned businesses and they are not as resilient as large banks. Nevertheless, because of their small size, it was easier for their shares to be sold to international banks. The opportunity now exists for multinational banks to penetrate the previously closed and protected Thai banking sector. The long-awaited concession to the World Trade Organisation (WTO) to open the financial sector has finally arrived through forced acceptance of foreign participation.

During 1999, Singapore's United Overseas Bank acquired 75 per cent of Radanasin Bank, which had taken over the defunct Laem Thong Bank in August 1998. Radanasin Bank's accumulated losses were five times its capital funds. The Netherlands' ABN Amro took over the majority of shares in the Bank of Asia. The Development Bank of Singapore bought a 75 per cent stake in Thai Dhanu Bank. Standard Chartered also bought 75 per cent of the shares of Nakornthon Bank in September 1999. The majority stake in Siam City Bank will be sold to a foreign bank in 2000.

The Bank of Thailand took over the Bangkok Metropolitan Bank (BMB) in December 1997 and its shares were written down from 11 billion to 11 million baht. The BMB had been in financial trouble even before the crisis. The bank's family-style management and heavy lending to its affiliates were the root of the problem. Thus, in 1994 when the Bank of Thailand allowed licences for offshore borrowing through the BIBF, the BMB was among the few banks that were denied a BIBF licence. In 1995, the BMB was refused permission to provide additional loans to its subsidiaries.

Along with another medium-sized bank, Siam City Bank, BMB is expected to be sold in 1999 to the Hong Kong and Shanghai Banking Corporation and GE Capital, the giant US financial firm. Both banks have NPLs above 70 per cent of their total loans. Most of their problem loans are over twelve months in arrears. In 1996, BMB pleaded guilty to charges of falsifying records and obstructing a probe by the US bank regulators. BMB closed its branches in San Francisco and New York and paid a fine of $3.5 million. The incident indicated the kind of corporate governance that prevailed in the Thai banking industry.

The Bangkok Bank of Commerce (BBC) was the first bank that showed signs of financial distress, but this occurred several years before the crisis of 1997. The Bank of Thailand did not effectively handle the case of BBC, and this proved to be costly. The Bank of Thailand responded to the problems of the BBC by injecting huge volumes of public funds into the BBC without changing management controls or increasing effective supervision. This led to cosmetic mismanagement and fraud. The BBC was the place where the confidence crisis started. In 1998 the BBC was finally ordered to cease operations.

Krung Thai Bank, a state-owned bank, has acquired the ailing First Bangkok City Bank, assuming the management of FBCB's assets. The approach to FBCB typified the traditional Thai means of solving a banking crisis: a state-owned bank would assume the control of a weak commercial bank. Ironically, KTB was established in the 1950s through the same approach of merging two troubled banks. As a state-owned bank that must maintain the public confidence in the banking system, KTB also had to take over the ailing Siam Bank. The Siam Bank itself was formerly the Asia Trust Bank, nationalised when it did not survive economic turmoil in the mid-1980s. Disposal of bad assets is crucial for the survival of KTB, whose problem loans were estimated to be as much as 80 per cent by value of its total loans. Although seriously considering selling its shares directly to international buyers, KTB has resisted selling shares in Thailand's bank sales dominated by international buyers.

When international banks buy a major stake in these ailing banks, separate asset management corporations (AMCs) will manage bad loans. In a typical deal with potential buyers, the Bank of Thailand can claim 95 per cent of the profits from the AMC to be made in the future, the remainder going to the new international buyers. In the case of losses, the Bank of Thailand would bear 85 per cent of the burden, the remainder borne by the new investors. The idea of sharing losses and profits makes selling banks that are technically bankrupt more attractive. If the Thai economy rebounds sharply, the burden of the Bank of Thailand would be lessened and the value of these banks to buyers will be much greater.

The remaining solvent banks are struggling to increase capital funds to meet the stringent requirements of the Bank of Thailand. They must raise their capital funds to meet the Bank of International Settlements standard and to provide allowances for non-performing loans. Since they suffer operating losses, their ability to increase provision for bad debts is limited. They can raise their core capital funds (tier-one) and supplementary funds (tier-two). The three largest private banks, Bangkok Bank, Thai Farmers Bank, and Siam Commercial Bank successfully mobilised capital funds by selling shares to international investors without having to lose management control.

Through aggressive strategies, six banks in the medium-sized group were able to gain market shares between 1990 and 1996. Heavy reliance on borrowed money allowed medium-sized banks to increase their lending volume at the expense of larger banks. Instead, Bangkok Bank and Thai Farmers Bank, which adopted more conservative strategies, streamlined their operations and focused on quality loans. Medium and small banks tended to commit technical errors in lending such as maturity and currency mismatching. Although economic recession affects all banks similarly, some banks are able to survive because they avoid having insider loans and loan concentration on the property market.

Medium-sized banks are having difficulty raising funds abroad and have to rely on public funds to match their efforts in raising funds to raise supplementary funds through selling Capital Augmented Preferred Shares and Stapled Limited Preferred Shares. The Thai Military Bank, in which the Royal Thai Army holds a 20 per cent share, is considering these options if it fails to raise its tier-one capital. Because interest rates on fixed deposits will decline to 4 per cent by the end of the year and the return from the stock market is not attractive, it is possible that some banks can succeed in raising capital funds through selling preferred shares.

Most banks have not provided sufficient allowances for non-performing loans. The full requirement of 100 per cent provision is required by the end of the year 2000. As long as a bank has to struggle to maintain a capital standard, it cannot have sufficient funds to increase its lending to the private sector. This is why raising funds from foreign investors is vital for the recovery.

The government was able to prevent a systematic banking failure as the contagion effects of bank runs began to spread from small to large banks. Panic set in with rumours of bank insolvency. The announcement of the government that it would guarantee all deposits in banks and finance companies halted the fear of depositors. All deposits of failed banks and finance companies were substituted by long-term promissory notes honoured by the Ministry of Finance.

A large number of Thai banks have been sold to international banks but there has been no strong public objection to these sales, a fact that has surprised some observers. Public confidence in weak banks can be restored with injection of sufficient funds from abroad. It is expected that foreign participation will also involve the transfer of technology, enhanced credit culture and intensified competition.

The temporary return to interest rate ceilings and capital control measures did not indicate a policy reversal toward the pre-liberalisation period of the 1980s. It suggests rather a temporary departure from the liberalisation process in order to gain policy autonomy to deal with short-term problems such as liquidity shortage and capital flight. In the long run, the liberalisation policy may be expected to be resumed, because the cost of controls is seen as exceeding their benefits. A turning back toward an inward-looking strategy of financial development should not be expected.

The policy perception in Thailand is that since it is impossible to eliminate fluctuations in capital flows, Thailand must learn to live with them. The prevailing view is that one cannot liberalise the financial sector without also liberalising foreign exchange markets. A flexible exchange rate system is seen as liberalisation in the foreign exchange market and this approach can be expected to be maintained. A currency board is seen as unnecessary for a country with fiscal discipline and price stability. An engineered weak currency to help exporters and poor farmers are seen as inappropriate and dangerous. Intervention by the central bank to achieve a significantly overvalued or undervalued exchange rate should be a policy of the past.

The financial crisis has radically altered the structure of the Thai banking industry. The excessive number of financial institutions has been reduced and the survivors have become more efficient and transparent. Stringent rules on loan-loss provisions and required capital adequacy ratio are now in place. The existing measures may be too restrictive in that they have contributed to a severe capital shortage. But once the Thai economy begins to recover, these prudential rules and regulations should create a stronger and healthier banking system, where market discipline prevails. Competition will be intensified by the arrival of new international banks that have major stakes in weak domestic banks. Bank governance should be improved, while transparency and accountability is strengthened.

The massive public spending to bail out troubled financial institutions will not be recovered. The total losses and liabilities of the Financial Institutions Development Fund are estimated at around 1.3 trillion baht (US$37 billion). Short-term liabilities amounted to 500 million baht, due to short-term borrowing from the bond repurchase market and 200 billion baht from guarantees to depositors of the fifty-six closed finance companies, whose promissory notes were transferred to Krung Thai Bank and Krung Thai Thanakit. The government has issued 500 billion baht to compensate for the Fund's losses. The interest on the debt comes from the fiscal budget, while the principal on liabilities remains outstanding. The Fund is the largest creditor of the fifty-six finance companies, holding 85 per cent of the total. Asset sales have raised 200 billion baht. By selling shares to international banks at losses, the Bank of Thailand hopes that the long-run gain to the Thai economy would offset the short-run losses.

Reforming the regulatory framework

In the year 2000 the government will propose three new draft bills to the parliament: a new Financial Institutions Act, amendments to the Bank of Thailand Act, and the Currency Act. The central bank will be given increased authority and flexibility in taking action against troubled financial institutions, without requiring approval from the Minister of Finance. Accountability, transparent rules and formalised codes of practice will be established to limit abuse of power and regulatory discretion. There will be new guidelines for financial institutions on investment limits and cross-shareholding regulations. Strict limits will apply to issuance of credit to directors and management. The Bank of Thailand will set capital adequacy rules where corrective action, regulatory intervention, and licence withdrawal are clearly specified. The BOT would require independent auditors to report instances of fraud in financial institutions and could authorise external auditing to include parent companies and subsidiaries of financial institutions. This new institutional regulatory framework should strengthen the financial infrastructure and enhance the regulatory independence of the central bank.

The Bank of Thailand has tried to strengthen its supervisory role by relying more on forward-looking analysis than examining bank accounts. This means that banking supervision must concentrate on lending procedures, asset qualities, and risk control. In the future, commercial banks must report their NPLs on a monthly basis to the Stock Exchange of Thailand. When the Deposit Insurance Agency is established in a few years' time, these banks will be rated according to their risks.

To improve management transparency and corporate governance, the Stock Exchange of Thailand now requires that each listed company set up a three-person audit committee, or face suspension for three months. The committee is to oversee and improve firms' internal controls and risk management, and is expected to enhance corporate governance.

The Bank of Thailand has established new rules designed to prevent conflicts of interest between banks and their borrowers. To reduce the extent of interlocking directorates', an executive of a commercial bank is not allowed to be a member of the board of directors of more than three companies. Since economic and financial power has already been concentrated in several families in Thailand, interlocking directorates can further enhance the monopoly power of certain firms by increasing the financial power of commercial banks. The regulation is well intended, but its implementation will be difficult, considering the power of the large banks.

Civil actions against executives of financial institutions

The Bank of Thailand has implemented a series of legal actions intended to demonstrate to the public that crime does not pay. Dozens of criminal cases have been filed by the BOT against former bank and finance company executives. Charges include fraud, banking violations, and damaging their companies. For example, Finance One's executives extended loans to its subsidiaries without collateral through purchases of promissory notes worth 2.1 billion baht. In other cases, some executives used their personal assets as collateral for loans when their companies borrowed from the Financial Institution Development Fund (FIDF). When they failed to redeem their assets, they were subject to prosecution. The civil actions against these executives seek compensation for damages amounting to several hundred billion baht. The FIDF has lent 1.12 trillion baht to failed financial institutions in such cases and is expected to lose more than 500 billion baht. After filing criminal charges, the BOT has frozen the assets of these executives and banned them from overseas travel.

In two unprecedented cases, the BOT filed cases against two of its own executives who, before joining the BOT, worked for these now-defunct financial institutions. It remains to be seen whether the BOT can continue to pursue this role without double standard. In one case, a former executive of the Krung Thai Bank, which obtained a 185 billion baht bailout from taxpayers using personal assets as collateral, has not been charged. The credibility of the BOT as an examiner and supervisor of financial institutions will be questioned unless the rule of law is seen to apply without exception.

BOND MARKETS

Many large corporations, such as Total Access Communication (TAC), Thailand's second largest mobile phone operator, were badly damaged by the currency depreciation. On 2 July 1997, the day of the floating of the baht, this company's debt increased from 25 billion baht to 55 billion baht due to its reliance on foreign sources of finance. Had the domestic bond market been sufficiently developed, large Thai corporations such as this could have survived massive currency depreciation.

Thailand's bond market is relatively small compared with other means of investment financing. Its size relative to GDP was 11.3 per cent in 1997 (Table 5.3). Bank loans have been the predominant source of funds, with a size relative to GDP of 124 per cent in 1997. This high level indicates a very high degree of over-lending and excessive indebtedness. Highly leveraged companies are vulnerable to interest rate shocks. The stock market boom of 1993, fuelled by foreign portfolio investment, led to a high ratio of market capitalisation to GDP, reaching 105 per cent in 1993. The asset price bubble led to overvaluation of collateral and to poor lending policies of commercial banks. The stock market crash in 1997 caused a sharp decline in the market capitalisation ratio.

A sharp increase in the activity of the bond market can be observed in 1999. The share of government bonds, which was as low as 2.5 per cent in 1997, rebounded sharply in 1999. The budget deficit requires the government to issue a large amount of bonds. There are some indicators that corporate bonds have become more popular.

Large corporations such as Siam Cement Co. have begun to issue debentures worth 56 billion baht with six years' maturation, carrying 8–10 per cent annual interest. This rate is lower than current long-term borrowing rates from commercial banks. When interest rates on bank fixed deposits declined to 3 per cent in 1999, the return from holding bonds became attractive. More than twenty large clients from commercial banks have issued debentures. The development of bond markets can help large corporations to refinance their debts and provide cheap funds for their operations. Thus, there is pressure for commercial banks to reduce their lending rates to compete with bond markets. Nevertheless, small and medium-sized firms cannot enter the bond markets nor can they rely on commercial banks' lending, due to their high risk premiums.

Non-performing loans

Because of over-capacity in the real estate sector, its incidence of non-performing loans is the highest among all sectors, reaching 72 per cent in July 1999. The foreign trade sector also suffered badly from the currency crisis. Nevertheless, its NPLs peaked at 48 per cent in February 1999 and declined to 29.2 per cent in July 1999, two years after the currency crisis. As exports showed sign of positive growth in 1999, the level of NPLs in this sector has declined markedly. In contrast, the financial sector, which has not directly received the full benefit of currency depreciation, suffered from a rising level of NPLs. While the level of NPLs in the infrastructure sector has stabilised, NPLs in the financial sector rose from 28.4 per cent in September 1998 to 42.8 per cent in July 1999 (Table 5.4).

The loan-loss provision of the banking sector is 70 per cent of the level required by the end of 2000. Thai commercial banks require an additional 100 billion baht to meet the provisioning requirement, assuming that the volume of bad loans remains unchanged. Since the incidence of NPLs has reached almost 50 per cent, it seems impossible to reduce the level substantially within a few years. In consequence, the return to a normal economic growth path would also be delayed as long as recapitalisation remains incomplete.

Table 5.3   Sizes of bond and capital markets, Thailand

	per cent of GDP				
	1992	*1993*	*1995*	*1997*	*1999*
Bank loans	76.4	84.1	101	123.9	112.2
Equities	52.5	104.9	85.1	23.5	35.4
Bonds	7.6	8.3	10.1	11.3	27.3
	per cent of total outstanding bonds				
Government	58.4	38.4	10.3	2.5	44.7
SOEs	39.0	51.5	56.1	53.7	25.4
BOT/FIDF			2.2	9.4	1.7
Corporate	2.6	10.00	31.5	34.3	28.2

Source: Bond Dealer Club, Bangkok.

The central bank set up a Corporate Debt Restructuring Advisory Committee in 1998 to coordinate debt talks among regulators, local and foreign banks and industrial debtors. Both creditors and debtors are committed to a negotiation deadline within seven months. The AMC would take action against debtors who cannot agree in principle on debt restructuring programs before the end of 1999. A decline in NPLs might therefore be expected at the end of 1999 after successful debt restructuring plans have been concluded. Nevertheless, restructured loans can become bad debts once again if the recovery is not sustainable.

The AMC, the bidder of last resort, obtained 190 billion baht of assets at auction from the Financial Sector Restructuring Authority. The AMC paid the FRA for only 17 per cent of the total value of the assets acquired through auction. Most of these acquired assets are from property investment. Seventy per cent of the acquired assets are tied up in land, 13 per cent in high-rise building projects, 5 per cent in golf courses, 5 per cent in housing projects, and 2 per cent in industrial plants. The AMC attempts to convert debts into assets and to restructure the balances. It has to cooperate with debtors to convert parts of its loans to equity, reschedule debt repayment periods and reduce loans for its debtors.

'Strategic' NPLs

The non-payment culture' that has emerged after the crisis also contributes to a high level of NPLs. Some borrowers who are able to repay calculate that if they default they may obtain a better deal from creditors through reduction of principle and interest and rescheduling loan periods. Some of these strategic NPLs are owed by politicians and well-known businessmen. This moral hazard issue is related to the fact that it is very difficult for creditors to take debtors to court and, if they do, creditors are likely to lose more than borrowers. Some of the collateral concerned has already depreciated to such an extent that foreclosure of those assets may not be the best solution for creditors. Strategic NPL debtors have some bargaining power and incentive to default. The degree to which the restructuring program may have increased incentives for strategic non-repayment of loans remains unclear.

Table 5.4 Sectoral non-performing loans, Thailand

	per cent of total outstanding loans		
	Sept. 98	*Feb. 99*	*July 99*
Real estate	56.7	71.4	72.2
Financial sector	28.4	37.9	42.8
Infrastructure	23.5	27.5	25.6
Imports/exports	38.1	48.1	29.2
Total NPLs	32.7	46.7	47.1

Source: Bank of Thailand.

In an effort to reduce strategic non-performing loans, thirteen Thai commercial banks have established a credit bureau to help them discipline borrowers and raise market efficiency. Local banks provide information to the credit bureau, and information will be shared among themselves. Borrowers with poor records would be charged higher borrowing costs or can be blacklisted by financial institutions. To reduce principal–agent problems, in particular for small and medium enterprises and individual major borrowers, the credit bureau can raise the lending efficiency of financial institutions in Thailand.

CONCLUSIONS

Capital controls

Considering the changes to the ease with which funds can now be moved internationally, it would seem likely that if the pre-1990 capital controls had been retained, or were reintroduced today, they would be even less effective than before in regulating capital flows. The economic debate on the efficacy of capital controls continues and dogmatic positions on either side of this discussion are surely unwarranted by the limited evidence available. Nevertheless, capital controls would not seem to be the answer to preventing the development of vulnerability to crisis in Thailand.

If Thailand's capital controls had been left in place in the early 1990s and not dismantled, as they were, it would seem likely that capital inflows would have been slower, but this alone would not have prevented the development of vulnerability. Still lacking were the properly enforced prudential banking regulations required to prevent over-exposure of domestic banks. This was a more important matter than whether capital controls remained in place. Similarly, Thailand would have been better served by the abandonment of the Bank of Thailand's obsession with pegged exchange rates and the attendant danger of exchange rate misalignment. If the exchange rate had been floated, or even devalued significantly, in mid-1996, it would seem likely that the crisis could have been averted.

Banking reforms

Progress with Thailand's banking reforms has been mixed. Fifty-six finance companies were closed and their assets were auctioned by the Financial Restructuring Authority. Seven non-viable commercial banks were integrated with state banks or recapitalised by the government for sale at a later date. Corporate debt restructuring has been less successful. By July 1999, unresolved NPLs still amounted to 47 per cent of total outstanding loans. Thailand's financial restructuring still has a long way to go.

NOTES

1   The helpful comments of Michael Hasenstab and Marina Moretti are gratefully acknowledged. The authors are responsible for all views presented and any errors.

2   See Warr (1999) for a description of the accumulation of the short-term capital stocks relative to reserves.

3   See Corden (1999) for a helpful discussion of the Asian crisis within this Keynesian framework.

4   Relaxed in 1990 to 15 days, following the acceptance by Thailand of IMF article XIII.

5   The exchange rate between the baht (the Thai currency) and the US dollar was held constant at 20 baht/dollar from the early 1950s until two devaluations in the early 1980s (10% in 1981 and 15% in 1984). From then until the float of 2 July 1997, the baht was officially pegged to a basket' of currencies, but the constancy of the rate at around 25 baht/dollar over this entire period demonstrated that the basket was dominated by the US dollar. Following the float, the baht depreciated to 55 baht/dollar in January 1998, but had stabilised at around 35 by August 1998 and remained at approximately that rate in late 1999.

6   For evidence, see Warr and Nidhiprabha (1996, Figure 8.2: 173).

7   See Warr and Nidhiprabha (1996: 172, Figure 8.1).

8   See Sachs, Tornell and Velasco (1996) for a fuller discussion of these concepts within the context of crisis vulnerability.

REFERENCES

Corden, W.M. (1999) *The Asian Crisis: Is there a way out?*, Institute of Southeast Asian Studies, Singapore.

Dornbusch, Rudiger (1997) A Thai–Mexico primer: Lessons for outmaneuvering a financial meltdown', *The International Economy*, September–October: 20–23: 55.

Edwards, Sebastian (1998) The Mexican Peso Crisis: How much did we know? When did we know it?', *The World Economy*, vol. 21, 1–30.

Ingram, James C. (1971) *Economic Change in Thailand: 1850–1970*, Stanford, California: Stanford University Press.

Khoman, Sirilaksana (1993) Education', in P.G. Warr (ed.) *The Thai Economy in Transition*, Cambridge: Cambridge University Press.

Kochhar, Kalpana, Dicks-Mireaux, Louis, Horvath, Balazs, Mecagni, Mauro, Offerdal, Erik and Zhou Jianping (1996) Thailand: The road to sustained growth', *Occasional Paper* no. 146, International Monetary Fund: Washington, DC, December.

Robinson, David, Byeon, Yangho and Teja, Ranjit (1991) Thailand: Adjusting to success, current policy issues', *Occasional Paper* no. 85, Washington, DC: International Monetary Fund.

Sachs, J., Tornell, A. and Velasco, A. (1996) Financial crises in emerging markets: The lessons from 1995', *Brookings Papers in Economic Activity*, no. 1, 147–215.

Siamwalla, Ammar and Setboonsarng, Suthad (1991) Thailand', in A.O. Krueger, M. Schiff and A. Valdes (eds) *The Political Economy of Agricultural Pricing Policy: Vol. 2, Asia*, Baltimore: Johns Hopkins University Press.

Vichyanond, Pakorn (1999) Financial reform in Thailand', paper presented to the conference Thailand Beyond the Crisis, Australian National University, Canberra, April.

Warr, Peter G. (1993) The Thai Economy', in P.G. Warr (ed.) *The Thai Economy in Transition*, Cambridge: Cambridge University Press: 1–80.

and Nidhiprabha, Bhanupong (1996)   *Thailand's Macroeconomic Miracle: Stable adjustment and sustained growth*, World Bank and Oxford University Press: Washington and Kuala Lumpur.

(1999) What happened to Thailand?', *The World Economy*, vol. 22, July, 631–50.

World Bank (1998) *Recovery in East Asia.*

6 Governance and the crisis in Indonesia

Hadi Soesastro

INTRODUCTION

The Indonesian economic crisis cannot be attributed to a single cause. Yet if a case is to be made for the overwhelming contribution of *poor governance* to the unfolding of an economic crisis, the Indonesian experience provides a clear example. Poor governance was largely responsible for the building up of vulnerabilities in the economy that made it crisis-prone. Poor governance was equally responsible for the gross mishandling of the financial crisis that resulted in an even deeper economic crisis and a serious political crisis. Poor governance also explains why current reform and recovery efforts and programs have been slow and frustrating, which perhaps could become a major source for their failure.

Thanks to the crisis, issues of governance are now on the national agenda. For some years prior to the crisis, the term governance' had been introduced in Indonesia and other developing countries by international development and aid agencies. But until the crisis broke it did not capture the attention and the imagination of the wider public as it was largely seen as an abstract concept. There is as yet no official Indonesian word for governance; unofficially, the word *penadbiran* has been introduced but it sounds alien to many. KKN has become a popular slogan that better conveys the notion of poor governance. KKN stands for *korupsi, kolusi, nepotisme* – or corruption, collusion and nepotism. These three words were originally used to characterise Soeharto's style of leadership, governing and governance, but remained in use under Habibie's transition government. Malaysians have also adopted the term KKN to express their displeasure with Mahathir's policies and style of governance. Thus, the notion of governance is already quite widespread and no longer elitist jargon in Indonesia and perhaps in the wider Southeast Asian region as well. This is a significant development because the impetus for good governance must be internally generated.

This development notwithstanding, the challenge for improving governance in Indonesia is a tall order. Elimination of KKN is seen as the main outcome of good governance. The fight against KKN has been couched within, and largely identified with, the package of total reforms, including political reforms. The capacity of the state and the society to undertake this total reform within a reasonable time frame is increasingly being questioned. The immediate question is how to approach the issues of governance in Indonesia and where the priorities should lie in promoting good governance.

Based on a series of meetings with Indonesian policy makers, Mishra (1999) identified the following issues of political economy. First is the issue of whether there exists a single, universal set of best practices that defines the core of good governance. Second, if indeed such a structure of governance exists, is it transferable to particular developing countries? Third, will governance become the new litmus test by which the efficiency of governments will be judged in the future? Fourth, will governance also become an overriding element of conditionality linked to development assistance? Mishra argues that the issue of governance must be tackled from a broader perspective of development policy. This would focus on the issue of the role of institutions in economic growth and development and the search for an optimal governance structure, including the optimal size of the state. It would also focus on ends and not just means of governance, and on the pathway of dependence of one governance structure on previous structures. Mishra's study points to the following conclusions: (a) there is no fool-proof linkage between specific institutional arrangements and economic performance; (b) there is a sequencing problem in institutional reform, and an effective state will be needed to prevent coordination failure and to play the role of key facilitator of institutional reform; (c) the governance agenda should not be overloaded; and (d) expectations of immediate gains from governance reform should not be too high.

This chapter underlines the need to address the issues of governance from the broader perspective of economic, social and political development. Improving governance in Indonesia is not simply a matter of finding technical solutions to an allocation or a transaction cost problem. It will require a process of working towards a new national consensus as it will involve fundamental changes about how the state and society will be organised. For instance, regional decentralisation issues will have to be addressed within the context of political, economic, social and even cultural demands for greater regional autonomy, which, in turn, will open up the debate on whether a federal state system would better accommodate such demands, rather than the present unitary state system. Can the society successfully undertake a constitutional reform without crafting a new consensus, based perhaps on a new social contract?

The following section discusses the relevant elements of governance through an examination of developments during the Soeharto regime that have resulted in poor and deteriorating governance. This will be followed by an examination of the process of economic reform and recovery that is greatly influenced by the complex interactions with political and social factors. The final section discusses the agenda for, and challenges towards, improving governance in Indonesia.

GOVERNANCE AND INDONESIA'S ECONOMIC CRISIS

Governance in the national agenda

The nation's agenda for improving governance should not be seen only as a short-term objective to restore confidence that has been shattered by the way the government has handled the crisis. It is true that in today's world of free capital movements the maintenance of market confidence is critical to economic prosperity. Governance indeed affects market confidence. But governance should be pursued, in the first place, to ensure economic sustainability.

Governance entails a concern with institution building, public sector reform and regulatory frameworks for ensuring competition and legal and property rights to its market-friendly agenda (World Bank 1991). It is also defined as the manner in which power is exercised in the management of a country's economic and social resources for development' (World Bank 1992). In its political aspects, governance is an all-embracing term that captures the essence of effective and efficient political leadership permeating all levels of society. The aim of governance is to create a transparent, fair and stable environment for economic activity to take place (Bhanu 1999).

In the context of its mandate, the World Bank (1992) has identified four components of governance, namely:

> *improving public sector management.* It is obvious that in developing economies there is a constant need to strengthen the capacity of the public sector to manage the economy and deliver public services;
> *accountability.* Public officials must be made responsible for their actions. At the core of accountability is government's responsiveness to the needs and views of the public for which the services are intended;
> *legal framework for development.* It is important to ensure that: (a) there is a set of rules known in advance; (b) the rules are actually in force; (c) there are mechanisms for ensuring the application of the rules; (d) conflicts are resolved through binding decisions of an independent judicial body; and (e) there are procedures for amending the rules when they no longer serve their purpose;
> *information and transparency.* The availability of information is crucial for the competitive functioning of a market economy. Allied with accessibility to information is transparency.

In all of the above, Indonesia's report card is poor. The World Bank, in a startlingly strong self-criticism, acknowledged at the beginning of 1999 that it had ignored widespread government corruption during Soeharto's rule (*Straits Times*, 12 February 1999). The new World Bank representative in Indonesia made the following remarks: We prided ourselves on working behind the scenes, with the government   We got things done that way. Now, I think we should have spoken out on corruption.' (*New York Times,*

5 September 1999). He was further reported as saying that Indonesia is a crucial test case of the World Bank's new willingness to challenge its partners around the world, because ending corruption has become essential.

In fact, the World Bank has gone beyond the concerns with corruption to point also to issues of political freedom, which are critical to the overall problem of governance. In a letter accompanying the report that reviewed the Bank's forty-four-year program in Indonesia, the authors stated: While the government's development strategy has had remarkably positive results, issues of poor governance, social stress and a weak financial sector were not addressed and contributed to the depth of the crisis. The bank's neglect of those issues and its underestimation of risks and lack of contingency planning dampened the overall effectiveness of its assistance' (*Straits Times*, 12 February 1999).

Corruption and civil service reform should definitely be at the top of the agenda for improving governance. Public sector reform has been included in Indonesia's development agenda for many years and a state minister has been charged with improving the performance of public administration and civil servants. Allegations remain strong, however, that at least 30 per cent of public funds for development expenditures are being siphoned off annually. This kind of corruption has been justified' by some on the grounds that civil service salaries are too low. It has been said that the average salary of low level civil servants is less than minimal physical needs (*kebutuhan fisik minimum*) and enables them to live for only two weeks in a month. It is common knowledge that development project funds are the main source for compensating for low salaries, especially of middle to lower level bureaucrats. Those at the top level have other sources. Tax and customs officials have the most lucrative sources at their disposal. Judges and officers in the Attorney General's office can occasionally make a big catch. Respected institutions such as the Central Bank and the National Planning Board (Bappenas) cannot declare themselves clean under close scrutiny. In fact, this practice of corruption no longer can be seen as compensating for the low salaries. In addition, perhaps ironically, it has produced the most skewed distribution of income in the civil service as compared with other sectors of activity.

The origin of the low official salaries of Indonesian civil servants was in the design of the budget, in which current expenditures were repressed in order to produce an ever-increasing amount of government savings, and to increase the share of the government in overall development expenditure. When domestic revenues are not increasing, civil service salaries, which account for a large portion of current expenditure, often remain stagnant.

In the late 1970s an experiment was conducted in the Ministry of Finance to raise the salaries of its employees nine-fold. An evaluation of the impact of this in terms of productivity (not in terms of eliminating corruption, which cannot readily be measured) showed no significant effect. Hence, the increase in salary was not applied to other government departments, but was retained in the Ministry of Finance. Even in the Ministry of Finance the raise in salary did not apparently produce a cleaner bureaucracy. This was clearly demonstrated by the decision in 1984 to de-activate the Customs Department and to replace it with a Swiss-based firm, SGS, which would undertake the inspection on behalf of the government. Increasing civil service salaries will not suffice to solve the problem. The measure is just one component of an anti-corruption strategy, which must include judicial reform and community efforts. The latter has recently come out strongly and spontaneously in reaction to Soeharto's KKN, and widespread fears of even greater corruption and the use of money politics under Habibie. The Bank Bali scandal confirms these fears and provided the momentum for such initiatives as the Indonesian Corruption Watch (ICW) and the Indonesian Transparency Society (*Masyarakat Transparansi Indonesia*), and even for non-government organisations (NGOs) like the Urban Poor Consortium to step up their activities.

Corruption and governance

The extent of corruption, by its nature, cannot easily be measured. Anecdotal evidence can be used to indicate the degree of corruption in a society. Systematic surveys of perceptions have been conducted by Transparency International, and the resulting Corruption Perception Index is currently a main reference for the business community, politicians and the media. Table 6.1 lists the Corruption Perception Index of eleven Asian countries and their ranking amongst eighty-five countries in the world. In 1998 Indonesia ranked lowest in East Asia, suggesting that problems of corruption in Indonesia are indeed very serious. If there is strong correlation between corruption and governance, which is likely to be the case, it also suggests the very poor state of governance in Indonesia.

Table 6.1   Corruption perception index, 1998

Country	Index(a)	Rank(b)
Singapore	9.10	7
Hong Kong	7.80	16
Japan	5.80	25
Malaysia	5.30	29
Taiwan	5.30	30
South Korea	4.20	43
China	3.50	52
Philippines	3.30	56
Thailand	3.00	62
Vietnam	2.50	74
Indonesia	2.00	80

Notes:
a Refers to perception of corruption ranging from 10 (highly clean) to 0 (highly corrupt).
b Ranking among 85 countries.
Source: Transparency International, in Tanzi (1998).

In the literature, the phenomenon of corruption has often been linked to the size of government, leading to the question of the optimal size of the state (Abimanyu 1999; Mishra 1999). It is to be noted, however, that some of the countries with the largest public sectors (Canada, Sweden, the Netherlands) belong to the least corrupt group. Thus, the solution to the problem of corruption is not as simple as reducing the level of taxation or public spending. Corruption is usually connected with the activities of the state and especially with the monopoly and discretionary power of the state. Tanzi (1998) lists various governmental activities that are a fertile ground for corruption. These include regulations and authorisations, taxation, spending decisions, provision of goods and services at below-market prices, other discretionary decisions, and financing of parties. In his view, the level of civil service salaries and the quality of the bureaucracy are only indirect causes of corruption. Other indirect causes of corruption relate to penalty systems; institutional controls; transparency of rules, laws and processes; and example by leadership. Perhaps it is more useful to address the problem of tackling corruption as involving two levels of problem. The first level is systemic' problems relating to the nature and style of managing state and society. In developing societies the government plays a predominant role. The second relates to organisational' problems such as public administration.

Good governance is widely identified with the following four attributes: transparency, accountability, efficiency and fairness. They are the outcome of developments in both the systemic level and the organisational level. Improving governance is all too often identified with efforts at the organisational level. Indeed, this is the level at which multilateral and other development agencies are able to participate. Sovereignty considerations have constrained them from involvement at the systemic level. This is where civil society can play its role.

Poor governance and the low quality of public sector management in Indonesia result mainly from developments at the systemic level, although many improvements need to made at the organisational level. The latter can contribute to changes at the systemic level, but perhaps only to a limited extent. An examination of the current setting for implementing a national agenda to improve governance would clearly show that the most serious problems and obstacles are at the systemic level. Perhaps the conditions prevailing today are less favourable than those at the beginning of the New Order some thirty-three years ago. A brief review of the salient developments affecting governance under Soeharto's rule is instructive. A more elaborate discussion of this can be found in Soesastro (1999c).

Governance and the rise and fall of Soeharto

In 1966, when Soeharto took over the leadership of the country, the first task was to restore macroeconomic stability and introduce market-oriented reforms. Improving governance was first attempted at the organisational level by bringing about discipline in the budget. In 1967 the government adopted a balanced budget policy, which became one of the important cornerstones of the New Order's economic management. This policy prohibited the domestic financing of the budget in the form of domestic debt or money creation. This policy was important to controlling inflation, but an equally important role of the balanced budget policy was to control government expenditures in view of the competing demands from various sectors within the government itself. From a political economy perspective, it provided the economic technocrats in the government with an important policy instrument to control the spending by the technical departments. To bring down inflation, the government also adopted a stringent monetary program. The exchange rate was adjusted and, following the devaluation in 1971, the capital account was fully liberalised. This open capital account was another significant cornerstone of the New Order's economic management.

The early years of the New Order government were marked by a style of economic management resembling the operations of an army unit being assigned the task of mobilising resources, having control over them and using them to achieve a specific objective. Soeharto, himself an army commander, was at the helm and immediately began organising groups to undertake specific tasks in mobilising resources. He retained full control over those resources by delegating their management to a number of his assistants. Later, he himself managed a large portion of the resources. In addition to macroeconomic stabilisation, the technocrats were assigned to mobilise foreign aid with the help of the International Monetary Fund (IMF) and the World Bank. Various individuals were dispatched as Soeharto's personal envoys, to lobby foreign governments for increased aid and to attract foreign companies to invest in the country. The President made a few of his army colleagues the heads of important state enterprises, not only to restore their functioning and economic health but also to mobilise resources for various non-budgetary expenditures. The use of 'tactical funds' was a common feature of management, which could have been borrowed from the practice of the military, and sowed the seeds of corruption and lack of transparency and accountability. The head of Pertamina, the state oil company, was given the task of providing supplementary resources for the armed forces, whose funding from the budget had been drastically reduced (see Chapter 7).

Soeharto himself formerly chaired the Economic Stabilisation Council, formed in 1968 to oversee the economic rehabilitation program. In later years, the main forum for economic policy coordination was the weekly cabinet meeting on economic affairs. The extent to which policies were discussed and debated among cabinet members and the President in these meetings has been questioned. Much remains to be revealed, but scant reports and recollections by former participants in the process have indicated that these meetings were mostly a formality. It appears that important matters were decided during bilateral meetings between the President and the relevant minister or ministers, and policy decisions were subsequently reported to the cabinet meeting prior to a public announcement.

This structure of centralised economic policy making seems to have worked well, at least in the early days. The key to success rests with the organisation of policy inputs to the President, who made the final decisions. The technocrats who were initially recruited as economic advisers to Soeharto became ministers and were given important portfolios. Working as a group, under the leadership of Widjojo Nitisastro, they were able to propose coherent policies that received the full support of the President. Being in charge of important economic ministries and with the group's cohesion, they could implement policies despite the weak bureaucracy. In addition, the team was successful in insulating' themselves from vested interests, which initially were far from complex, involving only the military and foreign corporations. These groups had direct access to the President.

Perhaps a major factor that has helped the technocrats insulate themselves from interference was the visible and swift results that were delivered by the reform programs they introduced. No other group could offer a superior alternative. However, the development agenda of the technocrats did not remain unchallenged for long. Within a few years the country was seen to have opened its doors too widely to foreign investment, particularly from Japan, arousing nationalist sentiments that culminated in the so-called Tanaka riots in early 1974. The riots, which were compounded by an internal political struggle among the political elite, came as a shock to the leadership. A series of economic policies were introduced in response, including more restrictive policies on foreign investment.

The direction of development was further altered as a result of the oil bonanza in the mid-1970s. With increased availability of resources, public enterprises began assuming a dominant role in a number of sectors, and public investments were increasingly directed into heavy industries. The civil service expanded rapidly, and bureaucratic intervention became rampant. To promote import substitution in government-initiated upstream industries, the incentive regime was made progressively more inwardly-oriented. Investment licensing and credit allocation at subsidised interest rates reinforced distortions in the trade regime. The oil boom increased the amount of resources at Pertamina's disposal. They were used to finance the development of heavy industries (Krakatau Steel), air transport (Pelita Air), a rice estate in Sumatra, hotels throughout Indonesia and other major projects. In addition, a new division of advanced technology was set up within Pertamina to create a position for the engineer Habibie, who had returned from Germany. It was the embryo of what later became the Agency for the Study and Application of Technology (BPPT).

With these augmented resources, Pertamina's head, Ibnu Sutowo, began to challenge the technocrats with an alternative vision of development. However, Pertamina's rapid expansion, including the development of its own fleet of tankers, led to a severe financial crisis when oil prices weakened. The technocrats were called upon to resolve the situation and, for a while, economic policy making was back to what it had been. New challenges arose. The economy became too dependent on oil and suffered from the Dutch disease' problem, which eroded the competitiveness of its non-oil sector. To protect the newly developed industries, protection was raised and a host of non-tariff barriers was introduced.

An import licensing system was introduced, with the intention of promoting import substitution in such basic goods as cement, fertilisers, chemicals, synthetic fibres, and iron and steel. An attempt by the Department of Industry to establish a system of administrative guidance' failed, and the import licensing system was misused to create import monopolies that were related to the power centre. The bureaucracy was powerless to facilitate a process in which powerful business groups were involved. Fair rules of the game could not be formulated or enforced under such circumstances. The import licensing system became the source of the high-cost economy. Gradually, exporters began to feel the negative effects of the import protection scheme and took up the fight to dismantle the system. As observed by MacIntyre (1992), these exporters later became valuable allies of the technocrats in undertaking reform. Government–business relations began to take on a new dimension. The influence of business became much more pronounced. This was a new challenge to economic governance. In the late 1980s, the Minister of Trade, Arifin Siregar, proposed the creation of a formal mechanism for government–business relations but, unfortunately, he did so in terms of the idea of Indonesia Incorporated'. The mechanism was strongly opposed in many quarters as it was seen as legitimising the practice of government–business collusion that by then had become very visible.

The technocrats were trying to deal with the excessive rent-seeking activities and to limit the damage caused by the policy of inwardly-oriented industrialisation (see Chapter 7). They made good use of three important disciplining devices to deal with government colleagues who favoured large, capital-intensive upstream projects and high technology ventures. These devices were the balanced budget, the open capital account, and a rule-of-thumb limiting the use of foreign capital, aimed at maintaining a maximum debt-service ratio of 20 per cent. These devices enabled the technocrats to maintain sound macroeconomic policies. Their inability to curb officially sanctioned' rent-seeking activities resulted in the high-cost economy. The weakening oil prices in 1982 thus came as a blessing in disguise. This allowed the technocrats to embark on a deregulation drive. As they encountered strong resistance to the deregulation of trade and industry, they were left with the financial sector to launch this process. The decision to liberalise the financial system was a daring move and went against the conventional wisdom that financial-sector liberalisation should not precede that of the real sector.

The continuing low oil prices helped to keep up the pressure for reform. They also allowed the technocrats to adopt a gradual approach to liberalisation. The government introduced the first package of trade and industrial deregulation in May 1986, allowing major exporters to procure foreign-sourced inputs directly rather than going through licensed importers. This was soon followed by the dismantling of the complex import licensing system and a further round of tariff reductions and the removal of non-tariff barriers to imports, including the dismantling of the monopoly on steel and plastic imports that was widely seen as a symbol of the emerging cronyism.

As it became more obvious that the President opposed further trade and industrial reform, the technocrats turned their attention to the financial system. The deregulation in October 1988 was heralded as the most sweeping initiative in that sector thus far. It removed most entry barriers. The number of banks increased from sixty-one in 1988 to about 230 in the mid-1990s. The assets and credits of private banks expanded rapidly. Soon concerns were expressed about the dangers of financial instability and distress because of an increase in problem loans and bank failures. In August 1990, one of the largest domestic private banks, Bank Duta, encountered problems caused by its foreign exchange dealings. Efforts were made to strengthen prudential regulations in 1991, but confidence in the banking system remained shaky.

The remarkable thing about the Bank Duta case was the manner in which it was rescued. Since the bank was partly owned by a number of foundations created by President Soeharto, he organised the rescue operation himself. He requested a close business associate to provide fresh capital to be injected into the bank in the shortest time possible; this met with a favourable response. Within a few months the associate was granted a licence to build one of Indonesia's largest petrochemical complexes, Chandra Asri. The project enjoyed foreign direct investment privileges and was subsequently given tariff protection. The then Minister of Finance, Mari'e Muhammad, who as stipulated by law was also *ex officio* head of the Tariff Board, was removed from the latter position because he opposed the tariff protection (see Chapter 7). The awarding of the protection was in violation of the spirit of AFTA, the ASEAN Free Trade Area, which had just been launched. It was even more awkward because it was announced only a few days after President Soeharto successfully engineered the Bogor Declaration of APEC towards open and free trade and investment in the region.

By the mid-1990s the technocrats were no longer so favourably placed to advise the President. Faced with a rapid deterioration in governance, they pulled together their remaining strength to make liberalisation of the economy a regionally-binding commitment (AFTA) or one based on a political commitment by the leader within the context of regional cooperation (APEC's Bogor Declaration). The financial crisis in 1997 was initially seen by the technocrats as a blessing in disguise as it could provide a new opportunity to redress problems and continue the deregulation process that had actually come to a halt. The technocrats misjudged the President's behaviour. The President's unwillingness to undertake the necessary reforms resulted in a gross mishandling of the crisis, which, in turn, produced the downward spiral in 1998.

The Bank Duta episode and subsequently the Timor national car project illustrate the direct involvement of, and intervention by, the President in business affairs, by-passing institutions and ignoring established rules and regulations, resulting in serious distortions in the economy. Such behaviour began to increase from the early 1990s and was largely unchecked. The political system was no longer functioning. Political, economic and legal institutions were no longer independent and could not function effectively. Yet this lack of effective governance did not discourage private foreign investors from entering the country. MacIntyre and Ramli (1997) offer three explanations for this puzzle. First, high rates of return to investors made them accept some increased costs associated with bribery and some increased risk associated with uncertainty over property rights. Second, relating to the nature of governance, President Soeharto's central position in Indonesia's political system can be likened to a unified monopolist. As such he was able to monitor and control circumstances so that the pricing of bribes by agencies did not drive down investments. Third, political stability and strong leadership provided an assurance that decisions would not be reversed. This perceived guarantee was strengthened by the open capital account, which created a powerful early warning of investor discontent and hence exercised strong discipline on government behaviour. MacIntyre and Ramli could have been correct in their assessment, but these factors no longer held after the crisis broke out. Recent interviews by this author with representatives from multinational corporations confirm this.

This brief review of developments shows that, in the beginning, the New Order government had to undertake the task of economic stabilisation and rehabilitation without having the necessary institutions in place. The government subsequently began rehabilitating the bureaucratic structure and building new institutions around it. Institutional development also took place in other fields, including that of politics. There was further progress in institutional development in the early years of deregulation. There was a qualitative shift from the use of informal, *ad hoc* and irregular mechanisms of economic policy making and implementation to the establishment, strengthening and exercise of more formal, structured and coherent arrangements. The establishment of more normal and regular processes of government and governance with accompanying institutional arrangements resulted in the emergence of a corporatist' state system, characterised by a strong role for the bureaucracy in an economy that is directed by a strong president.

Later phases saw clear stagnation in the process of institutional development, and perhaps even institutional involution' as institutions progressively lost their independence and became part of a system of government and governance that was increasingly more patrimonial and paternalistic in nature, and perhaps even more paranoid politically as the centre of that system became obsessed with the challenges of being able to stay in power. While the economy became more liberalised and open to the world over the years, much economic activity came to be conducted under a patrimonial system centring on the President, who was concerned about his control over the financial resources that were crucial to his ability to stay in power. The change described above did not occur abruptly. Perhaps this explains why it was not promptly recognised and did not have an immediate, negative impact on the economy. This was true until the crisis unfolded.

The fall of Soeharto has unleashed demands and the forces for total reform. Institutions will have to be renewed and resurrected. Soeharto's New Order inherited a bureaucracy and institutions that had been destroyed by years of ideological conflicts. Soeharto's New Order had left the country with a bureaucracy and institutions that had been severely weakened by KNN. The transition government of President Habibie made matters even worse as corruption became more rampant. The social fabric was also being destroyed and the country in great danger of disintegrating. This transition government has been replaced by a democratically elected government under the leadership of Abdurrahman Wahid, a nearly blind cleric, but widely accepted as an enlightened leader. However, the Habibie government has left many time bombs, even though it was in power for only seventeen months. The challenges to the new government will be enormous. Undeniably, the task of creating good governance will be hampered by its path-dependence on the previous governance structures. However, there should be belief and hope in the possibility of innovations in arrangements and structures that can influence the process towards establishing good governance.

THE CHALLENGES: REFORM AND RECOVERY

IMF-supported reform and recovery

The economic crisis has been deep. The year 1998 saw the worst economic performance of the past thirty-two years, with the economy contracting by about 14 per cent and an inflation rate of 70 per cent. Amongst the crisis-affected countries in East Asia, Indonesia has been hit hardest. The trigger was the contagion from Thailand, but the vulnerabilities that had been building up in the economy made it prone to the contagion. The economy has been growing too rapidly on a shaky foundation. The financial system was weak because of lax supervision and inadequate enforcement of prudential regulations. There was too much corruption in the system, and the private sector had embarked on heavy borrowing from abroad, some sizeable part of which was used to finance questionable investments. This brought corporate governance issues to the attention of the wider public and they, together with public governance issues, are now on the national agenda.

All the ills present in Indonesia were shared by other East Asian economies. However, in terms of a number of macroeconomic indicators, Indonesia did not do as badly as did some of its neighbours. The economy continued to grow at about 8 per cent until the second quarter of 1997. Inflation was low, and the budget deficit was relatively small. The deficit in the current account of the balance of payments was about 3 per cent of GDP, lower than the 8 to 9 per cent experienced by Thailand and Malaysia. Yet Indonesia was hit hardest. The question is, why? A series of mis-handlings by the government resulted in a loss of confidence. It was this loss of confidence that fed into the downward spiral. The need to restore confidence in the economy and in the government as a prerequisite for economic recovery was recognised quite early on. Rather than improving the situation, the last two governments under Soeharto (July 1997 to March 1998 and April 1998 to May 1998) and Habibie (June 1998 to October 1999) caused greater damage to the confidence in the market and of the population at large.

In restoring confidence in the economy, in October 1997 the government invited the IMF to come to Indonesia's assistance. This was not triggered by a huge loss of international reserves as was the case of Thailand and Korea. In fact, the Indonesian government made a clear decision not to use its reserves to shore up the currency. In dealing with the pressures in the foreign exchange market, it initially widened the intervention band, but in mid-August 1997 it abandoned the managed float to allow the currency to float freely. Prior to the IMF's involvement, the government had already adopted a tight monetary and fiscal policy. It had taken the necessary steps on its own, but it felt that it needed the IMF to deal with the contagion.

The contagion was caused not only by the herd behaviour of international investors, particularly portfolio investors and the hedge funds, but largely by the rapid loss of confidence on the part of Indonesians themselves. This resulted in large outflows of capital. Indonesians immediately detected that there were different appreciations of the crisis inside the government itself, and that the President's policies had begun to diverge from those of his economic team. While the monetary authority tightened the money supply, Soeharto openly demanded an end to that policy. It was obvious that Soeharto acted on the advice of his children, whose businesses were being affected by the high interest rates.

The IMF successfully produced a large financial package. This large package was meant primarily to deter speculators and, in doing so, it was also hoped that confidence would be restored. But the speculators were not the main cause for the huge outflows of capital.

The IMF-supported program for recovery, which included a huge financial package, did not produce the desired effect. Confidence was further weakened because the government, the President in particular, did not show any will to implement the agreement with the IMF in good faith. The recovery program included a number of structural reforms that involved the abolition of the monopoly by the State Logistics Agency (Bulog) in food distribution, and the termination both of the national car projects of one of Soeharto's sons and of Habibie's aircraft industry. Initially the IMF hesitated to include these projects in the program, but was convinced by the Indonesian negotiators (and the World Bank) that their inclusion was important to restore confidence. Those projects had become symbols of KKN and the abuse of power, and a willingness to tackle them would be a key to restoring confidence. The IMF and the Indonesian negotiators took a risk by incorporating them in the program. They thought that Soeharto was willing to give in and to take the necessary measures in the same way that he had been prepared to make the difficult decisions during the previous crisis situations of the mid-1970s and the mid-1980s. Soeharto continued to insist that those projects were sound and necessary for Indonesia. His unwillingness to change became all the more obvious in January 1998 following the signing of the second agreement with the IMF.

Many other decisions by Soeharto did further damage to the government's credibility. The early response to the crisis was to postpone and cancel a number of big projects, including a bridge to connect Sumatra and Peninsular Malaysia, the Jakarta Tower which was to have become the tallest building in Asia, and many others, in order to save foreign exchange and to further contain foreign borrowing. In early November 1997, however, the President decided to bring back to life about fifteen of those shelved projects, all of which were connected with his children and cronies. In January 1998, clearly on the advice of his children and in open confrontation with the IMF, Soeharto proposed the adoption of a Currency Board System (CBS). He might have believed that there would be an announcement effect of the policy that would result in a strengthening of the currency to about Rp 5,000/US$, at which point it would then be fixed. Finally, in the third week of January, Soeharto announced that he would have Habibie as his Vice-President, knowing that there were strong resentments towards Habibie. In reaction to this, the rupiah tumbled to an all-time low of Rp 17,000/US$.

The IMF also shared the blame. In retrospect, the IMF acknowledged that the proposal to liquidate the sixteen banks in November 1997 was a mistake, as it did not take into account the reactions of the people at large and of the market. As there was no deposit guarantee in place, only small depositors were being paid while large depositors lost their savings. This created a banking panic of unprecedented proportions since the public was also unsure which other banks would be closed down. The decision to close down the sixteen banks lacked clear criteria and transparency. Many other banks were suspected to be in a similarly dire situation. Even relatively healthy banks were affected by the bank runs. Indonesian banks were faced with a situation in which on the one side depositors withdrew their money and on the other side their debtors were unable to pay back their loans due to the crisis. Non-performing loans in the banking system rapidly increased from about 10 per cent at the onset of the crisis to about 60 per cent, and were reported to have reached 80 per cent in some state banks. This would logically result in a very severe banking collapse.

Yet, on the whole, the IMF instituted a reform and recovery program that has had the effect of disciplining economic policy in the country during the tumultuous changes of government. The IMF-supported recovery program placed binding constraints on the new government established by Soeharto following his re-election in March 1998. It had the same effect on the Habibie government that took over in late May 1998. Without the IMF program in place, many policies would have been introduced that would have caused greater damage to the economy. The IMF reacted to such policies by withholding the disbursement of its funds; that happened a few times under both Soeharto and Habibie. They were rather effective in containing policies that gave favours to particular business groups or that were populist in nature. However, the occasional stand-off with the IMF resulted in a loss of momentum for recovery.

The IMF-supported program is indeed quite wide-ranging. It is perhaps much more comprehensive than those for Thailand and Korea, particularly with regard to the structural reform component. In addition to the restructuring of the banking system, the structural reform program includes removing the monopolies and a whole range of measures to strengthen markets and to enhance transparency and accountability. These relate to the improvement of the bankruptcy law, the establishment of commercial courts, the drafting of a competition law, as well as guaranteeing the independence of the central bank. The program also strengthens the commitment to open economic policies. One major shortcoming of the program has been the belated inclusion of measures to help resolve the private sector debt and corporate restructuring. Both the government and the IMF refrained from doing so as they were cautious not to be drawn into providing bail-outs. This is understandable. However, they failed to appreciate the fact that the high debt overhead and foreign exposure of the corporate sector have turned the problem into a public policy issue that cannot be solved by the private sector itself.

The failure to address the problem of private sector debt has been a major reason for the slow process towards recovery. In addition, bank restructuring has proceeded slowly. Partly, this was due to the fact that so many banks had to be rescued and brought under the control of a new agency, the Indonesian Banking Restructuring Agency (IBRA). But IBRA was not free from political intervention by the government, as the Bank Bali scandal revealed. This poses a serious governance issue. The slow progress in bank restructuring has resulted in an inflation in the cost of restructuring. Current estimates suggest that the total cost of restructuring could range between 50 and 100 per cent of the country's GDP. This is a staggering amount. Part of the cost will be borne by the government, and public funds from the budget will have to be used for this. This poses a major political problem, as it would mean that other expenditures would have to be sacrificed. Political sentiments run deep on the issue and the government will have a hard time convincing the public that assistance to big businesses is not given at the cost of social programs that benefit the little people.

It is widely acknowledged that the bank restructuring and resolution of private sector debt are both keys to the restructuring. Banks have not been able to provide new credit and thus no new major investments have been undertaken by domestic investors. Working capital is also not easy to obtain, as banks continue to face problems of high non-performing loans. The dramatic reduction in deposit interest rates, from a peak of 70 per cent per year in August 1998 to about 14 per cent a year later, has reduced the cost of funds and lessened the interest burden of debtors, but it appears that investments have not been stimulated by this reduction. The country may indeed be in a liquidity trap'.

Both domestic and foreign investors are taking a wait-and-see' attitude. Political developments are a decisive factor influencing their investment decisions. Until the middle of 1999, foreign investment and domestic investment approvals have been far below those in 1998. Net foreign direct investment (FDI) inflows plummeted from US$6.5 billion in FY (fiscal year) 1996–7 to US$1.8 billion in FY 1997–8 and further to US$0.1 billion in FY 1998–9 (Table 6.2). Surprisingly, export-oriented investments have exhibited the same trend. It appears that the competitive exchange rate, produced by the large devaluation, has not been sufficient to attract export-oriented investments. Again, the uncertain political situation accounts for this. Indonesia's non-oil export performance has been disappointing. The first half of 1999 saw a further slowdown in export growth. This was partly due to weak commodity prices, and partly caused by weak demand in the region. This may suggest that the export sector cannot be relied upon to act as the engine of growth for economic recovery.

The exchange rate had begun to strengthen from June 1999, only to experience a weakening due to the Bank Bali scandal. Monetary stability is a necessary but an insufficient condition for recovery. Fiscal sustainability could be the main problem for the medium term. If economic growth remains low for a number of years, significant government revenues will not be able to be raised, even with improvements in tax collection and administration,

Table 6.2 Crisis and recovery, selected indicators

	96–97	97–98	98–99	99–00(p)
Index of real exchange rate	100	245	175	139
Inflation (% per year)	4.8	36.8	45.4	4 to 6
Nominal lending rate (% per year)	18.9	27.8	31.8	18 to 22
Net FDI (billion $)	6.5	1.8	0.1	0.6
Per capita GDP ($)	1159	412	571	745
Growth of GDP (%)	8.2	1.9	-14.6	2 to 4
As % of GDP				
Current account	-3.5	-2.0	3.7	2.0
Investments	33.4	29.8	13.6	17.4
Overall balance of the budget	1.0	0.0	-1.9	-5.1
Cost of bank restructuring	-	-	0.8	3.4
Government debt (incl. domestic debt)	22.9	65.2	74.9	97.8
Net external financing of the budget	-0.8	-0.2	4.6	3.5
External debt	49.2	166.2	128.5	96.6

Notes: p projections.

Source: Bappenas (1999).

as these continue to suffer from the entrenched corruption in the system. Oil revenues are a function of world prices, and recent projections show that they may weaken during the next two or three years. In addition, with the new formula for sharing the revenues from oil and gas exploitation with the producing regions, the share of the central government revenue will be reduced.

Foreign assistance is not likely to make up for the decline in the government's domestic revenues. Apart from aid fatigue in many donor countries, the government itself may adopt a policy of limiting its foreign borrowing in view of the fact that the country's external debt is already very high. Estimates suggest that, with an external debt at about 130 per cent of GDP, Indonesia is currently one of the most indebted developing countries in the world. Suggestions have also been made that the new government should explore the possibility of debt restructuring. This will not be an easy task as its acceptability by the international community is low. Last year the Paris Club of donors agreed to some selective debt rescheduling, but it is unclear whether this can be repeated. Whatever the case, fiscal constraints will pose a real problem for the new government. In macroeconomic terms, this means that the government cannot adopt a policy of fiscal expansion to stimulate the economy. More importantly, this also means that the government will have to sharpen its priorities in the use of its development funds.

Selected indicators of the crisis and the recovery are shown in Table 6.2. The turnaround in the current account in the balance of payments reveals the severity of the adjustment that has taken place. The current account was in deficit of about 3.5 per cent of GDP in 1996–7, but in 1998–9 the current account recorded a surplus of about 3.7 per cent of GDP. Some early signs of recovery since the second quarter of 1999 have produced cautious projections of a recovery in the year 2000, as shown in the projections for FY 1999–2000 by Bappenas (1999). Growth is expected to be between 2 and 4 per cent, and inflation between 4 and 6 per cent. Net FDI inflow is expected to increase to US\$0.6 billion from its all time low of US\$0.1 billion, but this remains far below that in 1996–7. Similarly, as a percentage of GDP, investments are expected to recover to 17.4 per cent from less than 14 per cent in 1998–9, but it will take time for the economy to return to an investment rate of more than 33 per cent of GDP, as experienced in 1996–7.

Sustainability of the recovery remains a major concern. The overall balance of the budget will be in deficit of about 5 per cent of GDP in 1999–2000. According to Bappenas projections, this deficit will remain high for the next three years. The cost of bank restructuring is projected to be around 3–3.5 per cent of GDP for the next six years. Government debt is approaching 100 per cent of GDP.

The most important task for the new government is to ensure that economic recovery will be sustainable. The agenda for achieving this is complex. It needs to cover all aspects – political, economic, and most importantly, improved governance and strengthening of the rule of law. The latter is critical to restoring confidence in the economy and in the government. There are concerns, however, that a quick recovery of the economy would leave the reform agenda unfinished.

The government of Abdurrahman Wahid has been given one hundred days by the public to begin to deliver on both economic recovery and serious efforts to eliminate KKN. The ability of the government to do so is somewhat in doubt because the cabinet has been seen as being too accommodating to the various political parties that have diverse interests and because most members of the cabinet do not have experience in government or a convincing track record. The first test for the government remains in the political field, namely how it will deal with Soeharto, the Bank Bali scandal, and the problem of Aceh.

The new political system is likely to be too fragile to ensure that the reforms will be implemented consistently. While it may not be to the liking of many, it is the IMF that can help maintain the momentum for reform. However, stronger forces to assure that this process will be kept on track must develop from within the society itself. This will involve the mass media and civil society.

Three preliminary conclusions can be drawn from this brief examination of the setting in which efforts to improve governance will take place. First, expectations must be modest. The focus should be on a few issues, of which tackling corruption appears to be most urgent. Second, efforts should be directed to establishing and strengthening a few key institutions, of which judicial institutions are an obvious target. Strengthening the integrity and independence of key economic institutions such as the Central Bank and IBRA is equally important. Third, the role of multilateral institutions such as the IMF is very important, but there is a limit to what they can do because of sovereignty considerations. Therefore internally there must be groups representing the interest of the society that can act as the vanguard for the needs and demands of good governance. Hence the critical role of civil society.

THE WAY AHEAD: EXPERIMENTATION AND INNOVATIONS

Enter the IMF with a governance agenda

The financial crisis brought the IMF right into the middle of the scene. The IMF-supported program for Indonesia's economic recovery was regarded as unusual as it incorporated many structural reforms that traditionally are outside its mandate. In addition to macroeconomic stabilisation and reform of the financial and banking system, the IMF-supported program also stipulates a continuation of the deregulation and liberalisation in international and domestic trade over a three-year period. This includes opening up wholesale and retail trade, and withdrawing all import and marketing monopolies (except rice) over the next three years, as well as phasing out price controls and domestic monopolies, including on cement and plywood. These measures are quite far-reaching and go beyond the many regional and international commitments that Indonesia has made. Perhaps equally, if not more, important is the program to strengthen institutional development in order to promote greater transparency and competition, more institutional autonomy, and a stronger legal and regulatory environment.

The IMF-supported program was critical for the maintenance of a coherent economic agenda during a period of turmoil and tumultuous changes of government. The IMF has been able to force the government to withdraw policies that do not conform to the overall program, by withholding the disbursement of funds. This happened several times in the last few months of the Soeharto government and under Habibie. The immediate impact of this has been the loss of momentum for recovery. Curiously enough, such IMF actions were not criticised by the public. In fact, its actions were supported by the public and the media as well as by leaders of the reformist' parties. The Bank Bali scandal that came to the attention of the public in mid-August forced the IMF to take a tougher stand with the government. The $70 million scandal, implicating many key government and Golkar officials as well as individuals who were known to be in Habibie's Success Team' for his re-election, severely damaged the credibility of the government as well as the IMF. Since the Habibie government was reluctant to uncover and resolve the scandal, the parliament took on the task of investigating the case. Its ability to act was limited. The IMF forced the government to invite an international auditor, PriceWaterhouseCoopers, to undertake the audit and to make the result public. When the audit was completed, the government refused to publicise the full report. This prompted the IMF to postpone the disbursement of funds. The IMF resumed its review and support only after the new government was in place.

Developments in Indonesia, as in Russia, pose a dilemma for the IMF. They are an important test for the institution. The Indonesian case was unfortunate because its warnings and threats appear to have been ignored by the previous government. The new government in Indonesia will have to clean up the mess left behind by previous governments. Cooperation with and support from the IMF will help. But how can the IMF help, in particular with improving governance?

According to James (1998), the IMF's interest in governance is now firmly embedded in its activities. Conditionality has come to the fore in each of four completely new areas. First, military spending was a central element in IMF discussions with the governments of Pakistan and Romania. Second, corruption is explicitly addressed in Africa and in Indonesia. Third, democracy is now being addressed. Fourth, especially in response to the East Asian crisis, it is also addressing the issue of crony capitalism'. As described by James, the gradual extension of the IMF into these areas is an immediate result of the new consensus about economic practice and of a new world political order that it has helped to produce. But it reflects something more profound – a realisation increasingly shared throughout the world that the world economy, and world institutions, can be a better guarantee of rights and of prosperity than some governments, which may be corrupt, rent-seeking, and militaristic. Economic reform and the removal of corrupt governments are preconditions both for the effective operations of markets and for greater social justice.

This new approach may sound impressive, but James correctly poses a few important questions. First, how even-handed can the IMF be in its treatment of all its members? In its dealings with Indonesia, which is not a small' country, the IMF often appeared too accommodating towards the government, but then, encouraged by Indonesians themselves (politicians, economists and media) took a tougher stand. Second, what is the IMF's institutional capacity for implementation? Again, in the case of Indonesia, with the incorporation of a comprehensive structural reform agenda, the IMF has embarked on a completely new area in which it has no previous experience. Third, will it be the case that the more the IMF is seen to extend its mandate, the more it will be expected to undertake? The suggestions that the IMF must integrate environmental and labour standards into its programs and that it must be responsive to social and humanitarian concerns could lead the institution into an expectations trap'.

The IMF must be wary about institutional over-extension. In July 1997, in coincidence with the onset of the crisis, the IMF Executive Board approved a Guidance Note on the role of the IMF in governance issues. The basis for the IMF's governance agenda is the conviction that greater attention to governance issues can make a contribution to macroeconomic stability and sustainable growth in member economies. It proposes to do this through different channels: policy advice, technical assistance, and promoting transparency in financial transactions (IMF 1997). In the context of Article IV on consultation discussions, IMF staff should point to reforms that can contribute to the promotion of good governance, for example, reduced scope for generalised rent seeking, enhanced transparency in decision making and budgetary processes, reductions in tax exemptions and subsidies, improved accounting and control systems, improvements in statistical dissemination practices, improvements in the composition of public expenditure, and accelerated civil service reform. In addition, they should bring to the attention of governments the potential risk that poor governance could adversely affect private market confidence. In regard to instances of corruption, IMF staff should continue raising these with the authorities. The IMF does not have the mandate to adopt the role of an investigative agency or guardian of financial integrity in member countries. In the case of IMF-supported programs, financial assistance from the IMF could be suspended or delayed on account of poor governance. Corrective measures that at least begin to address the governance issue will be necessary for the resumption of any support.

Staff must exercise judgment in assessing whether the actions adopted by the government concerned are adequate. Recent experience in Indonesia has shown that by doing so, the IMF has broadened its contacts with non-government people and institutions, including opposition parties and the NGOs.

The Indonesian experience may demonstrate that the IMF's effectiveness in contributing to good governance depends on circumstances. In bad times it can be effective; in good times its exhortations may fall on deaf ears. The new political parties in Indonesia, including those that form the new government, have pledged to continue to work with the IMF, at least under the existing three-year program. What will happen next is not clear.

Towards a regional surveillance mechanism

Indonesia, together with its ASEAN neighbours, has supported the development of a regional surveillance mechanism. This is one of the few regional initiatives in response to the financial crisis. If it is successful, it can complement the global surveillance under the IMF, especially in good or normal' times. A regional surveillance mechanism has a number of attractions. Battacharya and Kawai (1999) from the World Bank argue that in this increased financial independence, a currency crisis in one country can easily spread to other *neighbouring* countries. A regional arrangement for financial coordination could include modalities for mutual consultation, surveillance and collaboration. It should be consistent with multilateral arrangements. Dobson (1999) and Quibria (1999) are in favour of regionalising surveillance structures. This view proposes that the IMF surveillance should be made less centralised. The potential value of regional surveillance is that countries are reluctant to take outside advice of any kind, especially in good times. However, neighbours are the ones that have the greatest stake in each other's good policies, performance and, increasingly, governance.

The so-called ASEAN surveillance process is still in its infancy and will take time to evolve into an effective process that can have a positive influence not only on the financial management of its participants but also on economic governance in general (Soesastro 1999a). This is not surprising. The ASEAN finance ministers only held their first meeting in March 1997, a few months before the onset of the crisis. They then agreed to promote ASEAN financial cooperation in the area of finance. The activities are to include exchanges of views on macroeconomic policies, improving transparency of policies, regulations and rules affecting the financial sector, promoting ASEAN as an efficient and attractive financial and investment region, promoting public–private sector linkages in the area of finance, and developing ASEAN human resources in the area of finance. In subsequent meetings they considered the development of a regional surveillance mechanism, which was previously discussed amongst a subset of APEC members in Manila. In view of the slow moves by the so-called Manila Group, ASEAN ministers decided in February

1998 to move ahead immediately. They were not specific about the kind of surveillance to develop, but suggested the inclusion of new elements in the traditional scope of surveillance. The surveillance process is to be conducted within the general framework of the IMF, and ASEAN approaches to the Asian Development Bank (ADB) for assistance. The ASEAN Surveillance Process (ASP) was formally established in October 1998. The process will involve peer review and frank exchanges of views and information and, importantly, it will provide recommendations on possible actions that could be taken not only at the regional level but also in individual countries. The latter can be seen as a departure from ASEAN's principle of non-interference and, if indeed the ASP exercises this mandate, it will transform the nature of ASEAN. The first Ministerial Peer Review Process took place in March 1999 and discussed the first report of the ASP. Another report was prepared for a second meeting in late 1999.

The direction in which this process will evolve is still open. Suggestions have been made to develop the process as the core of a wider regional effort (East Asia or APEC) as well as to become an element of a regional financial architecture. The other possible elements of the regional financial architecture could be the establishment of a regional fund and exchange rate coordination (Soesastro 1999b). Initiatives towards a regional financial architecture, especially regional surveillance, could be seen as an innovation at the regional level that could help individual countries deal with governance issues, not only at the organisational level but perhaps also at the systemic level, because this process involves voluntary participation of governments. In this sense, it could complement the IMF surveillance, in particular during good times.

Strengthening civil society

The process of democratic consolidation and the nature of democracy that exists in a society are perhaps best reflected in the strength of its civil society. Civil society, together with state and market, is one of the three spheres' that interface in the making of democratic society (UNDP 1993). In the words of Barber (1998), civil society is an independent domain of free social life where neither governments nor private markets are sovereign'. Civil society has been called the private non-profit sector, the voluntary sector, or the third sector.

Civil society can influence resource allocations (Soesastro 1997). More importantly, civil society in East Asia today has acquired significance in the context of both democratic consolidation and improving governance. The latter results from a widespread agreement that the lack of good governance has been one of the main causes of the financial crisis in the region. The crisis has demonstrated also that good governance cannot be separated from political development, namely democratisation (Soesastro 1998). The process of democratisation in Indonesia has accelerated as a result of the crisis. This process has been sustained by the rise of a civil society that has become greatly aware of the importance of good governance. Civil society has become a code for a set of ideas related to participation, good governance, human rights, privatisation and public sector reform.

Much is being expected of civil society. In the first instance, it serves to promote democratisation; in fact, it is seen as a prerequisite for democracy. Diamond (1991) identifies six functions of civil society in shaping democracy: (a) to act as a reservoir of resources to check the power of the state; (b) to ensure that the state is not held captive by a few groups; (c) to supplement the work of political parties in stimulating political participation: (d) to stabilise the state because citizens will have a deeper stake in social order; (e) to act as a locus for recruiting new political leadership; and (f) to resist authoritarianism.

In addition, it is expected to provide services to the poor and underprivileged members of the society. It is expected to provide a social safety net for society. It should also help assure sustainability by engaging in capacity building and human resources development. Civil society faces the dangers of being overburdened and overloaded. Therefore, it is important to view civil society in the context of the developmental challenges in individual societies. By their nature, voluntary organisations are somewhat unstructured; they are disparate and atomised.

It is likely that the prevailing situation and environment in a society will influence the agenda and activities of organisations and movements as well as networks of organisations that constitute civil society. Both civil society organisations and agencies or foundations supporting the development of civil society have been preoccupied with two issues. First, is the importance of an enabling environment for civil society to develop. The second issue is the need to strengthen the management, funding and human resources of civil society organisations so that they are able to function effectively. Much attention has been given to the strengthening of non-governmental organisations, but civil society includes organisations that are not NGOs in the sense commonly used. Peasants who organise themselves to defend their land rights or to demand fair compensations for the land used for development projects are often overlooked.

Until recently, civil society has been regarded as an alien concept in Indonesia (Buchori 1999). The new, rather common Indonesian word for it, *masyarakat madani*, was originally used in Malaysia and introduced into Indonesia by Anwar Ibrahim in 1994 during the second Istiqlal Festival in Jakarta. It has been taken from the Arabic word *al-mujtamai al-Madani*, which in the Middle East has been used to convey the idea of civil society. This concept purports to include the civilianisation of the entire society, including the government. Consequently the government has made civil society its business. Presidential Decree No. 18/1999 of 24 February 1999 established a National Reform Team to work towards *masyarakat madani*.

There are concerns that through this decree the government is trying to co-opt existing civil society organisations.

Civil society in Indonesia is still weak. The main constraint has been political. The fall of Soeharto opened up a greater space for civil society. Although this unleashed a democratisation process, civil society continued to be seen by the transition government of Habibie as a serious threat to its survival, since civil society was at the forefront of the opposition to the Habibie government and its continuation in power. Buchori believes that civil society will survive and gradually develop in Indonesia, but that this will be critically influenced by the process of leadership transfer. Hikam (1999) is of the opinion that the role of civil society in Indonesia, as manifested mainly by NGOs, will increase because of current global and national trends towards de-bureaucratisation and decentralisation of decision-making processes in society.

NGOs are not a new phenomenon in Indonesia. Many traditional institutions have functioned as social empowerment agencies'. As described by Eldridge (1990), the main role of NGOs in Indonesia is to enhance the capacity for self-management among less advantaged groups, enabling them to deal with government agencies and other powerful forces on more equal terms. A more recent development in Indonesia is the emergence of issue-oriented NGOs'. They have arisen in response to the concentration of power and to the top-down' approach to development under Soeharto's New Order governments. These issue-oriented NGOs have gained prominence due in part to their efforts to provide alternatives to the society beyond the state's framework and strategy of development.

The active involvement of civil society in the change of government and in demands for reforms in all fields, including governance, has built up a momentum towards expanding the space for civil society. Civil society also participated actively in assuring that the recent general elections were conducted fairly and freely. Various election-monitoring groups were set up to prevent a recurrence of the practice of vote rigging by the state apparatus and the government party. The past year has seen the appearance of a number of watchdog' non-private organisations and activities. A number have focused on corruption and governance issues. But the very fact of the growth of such organisations and their activities in society could help promote good governance. Civil society can do much in raising governance issues at the systemic level.

REFERENCES

Abimanyu, A. (1999) 'Challenges toward good governance and anti-corruption – The case of Indonesia', paper presented at the Second Intellectual Dialogue on Building Asia's Tomorrow: Promoting Sustainable Development and Human Security, Singapore, 6–7 July.

Bappenas (1999) *Looking to the Future of the Indonesian Economy*, Jakarta.

Battacharya, A. and Kawai, M. (1999) International financial architecture and the role of the World Bank: Lessons from the East Asian crisis', paper presented at the 15th Annual Technical Symposium on international Finance and Financial Institutions: Analysis of the Asian Crisis, organised by The Center for Japan–U.S. Business and Economic Studies, New York University and Stern School of Business, 26 March.

Barber, B. (1998) *A Place for Us: How to make society civil and democracy strong*, Hill and Wang Publisher.

Bhanu, S. (1999) Research notes on governance, human security, social safety nets, human resources development and non-governmental organisations', Singapore: Institute of Southeast Asian Studies.

Buchori, M. (1999) Development of civil society and good governance in Indonesia', paper presented to the Global ThinkNet Paris Conference on International Comparative Study on Governance and Civil Society organised by the Japan Center for International Exchange and the Institut Francais des Relations Internationales, Paris, 18–19 March.

Diamond, L. (ed.) (1991) *The Democratic Revolution: Struggles for freedom and pluralism in the developing world*, Perspectives on Freedom no.12, Freedom House.

Dobson, W. (1999) What should we do with the IMF?', paper.

Eldrigde, P.J. (1990) NGOs and the state in Indonesia', *Prisma* 47: 34–56.

Hikam, M. (1999) Non-governmental organisations and the empowerment of civil society', in R.W. Baker, M.H. Soesastro, J. Kristiadi and D.E. Ramage (eds) *Indonesia – The Challenge of Change*, Singapore: Institute of Southeast Asian Studies.

IMF (1997) *Good Governance – The IMF's Role*, Washington, DC: International Monetary Fund.

James, H. (1998) From grandmotherliness to governance – the evolution of IMF conditionality', *Finance and Development* 35 (4).

MacIntyre, A.J. (1992) Politics and the reorientation of economic policy in Indonesia', in A.J. MacIntyre and K. Jayasuriya (eds) *The Dynamics of Economic Policy Reform in South-east Asia and the South-west Pacific*, Singapore: Oxford University Press.

—— and R. Ramli (1997) Investment, property rights, and corruption in Indonesia', paper presented at the World Bank/Foundation for Advanced Studies on International Development Workshop on Governance and Private Investment in East Asia, Hakone, 24–6 August.

Mishra, S.C. (1999) Government and governance: Understanding the political economy of the reform of institutions', paper presented to the LPEM/USAID conference on The Economic Issues Facing the New Government, Jakarta, 18 August.

New York Times (1999) Tougher talk for Indonesia', 5 September.

Quibria, M.G. (1999) The case for an Asian fund', *Asiaweek* 25 June.

Soesastro, H. (1997) Economics, the military and civil society', in S. Harris and A. Mack (eds) *Asia–Pacific Security – The Economics–Political Nexus*, St Leonards, NSW: Allen and Unwin Australia Pty Ltd.

(1998) Long term implications for developing countries', in R. McLeod and R. Garnaut (eds) *East Asia in Crisis: From being a miracle to needing one?*, Routledge.

(1999a) ASEAN during the crisis', in H.W. Arndt and H. Hill (eds) *Southeast Asia's Economic Crisis: Origins, Lessons and the Way Forward*, Singapore: Institute of Southeast Asian Studies.

(1999b) Creating a new economic environment: How bold can ASEAN be?', paper presented at the ASEAN 2020 Conference, organised by ASEAN ISIS, Singapore, 21–2 July.

(1999c) Government and deregulation in Indonesia', in C. Barlow (ed.) *Institutions and Economic Change in Southeast Asia,* Cheltenham, UK: Edward Elgar Publishing.

Straits Times (1999) World Bank admits to policy flaw', 12 February.

Tanzi, V. (1998) Corruption around the world', *IMF Staff Papers* 45(4): 559–94.

UNDP (1993) *UNDP and Civil Society*, New York: UNDP.

World Bank (1991) *World Development Report*, Washington, DC: The World Bank.

(1992) *Governance and Development*, Washington, DC: The World Bank.

7 Government–business relations in Soeharto's Indonesia

Ross H. McLeod

Indonesia has a reputation as one of the most corrupt countries in the world (Transparency International 1999). Unlike other countries that are regarded as highly corrupt, however, this was not incompatible with rapid economic progress over many years, and Soeharto's New Order regime clearly brought considerable material benefits to the majority of Indonesia's population. Some argue that endemic corruption was unsustainable and that it was responsible for the unravelling that has been seen since mid-1997, but while the nature of government–business relationships undoubtedly contributed in important ways to the crisis, the mechanisms by which this occurred have yet to be adequately described.

THE POLITICAL ECONOMY OF THE RENT-GENERATING GOVERNMENT

According to Mao Zedong (1961), Political power grows out of the barrel of a gun.' No fan of Chinese Communism, the pragmatic former President Soeharto may well have thought to himself: Quite so. But you need cash to buy the gun'. For much of the last three decades, Soeharto was not merely the leader of Indonesia's government: he *was* the government for all practical purposes. This chapter describes how he created a symbiotic relationship between government and business that gave him direct or indirect access to cash in abundance, and thus bestowed on himself the power to stay in office for such a long period. The ultimate objective is to reflect on how this system contributed to the current crisis, with a view to determining how government–business relations should be modified if Indonesia is to return to sustained economic growth.

A quarter of a century ago, Kreuger's seminal paper focused attention on the phenomenon of rent-seeking' behaviour, and implied that much of the blame for corruption in developing countries lies with the proliferation of economic controls following independence' (Kreuger 1974: 293). She noted the danger that if it comes to be perceived that

> wealthy individuals are successful rent seekers, whereas the poor are those precluded from or unsuccessful in rent seeking, the market

mechanism is bound to be suspect [in which case] the inevitable temptation is to resort to greater and greater intervention, thereby increasing the amount of economic activity devoted to [socially wasteful] rent seeking.

Apart from noting the possibility of a political vicious circle' in which intervention, followed by rent seeking, would generate more intervention, Kreuger had nothing to say about the reason for the initial intervention. Likewise, the World Bank's study of industrial licensing in Indonesia merely reported that

> the most frequent justification advanced for licensing and other regulation procedures is that it is desirable for the Government to build or cultivate the development of the industrial sector [i.e.] that the proper role of government officials is to provide leadership and direction to businessmen and to guide them in the right direction (World Bank 1981: 20),

but took these views as given. McCawley (1981: 77–8) also was concerned by the undesirable but increasingly interventionist tendencies of the Indonesian government during the 1970s, but made no attempt to explain them.

The notion that ill-advised intervention leads to rent seeking and corruption and that endemic corruption caused the crisis[1] suggests that crises can be avoided by eschewing such intervention, and encourages the view that crises already underway can be cured by getting rid of it. The latter view may have motivated the International Monetary Fund's (IMF) long list of policy changes demanded of Indonesia early in the current crisis (McLeod 1998: 45–7).

The following discussion turns the Kreuger notion of rent seeking as an unintended response to intervention on its head, seeing intervention instead as the means of deliberately generating and capturing rents. This is an idea I touched upon long ago when attempting to explain the Indonesian government's great propensity to control and regulate', noting that regulations have the potential to generate great benefits for both the bureaucrats who administer them and the firms favoured by them' (McLeod 1980: 136). Similarly, in relation to the state-owned banks, I have argued that their managers used their discretion to keep lending rates well below market levels in order to maintain a flow of rents to bank officials faced with the resulting excess demand for loans (McLeod 1999a: 266). Thus the view to be explored here is that the substantial government intervention that existed under Soeharto was in no sense an accident, but was consciously put in place for the purpose of generating the rents (cash') that Soeharto presumably wanted for their own sake, but also needed in order first to attain and then maintain a position of virtually unchallenged authority.

THE SOEHARTO–BUSINESS SYMBIOSIS

It is helpful to think of an autocrat such as Soeharto became as having the power to *privately* tax economic activity in general. In the period before he came to power (in the aftermath of the attempted coup against President Sukarno in 1965) the tax base had shrunk drastically, so the first challenge was to resurrect the economy from the crisis it was then undergoing.

Although the economy was then in a calamitous state, it was endowed with an abundance of natural resources, a huge population and a cheap labour force, all of which made it attractive to investors, including foreign investors. At the same time, the West was anxious to consolidate the move away from communism, to which Indonesia had become uncomfortably close under Sukarno. Given these circumstances it proved possible to revive the economy in a relatively short time by opening it to largely unfettered foreign investment (Sadli 1993: 43), and by welcoming a large inflow of international aid (Hill 1996: 78–81). Indeed, Soeharto exploited both these sources of funds with great skill throughout his entire term in office.

Soeharto also inherited a large state enterprise sector active in many fields of activity. This was useful in several ways. First, state-owned enterprises (SOEs) could be used to provide jobs for members of the armed forces upon their retirement from active duty, thus helping to ensure their loyalty to, and dependence on, the regime. Second, they could be used in similar fashion to provide jobs for relatives and friends of other Soeharto supporters, such as his ministers and senior bureaucrats. Third, they could be used to absorb high level military personnel who might be seen as potential threats to Soeharto's authority. (Thus the SOEs came to employ ex-military men at all levels, from security guards to managing directors and commissioners.) Fourth, they could be used as cash cows – by way of overpriced contracts with suppliers and under-priced contracts with customers.

In one way or another, the private corporate sector provided the primary medium through which Soeharto generated his family's enormous wealth and maintained his own power. Early on he realised the effectiveness of private sector monopoly privileges for generating rents. The earliest prototype emerged in 1968 – the first year of the New Order. It involved the restriction on imports of cloves – an essential component of Indonesia's *kretek* cigarettes – to just two firms, one owned by Soeharto business associate and now Indonesia's richest citizen, Liem Sioe Liong, and one by Soeharto's half-brother, Probosutejo (Backman 1999: 114; McDonald 1980: 120–1). Two years later, a far more important monopoly – that for importing wheat – was created for the benefit of Liem's burgeoning conglomerate (Schwarz 1994: 110–1), and this was followed years later by another monopoly on the import of soy bean cake, held by a firm owned by a number of Soeharto-associated conglomerates (Schwarz 1994: 133–5). In the 1990s, the same strategy was employed for the benefit of youngest presidential son, Tommy, who monopolised the domestic trade in cloves (Backman 1999: 267–9).

Such monopolies usually had some transparently spurious national interest rationale for the sake of appearances, but in the absence of a free press and an effective parliament, few voices were raised in opposition to them. Their purpose was to generate rents that were then shared between the favoured recipients and Soeharto and his family, or his supporters and theirs. Although there may be little evidence of anything so crude as direct payments as a *quid pro quo*, it is no coincidence that members of the first family came to be significant shareholders in the many firms that benefited from some kind of privilege granted by the government (Robison 1986: 343–50; Backman 1999: 255–99). Another technique for harvesting the rents generated by these privileges was for the favoured firms to donate' large sums to a number of foundations (*yayasan*) – tax-free entities cloaked as charitable institutions of one kind or another – controlled by Soeharto, and whose funds were deployed for purposes known only to himself.[2] An interesting point to note in passing is that there was nothing illegal in these arrangements: they were backed by laws and official decrees. This is one important reason why it will be difficult to find evidence of Soeharto having profited from corruption.

ASPECTS OF THE SOEHARTO SYSTEM OF RENT GENERATION

Various important features of Soeharto's Indonesia can be explained within the framework just outlined.

Centralisation of power

The Soeharto pattern of rent extraction at the commanding heights of the economy was successful, but for Soeharto to maintain his position as leader he would need plenty of support and not too much active opposition. Since the bulk of economic activity involved large numbers of relatively small firms, it would not be practicable for him to maximise the flow of rents unless rent generation and harvesting could be replicated at lower levels. The solution was a system akin to business franchising – or what Crouch (1979) has referred to as a patrimonialism'. Just as Soeharto used his position as head of the national government to bestow privileges on selected firms (cronies', as they have come to be known), so he effectively awarded franchises to other government officials at lower levels to act in similar manner. This included many of his ministers and senior bureaucrats, government administrators at all levels – from provinces down to rural villages – and top executives in the state enterprises and special government bodies such as the food logistics agency, Bulog, and the Agency for the Study and Application of Technology.

These franchises were not awarded free of charge; as with business franchises, there had to be benefits to both franchiser and franchisee. The payback could be in a multitude of forms: payment to a Soeharto-controlled *yayasan*; the provision of loans and award of contracts on favourable terms to first family members and business cronies by state banks, state enterprises and government departments; a flow of information to the top regarding individuals or organisations that might in any way threaten the existence of the system; a willingness to act against such individuals and organisations in order to protect the system; and of course clear loyalty to the head of the franchise whenever there might be a public outcry about the way the country was being governed.

This is not to suggest that all Soeharto appointees, all members of the bureaucracy, and all employees of the state enterprises played an active role along these lines. All that was necessary was that there should be sufficient people willing to play the game, so that opportunities for harvesting rents could be optimally exploited, and that those who might otherwise have opposed what was going on would have a good deal to fear from stepping out of line – whether in terms of forfeited promotion prospects or loss of their positions. Moreover, there were those who knew clearly what was going on and wanted no part of it, but thought that they had a better chance of changing the system for the better from within. A small number of officials had the courage to take a principled stand on various occasions during the three decades of the New Order, and suffered as a consequence, providing a cautionary example for others of like mind (Kenward 1999a). Thus the endemic corruption at all levels of the bureaucracy should not be interpreted as an unintended shortcoming of Soeharto's Indonesia. Rather, it reflected a conscious effort to generate and harvest rents from business (and, to a lesser extent, from individuals) at all levels.

Rule of law

To say that the rule of law under Soeharto was weak would be a gross understatement. Black letter law was largely a relic of the colonial era, and there was considerable reluctance to bring laws up to date or to introduce new laws in areas where modernisation of the economy and polity made this highly desirable. But it was not the case that written law was useless. The more serious problem was the ineffectiveness of law enforcement and the courts. Policemen rarely arrested or charged traffic offenders, supervisory officials rarely punished firms that violated regulations, and commercial disputes were rarely taken to the courts to be settled. Judges, public prosecutors, police and regulatory supervisors were all either Soeharto franchisees or else felt powerless to take a stand against the system.

None of this should be seen as an oversight, nor was the system anarchic. In the absence of properly functioning formal law, informal law naturally tends to take its place. The vacuum was filled by informal arbitration, with Soeharto and his franchisees playing the role of arbitrators and enforcers. Just as judges could enrich themselves by selling their judicial decisions, so Soeharto and his other franchisees could do so by making determinations' outside the courts that put an end to all kinds of matters in dispute.

Thus, for example, on occasion when a Soeharto minister was exposed as seemingly being involved in corruption, there was never the slightest suggestion that the case would be dealt with formally by the courts or the civil service. The matter would be passed to Soeharto, who would consider it for a while (allowing the minister to sweat for a few days), then announce his findings and the accompanying punishment – perhaps along the lines that there had been administrative errors' and that the minister would have to engage in a period of introspection' (*Jakarta Post*, 27 December 1995: 1). Dismissal was out of the question, much less a jail term. After all, being a franchisee conferred the right to plunder, and the right to protection by the franchise. But no doubt it served a useful purpose in reminding all ministers and other top officials that their position depended entirely on maintaining Soeharto's favour.

Reliance on the military

As noted above, the lack of rule of law did not imply anarchy. There was a type of quite effective informal law in action, relying on the ability of Soeharto to grant and withdraw his franchise, and ultimately on the coercive power of the military. The armed forces (including the police) were not invariably inept, but selectively so. In the normal course of events, the police appeared incapable of controlling the traffic. But at times when the former President had to travel from his residence to the Palace, for example, they and the military police combined would display the highest degree of effectiveness, closing down all intersections on the route so that their franchiser would have a clear run.

Soeharto made skilful use of the military, having demonstrated in 1965–6 that he would not hesitate to use it in the most brutal fashion against forces or groups that did not play by his rules (Crouch 1979: 575–6). Hundreds of thousands were murdered for the crime' of having supported the Communist Party (the main political party to oppose the military in seeking to determine Indonesia's political direction under Sukarno) while the military stood by and gave its tacit support (Cribb 1990).[3] Thousands of others were recorded as having had links to the Communist Party, and were jailed or at least excluded from participation in the bureaucracy. Indeed, even the children of such people were so excluded, for decades to come. And at times when other groups threatened the integrity and continuity of the regime – separatists in Aceh, East Timor and Irian Jaya; university students; militant labour; thugs and extortionists outside the franchise – Soeharto did not hesitate to unglove the iron fist of the military (see for example McDonald 1980: 127).

When he wanted it to be, Soeharto's law was chillingly effective. In the mid-1980s, at a time when petty crime by neighbourhood gangs was beginning to get out of hand, Soeharto simply unleashed the military – not to apprehend the offenders and bring them before the courts, but to apprehend and murder them, leaving their bodies to be found by the public so that word of their fate would quickly spread. Young men with tattoos on their arms – often associated with gang membership – burned them off with acid rather than risk assassination as a suspected neighbourhood thug.

Civil and military salaries

One of the most obvious explanations for the immense shortcomings of the Indonesian civil service is its salary structure. By comparison with the private sector where wage and salary rates reflect supply and demand, this structure is extremely compressed, with salaries of the very top officials only a relatively small multiple of those of clerks and office assistants with minimal education and skills. At the bottom end, wage rates have been, if anything, above market, meaning that there has never been any difficulty in recruiting individuals for these positions. Indeed, there has usually been an excess supply of applicants, and low level officials of personnel departments have not been slow to exploit the franchise right to harvest the rents from those keen to win secure jobs in the civil service and state enterprises.

At the top end, however, salaries have always been woefully inadequate – a small fraction of those available in the private sector for people with the levels of training and skills required in order to do these jobs properly. The result was not that there was any difficulty finding people to fill the positions, however. This could never be a problem, given the large numbers who made up the lower echelons, and who waited patiently for those at higher levels to retire or die and thus give them a chance of moving up the ladder. Rather, the problem has been that the people who moved up were to a large extent those who demonstrated by their conduct over many years that they were worthy of being awarded a Soeharto franchise – and, in many cases, who were willing to pay those who controlled promotions in order to be looked upon favourably.

The oft-heard complaint that low civil service salaries force' civil servants to be corrupt is unconvincing. It is contradicted by the facts that vast numbers of civil servants are not corrupt, and that many who rise high in the pyramid and amass enormous wealth do not then cease to be corrupt. Soeharto himself, of course, was a top-ranking civil servant, and his family's wealth became incalculably large, yet his rent-generating activities went from strength to strength the longer he remained in power. The point is that the system was designed precisely in order to attract and recruit people who were willing and able to play the game by Soeharto's rules. The eagerness to opt for a lowly paid civil service or military career, to pay bribes (in cash or in kind) to get a foot in the door, and to pay bribes again in order to get promotions, is most easily understood in the context of a system in which everyone knew that the civil service, the military and the state enterprises were all part of a huge franchising operation, in which one could expect to become increasingly wealthy if one signed on to the implicit franchise contract.

Land titling

One aspect of law that has been a perennial source of complaint is land titling. The transition from a traditional agricultural to a modern industrial economy creates a need for a modern system of recognising land ownership. In the modern economy it must be relatively easy to demonstrate ownership, to be able to use land as collateral for loans, to clear the way for construction on it, and to transfer such ownership in order that the land can always be easily put to its highest value uses. Efforts of the government under Soeharto to complete a national cadastral survey to this end were excruciatingly slow, for one main reason. A certificate that established clear ownership of land was valuable, and the franchisees in the Department of Agrarian Affairs were keen to harvest the rents potentially generated by their monopoly of the certification process. Unless current owners had a pressing need to possess such a certificate, therefore, they were prepared to put up with the risks of not having one, rather than pay the price for the rubber stamp and signature.

Thus it suited the interest of the entire franchise that land titles remained unclear, because rents could be generated as soon as there was a desire to transfer land from customary use to some new activity. Alternatively, control over land could be easily transferred from the weak to the powerful when clear title was lacking. This meant that firms that wished to develop land would be prepared to pay the franchise in order to gain access to it cheaply. The extraordinary system that emerged was that firms could approach the authorities with a development proposal involving land still under customary ownership, hoping to persuade the authorities that this proposal was in the national (or provincial) interest. If they were successful, they were granted a monopoly right to. acquire the land in question. In principle, proper compensation was supposed to be paid but, in practice, strong-arm methods were used in order to coerce customary owners to give up their land for a pittance, if for anything at all. In principle, such a system could be implemented even if clear title for the land in question already existed, but in practice the lack of title and the corruptibility of the courts gave the favoured developers the upper hand.[4]

The role of the technocrats

One of the seeming paradoxes of the Soeharto era was the role of the so-called technocrats' (or Berkeley Mafia') – a group of academics who had been sent overseas to undertake postgraduate study during the last few years of the Sukarno era, and who returned to their homeland when the Old Order was in the process of being taken over by the New (Sadli 1993: 40–2). They were quickly recruited by Soeharto to serve as his economic policy makers, and they were successful in rapidly restoring calm and stability to the economy after many months of hyperinflation (Arndt 1969: 2–3). Their informal leader, Professor Widjojo Nitisastro, and his close associate, Professor Ali Wardhana, ultimately outstayed their former boss, being kept on as advisers when Habibie took over from Soeharto in May 1998.[5]

Serving in key positions such as Planning Minister, Finance Minister, Minister for Mining, Coordinating Minister for Economic Affairs, and later as special advisers to the President, this group is generally given the credit for Indonesia's record of sustained rapid growth throughout the Soeharto era and, in particular, for their deft handling of earlier financial crises such as the state oil company, Pertamina, debt debacle of the mid-1970s (McCawley 1976: 2–6) and the drastic decline in oil prices in the mid-1980s (Muir 1986: 3–5). They are also widely respected for having always distanced themselves personally from the rent-generating franchise system: indeed, they are known to have done all that they could to oppose it. But although they won quite a number of significant battles, it is difficult to say whether they won or lost the war.

They can rightfully claim the credit for designing and implementing economic policies that brought immense material benefits to the Indonesian people over some three decades. On the other hand, it is hard to imagine that Soeharto could have amassed the wealth and power he did without them. As a military man, he had no training in economics other than what they taught him (Sadli 1993: 40–1), but he knew the importance of a healthy economy. Thus he allowed them just sufficient influence to keep the economy running reasonably smoothly at the macroeconomic level, while never allowing them seriously to threaten his rent generating activities in the micro-economy.

Having the Berkeley Mafia as his advisers had an additional benefit for Soeharto. From the outset, the international community was keen to do what it could to assist with Indonesia's rehabilitation after the downfall of Sukarno. Initially organised by a consortium of individual country donors known as the Inter-Governmental Group on Indonesia (McDonald 1980: 72–4), within a relatively short time the running had been taken over by the World Bank and the IMF, later to be joined by the Asian Development Bank (ADB). Having these institutions on side helped greatly to strengthen the Soeharto franchise.

First, the World Bank and, later, the ADB brought with them a large flow of loans that, with the aid of his franchisees in the bureaucracy, Soeharto was able to tax very successfully – mainly through the award of contracts at inflated prices to favoured companies. Second, with their generally glowing assessments of the way Indonesia was managed,[6] and backed by complementary expressions of approval from the IMF, the government was able to continue to tap large quantities of bilateral aid and to attract ever increasing private foreign capital inflows, including direct investment, portfolio investment and loans. Thus, when Soeharto announced his new cabinet in 1993 but neglected to mention whether the remaining active technocrats, Widjojo and Ali, would retain their policy-making influence as advisers to the government, there were immediate expressions of concern from the international community; the President quickly responded by confirming that they would indeed continue in these roles.

Foreign direct investment invariably took the form of joint ventures with domestic partners, and became an important channel for rent generation. All such investments had to be vetted by the Investment Coordination Agency (BKPM), and those over a certain value ultimately had to be approved by the

President himself. Not surprisingly, the foreign firms found it wise to respond positively to BKPM suggestions as to suitable domestic partners, or to seek out such partners at the outset as a means of ensuring the success of their applications – and, they hoped, to ensure their ongoing protection in the absence of rule of law. During the late 1980s and throughout the 1990s, virtually no large foreign investment was undertaken that had no first family involvement as the domestic partner. Meanwhile, foreign portfolio investment and loans naturally flowed to the favoured – and therefore most profitable – domestic companies.

RENT GENERATION

As Harrison (1966) wrote in relation to the taxation issue in the United Kingdom in the 1960s,

If you drive a car I'll tax the street,
If you try to sit I'll tax the seat,
If it gets too cold I'll tax the heat,
If you take a walk I'll tax your feet

In the search for new sources of rents – new components of the private tax base – few areas escaped unscathed. The granting of monopolies was by no means Soeharto's only means of generating and harvesting rents. As well as from smokers and consumers of noodles (that is, a large proportion of the population), rents were extracted from Haj pilgrims, cinema-goers, rattan producers, car drivers and motorcycle riders, travellers returning from overseas, small landholders and so on. Indeed, presidential grandson Ari Sigit came close to putting into effect the idea of taxing feet', by attempting to obtain a monopoly on the supply of shoes to all of Indonesia's schoolchildren, although the public outcry forced Soeharto to step in and abort the scheme (Backman 1999: 281–2). The range of techniques, some of which have been mentioned already, included the following:

Protection from imports. In conjunction with licensing to constrain domestic competition, favoured firms were granted protection from imports (Fane 1999: 655–7). A prime example is motor vehicle assembly, for which the real effective rate of protection in 1995 exceeded 600 per cent (Fane and Condon 1996: 48).

Awarding contracts without bidding. Private sector firms were awarded contracts by government departments and state enterprises without any genuine bidding process involving competition with other firms. The most egregious examples involve the giant state oil company, Pertamina, which favoured first family members with, amongst other things, contracts for the shipment of oil and gas exports (Backman 1999: 266).

Providing access to cheap loans. Favoured firms had ready access to state bank or even central bank loans at highly subsidised interest rates[7] – and were not forced to repay if investments did not turn out well. In the course of the crisis it became clear that the state banks were responsible for by far the bulk of bad loans (Pardede 1999: 26), a large proportion of which were owed by Soeharto family and crony companies (*Dow Jones Newswires*, 15 June 1999).

Granting rights to exploit natural resources. The award of rights to exploit natural resources without having to bid or to pay a reasonable level of royalties has been of immense benefit to the Soeharto franchise. Forest concessions are a prime example, as are the Freeport minerals concessions in Irian Jaya. A clear picture of the processes involved emerged from the Busang gold fiasco in 1996–7, when various first family members squabbled as to who would get access to the rents expected from what was then thought to be the world's largest gold deposit (McLeod 1997: 29–31).

Designation as mandatory partners in foreign joint ventures. Just as domestic firms could earn favours for themselves by donating shares in themselves to first family members, so foreign firms were willing to pay for the privilege of being permitted to establish new operations in Indonesia – perhaps with special facilities of various kinds – in much the same way. The construction of power generation plants is a good example.

Rights to take over land. The grant of rights to take over land, in practice without payment of fair compensation to the original occupiers, has been a method often used to generate rents. This has occurred with land around major cities, and also with tracts of forest to be converted into plantations.

Purchase of inputs at artificially low prices. In many cases firms have been favoured by being permitted to purchase inputs at artificially low prices from state enterprises – if they were paid for at all. Examples include cement manufacturers purchasing electricity from the state electricity company, PLN; airlines purchasing aviation fuel from Pertamina (Backman 1999: 275); and petrochemicals manufacturers purchasing petroleum feedstock – also from Pertamina.

Favourable treatment by the tax office. The business sector has always been able to reduce the amount of legitimate tax it paid, through negotiation of mutually beneficial outcomes with Soeharto franchisees in the tax office. In addition, at various times the Soeharto government made tax holidays available to firms it wanted to favour (Parker and Hutabarat 1996: 28–9).

Rights to collect taxes. In the later years of the Soeharto regime, the rent generation effort at times became so blatant as to encompass the imposition of new taxes collected by first family companies – a small portion of which was supposedly turned over to the government. The most famous instance was the sale by presidential grandson Ari Sigit of Rp 600 tax stickers for each bottle of beer to be sold in Bali, with just Rp 200 being turned over to the provincial government (Bird 1996: 25–6; Backman 1999: 278–9). The scheme met with such widespread disgust that the beer companies were able to mount a successful campaign to have it discontinued.

PRIVATISING THE LAFFER CURVE

The no longer fashionable Laffer curve describes the relationship between the tax rate applied to an economic activity and the tax revenue generated (McMullen 1981–2). As the rate increases, revenue increases – but at a decreasing rate, because the tax discourages the activity in question. Beyond a certain point, this induced shrinkage of the tax base outweighs the impact of further increases in the rate, and revenue begins to decline. Roughly speaking, the trick for the tax gatherer is to find the rate that maximises revenue. The same principle applies to the private sector criminal activity of extorting protection money' from legitimate businesses.

A clear understanding of this fundamental principle of taxation and extortion differentiates Soeharto from political leaders in a host of other developing countries, who simply stole on a scale so grand as to bring about severe economic declines – usually with the result that they forfeited their hold on power (and sometimes their lives). Soeharto always took the long-term view, in which sustained growth[8] was essential to the flow of rents and, consequently, his hold on power. In this sense, Indonesia under Soeharto was blessed' with a better class of corruption than many other countries.

An important feature of the business sector is that it is heavily dominated by firms owned by Chinese Indonesians. This small group, only about two to three per cent of the total population, had always suffered the rancour of large sections of the *pribumi* (indigenous) community. The manner in which Soeharto and those around him promoted the interests of a few prominent Chinese Indonesian families served to deepen resentment against this whole minority community, down to the smallest shop owner, and to others who had no business at all. The legal system did little to protect their interests, and it suited Soeharto and his franchisees to maintain this state of affairs. Given the Chinese Indonesian minority's vulnerability to outbreaks of mob violence and to extortion by neighbourhood thugs, they could always be expected to pay in various ways for protection.[9] On some occasions the violence that did occur was not spontaneous, but was deliberately engineered in order to create an artificial demand for protection. Nevertheless, Soeharto appreciated the importance of keeping extortion of the business community within tolerable limits.

For the favoured few, as we have seen, rents were generated by the franchise. For the many, however – ethnic Chinese and *pribumi* alike – payments to the franchise were obligatory unrequited transfers. Licences and permits of all kinds were subject to trivially small legal fees and much larger illegal levies. Again, it is no accident that the legal fees were always kept small: this was precisely what was required if the illegal surcharge was to be maximised within the Lafferian constraint.

Soeharto could not safely assume that his own implicit understanding of the Laffer curve was shared throughout the civil service. As noted already, from time to time ministers who became too greedy had to be pulled into line. And in one famous case, he had to move against the entire Customs Service (Dick 1985: 10), since the scale of its rent harvesting from importers had become so large as to pose a serious impediment to growth of the economy (McDonald 1980: 116). The import inspection function for all shipments over $5,000 in value was contracted out to the Swiss firm Soci t G n rale de Surveillance in April 1985. This early example of privatisation (of a function rather than an enterprise) seems to have been a great success from the wider economic viewpoint, but from the perspective of the franchise it was *too* effective and, over a period of several years, more and more of the work being done by SGS was handed back to the Customs Service (Parker and Hutabarat 1996: 29).[10] Nevertheless, the lengthy interruption to the flow of bribes to Customs officials sent a clear message to franchisees throughout the bureaucracy that excessive rent harvesting would not be tolerated.

ANOMALIES IN THE REGIME

Certain features of the regime and episodes of policy change appear (on the surface at least) to fit less comfortably with the outline presented above, including the role of Islam in Indonesian society; the New Order emphasis on expansion of the education system; extensive deregulation of both the real and the financial sectors in the mid- to late 1980s; the improvement in civil service salaries over time; and the rapacious rent harvesting activities of the first family. We now discuss each of these aspects in turn.

The role of Islam

Although Soeharto managed to emasculate, or prevent the emergence of, most of the institutions that are taken for granted in democratic societies, he had rather less success with organised religion. With by far the majority of the population professing to be Moslems, the top priority was to weaken any opposition to the franchise from the Islamic movement, and preferably to win its support. In the earlier years of the regime, the main emphasis was on the former. Soeharto had a strong ally in the Armed Forces (ABRI), which were suspicious of organised Islam and strongly opposed to the idea of Indonesia becoming an Islamic state, as some of the more radical Moslems advocated. The killing by ABRI of many Moslems during a demonstration in Tanjung Priok (Jakarta's port) in September 1984 (Schwarz 1994: 172–3) was only the most obvious example of the approach during this early period.

But harsh repressive measures always run the risk of amplifying and strengthening opposition rather than subduing it,[11] and Soeharto eventually moved to attempt actively to enlist the support of Moslems. He had always maintained a Department of Religious Affairs, headed by a Moslem, as an instrument for distributing patronage to organised Islam, and for monitoring and influencing its activities. Now he became more ostentatiously Moslem, undertaking the *haj* pilgrimage to Mecca, and encouraging his prot g

Habibie to establish the Indonesian Association of Moslem Intellectuals (ICMI). In 1993 he replaced a number of Christian members of Cabinet with Moslems (Schwarz 1994: 183–4).

Ultimately the new approach contributed to Soeharto's undoing. Although many individuals saw membership of ICMI as promising access to higher levels of the franchise, others who had come to despise the system bowed to pressure to join ICMI, but also saw it for what it was and gave it much less than fulsome support. Amien Rais, one of the key personalities in ICMI, became increasingly critical of the regime and built up a strong following. He was eventually forced out of the organisation, but then became an even more vocal and effective critic, and played a key role in Soeharto's downfall in May 1998. By contrast, the very widely respected and influential Moslem leader, Abdurrahman Wahid, always a force for moderation and religious tolerance, never gave his support to the overtly sectarian organisation (Schwarz 1994: 162–3).[12]

Expansion of the education system

By far the most vigorous opposition to the franchise came from the student movement. Soeharto was well aware of the potential threat this constituted, since it had played a key role in the eventual downfall of his predecessor, Sukarno. Yet governments under Soeharto always placed considerable emphasis on expanding the reach of the education system. By the time the current crisis began, most young children were attending primary school, and the government had committed itself to extending universal education right through junior secondary school (that is, up to year nine). Watching television broadcasts of students occupying parliament to demand his resignation in May 1998, the former President may well have wondered if his education policies had created a rod for his own back.

There were, nevertheless, good reasons for such a policy. Increased rent harvests required economic growth and modernisation of the economy. In turn, this required a rapidly growing workforce with literacy, numeracy and other skills that were lacking in the predominantly agricultural economy of the mid-1960s. Second, minimising opposition to the franchise from those who were not part of it required that the population in general would also need to enjoy some of the fruits of development; widening access to education (and health services) was an effective way to achieve this. From time to time the students raised their voice against the system, but were able to be intimidated into acquiescence. But as was the case with organised religion, ultimately the students whom the regime had educated turned on it with sufficient enthusiasm to play a major role in its defeat.

Deregulation

The 1980s saw a good deal of deregulation of the economy. In the field of international trade, non-tariff barriers were largely eliminated and the average level of tariffs was significantly reduced (Hill 1996: 114–6; Fane and Condon

1996). In the financial sector, entry to banking was opened up to new domestic and foreign competitors and many forms of controls were abolished, while most subsidised loan programs were discontinued; the stock exchange was also privatised and suffocating bureaucratic controls for the most part removed (Cole and Slade 1996; McLeod 1999a). Finally, the previous emphasis on state enterprises was replaced by a strong push to boost the relative importance of private sector business activity.

At first glance it might be thought that these developments would have weakened the Soeharto franchise. On the contrary, however, they were in fact indications of continuing adaptation to changing circumstances. For example, remembering that healthy economic growth was always potentially beneficial to the franchise, the reallocation of new investment from grossly inefficient state-owned companies to private enterprise held out the promise of larger rent harvests, notwithstanding the diminished usefulness of state firms for providing jobs for military retirees and relatives of other members of the franchise. Allowing private firms to compete with formerly protected state enterprises actually opened up new opportunities for generating and harvesting rents in fields as diverse as power generation, water reticulation and airline services, without incurring the burden of state enterprise inefficiency.

Similarly, the decline in oil export earnings in the 1980s was a threat to both the economy and the franchise, which could be offset if other sources of export revenue could be developed. The technocrats persuaded Soeharto that liberalising imports would indirectly promote exports, and he realised that the loss of rents from protected industries could be more than compensated for elsewhere. The state banks had been used to distribute rents derived from the oil boom and from aid revenues, but as the private sector conglomerates grew and oil revenues declined with falling oil prices, it became expedient to allow the conglomerates to tap the savings of the general public rather than those of the government through the expansion of existing and newly established private banks.

Improvements in civil service salaries and conditions

The discussion above suggested that low civil service salaries have the characteristic of attracting the kinds of individuals who are willing even to pay to seek such employment and to gain promotion, in the hope of eventually earning incomes as Soeharto franchisees far higher than their legal entitlements. At the same time, the system encouraged an attitude of always aiming to please one's superior officers, given their undoubted ability to influence one's career path.

This does not imply that there were no improvements in salaries and working conditions over the years. Soeharto could hardly have hoped to have maintained the support of non-corrupt civil service employees – presumably the large majority – in the absence of such improvements. Thus, as in the case of the provision of education, the task was simply to increase salaries rapidly enough to ensure the acquiescence of non-franchisees in the civil service, while not going so far as to require heavy levels of (legal) taxation to fund the implied budget outlays.

First family depredations

By contrast with Soeharto's willingness to bring ministers and other members of the bureaucracy to heel if their enthusiasm for rent harvesting became excessive, he seemed most reluctant to keep his own children (and grandchildren) under control. His late wife Tien had been known as Madame Ten Percent' because of her alleged propensity for skimming 10 per cent of the value of government projects with which she had some connection, but this tax rate' was reasonable in Lafferian terms. Several of the Soeharto offspring appear to have taken the view that 10 per cent was far too modest and by all appearances seem to have grabbed lustily for everything they could, without any concern for the longer-term consequences for the franchise their father had built.

This was not just a question of selecting tax rates so as to maximise revenue, but also concerned the political consequences of untrammelled greed and ostentation. Many members of the public were prepared to overlook the privileges enjoyed by Soeharto cronies and first family members, provided that they themselves were experiencing significant material advancement, that the scale of rent harvesting was kept within reasonable bounds, and that the wealth of the privileged few was not displayed too brazenly. However, as the kids' – as they became known – expanded their empires at breakneck speed, flaunting rather than trying to hide the special treatment they received and the fabulous wealth they acquired, significant resentment began to build.

Most of Soeharto's rent harvesting in earlier years did not impact obviously on the general public. The latter were not conscious of being the true owners of Indonesia's oil, gas, minerals and forests, for example, so if the franchise exploited these natural resources for its own benefit there was little sense of individual loss. If the state banks and other state enterprises made heavy losses requiring injections of new capital from time to time by the government, the general public knew little about what was happening and did not feel directly harmed. And if the grant of monopoly privileges resulted in unnecessarily high prices, the public had little awareness of the implied income transfers at their expense. But when Tommy Soeharto first monopolised the clove trade, and then pleaded with the parliament to require clove smallholders to destroy half of their crops because he found himself holding huge unsold stocks, it was hard to ignore the message that the first family had no compunction about profiting at the expense of the poor. The later attempt by his nephew to monopolise the supply of shoes to school children carried the same message. Public outrage blocked both proposals, and the political damage to the franchise was considerable.

WHY DID THE SYSTEM COLLAPSE?

It has been argued elsewhere (Fane and McLeod 1999; McLeod 1999b) that the crisis that engulfed Indonesia from mid-1997 can be explained in terms of widespread concerns about the ability of the government to properly manage an adverse macroeconomic shock. Specifically, if it were widely believed that the government might react to such a shock in a manner that would lead to a significant increase in the money supply, then such a belief could turn out to be self-fulfilling, because currency depreciation is the inevitable consequence of a loss of monetary control.

In terms of this analytical framework, the initial shock provided by the unexpected devaluation of the baht caused investors to fear a breakdown of monetary control. They reacted to this by rushing to buy foreign exchange, and the government responded by allowing the rupiah to devalue. While many observers (including the writer) thought the extent of the early devaluation absurd, since the fundamentals did not seem to justify it,[13] others guessed that the pressures that had been unleashed would result in a monetary blow-out. They maintained or increased their net holdings of foreign currency assets, and were soon proved correct. Base money doubled in the space of a few months, and the value of the currency plunged to previously unimagined depths (Pardede 1999: 7, 15).

This quick summary provides a purely economic explanation for the crisis, ignoring the political context. How does it fit with the above outline of the Soeharto regime? With the benefit of hindsight, it can be seen that many aspects of the regime are likely to have contributed strongly.

First, the franchise was dependent to an extraordinary degree on a single individual in his late seventies, and there was every reason to fear a lack of leadership if Soeharto were suddenly no longer in charge. No matter how widely the system may have been despised, it had proved remarkably successful, and most Indonesians had known no other. And for all his genius, Soeharto had failed to arrange for the smooth transfer to a successor of the giant franchise he had built up over three decades. When he fell ill and was forced to cancel a planned overseas visit around the beginning of December 1997, it was the first time that this had happened, and it brought home to people the realisation that the end of the era could be very close indeed (Soesastro and Basri 1998: 20). It was not until this time that the crisis truly began to get out of hand.

To make matters worse, by this time the blatant nature of the first family's rent-harvesting activities had become less and less possible to ignore, even by a heavily muzzled press and a compliant parliament. The longer Soeharto stayed in power, the more it seemed that he was intent on dynastic rule in which his position would eventually be taken over by one of his children or at least some strong supporter of the first family. His first daughter, Siti Hardiyanti Rukmana, had adopted a very high profile in the 1997 election campaign,[14] and her brother, Bambang Trihatmodjo, already had become treasurer of the Soeharto election machine, Golkar. The notion that the regime might outlive its creator was sufficiently unpalatable as to boost significantly the groundswell of opposition to it, which was amplified by the students and a growing number of vocal individual critics.

Second, the crisis saw Indonesia turn to the international community for assistance – the first time since the mid-1970s it had felt the need to do so – and this punctured the aura of economic invincibility that existed in the mid-1990s. Moreover, having acknowledged (perhaps unwarrantedly) its inability to deal with the crisis by itself, the government (under pressure from Soeharto) then did much to create the impression that it would not do all that it had promised its international saviour', the IMF, it would do (Soesastro and Basri 1998: 20). This raised the prospect that financial assistance would be halted and that the loss of the IMF imprimatur would discourage investors from returning to Indonesia – even to purchase assets now available, in theory, at fire-sale prices.

Third, there were clear indications that the delicate working relationship between Soeharto and the technocrats, including their colleagues in the central bank, was being heavily strained. These economic policy makers had successfully encouraged the international financial institutions to present a long list of demands for microeconomic reform in return for their assistance (Soesastro and Basri 1998: 10–11). These reforms struck at the very heart of the franchise, yet had only the most tenuous connection with overcoming the crisis. In retrospect it is obvious that Soeharto and his franchisees could not have been expected to acquiesce in the face of the wholesale dismantling of the system. Indications of the strength of resistance came with the mysterious, fatal fire that engulfed the top few levels of the central bank's brand new office building early in December 1997, shortly after the forced closure of sixteen private banks, and with the purge by the President of the entire Board of Directors of the central bank during the following three months (Kenward 1999b: 121–2).

Fourth, the multiple burdens of depreciation, very high nominal interest rates, and falling private sector and government spending made it certain that widespread corporate distress would soon follow and, in turn, that loans from banks would not be repaid. In the case of the state banks, with their huge portfolios of loans to favoured firms, no one should have been in any doubt that in the time-honoured tradition, taxpayers rather than the borrowers would be called upon to cover the losses. And in the case of the private banks, the near-universal practice – at least among the large, conglomerate-owned banks – of lending heavily to affiliated firms meant that their owners had no funds of their own effectively at risk;[15] they therefore had little reason to do other than walk away from their bank's losses, leaving them for the government to worry about. Thus the absence of the rule of law and the corruption of the state banks meant that banks would not foreclose on defaulters, making it almost inevitable that the central bank would bail them out, and that this would lead to a loss of monetary discipline.[16]

Clearly, then, there were important aspects of the system that ultimately made it vulnerable to collapse. Soeharto had ensured that the only powerful institution was the armed forces. Political parties were emasculated; the parliament, the bureaucracy and the law were corrupted; the media were tightly controlled; the union movement was rendered virtually non-existent; and social organisations of all kinds (other than organised Islam) were never permitted to have a major impact. Individuals were drawn into the system or intimidated into accepting it as a fact of life. But although Soeharto could control most things, he could not control capital, which could vote with its feet in that most democratic arena: the global financial market. Capital could leave at any time, partly because of the government's policy since the early 1970s of keeping the capital account largely open, and partly because Indonesia's strong links with the overseas Chinese business community (especially in Singapore and Hong Kong) made it virtually impossible to do otherwise. It is interesting that the technocrats persuaded Soeharto to adopt this policy far earlier than other developing countries did, in order to provide a disciplining measure on macroeconomic management. The policy was all too effective: Indonesia was indeed disciplined' by the financial markets when ultimately they decided that the regime was inherently unstable.

LOOKING TO THE FUTURE

It is easy to point out the main areas of government–business relations in need of reform under the new presidency of Abdurrahman Wahid. In general, the government should cease acting in ways that generate rents for favoured firms. It should minimise its control and regulation of business activity except where there is a clear market failure justification, in order to limit the scope for extortion by government officials. It should minimise its own involvement in business activity, particularly in key fields such as banking and natural resources. It should provide a legal system, encompassing well-written laws and a properly functioning court system and police force, to protect property rights. And it should require that banks are adequately capitalised, so that owners have a genuine stake in their prudent management. If ever there was a belief that these things were unimportant in the Asian way' (or Indonesian way') of doing things, the crisis surely has exposed it as a myth.

To say that these kinds of reforms are highly desirable, however, begs the question as to whether they are likely to be implemented. The Soeharto franchise served its members well, and they will make every effort to try to put it back on its feet. On the other hand, Indonesia completed the first genuinely democratic popular elections of parliamentary representatives for several decades in June 1999, culminating in the election of new speakers of the People's Consultative Assembly (MPR) and House of Representatives (DPR), and a new President and Vice-President. Successful completion of this process appears to signal the dawn of a new era in which the executive is accountable to the parliament and the parliament is accountable to the people. Prospects for the civilianisation of government and for expansion of the rule of law also seem to have improved by virtue of the failure of the Armed Forces to capture any of these four influential positions.

Reform, and the realisation of genuine and lasting democracy, could be hastened by radical change in the salary structure of the civil service and the military, combined with far greater emphasis on accountability. As argued above, low salaries are bound to attract relatively many of the kinds of individuals who are willing to become active members of the franchise. Market-related salaries, on the other hand, would attract many more people who would be satisfied with their formal remuneration, and therefore not use their time to augment it in the ways outlined here: in short, they would see themselves as employees, rather than franchisees.

The suggestion that higher level salaries should be increased by orders of magnitude, while those at the lower level should be held constant if not actually reduced, is typically met with incredulity: the budgetary consequences would be intolerable; it would be unfair to those in the lower echelons; and it would be contrary to the (greatly overstated) public sector ethos of sacrificing one's personal interests in order to serve the people. But those who have supported the current salary structure while at the same time railing against the corruption, collusion and nepotism of the Soeharto regime, would do well to ponder their own unwitting contribution to maintaining it.

If far-reaching reform is to be achieved by the new government, it will need to effect very large salary increases for those at the higher levels of the bureaucracy and the military – while simultaneously making it plain, and acting to ensure, that the ways of the past are to change drastically along the lines indicated. But in the current circumstances in which the civil service and the state enterprises are reviled for their corruption, and the military for having brought shame on the nation by its actions in East Timor, such a strategy is unlikely to commend itself.

NOTES

1   For example, according to Hughes (2000), Large inflows of foreign capital into uneconomic crony investments exacerbated the build-up of non-performing loans in the financial sectors. International competitiveness was undermined and institutional structures became so impaired that economic collapses became inevitable'.

2   According to McDonald (1980: 121), the monopoly clove importers were supposedly restricted to a 2% handling margin, while the remaining profit went to a Soeharto *yayasan*.

3   Similar behaviour was observed more than three decades later in East Timor, after a large majority of its population voted for independence in August 1999.

4   Thus when Soeharto fell from power there was an immediate move by former peasant landholders to reclaim the land in West Java from which they had been evicted many years earlier to establish the President's own cattle ranch (*Business Recorder*, 18 June 1998). Elsewhere there were similar moves to reclaim land that had been expropriated and turned into golf courses.

5   This, despite the fact that they had done all they could under Soeharto to block Habibie's big spending plans on high technology projects (Schwarz 1994: 92–7)!
6   Less so in the last few years of the regime.
7   Both the original and more recent clove import monopolies mentioned previously were financed with cheap loans from the central bank, thus providing a double-barrelled handout to the recipients.
8   If not ecologically sustainable development.
9   Extortion of *pribumi* firms was not unknown, of course, but there is little doubt that Chinese Indonesians bore a disproportionate share.
10   As MacIntyre (forthcoming) put it when discussing this and other examples of Soeharto exercising control over corruption: None of these interventions was designed to *eliminate* corruption [i.e. rent harvesting, in the terminology used here] – the entire regime was built upon maximising corruption – but all had the effect of *curtailing* corruption that had become sufficiently costly or disruptive as to pose a serious threat to continued investor confidence '.
11   ABRI has been slow to learn this lesson in the provinces of Aceh, East Timor and Irian Jaya, where its brutal attempts to suppress separatist movements over the years only served to harden the will of the people for independence.
12   Wahid was to go on to become President, and Rais Speaker of the MPR, in October 1999, giving both the opportunity to dismantle the Soeharto franchise.
13   The central bank had been accumulating foreign reserves at a rapid rate for months beforehand in order to prevent *appreciation* of the currency (McLeod 1997: 22–3).
14   She was appointed as a minister in the short-lived March 1998 Soeharto cabinet, after the crisis was well under way, sending a clear message to the IMF–technocrat alliance that its attack on the franchise would be strongly defended.
15   By way of explanation: if the bank's owners subscribe Rp1 billion in capital, but then receive a loan of Rp1 billion (or perhaps considerably more) from the bank, they have no funds directly at risk in it. If the bank fails, the only thing they have to fear is claims from its creditors – depositors or the government, should it step in and cover the bank's losses. Given Indonesia's weak legal environment and corrupt and ineffective bureaucracy, this would have given little cause for concern.
16   It is possible to bail out banks without increasing the money supply (McLeod forthcoming) but this policy option was overlooked or ignored.

REFERENCES

Arndt, H.W. (1969) Survey of recent developments', *Bulletin of Indonesian Economic Studies* 5(2): 2–16.
Backman, M. (1999) *Asian Eclipse: Exposing the dark side of business in Asia*, Singapore: Wiley.
Bird, K. (1996) Survey of recent developments', *Bulletin of Indonesian Economic Studies* 32(1): 3–32.
Cole, D.C. and Slade, B.F. (1996) *Building a Modern Financial System: The Indonesian experience*, Cambridge: Cambridge University Press.
Cribb, R.B. (ed.) (1990) *The Indonesian killings of 1965–1966 : Studies from Java and Bali*, Clayton: Monash University, Centre of Southeast Asian Studies.
Crouch, H. (1979) Patrimonialism and military rule in Indonesia', *World Politics* 31(4): 571–87.
Dick, H.W. (1985) Survey of recent developments', *Bulletin of Indonesian Economic Studies* 21(3): 1–29.

Fane, George (1999) Indonesian economic policies and performance, 1960–98', *The World Economy* 22(5): 65–8.

and Condon, T. (1996) Trade reform in Indonesia, 1987–95', *Bulletin of Indonesian Economic Studies* 32(3): 33–54.

and McLeod, R.H. (1999) Lessons for monetary and banking policies from the 1997–98 economic crises in Indonesia and Thailand', *Journal of Asian Economics* 10(3): 395–413.

Harrison, G. (1966) Taxman', from The Beatles' album *Revolver*, Parlophone.

Hill, H. (1996) *The Indonesian Economy since 1996: Southeast Asia's emerging giant*, Cambridge: Cambridge University Press.

Hughes, H. (2000) The evolution of dual economies in East Asia', in Deepak Lal and R.H. Snape (eds), *Trade, Development and Political Economy: Essays in Honour of Anne Kreuger*, UK: Macmillan.

Kenward, L.R. (1999a) Vulnerability to financial crisis: Evidence from Indonesia', *Bulletin of Indonesian Economic Studies* 35(3):

(1999b) What has been happening at Bank Indonesia?', *Bulletin of Indonesian Economic Studies* 35(1): 121–7.

Kreuger, A. (1974) The political economy of the rent-seeking society', *American Economic Review* 64(3): 291–303.

MacIntyre, A. (forthcoming) Investment, property rights and corruption in Indonesia', in J.E. Campos (ed.) *Corruption: The boom and bust of East Asia*, Washington DC: The Brookings Institution.

Mao Zedong (1961) Problems of War and Strategy', speech, 6 November 1938 (published in *Selected Works*, vol. 2).

McCawley, P. (1976) Survey of recent developments', *Bulletin of Indonesian Economic Studies* 12(1): 1–43.

(1981) The growth of the industrial sector', in A. Booth and P. McCawley (eds) *The Indonesian Economy During the Soeharto Era*, Kuala Lumpur: Oxford University Press.

McDonald, H. (1980) *Suharto's Indonesia*, Blackburn: Fontana Books.

McLeod, R.H. (1980) *Finance and Entrepreneurship in the Small-Business Sector in Indonesia*, PhD dissertation, Australian National University.

(1997) Survey of recent developments', *Bulletin of Indonesian Economic Studies* 33(1): 3–43.

(1998) Indonesia', in R.H. McLeod and R. Garnaut (eds) *East Asia in Crisis: From being a miracle to needing one?*, London and New York: Routledge.

(1999a) Control and competition: Banking deregulation and re-regulation in Indonesia', *Journal of the Asia Pacific Economy* 4(2): 258–97.

(forthcoming) Lessons from Indonesia's crisis', in D. Wilson, D. Dasgupta and M. Uzan, *Capital Flows without Crisis? Reconciling Capital Mobility and Economic Stability*, Routledge.

McMullen, B.S. (1981–2) The Laffer Curve: Fact or convenient fantasy', *Economic Forum* 12(2): 113–5.

Muir, R. (1986) Survey of recent developments', *Bulletin of Indonesian Economic Studies* 22(2): 3–27.

Pardede, R. (1999) Survey of recent developments', *Bulletin of Indonesian Economic Studies*, 35(2): 3–39.

Parker, Stephen and Hutabarat, Posma (1996) Survey of recent developments', *Bulletin of Indonesian Economic Studies* 32(3): 3–31.

Robison, R. (1986) *Indonesia: The rise of capitalism*, Sydney: Allen and Unwin.

Sadli, M. (1993) Recollections of my career', *Bulletin of Indonesian Economic Studies* 29(1): 35–51.

Schwarz, A. (1994) *A Nation in Waiting: Indonesia in the 1990s*, Sydney: Allen & Unwin.

Soesastro, H. and Basri, M. Chatib (1998) Survey of recent developments', *Bulletin of Indonesian Economic Studies* 34(1): 3–54.
Transparency International (1999) Press Release: New Poll Shows Many Leading Exporters Using Bribes, http://www/transparency.de/documents/cpi/index.html, 26 October, accessed 27 October 1999.
World Bank (1981) Indonesia: Selected Issues of Industrial Development and Trade Strategy, Report no. 3182–IND, Annex 3, Industrial Licensing, Washington, 15 July.

8 The Malaysian experiment[1]

Prema-chandra Athukorala

INTRODUCTION

Malaysia's approach to management of its financial crisis represented a significant departure from the orthodox, IMF-centred approach to crisis management. This chapter documents the 'Malaysian experiment' and provides a preliminary analysis of its outcome as reflected in the recovery process in Malaysia during the first full year of its implementation. Where relevant, the Malaysian experience is compared and contrasted with the experience of Thailand and South Korea (henceforth referred to as Korea) under IMF-supported reform programs.

The next section provides an overview of Malaysia's initial policy responses to the crisis, with emphasis on the political and institutional underpinnings of the subsequent policy shift. This is followed by a discussion of the nature of the new policy package built around capital controls. The recovery process following the policy shift is then examined, followed by a critical examination of the role of capital controls and other related elements of the policy package in the recovery process. The final section draws inferences and policy lessons.

INITIAL POLICY RESPONSE

Unlike Thailand, Indonesia and Korea, Malaysia succumbed to the crisis with little foreign debt exposure of its banking system.[2] For this reason, it was able to 'muddle through' without an IMF-sponsored rescue package. The initial response of the Malaysian government to the outbreak of the currency crisis was one of denial. Given the perceived soundness of economic fundamentals, Prime Minister Mahathir's immediate reaction was to pounce on currency speculators and attempt to punish them through several initiatives of direct government intervention in the operation of the share market.

After a period of policy indifference of over five months, a major policy package was announced by the then Finance Minister Anwar on 5 December 1997. According to many commentators, this statement was 'IMF policy without the IMF'. However, the government quickly backtracked from this policy stance in favour of *ad hoc* counter-cyclical measures with a view to avoiding a recession–deflation spiral' (BNM 1999: 4). Increases in interest rates (market determined, rather than policy driven), coupled with rapid contraction in economic activity were quickly reflected in a massive build-up of non-performing loans (NPLs) in the banking system and corporate failures. On 5 May 1998, Prime Minister Mahathir made it clear that he disagreed with the IMF on the need to raise the interest rate further'. A National Economic Recovery Plan designed to manage the crisis without IMF involvement, primarily through domestic demand expansion was announced in mid-July (NEAC 1998).

In the absence of a clear policy anchor, this policy tinkering was ineffective in avoiding further economic collapse, let alone generating recovery. By August 1998, the economy was in recession. According to national account estimates released in the last week of August, the economy had contracted by 6.8 per cent in the first quarter of 1998, compared with a 2.8 per cent contraction in the previous quarter. The net NPL ratio of the banking system had risen from 4.1 per cent of total outstanding loans at the end of 1997 to 9 per cent at the end of 1998, and international credit rating agencies placed the figure at much higher levels (Soros 1998: 144). To make matters worse, the much hoped for export-led recovery was not on the horizon, despite massive improvement in competitiveness achieved through currency depreciation. Business confidence in manufactures as measured by the Business Confidence Index (BCI) of the Malaysian Institute of Economic Research (MIER) had dipped sharply for three consecutive quarters. MIER's Consumer Confidence Index was also at an all-time low. Net private short-term capital registered a deficit of US$2.3 billion in the first quarter of 1998, a reversal from the net inflow of one billion in the previous quarter. In constrast to the other crisis' countries in the region, in Malaysia the recession-induced current account surplus did not provide a respite in terms of an improvement in foreign reserves given capital flight.

A striking feature of capital outflows from Malaysia was that they largely took the form of ringgit (rather than foreign currency) flowing into Singapore. These flows were triggered by very attractive money market rates of between 20–40 per cent in Singapore, which provided a hefty premium over a domestic rate of about 11 per cent, coupled with a weakening exchange rate for the ringgit.[3] As much as RM35 billion (US$8.2 billion) ended up in Singapore at the height of the crisis in mid-1998 (Ariff 1999). This amounted to over 65 per cent of the total domestic supply of narrow money (M1) and 12 per cent of broad money (M2) in Malaysia. Policy makers became increasingly concerned about the internationalisation' of the national currency, which carried a potential threat to economic stability and monetary policy autonomy. The strong demand for offshore ringgit and the consequent build-up of offshore ringgit deposits increased the vulnerability of the ringgit, undermining the effectiveness of monetary policy (BNM 1999: 10).

THE EXPERIMENT

By the third quarter of 1998, policy choices available to the Malaysian government had become severely limited. Further easing of monetary conditions to boost aggregate demand and provide the highly leveraged domestic firms with a breathing space would have intensified capital flight, weakening the ringgit further and precipitating a share market collapse. To make matters worse, a plan to issue sovereign bonds in the United States and Europe to raise US$2 billion for implementing the banking sector restructuring program had to be shelved in late August because of unanticipated downgrading of Malaysia's credit rating by international rating agencies. These developments propelled a serious re-thinking of policy directions.

As Bank Negara Malaysia (BNM), the Central Bank, correctly observed in its *1998 Annual Report*, the root cause of the worsening economic situation was the market perception that Malaysia would be less committed to structural reforms as it was not under an IMF program (BNM 1999: 5). However, entering into an IMF program was not politically acceptable to the Malaysian leadership.[4] Given the intimate links between business and government forged under the New Economic Policy (NEP) over the previous two-and-a-half decades, the positive stabilising impact of such a move had to be weighed against its negative effect on politically connected business groups and the sociopolitical stability of the country (Crouch 1998). Macroeconomic policy that aimed to adjust the economy through market-determined interest rates was bound to have a severe effect on debt-ridden private sector firms and the viability of their banks. These were already suffering from the burst of the real estate bubble and the share market crash. Prime Minister Mahathir summed up his position on this issue:

> If we do not lower interest rates, not only will companies, but also banks and the government will encounter financial difficulties. When our financial position becomes very serious, we will have no option but to seek IMF assistance. We will then be subject to IMF's dictates. (Government of Malaysia 1998: 13)

In this context, Dr Mahathir opted to abandon policy tinkering along conventional lines in order to stimulate the economy through fiscal and monetary expansion, while insulating the domestic interest rate from short-term capital mobility through capital controls.[5] While Dr Mahathir's expression of interest in capital controls dates back to early in the crisis (Athukorala 1998), the new policy received a measure of legitimacy from recent developments in the international economic policy debate on crisis management. In particular Krugman's (1998) controversial piece in *Fortune* that argued for using capital controls as a crisis management tool received wide attention in the Malaysian policy debate and news media.[6] There was also growing attention in the financial press to the fact that China and Taiwan, the two economies in the East Asian growth league with controls on short-term capital movements, had fared much better than the rest of the region during the crisis. The experience of countries like Chile and Slovenia in using capital controls to manage shorter-term capital inflows also received wide attention.[7]

As a first step, offshore trading of Malaysian company shares was made illegal on 31 August 1998, in a move to control speculative trading in the over-the-counter (OTC) share market in Singapore, where short-selling of Malaysian shares continued despite prohibition of such activities in Malaysia.[8] This was followed by the imposition of stringent controls over short-term capital outflows (1 September) and fixing the exchange rate at M$3.80 per US$ (effective 2 September).

The new capital controls banned trading in ringgit instruments among offshore banks (including banks in Labuan offshore centre) and stopped Malaysian financial institutions offering domestic credit facilities to non-resident banks and stockbrokers. The use of the ringgit as an invoicing currency in foreign trade was banned with immediate effect, and legal tender on all ringgit deposits held outside the country was abolished with effect from 30 September. A twelve-month withholding period was imposed on repatriation of proceeds (principal and profit) from the sale of Malaysian securities by foreign investors. The other new capital and exchange controls included restrictions on overseas investments by residents exceeding RM 10,000, a requirement to repatriate all overseas ringgit within one month, and a limit of RM1,000 on the approval of foreign exchange for overseas travel and investment by the Malaysians.

The controls were confined to short-term capital flows only. With the exception of limits on foreign exchange for foreign travel by Malaysian citizens, there was no retreat from the country's long-standing commitment to an open trade and investment policy. No new direct controls were imposed on import and export trade. Foreign investors in Malaysia are free to repatriate dividends and equity related to their direct investment in the country. Immediately following the imposition of capital controls, BNM introduced new regulatory procedures for monitoring repatriation of profits and capital by foreign companies operating in Malaysia. These were swiftly removed in response to protest by these firms (Zefferys 1999).

In early February 1998, the Malaysian government announced modifications to the restriction on foreign portfolio investment, with the intention of promoting a long-term view by foreign investors. The original twelve-month withholding period was replaced with a graduated levy. Under this modification, portfolio capital invested in the country before 15 February 1999 would become subject to a three-tier graduated exit levy (10, 20 and 30 per cent) depending on the length of the period between funds being brought in (after 1 September 1998) and repatriation. For funds brought in after 15 February 1999, the principal could be repatriated without a levy but the profit would be subject to a 30 per cent levy if repatriated in less than a year, and 10 per cent otherwise. Unlike the original controls, the new revision was implemented after consulting investors (Merrill Lynch 1999). Although some commentators have treated it as a backsliding, the new capital tax appears a pragmatic move towards greater flexibility with a view to bringing fresh capital into the country to aid the adjustment process. It was also an attempt to modify the original scheme to make it an effective tool for managing capital inflows in the recovery phase with a view to avoiding unhealthy pressure through the resumption of capital inflows on the exchange rate. In August 1999, the exit taxation of portfolio capital was further simplified by replacing the two-tier profit tax with a unified 10 per cent levy.

With the policy autonomy gained through capital controls, the government swiftly embarked on an expansionary macroeconomic policy package. BNM reduced its three-month intervention rate (on which interest rates are based) from 10 per cent to 9.5 per cent and cut the statutory reserve ratio to 6 per cent from 8 per cent a week before the introduction of capital controls in order to inject liquidity into the debt-ridden banking system. After three successive cuts during the ensuing months, the three-month intervention rate stood at 6.0 per cent by early July 1999. The statutory reserve ratio by that time was a mere 4.5, compared with a pre-crisis level of 10 per cent. On 9 September BNM advised banks to expand their loans at a rate of 8 per cent a year. This was accompanied by a revision to the formula used in computing the base lending rate (BLR)[9] so that reductions in the intervention rate are better reflected in the cost of bank credit. Several other measures were introduced to encourage credit expansion. These included relaxation of credit limits on commercial bank and financial company lending for purchase of property and shares, easy financing for purchase of cars, special loan schemes for assisting smaller industries and low-income groups and relaxing credit limits on credit cards (see Yap 1999 for details).

The 1999 Budget, presented by Dr Mahathir on 23 October, proposed a stimulus package that called for a deficit of 6.1 per cent of GNP, compared with a 1.9 per cent deficit in 1998. It proposed no major spending proposals beyond MR4 (US$1) billion earmarked for road and rail projects. The major economic stimulants took the form of tax reductions. Among them, the key element was a total waiver of income tax in 1999.[10] There were also tax breaks for industries of national and strategic importance' and import duty reduction on machinery and equipment imports.

The fiscal deficit is to be financed mostly by issuing Malaysian Government Securities (MGS) to be absorbed largely by provident, pension and insurance funds. Only about a third of the financial needs are to be raised externally, mainly from bilateral and multilateral sources. In 1998, gross foreign borrowing amounted to RM4 (US$1.1) billion, including RM1.2 (US$0.3) billion from the World Bank to finance projects to review the economy and as assistance to vulnerable groups, and RM2.4 (US$0.6) billion from the Japanese government. A syndicate foreign currency loan of RM5.1 (US$1.3) billion was obtained from twelve locally incorporated foreign banks.

Speedy implementation of the programs (initiated in early 1998) for dealing with NPLs of banks, recapitalisation of debt-ridden banks and corporate restructuring were the other key elements of the reform package. The financial requirement for acquiring NPLs by the Pengurusan Danaharta Nasional Berhad (the National Asset Management Company) was estimated at RM15 (US$4) billion. As at 31 March 1999, Danaharta had acquired a total of RM23.1 (US$6.1) billion NPLs, amounting to 31.8 per cent of the total NPLs in the banking system. Recapitalisation of banks under Danamodal Nasional Berhad (the Bank Restructuring Company) is to be completed before the end of 1999. As at 31 March 1999, Danamodal had injected RM6.4 (US$2) billion into ten banking institutions. The risk-weighted capital adequacy ratio of the banking system had increased from 8.2 per cent in August 1998 to 12.7 per cent in July 1999. The NPL ratio (on a three-month basis), which reached a peak of 15 per cent in the last quarter of 1998, had stabilised at around 13 per cent by mid-1999.

As at 31 May 1999, the Corporate Debt Restructuring Committee (CDRC) had received sixty applications involving corporate debts amounting to RM32.5 (US$9) billion. Of these, six cases were withdrawn or rejected as non-viable, eleven cases involving RM10.9 (US$2.9) billion were completed, and the balance, involving debts totaling RM 3.3 (US$1) billion, were to be settled by the end of June 1999.

SIGNS OF RECOVERY

In the first quarter of 1999 the year-on-year rate of contraction of the Malaysian economy moderated to –1.2 per cent from –10.3 per cent in the previous quarter (Table 8.1). In the second quarter, the economy recorded 4.1 per cent growth, ending the year-long recession that started in the second quarter of 1998. The government growth forecast for 1999 is 4.1 per cent. Many independent analysts predict an average growth rate of 9 per cent or more in the next two quarters, leading to a full-year growth rate of 5 to 6 per cent in 1999, compared with a 6.5 per cent contraction in 1998.

Signs of recovery first emerged by the first quarter of 1999 in the services sector (particularly in financial services) and domestic market-oriented industries. By the second quarter, recovery had become more broad based, with export-oriented manufacturing showing impressive output growth. In that quarter, total manufacturing output expanded by 12 per cent year-on-year, contributing to nearly half of total GNP growth. Both domestically-oriented and export-oriented industries have contributed to this growth. The significant pick-up in export-oriented manufacturing is in sharp contrast to the experience of neighbouring Thailand, perhaps reflecting the competitive edge gained through the currency peg (see below).

On the expenditure side, private consumption was seen to stabilise in the first half of the year and is expected to pick up strongly in the second half of the year. The Consumer Sentiment Index compiled by the Malaysian Institute of Economic Research showed a clear upward movement in the first quarter of 1999. Other private consumption indicators, such as sales and production of passenger cars, sales tax and import of consumer goods, have recorded an improvement in the first quarter of 1999.

As yet, there are no clear signs of recovery in private investment. Only public investment has begun to increase, reflecting the new investment drive. MIER's Business Confidence Index, which recorded a steep decline for three consecutive quarters starting from the second quarter of 1997, recorded a turnaround in the fourth quarter of 1998 and improved further in the first quarter of 1999, suggesting that private investment will pick up in the second half of the year. The delayed recovery of private investment is consistent with the existing excess capacity and stock overhang in the economy. According to the MIER's Survey of Business Sentiment, capacity utilisation in the first quarter of 1999 was 75 per cent, compared with an average of 85 per cent for the boom years of 1987–96.

According to the Survey of Retrenchments (conducted by the Department of Labour) there has been a significant decline in worker layoffs in recent months. Weekly worker layoffs occurred at a rate of over 500 a week in 1998, reached a peak of 2,637 in the third week of March 1999 and then declined to 274 in the last week of June 274 (*Business Times*, 1 July 1999).

The rate of inflation (measured by the consumer price index) declined to below 3 per cent in May 1999 from a high of 5.8 per cent in July 1998, despite the heavy emphasis on fiscal and monetary expansion as part of the recovery strategy. Rapid expansion in domestic output backed by ample availability of cheap bank credit, still sizeable excess capacity production in the economy and the effective nominal anchor' provided by the fixed exchange rate seems to have underpinned the moderation of inflation. An added factor appears to be the government policy towards migrant workers. Despite initial moves to repatriate a large number of foreign workers, mostly from the construction sector, the authorities have continued to allow the importation of foreign workers in large numbers for employment in traded-goods sectors, export-oriented manufacturing in particular. This policy has been instrumental in keeping a lid on wage growth.

Merchandise imports, which continuously declined for over a year from the onset of the crisis, have begun to pick up in recent months. Total imports in the first half of 1999 were 11 per cent higher than the corresponding period in the previous year. This was, however, overwhelmed by export growth (16 per cent) generating an increase in the trade balance of 5.5 per cent. There was no significant change in the net balance of the services account. The net capital account balance indicated a minor improvement in the second quarter, thanks to an increase in portfolio capital inflows following the relaxation of capital controls in March. Total net foreign reserves almost doubled from $16 billion in August 1998 to $32 billion in August 1999, the largest percentage increase among the five crisis countries.

Table 8.1 Selected economic indicators, Malaysia, 1997Q1 – 1999Q2[a]

	1997 Q1	Q2	Q3	Q4	1998 Q1	Q2	Q3	Q4	1999 Q1	Q2
Growth of GDP (%)	8.6	8.4	7.7	5.6	-3.1	-5.2	-10.9	-10.3	-1.3	4.1
Growth by sector[b] (%):										
Agriculture, forestry and fishing (9.8)	1.8	3.9	-1.5	-2.1	-.2	-6.9	-.4	-4.7	-3.5	8.7
Industry (41.5)	10.2	8.4	9.1	8.8	-5.6	-9.4	-16.2	-15.4	-3.1	5.7
Mining and quarrying (7.7)	-0.5	2.6	1.9	8.1	0.6	0.3	1.2	5.1	-2.3	-6.0
Manufacturing (29.1)	11.8	9.6	11.3	9.2	-5.8	-10.3	-18.9	-18.6	-1.1	10.4
Construction (4.7)	17.5	10.8	7.3	7.8	-14.5	-19.8	-28	-29	-16.6	-4.0
Services (48.7)	11.4	11.7	10.6	6.4	2.2	1.9	-3.7	-3.4	0.6	0.6
Growth of manufacturing production[c] (%)										
Export oriented (weight: 0.52)	13.3	12.7	9.6	10.8	0.1	-5.3	-11.3	-12.2	-1.0	16.7
Domestic oriented (weight: 0.48)	13.3	10.4	9.7	9.3	-6.1	-12.8	-15.6	-18.3	0.4	14.6
MIER Consumer Sentiment Index (1988 = 100)	127.2	133.4	122.1	104.9	88.5	79.1	80	80.5	84	101.6
MIER Business Conditions Index (1988 = 100)	62.9	65.2	57.5	49.6	41	42.3	41.8	44.7	48.5	60.3
MIER Mfg capacity utilisation index (1998 = 1,000)	87.4	86.1	87.4	85.4	80.6	76.4	76.6	76.4	77.9	92.4
Inflation rate (%):										
Consumer price	3.2	2.5	2.3	2.7	4.3	5.7	5.6	5.4	4.0	2.7
Producer price	2.7	-0.5	1.0	7.2	11.9	13.9	13.9	3.9	-4.1	-5.0
Domestic goods	3.0	-0.9	0.6	7.5	12.0	14.5	15.0	3.8	-4.0	-5.0
Imported goods	1.4	1.0	2.7	5.9	11.3	11.3	9.6	4.8	-0.3	-0.8
Growth of money and credit (end of period) (%)										
M3	19.3	21.8	20.1	18.5	13.7	7.3	4.0	2.8	3.9	7.5
Loans extended by banking system	24.6	23.2	21.2	26.5	16.9	10.3	4.5	-1.6	-4.3	-3.2
Manufacturing	17.2	16.4	18.3	18.3	19.5	13.2	10.2	0.9	-9.0	-6.1
Property	27.2	26.8	29.2	33.6	27.6	19.8	14.2	4.7	0.5	-2.0
Loans approved by the banking system										
Manufacturing	–	–	–	–	-56.4	-86.0	-68.5	-16.9	33.0	78.5
Property	–	–	–	–	-70.1	-85.7	-84.2	-62.0	22.0	67.0

	1997				1998				1999	
	Q1	Q2	Q3	Q4	Q1	Q2	Q3	Q4	Q1	Q2
Share market performance										
KLSE Composite	1,203	1,077	815	594	720	456	374	586	503	870
Market capitalisation (Ringgit billion)	844.5	744.5	584.5	375.8	452.9	285.8	249.1	374.5	317.9	
Balance of payments (US$ million)										
Trade balance	1,659	-770	1,499	1,433	2,883	3,733	5,379	5,929	4,663	5,204
Exports	19,367	19,407	20,339	18,801	17,330	17,422	19,135	19,531	18,127	19,995
Imports	17,708	20,177	18,840	17,368	14,446	13,689	13,756	13,602	13,464	14,791
Services and transfers (net)	-2,649	-2,663	-1,966	-1,983	-1,240	-1,536	-2,079	-2,851	–	–
Current account	-990	-3,033	-780	-550	1,643	2,197	3,300	3,078	–	–
Capital account balance	4,188	1,574	-5,357	2,336	-1,945	-400	-1,874	613	–	–
Long-term capital (net)	2,361	3,302	-190	1,542	372	785	-667	1,202	–	–
Private short-term capital (net)	1,827	-1,728	-5,167	794	-2,317	-1,185	-1,207	-589	–	–
Errors and omissions	-2,339	878	2,960	-2,583	-162	-1,560	4,226	1,032	–	–
Overall balance = Change in reserves	859	-580	-3,177	-797	-464	237	6,128	4,723	1,540	3,428
Gross official reserves	20,097	19,517	16,340	15,543	15,079	15,316	21,444	26,167	27,707	31,135

Notes

a All growth rates on a year-on-year basis.
b Sectoral shares in GDP in 1996 are given in brackets.
c Based on manufacturing production index (1993 = 100). The weight attached to each category in the total index is given in brackets.
– Data not available.

Source: Compiled from Bank Negara Malaysia, *Monthly Statistical Bulletin* (updated for the latest quarters using data from the Bank's web site: www.bnm.gov.my) and MIER, *Monthly Economic Monitor* (various issues).

HAS THE EXPERIMENT WORKED?

It is evident from the above discussion that following the imposition of the capital-controls-based reform package, the Malaysian economy has begun to show strong signs of recovery. But how far has the radical policy shift actually contributed to the turnaround?

Many observers have attempted to answer this question through simple comparisons of the recovery experiences of crisis-hit countries using readily available performance indicators. A common inference from such comparisons is that controls have not made a distinct' contribution to the recovery process in Malaysia – not only Malaysia but also the other crisis-hit countries that maintained open capital accounts throughout have started to show signs of recovery (Hiebert 1999; IMF 1999b; Miller 1999, Lim 1999). Taking this a step further, some argue that Malaysia's recovery would have been faster under an IMF-centred policy package because, unlike Thailand, Korea and Indonesia, it really did not have a serious crisis to begin with (*Economist* 1999; Lim 1999).

These comparisons ignore the important fact that the economies under consideration are vastly different in terms of the sources of vulnerability to the crisis, and the nature of the economic structure, which determine flexibility of adjustment to a crisis. Put simply, details differ in important ways from one country to another, and readily available performance indicators do not capture these differences (Cooper 1998). Moreover, the view that Malaysia did not have a crisis in the first place is primarily based on Malaysia's relatively low foreign debt levels. It ignores the explosive mix of share market bubble and domestic credit boom that had developed in Malaysia in the lead-up to the crisis (Athukorala 1999).[11] In any case, the view that the severity of a speculative attack on the currency of a country is proportional to the degree of vulnerability is not convincing. If foreign lenders suspect an impending crisis, they do not expect to be told how serious the problem may become. They will simply withdraw their funds as rapidly as possible, thus turning a suspected financial problem into a financial rout (Cooper 1998). Given these considerations, an inter-country comparison can yield meaningful inferences only if economic adjustment under alternative policies is carefully studied, emphasising the fundamental differences in economic structures and original sources of vulnerability to the crisis. The time is not ripe for an in-depth comparative case study of this nature. We have to wait until the recovery process becomes well rooted and policy responses are well embedded in economic data. Here, a preliminary analysis of how capital controls have impacted on the adjustment process in Malaysia is attempted. The approach is to examine whether the original expectations (mostly negative) about the fate of the reform program were consistent with the actual experience.

Capital controls and monetary policy autonomy

A major doubt about the effectiveness of capital controls as a crisis management tool relates to presumably ample scope for avoidance and evasion, which can negate the expected monetary policy autonomy (Hale 1998; Edwards 1999). The general argument is that the more extensive are trade and investment links, the more difficult and costly it is to control capital account transactions because of the multiplication in the number of arbitrage possibilities that arise in the course of normal business. The problem with this argument is that it is based on a misleading mixing of placing funds abroad retail' by manipulating current account transactions and exporting capital wholesale' (Williamson 1993: 36). There is ample evidence from both developed and developing countries that capital controls are in fact effective in substantially reducing, if not preventing, capital flows of the latter type, in particular placement abroad of institutional savings (Eihengreen 1998; De Gregorio *et al.* 1998; Radelet and Sachs 1998). The evidence from capital controls in Malaysia is consistent with this evidence.

The indications are that controls helped the government to lower interest rates and encourage a revival of domestic consumption and investment without precipitating capital flight. Following the imposition of capital control measures, the net international reserve position of the country went up from US$20.2 billion in August 1998 to US$29.8 billion in May 1999. Short-term capital flows stabilised in the first quarter of 1998. Thus the foreign reserve position began to move in tandem with the surplus in the current account. As foreign exchange controls were carefully targeted only at short-term investment flows, and trade and foreign direct investment (FDI) related transactions continued to remain liberal, the policy shift did not result in the emergence of a black market for foreign exchange.

Easing of monetary policy relying on the respite provided by capital controls seems to have improved liquidity conditions and lowered the cost of credit in the economy. Reduction in nominal domestic deposit rates, combined with the marginally higher domestic inflation rate, was reflected in a significant narrowing of real interest rate differentials with other countries. In December 1997, the real interest rate differential with the United States was +1.9 per cent, and +0.6 per cent with Singapore. These differentials further increased to 2.7 per cent and 1.7 per cent in February 1998. This pattern was reversed under the new policy regime. The real differential with the United States turned negative in September 1998 and was –2.3 per cent by early 1999. Against that of Singapore, the differential turned negative earlier, around late June 1998, when Singapore raised its interest rates. This differential widened to –2.6 per cent in October and then moderated to –2.0 per cent by early 1999 (BNM 1999). Figure 8.1 compares the differentials between the real domestic money market rate against the world rates (proxied by the US rate) for Malaysia and Thailand, using monthly data over the period January 1996 to March 1999. In both countries, the real interest rate differential has turned out to be negative from about the last quarter of 1998, but the magnitude of the differential has been distinctly larger in Malaysia after August 1998.

Figure 8.1 Real interest rate differential against the United States[a], Malaysia and Thailand, January 1996 – March 1999

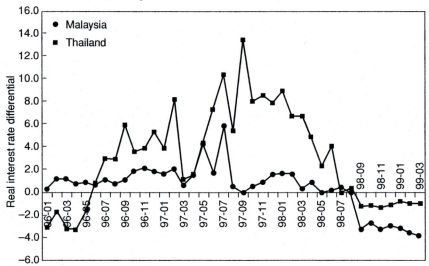

Note: [a] The difference between the money market rates of the given country and that of the United States is adjusted for the inflation differential.
Source: IMF, *International Financial Statistics* database.

FIXED EXCHANGE RATE AND EXPORT-LED RECOVERY

Fixing of the exchange rate at 3.80 ringgit per US$ was originally considered by many observers as a risky strategy. The new fixed rate was implemented as part of a policy package whose prime aim was to artificially inflate the economy through pump priming'. Under this strategy, there was the possibility that domestic inflation would result in real exchange rate appreciation, shifting the cost of adjustment disproportionately onto the tradable sector, hindering an export-led recovery.

As yet there are no indications of this pessimistic scenario unfolding. Domestic inflation pressures have continued to moderate. The rate of CPI inflation (year-on-year) declined from 5.3 per cent in January 1999 to 2.9 per cent in May, raising the prospects of an average inflation rate of about 2.5 per cent for the whole year. Meanwhile, the producer price index has shown a declining trend from February onwards. From a growth rate of 1.2 per cent (year-on-year) in January, it recorded a negative rate of 4.2 per cent in April, with the domestic component of the PPI declining faster (–5.2 per cent) than the import component (–3.2 per cent). Under these circumstances, the fixed exchange rate so far seems to have assisted Malaysian exporters by making their product relatively more competitive than the other crisis-affected countries in Asia (Figure 8.2). In Thailand and Korea, while domestic price trends have been similar to those in Malaysia, appreciation of the nominal exchange rate propelled by the resurgence of short-term capital flows seems to have begun to be reflected in an appreciation of the real exchange rate.

Controls and foreign direct investment

Many commentators expressed fears that capital controls would hamper economic recovery by adversely affecting foreign direct investment in Malaysia (*Economist* 1999: 79; Hale 1998). It was argued that a policy measure that constituted a significant departure from a long-standing commitment to economic openness could have an adverse impact on the general investment climate of the country. Moreover, in Malaysia, the decision to impose controls appeared so sudden and arbitrary that it called into question the general credibility of the government's whole framework for foreign investment. Whether this would translate into a significant reduction in FDI flows remained debatable at the time. The pessimistic view was based on an inappropriate aggregation of FDI with portfolio investment and short-term bank credits. FDI flows are determined by long-term considerations governing international production decisions of multinational enterprises (MNEs), not by financial panics and related short-term economic changes. What is of

Figure 8.2 J.P. Morgan real exchange rate index,[a] Malaysia, Korea and Thailand, January 1996 – June 1999 (1996 = 100)

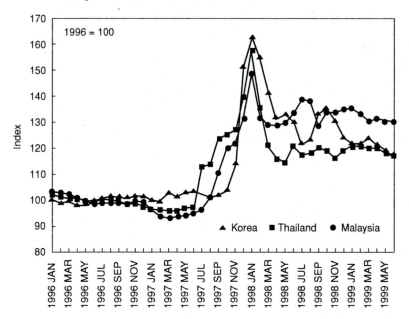

Note: [a] Producer price of the given country relative to that of its trading-partner countries – both expressed in a common currency. Producer price is measured net of food. The original index has been inverted here so that an increase in the index indicates an increase in relative competitiveness (real depreciation).

Source: J.P. Morgan web site <http://www.jpmorgan.com>.

primary importance in attracting FDI, in terms of the external economic policy of a country, is a firm commitment to the maintenance of an open current account (Bhagwati 1998b).

There are no data on realised (actual) investment to examine this issue systematically. However, the available data on the value of investment applications and approvals do not point to a major reversal in investment flows (Table 8.2). Based on data for the first five months, there is a strong likelihood that FDI approvals in 1999 could reach about the same level as in 1998. The total value of proposed new investment, a better indicator of investor response to more recent policy changes, has declined against 1997 at a rate faster than the total value of approved investment. Perhaps investors are still worried about future policy directions.

There are two factors other than capital controls that may have adversely affected investment trends. First, given excess capacity in domestic manufacturing, it is unlikely that domestic-market-oriented FDI will increase in the recovery process. This view is consistent with the trends in investment by local investors. According to the data reported in Table 8.2, from 1997 domestic private investment (which is overwhelmingly domestic market oriented) has grown at much slower rate than FDI. Second, investment flows from Japan and Taiwan, which together accounted for nearly a half of total investment flows to Malaysia, have slowed, probably because of their own economic troubles. During January–May 1999, approval of investment from these two countries fell by 64 and 70 per cent, respectively, compared with the same period in the previous year.

According to balance-of-payments records, FDI inflows to Thailand and Korea have increased in recent months, at a faster rate than those coming to Malaysia. These figures need to be interpreted cautiously because, in the two former countries, acquisition by foreign companies of assets or equity of domestic companies has been a major component of foreign capital inflows. For instance, during the period from 1 January to 15 April in 1999,

Table 8.2   Investment applications and approvals in manufacturing, Malaysia (US$ billion)[a]

	1996	1977	1998 Q1	Q2	Q3	Q4	1999 Q1	Q2
Applications	16,723	12,245	1,235	1,762	815	1,157	1,000	974
FDI	7,145	5,134	710	1,102	552	973	526	631
Local	9,578	7,111	525	660	263	184	474	343
Approvals	13,600	9,213	2,947	1,278	1,868	842	1,606	632
FDI	6,765	4,176	1,262	527	1,368	264	1,395	448
Private domestic	6,835	5,037	1,685	751	500	578	211	184

Note: [a] Original values in ringgit were converted into US$ using the period-average exchange rate (line *rf* in IMF, *International Financial Statistics*, March 1999).

Source: Malaysia Industrial Development Authority (MIDA) press releases.

capital inflows relating to these activities amounted to US$27 billion in Korea and US$20 billion in Thailand, compared with US$2 billion in Malaysia (*Far Eastern Economic Review*, 17 June: 38). Unlike Korea and Thailand, Malaysia has not promoted acquisition/takeover by foreign companies as part of the ongoing process of corporate and banking restructuring. This significant difference in policy orientation is important for any meaningful comparison of FDI flows to these countries during the post-crisis period.

A questionnaire survey of firms conducted by MIER in late 1998 failed to detect any significant impact of new capital controls on operational and investment decisions of both local and foreign firms (MIER 1999).[12] The majority (about 60 per cent) of firms nominated political stability, rather than capital controls, as the most important criteria for investing in Malaysia in the future. Over 85 per cent of firms (90 per cent of firms with FDI) disclosed plans to maintain investment levels in the next 1–3 years.

PORTFOLIO INVESTMENT

When the capital controls were first introduced (and even after the new levy was introduced on 15 February), many observers were concerned about potential massive outflows of short-term foreign debt and portfolio investment after 1 September 1999.[13] However, the ending of the one-year moratorium turned out to be a non-event. According to BNM data, total portfolio capital outflow in the first three days of September amounted to only $456 million, compared with a total stock of about $10 billion potentially movable foreign portfolio investment that remained in the country at the time the restriction was lifted (IMF 1999a: 98). This suggests that investors do not find it difficult to factor in the new profit tax on portfolio investment, as the ground rules are now more transparent in a context where signs of economic recovery are already clearly visible (discussed below).

Following the imposition of capital controls on 1 September 1998, Malaysia was dropped from the country coverage of MSCI and International Finance Corporations (IFC) capital market indices. Lack of transparency in new measures at the time controls were imposed was as much an issue as the nature of the controls themselves. It is pertinent to mention here that the imposition in the early 1990s of capital controls on repatriation of existing capital that involved a lock-up of five years did not lead to an exclusion of the Chilean market from these indices. Presumably this was because transparency was not an issue in Chile. When Malaysia introduced market-friendly changes to capital controls in February 1999, market analysts anticipated that Malaysia would soon be reinstated in these indices once the changes became well rooted and the economy began to show clear signs of recovery (Merrill Lynch 1999). In line with these expectations, MSCI announced on 3 August 1999 that it would reinstate Malaysia in its All Country Far-East Ex-Japan Index and Emerging Market Free Index with effect from February 2000. This decision, coupled with the ending of uncertainty about the possible outcome of the lifting of one-year moratorium on portfolio investment locked in the country (see below), is likely to boost the recent pickup in fresh portfolio capital inflows to Malaysia.

Investors seem to have responded favourably to the change in capital control measures introduced in February 1999.[14] During the period from 15 February to 9 June 1999, the net cumulative portfolio capital inflow to Malaysia amounted to nearly US$3 billion. About 6,000 new accounts were opened for the inflow of new capital after 15 February 1999. The new levy, unlike the original twelve-month withholding period, permits investors to take investment decisions in line with recovery prospects, while factoring the levy into their estimates of potential returns on investment in Malaysia. Increases in capital flows under the new exit levy imply that the term structure of inflows would have changed in favour of investments with a longer maturity period. This has been the experience of countries such as Chile and Colombia under capital inflow tax regimes (De Gregorio *et al.* 1998; Cardeas and Barrera 1998; von Furstenberg and Ulan 1998).

CONCLUSION

Once the Malaysian authorities decided to deviate from the IMF route and follow the conventional Keynesian recipe for crisis management, capital controls provided a conducive setting for the effective pursuance of such policies. The new policy has prevented capital outflows and permitted sustaining significant interest rate differentials with the rest of the world. Against the popular perception that short-term capital flows cannot be controlled in a highly trade-oriented economy, the Malaysian evidence suggests these flows can be regulated (at least on the margin), provided the controls are specifically targeted at capital account transactions. Some commentators have referred to the imposition of controls on capital outflows by the Malaysian government as a ritualistic locking of the stable after the horse has bolted. This is misleading, in that the purpose of controls was to set the stage for monetary expansion by preventing an outflow of local and foreign-owned funds, in response to lowering of domestic interest rate relative to world market rates. The potential threat of such an outflow was much greater in Malaysia than in the other crisis-hit countries because of the pivotal role played by the Singapore money market as a convenient alternative to the domestic market for the Malaysian investor.

So far, the fixed exchange rate has helped the recovery process by preventing premature exchange rate appreciation as part of the improvement in market sentiments about recovery prospects. It has also provided an effective nominal anchor for inflation expectations. However, as the recovery process gathers momentum, it will become difficult to maintain international competitiveness unless the fixed rate is supplemented by sterilisation of increasing foreign reserves or a shift to a more flexible rate. The choice between these two alternatives will soon become a challenge for the Malaysian authorities. In this connection, it is important to note that capital controls are needed in order to maintain a fixed (or an adjustable peg) exchange rate, because without such controls, it is difficult to cope with the flight of hot money. But it is not technically impossible to have a flexible exchange rate while retaining controls on capital transactions (Mead 1951: Chapter 22).

There is little evidence to suggest that controls on short-term capital flows have adversely affected Malaysia's image as a favourable location for foreign direct investment. On the contrary, there is anecdotal evidence that foreign investors, particularly those involved in export-oriented production, favour capital controls and a fixed exchange as sources of stability in the investment climate. The time-honoured (yet much neglected) view in the current debate on crisis management that, in terms of underlying determinants of mobility, long-term investment (FDI) is quite different from hot money' (Mead 1951: 298) is reconfirmed by the Malaysian experiment.

Neither have foreign portfolio investors completely deserted Malaysia. 1 September' was virtually a non-event, despite the earlier fear that investors would pull out the funds that had been trapped in the country. The shift in the capital control regime in March 1999 from a one-year withholding period to a market-friendly graduated tax seems to have helped in regaining the confidence of portfolio investors while influencing the term structure of such inflows. The lesson is that the use of capital control is unlikely to have an adverse lingering effect on foreign portfolio investment, provided timely steps are taken to infuse greater flexibility and transparency into the regulatory mechanism, and the reform process (of which controls are a part) brings about speedy economic recovery and restores opportunities for profitable investment.

An important issue that we have not addressed in the chapter is the long-term growth implications of crisis management behind closed doors. If the Malaysian authorities have made use of the breathing space provided by capital controls to rescue companies and banks that were rendered illiquid (unable to roll over short-term credit) by the financial panic but were otherwise viable, then the underlying growth prospects of the economy will remain intact. Alternatively, if bailouts assisted inefficient (mostly politically linked) firms whose insolvency was hastened by high interest rates and lower aggregate demand, then growth prospects will have been impaired. Such a rescue operation may also induce moral hazard by encouraging firms/banks to continue engaging in risky acts, in the hope that they will be rescued in the event of similar future crises. There is ample anecdotal evidence of inappropriate rescue operations (Ariff 1999). Danaharta has not revealed details of the bad debt acquired, beyond the names of the banks selling the bad loans, the value of the loans and the discount rates. Significant differences in discount rates across various assisted banks remain unexplained. Similarly, the criteria used by Danamodal in its decisions as to which banks should be given priority in injecting capital remain largely unexplained (Yap 1999).

With emerging signs of recovery in Malaysia, foreign analysts have begun to acknowledge that the radical reform measures have worked (or are doing no demonstrable harm) despite their initial scepticism. Major credit-rating agencies, which downgraded Malaysia's international credit rating immediately following the imposition of capital controls, have now come up with more optimistic assessments of prospects. A US$2 billion global bond issued by the Malaysian government in May 1999 was three times oversubscribed, reflecting renewed confidence by global investors in the economy. The IMF, in its Public Information Notice on the recent *Article IV Consultation with Malaysia*, commended the Malaysian authorities for using the breathing space [provided by the policy measures introduced in September 1998] to push ahead with a well-designed and effectively implemented strategy for financial sector restructuring'. Furthermore, with regard to macroeconomic policy, some IMF Directors supported the adoption of an expansionary policy stance, which they considered appropriate to reverse the sharp contraction of economic activity, particularly in view of the absence of inflation pressure (IMF 1999a). The Washington-based private think-tank, Economic Strategic Institute, recently noted that despite the bad press it gets as a result of Prime Minister Mahathir's critical comments about speculators, Malaysia is the best story in the region' (Economic Strategy Institute 1999).

Even if one does not accept the argument that controls have played a special role' for want of counterfactuals, the fact that the dire consequences predicted in the short term about the fate of Malaysia's non-standard policy response did not materialise cannot be ignored. In other words, the new policy measures have at least been successful in avoiding further economic disruption – collapse of companies and banks – leading to massive unemployment and economic hardship. This itself is an achievement of immense significance because, quite apart from economic efficiency considerations, social harmony is an overriding concern governing economic policy making in ethically diverse Malaysia (unlike in more ethnically homogenous countries like Thailand and Korea). Even if one ignores the bloody racial riots in 1969 as a distant event, the imminent ethnic conflict brought about by the modest economic downturn is the mid-1980s cannot be entirely overlooked (Crouch 1996).

It is, of course, hazardous to draw general policy lessons from the study of an individual country case. With the benefit of hindsight, one can reasonably argue that a number of factors specific to Malaysia as well as to the timing of policy reforms may have significantly conditioned the actual policy outcome. As noted, thanks to long-standing prudential controls on foreign borrowing, Malaysia succumbed to the crisis with limited foreign debt exposure. With a vast domestic revenue base and ready access to captive' domestic financial sources (in particular the Employees' Provident Fund (EPF) and the oil-rich Petronas), the Malaysian government was better placed than perhaps any other crisis country to make a decisive departure from the conventional, IMF-centred approach to crisis management. The implementation of new controls was also greatly aided by a well-developed banking system, which was able to perform most of the new functions smoothly in the normal course of its business. The imposition of capital controls coincided with a significant upturn in manufactured exports (mostly as a result of dramatic recovery in the world electronics trade). So there was no shortage of foreign exchange. The particular exchange rate parity, presumably chosen arbitrarily by Malaysian policy makers, eventually turned out to be a highly realistic rate, as the market panic against Asian economies began to subside and the yen began to appreciate against the US dollar. Given the availability of ample foreign exchange for trade and FDI-related activities at a realistic exchange rate, there was no panic buying leading to foreign exchange manipulation. Any policy inference from the particular Malaysian experience needs to be appropriately qualified by these specific circumstances.

Finally, the inference that capital controls have helped crisis management in Malaysia by no means implies that these controls should be retained after the economy recovers. Despite its underlying logic in a crisis context, the new strategy is costly in terms of long-term growth. The rationale behind the imposition of capital controls is to avert a painful economic collapse and to provide a conducive setting for the implementation of the required adjustment policies, in particular banking sector restructuring. The danger is that the complaisance induced by possible temporary recovery through expansionary policies may lead to postponement of long-term structural reforms, and thus to long-term economic deterioration. Moreover, any form of market intervention of this nature involves economic costs associated with bureaucratic controls and related rent-seeking activities. Prolonged use of controls is likely to compound these costs. The greatest challenge for Malaysian policy makers is, therefore, to strengthen the domestic financial system and to regain macroeconomic prudence, which sadly dissipated during the period of growth euphoria in the early 1990s, in order to set the stage for an orderly exiting from capital controls.

NOTES

1   This chapter is a revised version of a paper presented at the conference on Reform and Recovery in East Asia: The Role of the State and Economic Enterprise, hosted by the Asia Pacific School of Economics and Management, Australian National University and the IMF Regional Office for Asia and the Pacific, 21–2 September 1999, Australian National University, Canberra. Thanks are due to Mahani Zainal Abidin, Max Corden, Peter Drysdale, David Nellor and other conference participants for helpful comments.
2   For details on the macroeconomic conditions in Malaysia in the lead-up to the crisis and initial policy responses, see Athukorala (1998).
3   Why ringgit deposits fetched such high offshore rates (in Singapore) remains a puzzle. One possible explanation is that this was because of high demand for the ringgit on the part of hedge funds, which were trying to close out their short positions in that currency (EIU 1998).
4   A widely expressed view in pro-government news commentaries in Malaysia was that Malaysia would not have been eligible for IMF support even if it had wanted to seek such support because of its relatively strong balance-of-payments position and it relatively low foreign debt (BNM 1999: 5; NEAC 1999: 1).

This view is not consistent with the facts related to both Malaysia's economic conditions and general IMF practices in assisting member countries in the event of an economic crisis. The Philippines, for example, has continued to receive financing from the IMF, even though its balance of payments position is relatively sound (compared with Thailand and Korea) and its external debt burden is low. Balance-of-payments need is only one of the eligibility criterion, and even in relation to that, Malaysia's reserves have not been extraordinarily high. If it had wished, Malaysia could have entered an IMF program with financial support for crisis management, involving recapitalisation of banks and corporate restructuring.

5   To set the stage for the policy turnaround, Anwar (who had been pushing reforms along the IMF lines) was sidelined from the policy scene by the appointment of Daim Zainuddin (Mahathir's long-time policy adviser) as the Minister of Special Functions, a portfolio newly created for handling crisis management. On 3 September, Anwar was removed from the positions of Deputy Prime Minister and Finance Minister. He was subsequently expelled from the United Malay National Organisation (the major party in the ruling coalition). On 8 September, Mahathir appointed himself the First Finance Minister. This position was subsequently assigned to Zainuddin, in addition to his role as the Minister of Special Functions. One interpretation of the almost simultaneous sacking of Anwar and the announcement of a new reform package is that the prime motive for the latter was to set the stage for sacking Anwar without a visible display of market disappointment and precipitation of currency and share market collapse.

6   It is, however, not correct to name Krugman as the intellectual architect of the Malaysian experiment, as some authors have done (e.g. Miller 1999; Hale 1998). Apparently the decision to introduce capital controls was made by the National Economic Action Council on 6 August (Mahathir 1999), before the Krugman article appeared. Recently, Krugman stated in Singapore that It was a shock that while I was speculating idly about that [capital control], Dr. Mahathir was about to do it' (*New Straits Times*, 26 August).

7   It is also important to note that capital controls as a balance-of-payments management tool is not new to Malaysia. For instance, in early 1994, Bank Negara Malaysia successfully used temporary capital controls to avert successfully a speculative attack on the ringgit. The restrictions included ceilings on external liablities of commercial banks, a ban on sales of short-term debt instruments to foreigners, restricting ringgit deposits of foreign institutions to non-interest-bearing accounts, prohibiting non-trade-related currency swaps, and a new maintenance charge on non-interest-bearing foreign deposits. Once speculative pressure subsided and the exchange rate returned to the level of late 1993, BNM gradually removed the controls and freed up capital flows, completely lifting all restrictions by August 1994 (World Bank 1996: 67–8).

8   At the time, shares of about 15% of listed Malaysian companies were traded on the OTC market (*Financial Times*, 1 September).

9   The benchmark interest rate prescribed by BNM for lending institutions with a view to avoiding unhealthy competition in credit markets.

10   The waiver was part of a change in Malaysia's tax assessment system beginning in the year 2000 from one based on income derived in the previous year to income derived in the current year.

11   Interestingly, on these grounds, the international financier George Soros (1998: Chapter 7) treats the economic situation in Malaysia in the lead-up to the crisis as untenable as (if not more untenable than) than in Korea, Thailand and Indonesia.

12 Some 135 firms, accounting for over 60% of total manufacturing output in the country, responded to the questionnaire. Of these firms, 77 had foreign capital participation (wholly foreign owned – 33; joint ventures – 44) and 56 were fully locally owned.
13 The amount of portfolio capital trapped in the country by capital controls was estimated to be over US$14 (BNM 1999).
14 Figures given in this paragraph are from Bank Negara Malaysia Press release, 24 June 1999, <http://www.bnm.gov.my>.

REFERENCES

Ariff, Mohamed (1999) The financial crisis and the reshaping of the Malaysian economy: Trends and issues', Kuala Lumpur: Malaysian Institute of Economic Research, unpublished paper.

Athukorala, Prema-chandra (1998) Malaysia', in Ross H. McLeod and Ross Garnaut (eds) *East Asia in Crisis: From being a miracle to needing one?*, London: Routledge, 85–101.

—— (1999) Capital mobility, crisis and adjustment: Evidence and insights from Malaysia', paper presented at the conference on International Capital Mobility and Domestic Economic Stability hosted by the Reinventing Bretton Woods Committee, World Bank and Australian National University, 13–16 July 1999, Australian National University, Canberra.

Bhagwati, Jagdish (1998a) The capital myth: The difference between trade in widgets and dollars', *Foreign Affairs* 77(3): 7–12.

—— (1998b) Asian financial crisis debate: Why? How severe?', paper presented at the conference on Managing the Asian Financial Crisis: Lessons and Changes organised by the Asian Strategic Leadership Institute and Rating Agency Malaysia, 2–3 November, Kuala Lumpur.

BNM (Bank Negara Malaysia) (1999) *Annual Report of the Board of Directors for the Year Ended 31 December 1998*, Kuala Lumpur: BNM.

Cardenas, Mauricio and Barrera, Felipe (1998) On the effectiveness of capital controls: The experience of Colombia during the 1990s', *Journal of Development Economics* 54: 27–57.

Cooper, Richard (1998) Comments on the paper by Radelet and Sachs', *Brookings Papers on Economic Activity* 2: 90–2.

Crouch, Harrold (1998) The Asian economic crisis and democracy', *Public Policy*, 11(3): 39–62.

—— (1996) *Government and Society in Malaysia*, Sydney: Allen and Unwin.

Danaharta (National Asset Management Company, Malaysia) (1999) *Operations Report, 20 June – 21 December 1998*, Kuala Lumpur.

De Gregorio, Jose, Edwards, Sebastian and Valdes, Rodrigo O. (1998) Capital controls in Chile: An assessment', paper for the 1998 IASE–NBER Conference, Center for Applied Economics, Department of Industrial Engineering, Universidad de Chile, Santiago, mimeo.

Economic Strategy Institute (1999) *State of Asia*, Washington DC: Economic Strategy Institute.

Economist (1999) The road less traveled', 1 May: 79.

EIU (Economist Intelligence Unit) (1998) *Country Economic Report: Malaysia and Brunei*, 3rd Quarter 1998, London: EIU.

Edwards, Sebastian (1999) A capital idea? Reconsidering a financial quick fix', *Foreign Affairs* 78(3): 18–22.

Eihengreen, Barry (1998) *Globalizing Capital: A history of the international monetary system*, Princeton, NJ: Princeton University Press.

Government of Malaysia (1998) *The 1999 Budget Speech*, 23 October, Kuala Lumpur: Ministry of Finance.

Hale, David (1998) 'The hot money debate', *The International Economy*, November/December: 8–12 and 66–9.

Hiebert, Murray (1999) 'Capital idea?', *Far Eastern Economic Review*, 1 July, 162(26): 55.

IMF (1999a) Public Information Notice No. 99/88: IMF Concludes Article IV Consultation with Malaysia, Washington, DC: IMF (www.imf.org/external/np/sec/pn/19999/pn9988.htm).

—— (1999b) *International Capital markets: Developments, prospects, and key policy issues*, Washington, DC: IMF.

Krugman, Paul (1998) 'Saving Asia: It's time to get radical', *Fortune* 138(5): 74–80.

—— (1999) *The Return of Depression Economics*, New York: Norton and Company.

Lim, Linda (1999) 'Malaysia's response to the Asian Financial crisis', statement before the Subcommittee on Asia and the Pacific Committee on International Relations, US House of Representatives, June, http://www.house.gov/international relations.

Mahathir, Dato' Seri Bin Mohamad (1999) 'Why Malaysia's selective currency controls are necessary and why they have worked', paper presented at the Symposium of the First Anniversary of Currency Control, 2 October 1999, Nikko Hotel, Kuala Lumpur.

Mead, James (1951) *The Theory of International Economic Policy, Volume 1: The balance of payments*, London: Oxford University Press, Chapter XXII.

Merrill Lynch & Company (1999) 'Malaysia: Relaxation of capital controls', 5 and 9 February, Kuala Lumpur.

Miller, Merton H. (1999) 'Reflections of a retiring keynote speaker', keynote address at the 10th Annual Conference of PACAP/FMA, Singapore, July 1999.

MIER (Malaysian Institute of Economic Research) (1999) *The Impact of Currency Control Measures on Business Operation*, Kuala Lumpur: MIER.

NEAC (National Economic Action Council) (1998) *National Economic Recovery Plan: Agenda for Action*, Kuala Lumpur: Prime Minister's Department.

—— (1999) 'Prof. Merton is wrong', Kuala Lumpur, <http://neac.gov.my>.

Radelet, Steve and Sachs, Jeffrey (1998) 'The East Asian financial crisis: Diagnosis, remedies, prospects', *Brookings Papers on Economic Activity* 2: 1–89.

Searle, Peter (1999) *The Riddle of Malaysian Capitalism: Rent-seekers or Real Capitalists?*, Sydney: Allen & Unwin.

Soros, George (1998) *The Crisis of Global Capitalism*, London: Little, Brown and Company.

von Furstenberg, George M. and Ulan, Michael K. (1998) 'Courage and conviction: Chile's Governor Zahler', in George M. von Furstenberg and Michael K. Ulan, *Learning from the World's Best Central Bankers*, Boston; Kluwer Academic Publishers: 39–74.

Williamson, John (1993) 'A cost benefit analysis of capital account liberalisation', in Melmut Reisen and Bernhard Fischer (eds) *Financial Opening: Policy issues and experiences in developing countries*, Paris: OECD: 25–34.

Yap, Michael Meow-Chung (1999) 'Financial crisis in Malaysia: Adjustment through unorthodox policy', paper presented at the Malaysia Forum, Department of Economics, Research School of Pacific and Asian Studies, Australian National University, 24 June.

Zefferys, Nicholas (1999) 'Doing business in Malaysia: An American ground level perspective', presentation by President of the American Malaysian Chamber of Commerce to foreign journalists visiting Malaysia, www.neac.gov.my.

9 Reform and the corporate environment in the Philippines[1]

Angelo A. Unite and Michael J. Sullivan

INTRODUCTION

Literature discussing the recent Asian financial crisis points to several competing hypotheses on the causes of the financial turmoil that beset countries in the region. The often-cited reasons for the crisis include macroeconomic mismanagement; regulatory and supervisory weaknesses in the financial sector, specifically the banking system; and breakdowns in the corporate governance system. The importance of corporate governance is highlighted by Jim Wolfensohn, the World Bank president, who stated that the proper governance of companies will become as crucial to the world economy as the proper governing of countries'. Furthermore, in the case of the Philippines, Lamberte (1999) asserts that there are three main factors that contributed to the vulnerability of the Philippine economy to the Asian financial crisis: inappropriate exchange rate policy, inadequate prudential regulations for banks, and poor corporate governance. Consequently, much of the current focus of international financial organisations, international coalitions and financial and economic experts is on the corporate governance systems present in these various Asian countries. In particular, there are calls for improvements in the corporate governance practices and structures as a means of restoring financial stability and growth in the Asian region (Symposium Report on Corporate Governance in APEC 1998). The crucial role of improved corporate governance in assisting affected countries to rebuild competitiveness, restore investor confidence and promote sustainable economic growth is emphasised by the fact that the World Bank and the IMF are currently implementing corporate governance reform in these still ailing markets (Dubiel 1999).

Relationships between a country's political governance and its corporate governance system have a fundamental effect on the performance of that country's economy. Recently, the economic liberalisation that has occurred in many Asian countries has resulted in higher rates of economic growth. However, as this economic liberalisation results in a reduction of governmental impediments, it also acts to erode the effectiveness of governmental oversight, which is important. In this chapter we discuss the corporate governance system of the Philippines, the relationship of this system with Philippine political governance, and how corporate governance affects economic activity. We conclude by focusing on the role of monitors and argue for the necessity of a governmental role in this monitoring activity as a means of making the Philippine corporate governance system more effective and thus reducing the economy's vulnerability to future economic shocks.

First, we define corporate governance as a unique concept separate from the political governance system of a nation-state. Within this context, we discuss corporate governance issues underlying macroeconomic stability, and the vulnerability of the Philippine corporate and financial sectors to external economic shocks. Then we define various forms of corporate governance, with specific attention to the form of corporate governance in the Philippines. Next, we discuss the role of a monitor within any system of corporate governance. Again, focusing on the Philippines, we highlight possible corporate monitors and discuss their effectiveness. Then we discuss current trends in the corporate governance structure of the Philippines and how this structure is affected by recent regulatory changes. We conclude with general public policy recommendations that may be employed to increase the effectiveness of corporate monitoring systems within the Philippines and how the resulting improvements in the country's corporate governance structure can reduce, if not eliminate, the economy's vulnerability to the adverse effects of future external shocks.

CORPORATE GOVERNANCE

What is corporate governance?

Corporate governance can be defined as the relationship between corporate stakeholders and managers and how these participants determine the direction and performance of the corporation (see Sullivan and Unite 1998).[2] Corporate stakeholders can include both holders of equity and debt, as well as employees and suppliers. In other words, corporate governance focuses on who controls corporate assets and on the decision-making process regarding where capital funds are allocated.

An understanding of corporate governance is important for many reasons. First, understanding a nation's corporate governance system is imperative for understanding capital flows within the economy. Second, the corporate governance system, to a large extent, will determine which segments of society derive economic advantages and which segments of society are at an economic disadvantage. Finally, this understanding will give policy makers an opportunity to more completely evaluate economic needs and may lend insight into the usefulness of specific regulatory changes. Another important aspect of any corporate governance system is its dynamic nature. This is especially true in today's age of increasing globalisation, economic liberalisation, and the trend in many economies towards greater privatisation.

Sound corporate governance and macroeconomic stability

Among the countries in Southeast Asia, the Philippines was less severely affected by the financial crisis that beset this region in the latter half of 1997. Reasons cited include the strong economic fundamentals present and a better bank regulatory environment.

Sicat (1998) argues that the Philippines eluded the worst consequences of a full-scale crisis because it had relatively strong economic fundamentals, including a reformed financial sector at the onset of the regional crisis'. This economic strength is based on four years of fiscal surplus starting in 1994, a reduction in external debt since the mid-1980s, low inflation, and a resulting improved standing with international credit agencies. Moreover, Sicat contends that as a result of the painful experience brought about by an earlier 1980s crisis, the government embarked on structural reforms which helped to maintain prudent fiscal management, to promote accountability of the government, and to encourage greater political openness and democracy'. This economic improvement has been further bolstered by liberalisation in the financial and corporate sectors that encouraged greater competition, both domestic and foreign. Reformed bank regulation also acted to limit the exposure of Philippine banks to property sector loans. For example, a survey of twenty-one banks conducted by the central bank in 1996 revealed that loans to the real property sector accounted for only about 10.9 per cent of total portfolio. In contrast, Thai finance companies' exposure to real estate loans was a much greater 2 per cent. Wolfensohn (1998) confirms this view, pointing out that the Southeast Asian countries that suffered most had the highest debt-to-equity ratios. In 1996 debt-to-equity ratios were 3.5 to 1.0 in South Korea, 1.9 to 1.0 in Indonesia, and 2.3 to 1.0 in Thailand, while less affected countries, such as Taiwan, Singapore, and the Philippines, had ratios no greater than 1.0 to 1.0.

Perceived benefits from this banking reform have been echoed by Chaterjee (1999) and Garnaut (1998). Chaterjee argues that one reason why the financial crisis affected the Philippines least is because it had the highest degree of openness in the banking sector, the highest profitability, and better regulation and supervision'. Garnaut (1998) asserts that the country differences in the magnitude of the initial economic response brought by the regional currency shock are a function of the quality of a country's financial institutions and regulation. In particular, he mentions that the weaknesses in the financial systems, and the economic consequences, were moderate in Singapore and Hong Kong, somewhat greater in the Philippines and Malaysia, severe in Thailand and Korea, and catastrophic in Indonesia'.

Although the Philippine economy fared better than many of its regional neighbours, the crisis exposed flaws in the Philippine corporate governance system as well as weakness in its financial sector (Lamberte 1999). In turn, a major contributory factor in the Philippine's vulnerability to contagion effects associated with the crisis are weaknesses in corporate governance structure, specifically improper alignment of incentives and inadequate disclosure (see, for example, Lamberte 1999). However, it is important to note that the lack of a sound corporate governance system is not unique to the Philippines. Alburo (1998) argues that the crisis was partly triggered by cronyism and corruption in the affected Asian economies, and the lack of effective governance among the institutions concerned. More importantly, his analysis suggests that, given the Philippine experience, strong fundamentals do not provide automatic immunity' to adverse external shocks. This sentiment is echoed in the 1998 Corporate Governance in APEC Symposium Report, which indicates that poor corporate governance was among the factors that contributed to the vulnerability of Asia's corporate and financial sectors to the regional financial crisis. The report likewise highlights the role of improved corporate governance systems in the recovery of the economies adversely affected by this crisis.

Inadequate disclosure of a corporation's financial position, often referred to as a lack of transparency, enables managers to pursue non-profit maximising activities, such as over-expansion and diversification. Lamberte (1999) argues that this was the case in the 1990s when many Philippine corporations expanded well beyond their core competencies. Evidence supporting this claim can be gleaned from the fact that the number of firm closures doubled, and the number of firms laying off workers increased threefold from 1997 to 1998. The lack of accurate information about firms' financial health, viability and future growth potential creates a severe information asymmetry between small investors and majority shareholder-managers. This information asymmetry inhibits an investor's ability to assess firm risk level accurately and may act to promote contagion investment practices.

While the recent crisis has exposed flaws in financial and corporate sectors and problems associated with corporate governance systems throughout the region, foreign investors have taken a more cautious investing posture in these markets. To regain investor confidence, corporate governance systems are one aspect that must be improved. If these necessary improvements in the Philippine corporate governance system are not implemented, the economy's recovery and future growth may be jeopardised, since, as Lamberte (1999) argues, the corporate sector has become a principal engine of growth in the Philippines especially in the 1990s when this sector grew significantly in terms of number and asset size'.

The next section identifies and describes the corporate governance structure currently in place in the Philippines, to shed light on the weaknesses of the system and to serve as a reference point to discuss the appropriate reforms that may lead to effective corporate governance.

SYSTEMS OF CORPORATE GOVERNANCE

It is commonly thought that there are three general systems of corporate governance. These systems are not completely distinct; moreover, they are dynamic, being influenced by economic, historical and political forces. It should be noted, however, that there is no single ideal model of a corporate governance system; different forms will be appropriate in different countries at different times. We define these general systems of corporate governance as based on the capital market, the industrial group, and the entrepreneurial corporation.

The capital market based system can be found in the United States, Great Britain and Canada. The features of this system include a reliance on the marketplace to allocate resources and to determine asset prices. The economy consists of a large number of independently traded companies with easily transferable ownership rights. This system allows extensive use of public markets to raise funds. Most large, publicly traded companies rely on professional managers. To maintain public confidence in this marketplace-driven system, policy makers implement laws and regulations to protect small investors. As such, information disclosure is mandated and the court system enforces that the information disclosed is reliable.

Forms of the industrial group based system of corporate governance can be found in Japan and South Korea. In economies where this system is found, large industrial groups control economic activity. These prominent industrial groups are typically centred on a large commercial bank, which acts as the primary source of funds and also exerts some measure of managerial control. It is not unusual to find that these groups are diversified both horizontally and vertically, and all aspects of sourcing, production and marketing derive from group companies. In addition, group relationships are cemented through interlocking directorships, cross-shareholdings, joint ventures and product development agreements. This system allows rapid economic development by focusing manufacturing on export products.

The entrepreneurial corporation based system is found in many emerging market economies, including the Philippines. Corporations in economies with this system typically have concentrated ownership, where the control of companies is often by the founding family. As such, there is little reliance on professional managers, and information disclosure is minimal or unreliable. Capital markets are underdeveloped, and the primary source of corporate funds is from family assets or one of the few larger banks that may be found in the economy. For example, the entire Philippine public equity market as represented by the Philippine Stock Exchange (PSE) has only 221 listed companies, of which less than half are actively traded (traded on at least 200 days out of a total of about 250 trading days in a year). Total market capitalisation is US$31.3 billion, with the ten largest stocks making up 60.2 per cent of market capitalisation (Philippine Stock Exchange 1998). In addition, less than 0.5 per cent of the Philippine population own publicly-traded equity (Llave 1997). Mangaran (1993) and Lamberte and Llanto (1993) cite some possible reasons for the low supply of publicly listed shares. Many Philippine firms are either closely held by a few individuals or are family controlled. This creates a reluctance to go public, for fear of losing ownership control as well as exposing their business operations to public scrutiny. A second reason is that some owners of non-listed firms allegedly understate earnings to reduce their tax obligations.

The effectiveness of the entrepreneurial corporate based system depends upon the strength of intermediaries in the economy. There are cases where a strong independent banking sector effectively monitors corporate activity by analysing the economic viability of projects financed with borrowed funds. In cases where intermediaries are unable to function as corporate monitors, or where regulatory supervision is ineffective, the entrepreneurial corporate based system is subject to severe breakdown. For example, economic power is often concentrated in a few corporate family groups that also have strong ownership ties with major banks, resulting in severe conflict-of-interest problems.

The Philippine system of corporate governance

In the case of the Philippines, companies owned by family groups control a large proportion of productive assets. The control of assets is important because the controlling party determines how these assets are deployed, the economic returns these assets produce, and who garners the resulting benefits. We conjecture that the long-term effectiveness of any system of corporate governance is dependent on how effectively this system is monitored and what incentives are provided to coerce those controlling corporate assets to efficiently deploy assets and to align their goals with the economic goals of the state.

We find that even the larger corporations are often part of a corporate group that is controlled by the founding family. For example, of 196 companies listed on the PSE for which we have data at the end of 1997, we identify twenty-nine corporate groups with interest in at least one of these listed companies (see Table 9.1). The breadth of holdings of family domestic

Table 9.1   Major family domestic corporate groups in the Philippines with holdings in 196 PSE-listed companies

Aboitiz	Lopez (ABS-CBN)
Alcantara	Ortigas
Ayala	Pangilinan (First Pacific)
Cervantes (Matrix)	Puyat
Cojuangco	Ramos
Concepcion (RFM)	Soriano
Consunji	Sy (Shoemart)
Del Rosario	Tan, Andrew (Megaworld)
Gatchalian (Wellex)	Tan, Lucio
Go, George (Gotesco)	Tan Yu (AsiaWorld)
Go, Jonathan and David (Guoco)	Ty (Metrobank)
Gokongwei	Uytengsu
Gotianun (Filinvest)	Villar
Gow	Yuchengco (Pan Malayan)
Lim (Solid)	

corporate groups is further demonstrated in Table 9.2, which lists thirteen of the largest groups. It is shown these thirteen corporate groups are each composed of many large companies (publicly traded and privately held) totalling 392 companies from eighteen different major industries.

While focusing only on PSE-listed companies, we find that the top owner is shown to have, on average, a 37.7 per cent ownership interest. This is telling, since PSE-listed firms are expected to be more widely held than non-listed firms. As shown in Table 9.3, this ownership concentration rises quickly to 64.7 per cent when considering the largest five stockholders, and to nearly 80 per cent when considering the top twenty. This heavy ownership concentration, together with the prevalence of group ownership, supports the belief that an inordinate proportion of company assets is controlled by a few.

Further evidence of the concentrated ownership of corporate assets in the Philippines can be gleaned from information reported in Tables 9.4 and 9.5. Table 9.4 shows that seventy-five of these 196 PSE-listed firms are effectively controlled by family domestic corporate groups.[3] Furthermore, another thirty companies are partially owned by related companies, twenty-seven are controlled by foreign interests, and eight are subject to shared control by family groups and foreign interests. This leaves only fifty-three of the 196 listed firms which we consider to be controlled by non-affiliated interests. Table 9.5 reports the percentage ownership by categories of the

Table 9.2 Breadth of corporate group control of corporate assets

Group name	Number of major companies	Major industries[a]
Lopez	30	1,2,3,4,10,13
Soriano	25	1,3,5,6,8,11,12,14
Cojuangco	45	1,3,5,9,11,13,14,15
Ayala	57	1,3,8,10,11,12,13,14
Concepcion	18	3,5,8,14,15,16
Sarmiento	18	3,8,9,12,13,15
Aboitiz	28	1,2,3,5,7,13
JAKA	25	3,5,8,9,12
Solid	25	3,13,17,18
Floirendo	21	3,12,14,18
Gokongwei	37	1,2,3,8,9,11,16
Yuchengco	54	1,2,3,6,8,11,12,13
Gotianun	9	3,8,9

Note: [a] Major industries coding: 1= banks, 2= energy, 3= food and agriculture, 4= broadcasting, 5= transportation and shipping, 6= mining, 7= construction, 8= real estate, 9= manufacturing, 10= information technology, 11= insurance, 12= brokerage and financial services, 13= import and export, 14= tourism and hotel, 15= basic industries, 16= telecommunications, 17= electronics, 18= automotive.

Source: Business World, Philippines, Inc.: Who Owns the Philippines', 7th Anniversary Report, 1994, Manila, Philippines.

top twenty owners. As shown, domestic corporate groups own, on average, over 32 per cent of PSE-listed company shares. If we consider insider ownership, in addition to this group ownership, we see that average ownership by the closely-held interest amounts to nearly 50 per cent.

The conclusion we draw from these data is that family domestic corporate groups control the bulk of corporate assets in the Philippines. Since these groups are often still controlled by the founder or their immediate descendant, we assume decisions as to where corporate assets are deployed are based on the needs of these controlling families, which may not necessarily intersect with the goals of the broader economy. Therefore, corporate decisions will be biased towards these controlling families unless an effective monitor that can focus corporate decision making towards these broader economic interests exists.

Table 9.3   Stock ownership concentration of 196 PSE-listed companies

Ownership concentration	Percentage owned
Top owner	37.67
Top 5 owners	64.70
Top 10 owners	73.25
Top 20 owners	79.89

Note: Based on 20 largest ownership positions.
Source: Investments Guide 1997.

Table 9.4   Ownership control of 196 PSE-listed companies by family domestic corporate groups, foreign interests, related companies and government[a]

Ownership control [b]	Number
Family domestic corporate groups	75
Foreign interests	27
Shared between family groups and foreign interests	8
Related companies	30
Government	3
Non-affiliated interests	53
Total	196

Notes:
a Based on 20 largest ownership positions.
b The party with effective control (greater than 20%) of 196 PSE-listed companies.
Source: Investments Guide 1997.

THE ROLE OF A MONITOR

The effectiveness of any system of corporate governance hinges on the presence of an effective corporate monitor. The role of a monitor is essential as a means of ensuring that corporate managers utilise funds in a productive manner. At the extreme, the lack of an effective monitor allows the misallocation of valuable economic resources to benefit a few in society at the expense of the economy as a whole. Even when the lack of an effective monitor does not result in widespread economic

Table 9.5   Ownership profile of 196 PSE-listed companies[a]

Ownership type	*Percentage*
Foreign[b]	6.97
Financial institutions[c]	1.16
Investment companies[d]	8.90
Domestic corporations[e]	2.61
Insiders[f]	15.41
Domestic corporate groups[g]	32.49
Blind accounts[h]	8.06
Government[i]	2.04
Individual investors[j]	2.25
Total	79.89

Notes:

a Based on 20 largest ownership positions.

b Foreign ownership includes shares owned by international development banks, foreign insurance companies, foreign brokerage companies, 50% of mutual fund ownership, foreign corporations, foreign banks, and non-Filipino owned Philippine Central Depository (PCD) registered shares.

c Financial institutional ownership includes shares owned by domestic insurance companies and domestic banks.

d Investment company ownership includes shares owned by domestic brokerage companies, retirement funds, investment companies, investment houses and real estate development companies.

e Domestic corporation ownership includes shares owned by domestic corporations and holding companies.

f Insider ownership includes shares owned by directors, relatives of directors, and management.

g Domestic corporate group ownership includes shares owned by family group companies, the domestic parent company, and the foreign parent company.

h Blind account ownership includes shares owned by blind numbered accounts and Filipino-owned PCD registered shares.

i Government ownership includes shares owned directly by the government, social security system, GSIS, AFP, the Development Bank of the Philippines, a university, or religious organisation.

j Individual investor ownership includes shares owned by individual investors and 50% of mutual fund ownership.

Source: Investments Guide 1997.

abuse, the resulting absence in monitoring can lead to inability of investors and other stakeholders to evaluate corporate activity accurately.

For example, the United States and Japan employ vastly different systems of corporate governance, but both are quite successful because they have effective monitoring systems. In the United States, a well-developed capital market, along with a high degree of mandated information disclosure and resulting transparency, allows a diverse array of stockholders to monitor activities of corporate managers. In addition, a strong legal system and an active market for corporate control allows stockholders to enforce their will, while the goals of managers and owners are aligned through incentive-based contracts. In Japan, *keiretsu* groupings, with their interlocking directorships, cross-shareholdings and lender relationships, allow the main banks to collect vast amounts of information on group companies, and therefore, to monitor how effectively these companies employ assets. The desire to adhere to *keiretsu* group goals provides the incentive for professional managers to direct asset use for the benefits of the group. Also, strong government oversight by the Ministry of Finance allows this government agency the ability to implement policies and regulations that focus resource activity in certain directions that are determined to be in the state's interests.

Within the broadly defined entrepreneurial corporation based system, potential sources for an effective monitor include strong independent banks, powerful government regulators, or competitive forces. In the succeeding discussions, we demonstrate the nature of the Philippine corporate governance system and the weaknesses that hinder the effectiveness of this system. Specifically, we demonstrate the inability of any of these potential monitors to fulfil the monitoring role adequately.

In the Philippines, larger banks are often, at least partially, owned by the economically dominant family corporate groups. This creates an obvious conflict of interest for these banks to act as corporate monitors, since the managers of these banks may be related or appointed by the family corporate group or are in some sense subservient to these family corporate groups. Second, although regulation is in place to certify some sense of economic propriety by corporate groups, the present weak bureaucracy cannot ensure enforcement. Problems such as low pay, inadequate training, and corruption act to undermine regulators' ability to monitor effectively. Finally, there has been a historic lack of competition for domestic corporations (McCoy 1994). Part of this lack of competition results from restrictions applied to foreign corporations, discouraging or completely excluding these corporations from operating in the Philippines. In addition, large domestic family corporations have often been able to avoid domestic competition. Governmental privilege has historically enabled corporate groups to dominate certain industries, either nationally or regionally without facing a competitive threat (McCoy 1994).

The role of banks as corporate monitors

Large commercial banks are in a position to act as monitors of corporate activity. As discussed earlier, in the Philippines many of these banks are influenced, if not controlled, by the large family-owned corporate groups. Tables 9.6 and 9.7 provide information on group ownership of sixteen large commercial banks, the percentage of that group ownership, and total assets over the years from 1990 to 1998. These banks are all publicly traded, all belong to the top 1,000 corporations in the Philippines, and their total assets constitute on average roughly 70 per cent of the total assets of the entire commercial banking sector over the period. We find that ten of the sixteen commercial banks are subject to significant group ownership. This highlights the obvious problem of relying on banks to act as corporate monitors. In addition, when we consider ownership of related parties, including affiliated companies and insiders, we find that a related party effectively controls every one of these large commercial banks. Table 9.7 shows the relative sizes of these commercial banks, indicating that a majority of Philippine commercial bank assets are controlled by a few.

Further evidence on the inability of banks to function effectively as corporate monitors in the Philippines is presented by Rivera and Koike (1995), who investigate the corporate holdings of the so-called six *taipan* families: namely the Chinese-Filipino business families headed by Lucio Tan, John Gokongwei Jr., Alfonso Yuchengco, George Ty, Henry Sy and Andrew Gotianun. They show that each of these families has a flagship firm engaged in commercial banking (see Table 9.8). For example, the top Philippine commercial bank in 1993, based on gross revenues and total assets, was Metropolitan Bank & Trust Co., controlled by *taipan* George S.K. Ty.

Why do these domestic family corporate groups have large ownership interests in banks? The answer is that the benefits of controlling a large commercial bank in the Philippines are twofold. First, control of a large commercial bank by a corporate group provides a ready source of funds. The obvious concern with this arrangement is that banks will favour lending based on corporate affiliation rather than merit, which would presumably lower the quality of the banks' loan portfolio due to incomplete analysis of a borrower's loan application. Second, ownership in a large commercial bank has been shown to be very profitable, due to high interest rate spreads. A 1991 Citibank report stated that interest rate spreads of Philippine banks are some of the highest in the region (Hutchcroft 1998). This report attributes these spreads to high reserve requirements, regulations and oligopolistic market power. Oligopolistic market power allows banks to profit at the expense of depositors and small independent borrowers. Such evidence that corporate groups and related parties effectively control banks suggests the possibility that an external shock that initially hits the banking system can lead to dire consequences in the corporate sector and vice versa.

Table 9.6 Total assets of 16 selected domestic commercial banks, 1990–8 (billion pesos)

Bank name	1990 TA	%	1991 TA	%	1992 TA	%	1993 TA	%	1994 TA	%
Philippine National Bank	73.5	20.1	93.8	22.0	97.6	20.7	131.8	22.5	148.2	20.0
Bank of Philippine Islands	54.9	15.0	63.0	14.8	70.7	15.0	81.9	14.0	95.8	12.9
Metropolitan Bank & Trust Co.	48.5	13.2	54.8	12.9	63.3	13.4	88.9	15.2	120.0	16.2
Far East Bank & Trust Co.	43.1	11.8	45.7	10.7	46.6	9.9	52.2	8.9	69.2	9.4
Philippine Commercial Intl Bank	33.1	9.0	36.7	8.6	41.1	8.7	48.3	8.2	73.1	9.9
Rizal Commercial Banking Corp.	21.0	5.7	26.7	6.3	31.4	6.7	39.7	6.8	52.8	7.1
Equitable Bank	16.9	4.6	19.4	4.6	22.2	4.7	26.6	4.5	30.7	4.1
Prudential Bank	14.1	3.8	15.0	3.5	14.3	3.0	16.0	2.7	17.6	2.4
Solidbank	13.6	3.7	14.5	3.4	15.5	3.3	18.1	3.1	21.8	2.9
China Banking Corp.	11.8	3.2	15.5	3.6	17.4	3.7	20.9	3.6	29.0	3.9
Security Bank Corp.	7.9	2.2	9.5	2.2	11.1	2.4	15.8	2.7	20.3	2.7
Philippine Bank of Communications	7.3	2.0	8.3	2.0	9.9	2.1	11.0	1.9	12.0	1.6
Union Bank of the Philippines	6.9	1.9	7.5	1.8	12.8	2.7	13.7	2.3	26.3	3.6
The Philippine Banking Corp.	5.9	1.6	6.0	1.4	6.2	1.3	6.9	1.2	6.6	0.9
Philippine Trust Co.	5.6	1.5	6.7	1.6	8.1	1.7	9.3	1.6	10.4	1.4
Urban Bank, Inc.	2.2	0.6	2.6	0.6	3.4	0.7	4.6	0.8	6.1	0.8
Total	366.3	100	425.7	100	471.6	100	585.7	100	739.9	100

Table 9.6 — cont'd.

Bank name	1995 TA	%	1996 TA	%	1997 TA	%	1998 TA	%
Philippine National Bank	167.2	17.1	196.9	15.8	248.5	15.7	200.6	13.1
Bank of Philippine Islands	148.8	15.2	175.2	14.0	204.2	12.9	218.9	14.3
Metropolitan Bank & Trust Co.	175.5	18.0	223.9	17.9	273.2	17.3	290.3	18.9
Far East Bank & Trust Co.	90.7	9.3	123.8	9.9	157.1	9.9	136.5	8.9
Philippine Commercial Intl Bank	94.2	9.6	125.3	10.0	144.4	9.1	148.7	9.7
Rizal Commercial Banking Corp.	65.6	6.7	80.3	6.4	105.7	6.7	109.9	7.2
Equitable Bank	44.6	4.6	63.0	5.0	104.7	6.6	109.1	7.1
Prudential Bank	19.7	2.0	22.4	1.8	26.3	1.7	25.4	1.7
Solidbank	29.6	3.0	38.7	3.1	54.1	3.4	52.7	3.4
China Banking Corp.	33.1	3.4	46.4	3.7	70.0	4.4	57.1	3.7
Security Bank Corp.	27.4	2.8	40.8	3.3	59.1	3.7	55.6	3.6
Philippine Bank of Communications	16.3	1.7	23.1	1.8	31.6	2.0	34.5	2.3
Union Bank of the Philippines	32.7	3.3	49.8	4.0	54.1	3.4	46.2	3.0
The Philippine Banking Corp.	10.4	1.1	14.3	1.1	16.1	1.0	13.9	0.9
Philippine Trust Co.	12.9	1.3	15.3	1.2	19.3	1.2	21.5	1.4
Urban Bank, Inc.	8.1	0.8	10.1	0.8	12.2	0.8	11.9	0.8
Total	976.8	100	1249.3	100	1580.6	100	1532.8	100

Sources: Annual Audited Financial Statements submitted to the Securities and Exchange Commission and the Philippine Stock Exchange; *Investments Guide* 1996 and 1997, Makati City, Philippines: Philippine Stock Exchange.

Table 9.7 Ownership of 16 selected domestic commercial banks, 1998

Bank name	Group[a]	Group ownership %	Related party ownership %[b]
Philippine National Bank	1	48.9	48.9
Bank of Philippine Islands	3	44.7	46.5
Metropolitan Bank & Trust Company	2	11.2(?)	49.2
Philippine Commercial Int'l Bank	4,5	37.5	57.0
Far East Bank & Trust Co.	5,7	26.4	51.1
Rizal Commercial Banking Corporation	6	48.9	68.3
Equitable Banking Corporation	8	45.0	49.8
Prudential Bank		0.0	46.5
Solidbank		0.0	32.8
China Banking Corporation	6,7	19.4	33.5
Security Bank Corporation		0.0	22.7
Philippine Bank of Communications		0.0	37.3
Union Bank of the Philippines	9	38.5	61.4
The Philippine Banking Corporation		0.0	58.8
Philippine Trust Co.	10	46.6	59.2
Urban Bank, Inc.		0.0	54.7
Total		22.9	48.6

Notes:

a 1= Govt; 2= Ty; 3= Ayala; 4= Lopez (Benpres); 5= Gokongwei (JG Summit); 6= Yuchengco; 7= Sy; 8= Del Rosario; 9= Aboitiz; 10= Yap.

b Family domestic group company ownership, insider ownership, and affiliated company ownership.

Source: Accomplished SEC Form 11-A (Annual Report Pursuant to Section 11 of the Revised Securities Act and Section 141 of the Corporation Code) for the year ended 1998 submitted to the Securities and Exchange Commission and the Philippine Stock Exchange. Note that although the Accomplished SEC form is dated year ended 1998, some banks reported ownership data as of the first quarter of 1999.

The role of government and the market as corporate monitors

Regulations and oversight by a governmental agency are other means of certifying some sense of economic propriety by corporate groups. However, a weak Philippine bureaucracy has historically proved unable to ensure enforcement.[4] Problems such as low pay, inadequate training and corruption act to undermine regulators' ability to effectively monitor corporate activities. While regulation of the Philippine equity market is modelled after that of the United States, there is no commensurate enforcement, market liquidity and implementation of accounting standards (Saudagaran and Diga 1997). In addition, because the accuracy of financial statement reporting is questionable, transparency remains a problem. For example, Saudagaran

Table 9.8 Ownership percentages of the six *taipan* in commercial banks, end
1994

Family group	Commercial bank	Ownership
Yuchengco	Rizal Commercial Banking Corporation	24.8%
Tan	Allied Banking Corporation	None reported
Gokongwei	Far East Bank and Trust Co. Philippine Commercial International Bank	18.82% 23.4%
Ty	Metrobank and Trust Company	78%
Gotianun	East West Bank	80%
Sy	Banco de Oro China Banking Corp. Far East Bank and Trust Co. Philippine National Bank	Majority 14% 7%

Source: Rivera and Koike (1995).

and Diga report that in a study of forty-one developed and emerging markets, the Philippines has been shown to rank comparatively low in financial disclosure. They conclude that financial information availability, defined as that information being adequate, timely and conveniently accessible, is inferior in many emerging market countries (including the Philippines) compared with developed market countries. In addition, due to this limited transparency, market forces cannot be relied upon to monitor corporate managers.

Another problem that undermines the role of the market as an effective corporate monitor in the Philippines is the lack of legal protection.[5] Minority investors and other stakeholders typically have little legal recourse when majority investor-managers make decisions benefiting themselves at the expense of these other stakeholders. At the extreme, unchecked discretionary action by majority investor-managers can lead to breakdowns in an economic system. The severity of the effect on an economy depends on the extent of these managers' self-indulgence. According to Lamberte (1999), there were several cases in the Philippines in which management and controlling owners of corporations misused corporate assets (e.g. by expanding plant capacity without rigorous feasibility study, buying or establishing subsidiaries), often appropriating for themselves hefty salaries and bonuses despite deteriorating corporate financial conditions'.

Finally, there has been a historical lack of competition for domestic corporations (McCoy 1994). Part of this has been the result of restrictions applied to foreign corporations, discouraging or completely excluding these corporations from operating in the Philippines. In addition, the large, domestic family corporations have to a large extent avoided domestic competition. Governmental privilege has historically enabled corporate groups to dominate certain industries, either nationally or regionally, without facing threat of competition (McCoy 1994). Although the 1990s saw a plethora of reforms aimed at liberalising domestic markets, the current legal, regulatory and institutional framework for competition is highly diffused and weak in preventing anti-competitive behaviour' (Lamberte 1999).

In summary, it is imperative that governments build the right legal and institutional environments that will act to encourage good corporate governance practices. This environment can be further advanced by business leaders through self-regulation and the establishment of tough rules for transparency and disclosure.

CURRENT TRENDS

The previous analysis discussed possible shortcomings of the corporate governance system in the Philippines and how these shortcomings may have contributed to vulnerability to the regional economic crisis. In this section we discuss steps taken by the Philippine government, and evolution in the corporate governance system that may strengthen the Philippine corporate governance system and thereby reduce the country's vulnerability to future external shocks.

The Philippine government, starting with the Ramos administration from 1992 to 1998, has focused on economic liberalisation. Many of the protectionist policies implemented by prior administrations began to be reversed during this period. More recently, the Estrada administration has continued this liberalisation of commercial banking and foreign entry into many areas of the general economy. As part of these liberalisation measures, the central bank, Bangko Sentral ng Pilipinas (BSP), has focused on strengthening commercial banks by increasing capital requirements, promoting mergers and allowing foreign entry. For example, in March 1998, the BSP (through Circular No. 156) mandated commercial banks to increase their capital by 20 per cent for expanded commercial banks (to P5.4 billion) and by 40 per cent for regular commercial banks (to P2.8 billion) for compliance by the end of December 2000. These higher capital requirements resulted in capital infusions, and in some cases have motivated commercial banks toward mergers and acquisitions, as banks look for strategic partners to help increase their capital base. Several bank mergers have been announced or proposed in 1999 and this merger activity appears to be accelerating. For example, mergers have been completed between Equitable Banking Corporation and Philippine Commercial International Bank, Global Banking Corporation (a commercial banking arm of Metropolitan Bank & Trust Co.), and the Philippine Banking Corporation, Prudential Bank and Pilipinas Bank, and the Bank of the

Philippine Islands (BPI) and Far East Bank and Trust Co. (FEBTC). Market analysts expect the mergers and acquisitions frenzy to continue during the year 2000 (*Business World 2000*).

The BSP has offered other incentives for bank mergers. These include lengthening the allowable amortisation period and loan loss provisions for merged institutions, primarily in cases where the bank being acquired is financially troubled. The recently installed BSP Governor, Rafael B. Buenaventura, was quoted as saying that he foresees a future where there will only be four to six large domestic banks which, along with a few foreign banks, will control close to 80 per cent of the total resources of the banking system (*Business World* 1999). This larger asset base is thought to be a means of assisting commercial banks to compete regionally.

Industry restructuring is taking place in two important directions. First, the government has made the decision to exit the banking business, and plans to sell its interests in Philippine National Bank (PNB). It was announced on 16 August 1999 that PNB had started cleaning up its balance sheet by transferring some P260 million (US$6.6 million) worth of aviation assets to its holding arm (*Business World* 1999). This is expected to be a first step in readying PNB for privatisation in the year 2000. Second, many of the family domestic corporate groups are selling interests in the commercial banking business. Family corporate groups, such as those headed by Eugenio Lopez Jr., John Gokongwei and Henry Sy, have announced plans to sell their interests in major commercial banks, with the intention of focusing on core business within their corporate conglomerate. Motivation to sell may be based on increasing pressure for more transparency, discussion of higher taxes on certain segments of bank business, and restrictions imposed by higher capital requirements.

There has also been a trend towards allowing greater competition in the banking sector by foreign interests. In October 1994, the entry of foreign banks to operate in the Philippines was liberalised via Republic Act No. 7721. This Act allowed the entry of ten additional foreign banks, with each having rights to up to six branches. In addition, foreign banks are allowed to enter the Philippine market by purchasing up to 60 per cent of the voting stock of an existing domestic bank or setting up locally incorporated subsidiaries, up to 60 per cent of which may be foreign owned. Table 9.9 shows the trend from 1990 to 1998 towards an increase in the number of foreign commercial banks. As shown, there were only four foreign, compared with twenty-six domestic, commercial banks in 1990 (13.3 per cent of the total). These foreign commercial banks held less than 7.0 per cent of total deposits and had only 12 per cent of total assets. By the end of 1998, foreign commercial banks made up thirteen of fifty-three commercial banks (24.5 per cent of the total). The share of total deposits held by foreign banks increased to 8.5 per cent, and total assets increased to 15.2 per cent. Important aspects of this foreign competition are the high level of managerial professionalism and diverse ownership structure of these foreign banks that naturally encourage improved underwriting criteria and, in general, sounder

Table 9.9   Number, total assets and total deposits of foreign commercial banks and all commercial banks

Year	Foreign commercial banks			All commercial banks		
	Number	Total assets[c] (million pesos)	Total deposits[c] (million pesos)	Number[a,b]	Total assets[c] (million pesos)	Total deposits[c] (million pesos)
1990	4	66,613	22,610	30	553,331	325,169
1991	4	64,196	22,983	31	627,331	383,175
1992	4	63,705	26,043	32	735,856	452,511
1993	4	75,956	32,905	32	919,055	585,688
1994	4	86,522	42,073	33	1,133,283	726,201
1995	14	115,466	42,007	45	1,447,118	904,158
1996	13	202,977	51,680	49	1,925,529	1,140,606
1997	14	350,533	104,837	54	2,565,191	1,502,221
1998	13	387,734	134,244	53	2,555,877	1,586,094

Notes:
a Head Offices only.
b Includes three specialised government banks: Land Bank of the Philippines, Development Bank of the Philippines, and Al-Amanah Islamic Bank of the Philippines.
c For 1997 and 1998, the Supervisory Reports and Studies Office of the Bangko Sentral ng Pilipinas included the total assets and total deposits of ING Banking Group, Ltd., a branch of a foreign bank, in the domestic expanded commercial banks' total assets and total deposits, and excluded these from the total assets and total deposits of the foreign commercial banks. We adjusted these reported figures by adding the total assets and total deposits of ING Bank to the total assets and total deposits of the foreign banks category and deducting the same from the total of the domestic banks category. The figures for ING Bank's total assets and total deposits were obtained from the bank's published statements of condition as of 18 December 1997 and 24 December 1998 submitted by ING to the Bangko Sentral ng Pilipinas. For total assets these are P62,188 million for 1997 and P77,317 million for 1998, and for total deposits P1,882 million for 1997 and P6,060 million for 1998.

Sources: Figures for the years 1990–6 are from *The Philippine Financial System Fact Book 1996*, Supervisory Reports and Studies Office, Bangko Sentral ng Pilipinas; Figures for 1997 are from *Executive Highlights: The Philippine banking system*, 31 December 1997, Supervisory Reports and Studies Office, Bangko Sentral ng Pilipinas; Figures for 1998 are from *Executive Highlights: The Philippine banking system*, 31 December 1997, Supervisory Reports and Studies Office, Bangko Sentral ng Pilipinas.

banking practices. Kroszner (1998) argues that an increase in foreign bank penetration in emerging markets can generate a virtuous circle in that foreign banks tend to be less politically connected and less likely to be able to capture the regulatory authorities. In addition, they are less likely to succumb to pressure for directed lending by government'. We expect that the governance system of foreign banks will reduce relationship-style banking.

These trends are encouraging for the resolution of problems historically hindering the effectiveness of Philippine corporate governance. The combination of a stronger banking industry, separation of banking from industry and foreign competition may provide the opportunity for commercial banks to begin acting effectively as corporate monitors. In the future, commercial banks may have both the ability and incentive to evaluate lending applications better and, therefore, may have some influence over where funds are allocated through the economy. More importantly, a strong and independent banking system will be more resilient to future external shocks.

FUTURE ISSUES

All systems of corporate governance are constantly evolving. This dynamism is especially true for systems in emerging market economies. In the long run these changes may be expected as part of the natural progression faced by any emerging market economy. Often the catalyst for advances in corporate governance systems can be attributed to policy changes that derive from global influences and a changing political environment.

The increased emphasis on economic globalisation has been an important influence on changing the nature of corporate governance, where this globalisation has brought both increased foreign competition and opportunities. Regulatory impediments to foreign competition are fast being eroded in many areas by changing technologies. This reduces or even eliminates the effectiveness of any regulatory restrictions and forces economies to open markets to foreign competition. In addition, to take advantage of economic opportunities in other countries, trade agreements often stipulate reciprocal opportunities or open markets. Globalisation has induced additional exchange rate pressures; this often leads economies to introduce forms of economic liberalisation that result in more open markets and therefore competition.

The more open political environment in the Philippines has also been an important reason for the changes occurring in the country's corporate governance system. Economic growth has been increasingly emphasised, and reliance on economic liberalisation has been the focus of this emphasis. Economic problems resulting from a closed economic policy, crony relationships and government takeover of certain key companies have motivated this liberalisation.

The Philippine economic structure has seen some important recent changes that may improve its system of corporate governance by creating more efficient forms of corporate monitors. Bank liberalisation allowing increased foreign competition, the demand for higher capital requirements and improved enforcement of bank regulation provide banks with greater independence; this, in turn, may promote improved lending practices and reduce the prevalence of relationship banking. In fact, recent trends demonstrate that many of the large family corporate groups are choosing to leave the banking industry.

Little has been done on the enforcement side regarding accuracy in financial statement reporting. Governmental oversight bodies, such as the BSP, the Securities and Exchange Commission (SEC) and the PSE lack the ability or power to properly scrutinise the organisations they are mandated to supervise. A helpful step would be to arm these regulators with the information they need to evaluate banks, corporations and individuals. Therefore, mandates to improve transparency would help improve the ability of regulators to monitor effectively.

There are initial indicators of transparency advocacy. The BSP has implemented measures to improve transparency in the banking system and promote market discipline via a number of circulars and memoranda issued during 1998 (BSP 1998). These include, among others, requirements for banks to disclose in their published statements of condition certain information that serves as alternative measures of the risk position of banks' loans portfolios (for example, amount of non-performing loans and ratio to loan portfolio, amount of classified loans and other risk assets, general and specific loan reserves, current level of restructured loans with and without uncollected capitalised interest, and total allowance for probable losses). Other measures seem to be directed at reducing relationship-based banking and increasing the ability of BSP bank supervisors to detect abuses on loan limit by directors, officers, stockholders and related interests (DOSRI). Efforts to reduce relationship-based banking are: first, the requirement for banks to post within the bank's offices and branches relevant information related to interest on loans, and second, the requirement for any director, officer, stockholder or related interest to waive secrecy of their deposits if they borrow an amount in excess of 5 per cent of the capital and surplus of their bank, or the maximum amount permitted by law. Recently, a more recent BSP circular (No. 208, 17 August 1999) requires that, commencing in the year 2000, all banks (both PSE-listed and non-listed banks), include information about their DOSRI loans, and the ratio of these loans to their total loan portfolio, in the quarterly statements of condition which they must publish in local broadsheets. The new circular also mandates banks to inform the public on the amount of the DOSRI loans and advances that have become past due (*Business World* 1999).

Literature on the recent Asian financial crisis often cites regional contagion as the driving mechanism for the spread of the turmoil among the countries in the region, even to economies with relatively favourable economic fundamentals, such as the Philippines. We argue that a potential source of such contagion effect on the Philippines is the lack of sound corporate governance in Philippine corporations. The previous analysis of the Philippine corporate governance structure points to the lack of transparency and the absence of strong institutional and regulatory frameworks to invoke such transparency. In turn, these imperfections in the corporate governance system may hinder its evolution into a more effective system that may mitigate much of the vulnerability of the economy to future external shocks. Considering that, within the current corporate governance system, the government appears to have fewer conflicts of interest than the banking system or the market, there is a leading role for the government, whereby more timely and accurate information, greater transparency, and improved enforcement of regulation and laws are mandated. Such a role by the government is consistent with the rationale behind The Corporation Code of the Philippines which is to establish a new concept of business corporations so that they are not merely entities established for private gain but effective partners of the National Government in spreading the benefits of capitalism for the social and economic development of the Nation'.

We posit that increased and timely disclosure of material information by Philippine corporations will help mitigate adverse effects of any future regional economic crisis, by reducing information asymmetry between corporate stakeholders and controlling managers. This improved transparency will enable investors to make more informed decisions and therefore minimise over-reaction to economic shocks. We also believe improved transparency may broaden interest in stock ownership, which is expected in turn to create pressure for additional improvements in transparency, as well as improvements in legal protection for small investors. Liberalising rules for foreign ownership of domestic companies and foreign entry into the Philippine market may also bring economic benefits. Increased foreign ownership may reduce the influence of family groups and, in turn, change the management–shareholder relationship away from stable business relationships to a greater emphasis on firm performance. Foreign ownership will also create demand for a monitoring role, and as such create additional demand for improved transparency.

To conclude, as Wolfensohn, president of the World Bank says, If the rules of the game are not improved, economic growth will remain skewed to a small number of wealthy countries. Good corporate governance can make a difference by broadening ownership and reducing concentrations of power within societies. It bolsters capital markets and stimulates innovation. It fosters longer-term foreign direct investment, reduces volatility, and deters capital flight. Moreover, it is only when high corporate standards are adopted that the public will trust their savings to companies to provide their pensions. This is a daunting concern for countries with weak social-security systems.'

NOTES

1 This chapter is based on a paper presented at the International Conference on Reform and Recovery in East Asia: The Role of the State and Economic Enterprise held on 21–2 September 1999 at the Australian National University, Canberra, Australia. We thank Hal Hill, Peter Drysdale, Ponciano Intal Jr. and conference participants for helpful comments.

2 Wolfersohn (1998) defines corporate governance in a similar manner and highlights the importance of a strong system. Corporate governance has both internal and external dimensions. Internally, it refers to the checks and balances of power within a corporation; in particular between management, employees, the board of directors, shareholders, and debt holders. It affects how vast amounts of capital are raised, where that capital is directed, the concentration of market power in the economy, and how firms interact with the state. Equally important, however, is that corporate governance affects how we on the outside – shareholders, regulators, workers or citizens – are able to influence the conduct of these powerful actors in the global economy.'

3   Absolute control is considered to be ownership levels greater than 50 per cent, while effective control is considered as ownership levels greater than 20 per cent (LaPorta, Lopez-De-Silanes and Shleifer 1999).

4   This problem is not unique to the Philippines. Although Shleifer and Vishny (1997) surmise that most advanced market economies solve corporate governance problems at least reasonably well, the mechanisms necessary to solve corporate governance problems are often seriously flawed in less developed countries. For example, Barca (1995) and Pagano, Panetta and Zingales (1995) have shown that Italian corporate governance mechanisms are so undeveloped that the flow of funds is drastically impeded.

5   We define the legal rights of stockowners as (a) the right to vote (by mail or in person), (b) board composition (insider/outsider), (c) the right to sue corporations (class action lawsuits), and (d) the legal rights of creditors (bankruptcy laws).

REFERENCES

Alburo, F. (1998) Economic turmoil in Asia: Prospects for FDI flows', *The Philippine Review of Economics & Business* 35: 222–47.

Bangko Sentral ng Pilipinas (BSP) (1998) *Sixth Annual Report.*

Barca, F. (1995) On corporate governance in Italy: Issues, facts, and agency', unpublished manuscript, Rome: Bank of Italy.

Business World (1999, 2000) various issues, Manila: Business World Publishing Corporation.

Canlas, D. (1999) Banking risks, financial crises, and bank regulations in the Philippines', in D. Canlas and S. Fujisaki (eds) *Studies in Governance and Regulation: The Philippines*, Tokyo: Institute of Developing Economies.

Chaterjee, S. (1999) Lessons of the financial crisis: Case study of Indonesia', paper presented at the International Conference on Overview of Economic Crisis and Policy Options in Asia, Kyung Hee University, Seoul Korea, 20–1 April 1999.

Cheng, H.L. and Woodruff, C. (1998) Managing corporate distress in the Philippines: Some policy recommendations', Working Paper of the International Monetary Fund.

Corporate Governance in APEC: Rebuilding Asian Growth Symposium Report (1998) proceedings of a symposium held in Sydney, Australia, 1–3 November.

Dubiel, S. (1999) Corporate governance: Pushing ahead without best practices', *Economic Reform Today* 1: 14–7.

Fabella, R. (1998) Bubbles, monetary management and the Asian currency crisis', *The Philippine Review of Economics & Business* 35: 208–21.

Fukao, M. (1998) Japanese financial instability and weaknesses in the corporate governance structure', working paper, Keio University.

Garnaut, R. (1998) The financial crisis: A watershed in economic thought about East Asia', *Asian–Pacific Economic Literature* 12: 1–11.

Gonzalez, E. (1999) The crisis of governance in Asia: The long road for the Philippines', in *Reconsidering the East Asian Economic Model: What's ahead for the Philippines?*, E. Gonzalez (ed.) Pasig City: Development Academy of the Philippines.

Hesse, H. and Auria, L. (1998) The financial crisis in Southeast Asia: Causes and effects on the global economy', *Economics: A Biannual Collection of Recent German Studies* 57: 45–70.

Hutchcroft, P. (1998) *Booty Capitalism: The Politics of Banking in the Philippines*, Manila: Ateneo de Manila University Press.

Investments Guide (1997) Third Edition, Makati City, Philippines: Philippine Stock Exchange.

Kroszner, R. (1998) On the political economy of banking and financial regulatory reform in emerging markets', unpublished manuscript, Graduate School of Business, University of Chicago and NBER.

Lamberte, M. (1999) The Southeast Asian economic crisis and policy options: The Philippine case', paper presented at an international conference on Overview of Economic Crisis and Policy Options in Asia, Kyung Hee University, Seoul, Korea, 20–1 April 1999.

Lamberte, M. and Llanto, G. (1993) A study of financial sector policies: The Philippine case', Conference Proceedings, Asian Development Bank Conference on Financial Sector Development in Asia, Manila, Philippines, 1–3 September.

LaPorta R., Lopez-De-Silanes, F. and Shleifer, A. (1999) Corporate ownership around the world', *Journal of Finance* 54: 471–517.

Llave, R. (1997) The PSE: Quality as the banner towards the new millennium', in *Philippine Financial Almanac: 1997–1998 Edition*, Manila: Ventures Unlimited.

Mangaran, P. (1993) Arbitrage pricing theory and common stock returns', unpublished dissertation, University of the Philippines.

McCoy, A. (1994) *An Anarchy of Families: State and family in the Philippines*, Manila: Ateneo de Manila University Press.

Monks, R. and Minow, N. (1995) *Corporate Governance*, Massachusetts: Blackwell.

Pagano M., F. Panetta and L. Zingales (1998) Why do firms go public? An empirical analysis', *Journal of Finance* 53: 27–64.

Philippine Stock Exchange (1998) *Fact Book 1997*.

Reisen, H. (1998) Domestic causes of currency crises: Policy lessons for crisis avoidance', Technical Papers no. 136, OECD Development Centre.

Rivera, T.C. and Koike, K. (1995) The Chinese-Filipino business families under Ramos government', Institute of Developing Economies Joint Research Program Series no. 114.

Salda a, C. (1999) Philippine corporate governance environment and policy and their impact on corporate performance and finance', report submitted to the Asian Development Bank under RETA 5802: A Study of Corporate Governance and Financing in Selected Developing Member Countries, 19 October.

Saudagaran, S.M. and Diga, J.G. (1997) Financial reporting in emerging capital markets: Characteristics and policy issues', *Accounting Horizons*: 41–64.

Shleifer, A. and Vishny, R. (1997) A survey of corporate governance', *Journal of Finance* 52: 737–83.

Sicat, G. (1998) The Philippine economy in the Asia crisis', *ASEAN Economic Bulletin* 15: 290–6.

Sullivan, M. and Unite, A. (1998) Corporate governance, Philippine style: Who controls the ball?', *DLSU Business & Economics Review* 10: 31–8.

Symposium Report on Corporate Governance in APEC (1998) Rebuilding Asian Growth', Australian APEC Study Centre, December 1998.

Villacorta, W. (1999) The strategic implications of the Asian financial crisis: A Philippine perspective', paper presented at an International Conference on European Union, United States, and ASEAN: Exploring New Strategies for Cooperative Engagement in the 21st Century, Kuala Lumpur, September 1999.

Wolfensohn, J. (1998) A battle for corporate honesty', *The Economist: 1999 Annual*, London: The Economist Newspaper.

Yasay, P. (1997) Liberating the Philippine capital market', in *Philippine Financial Almanac 1997–1998 Edition*, Manila: Ventures Unlimited, Inc.

10 State-owned enterprise and bank reform in China: conditions for liberalisation of the capital account

Yiping Huang and Ligang Song[1]

INTRODUCTION

China's economic reform has been a process of redefining the relationship between the state and economic enterprises. In the pre-reform Chinese economy, the state was a direct administrator of economic enterprises through application of comprehensive economic plans. This resulted in huge technical and allocative inefficiency. The objective of reform was to improve economic efficiency and generate the momentum for growth. This was partly to be achieved through withdrawal of the state from commercial decisions and transformation of enterprises and banks into truly independent identities.

The transition of the Chinese economy has been slow but fruitful, compared with that of the European transitional economies. During the first twenty years of reform, real GDP growth averaged 9.5 per cent annually. The Chinese reforms have not only improved significantly the living standards of one-quarter of the world's population but also offered a useful model for other economies in transition.

Reforms in some areas have been less successful than in others, and two of the obviously less successful examples are the state-owned enterprises (SOEs) and the state-owned banks (SOBs). After twenty years of reform, SOEs are still trying to eliminate the soft-budget' problem and their financial position has deteriorated consistently (Huang 1999). SOBs suffer from serious weaknesses such as large non-performing loans, under-capitalisation and financial deficits (Lardy 1998). While the state sector now only accounts for about 30 per cent of the Chinese economy, it is responsible for nearly 80 per cent of total bank loans. Together, SOEs and SOBs are responsible for China's financial fragility, which not only reduces domestic efficiency but also holds considerable dangers for the whole economy should the capital market be opened to the outside world.

Capital market liberalisation has always lagged behind trade reform in China. This appears to be the preferred order of reform in the light of recent experiences in East Asia. Recent Asian experiences also show that successful reform of SOEs and SOBs must precede the liberalisation of the capital account (Garnaut 1998). China was fortunate to have capital account controls and other macroeconomic strengths when the East Asian financial crises began. Eventually, however, the capital account has to be liberalised in order to take full advantage of the international capital market and to allow China's deeper integration into the global economy. More importantly, time is very limited for China to implement such reform. Although capital controls were in place, capital flight through informal channels has been significant, almost similar or even greater than capital inflow (Sicular 1998; Li 1998).

The objective of this paper is to analyse the importance of SOE and SOB reform as an important condition for opening up the capital market and the necessary reform steps needed to meet this condition. The next section examines the changing relationship between the state and economic enterprises during the reform period. The third section discusses how that changing relationship contributed to the growing financial fragility in the Chinese economy. The fourth section explores the conditions for capital account liberalisation and requirements for further SOE and SOB reforms. The final section provides some concluding remarks.

REDEFINING THE STATE–ENTERPRISE RELATIONSHIP

Enterprises in pre-reform China were run like workshops of the state economy. The state determined the levels of production activities for individual enterprises, supplied all the inputs, including raw materials, capital and labour, and distributed all the outputs. All profits were remitted to the state while deficits were balanced from state budgets. The banking sector played only an insignificant role in the allocation of capital. There was only one bank, the People's Bank of China (PBC), which was responsible for the allocation of a small proportion of working capital. Other forms of financial institution did not exist.

When China embarked upon economic reform in the late 1970s, the improvement of SOE productivity and efficiency was seen as the key to success. The absence of autonomy and incentives was widely recognised as central problems of the pre-reform SOE institutions (Lin, Cai and Li 1999). Potential reform measures, however, had to satisfy one important pre-condition – to maintain the dominance of state ownership and the role of central plans. Reformist economists thus proposed to transform the SOEs from administrative units into independent economic identities' of the socialist economy (Xue 1981). Initial reforms thus focused on providing the SOEs with a degree of autonomy and incentives through limited modifications of the existing system.

SOE reform started first in Sichuan province when a handful of SOEs experimented with a program of expanded autonomy in 1978. This program was extended to a large number of SOEs all over China in the following years. The core of the program included profit retention, accelerated depreciation, freedom to sell above-plan output and the right to appoint middle-level management. By June 1980, about 6,600 SOEs, or 16 per cent of total industrial SOEs, were participating in this reform program. In 1981,

42,000 SOEs adopted the system of responsibility for profits and losses'. In May 1984, SOEs were allowed scope for independent decision making in production and output marketing; this policy was extended to fourteen areas in 1992.[2] To complement the reforms focusing on autonomy and incentives, the government also introduced two steps of tax for profit' reforms – the first in February 1983 and the second in September 1984. At the end of 1984, the loan for grant' reform was also announced. All state investment would henceforth be financed by loans from the state banking system rather than by grants from the state budget.

From the mid-1980s, it became increasingly clear that while the SOEs had begun to enjoy a degree of autonomy and incentive setting, accountability was not adequately imposed. Realisation of this missing ingredient prompted more radical reform proposals that would strengthen the link between enterprise performance and personal reward, for example, the contract system (Yang 1990), the shareholding system (Li 1987) and the asset responsibility system (Hua *et al.* 1986). Bankruptcy was also discussed as an important measure to improve the efficiency of SOEs at that time.

SOE reform in the second half of the 1980s was dominated by the contract responsibility system (CRS), although there were experiments with other reforms in a smaller number of SOEs. The contract system was favoured at that time, partly because of its maintenance of state ownership, and partly because of its success in the agricultural sector. Between 1986 and 1988, the proportion of SOEs implementing CRS rose from 6 per cent to 93 per cent. While the contracts varied in detail across industries and regions, they specified a set of mechanisms for the division of profits between the state and the enterprises, for distribution of wages and bonuses, and for technological innovation (Xu and Li 1996).

The contract system did not improve the performance of the SOE sector significantly. By the early 1990s, there were three main competing opinions on SOE reform. The first camp sought to transform the SOEs management mechanism by extending enterprise autonomy further (Zhou 1996). The second advocated the elimination of the social welfare functions of the SOEs so that they could compete with non-state firms on an equal footing (Lin, Cai and Li 1997). And the third viewed the solution as lying in the establishment of internal corporate governance through privatisation or divestiture (Wu 1993; Zhang 1997). These recommendations aimed at either strengthening the monitoring of the firm or improving enterprises' independent decision making, or both.

From 1994, the government adopted a new reform strategy of emphasising efficiency improvement in large SOEs and liberalising medium-sized and small ones. The shareholding system became the dominant institution for restructuring the SOEs during this third stage. The state would retain ownership of the largest 1,000 SOEs and used preferential policies to nurture them to critical production levels where economies of scale can (supposedly) be reached (World Bank 1996; Sachs and Woo 1997). While the definition of the size categories is vague, leaving room for different interpretations across administrative regions, the new strategy does provide the necessary incentives and autonomy for local governments to adopt different approaches. Even though discussions of privatisation by government officials are rare, a process of privatisation of small and medium-sized SOEs is now underway.

The reform period also witnessed a dramatic process of financial development and financial deepening. PBC became the central bank in charge of supervision of the financial system and coordination of the monetary policies in 1983. The state banking sector was gradually built around the four large SOBs – the Agricultural Bank of China (ABC), the Bank of China (BOC), the Industry and Commerce Bank of China (ICBC) and the China Construction Bank (CCB, formerly the People's Construction Bank of China). The rural and urban credit unions were transformed and consolidated. In the loan-for-grant' reform in 1983 and 1984, the government transferred its responsibility of supplying funds for SOEs from the state budget to the SOBs. Other financial institutions were also developed, including a number of insurance companies, the two stock exchange centres in Shanghai and Shenzhen and an increasingly active bond market. In 1994, the government established three new policy banks, the National Development Bank (NDB), the China Import–Export Bank (CEIB) and the China Agricultural Development Bank (CADB). Reform of the foreign exchange system started with the introduction of the dual-track policy. The official and secondary market rates were unified at the beginning of 1994 and, following that, free convertibility of the Chinese currency under the current account was realised in 1996. At the same time, a large number of foreign banks and other financial institutions entered the Chinese market.

Financial reform has been accelerated since the onset of the East Asian financial crisis. In order to improve independent monetary policy making, the provincial branches were replaced by the regional headquarters of the PBC. Supervision of financial institutions, in particular, was strengthened. The credit plan is being phased out, and bank managers have increasingly been given more autonomy in determining loan sizes and interest rates. A new accounting system was introduced in 1998 which classifies loans according to risk instead of size or type of borrower.

The previous SOE and SOB reforms focused on instituting new instruments to improve autonomy, incentives, responsibility and monitoring of enterprises and banks. State ownership was taken as a precondition of the reforms. That approach, unfortunately, failed to achieve its objectives. Though both enterprises and banks enjoy more autonomy and a better incentive structure, their decisions are still subject to restrictions imposed by government policy. Neither SOEs nor SOBs can easily dismiss redundant workers or dispose of redundant assets. Their managers are still appointed by the government, which forms a major barrier to commercialisation. For stability reasons, SOEs have to continue production even when they make losses and SOBs are burdened with policy loans even if projects are not financially viable. More importantly, because the state cannot monitor and manage effectively, responsibilities of enterprises and banks are difficult to enforce.

Changes in the relationship between the state and economic enterprises were gradual, but the directions were clear. Enterprises' autonomy is much greater than in the pre-reform period. According to a survey of 1,650 SOEs by the China Entrepreneurs Association in 1994, most of the surveyed firms enjoyed autonomy in production decisions, output pricing, output marketing, purchase of raw materials, wages and bonuses and internal organisation. The least satisfactory areas included scope to refuse unregulated levies, importing/exporting, amalgamation and acquisition, and disposing of redundant assets (Song and Wei 1996). The state still plays an important role in the banking sector. Only one small bank, Minsheng Bank, was founded by non-state organisations, and foreign banks are largely banned from RMB businesses. But gradually, managers of state banks gained a degree of autonomy in making lending decisions.

Outside the state sector, market mechanism quickly replaced the state plan in economic transactions. In 1978 when reform began, the state controlled 100 per cent of the total transactions relating to industrial production and 97 per cent of total retail sales. By 1990, these shares had fallen to 45 per cent and 31 per cent, respectively (Lau, Qian and Roland 1997). In the late 1990s, market channels handled more than 95 per cent of total commodity transactions. Bank loans which bear interest payments replaced budget grants as the major form of capital supply. Banks now account for about 85 per cent of China's total financial intermediation (Huang and Yang 1998).

The government made significant efforts to increase SOEs' and SOBs' financial independence and to eliminate the soft budget' problem. These efforts were clearly seen in the reform measures such as the responsibility system, the contract system and the shareholding system for the SOEs. But they were more amply demonstrated by two important reforms around the mid-1980s. One was the loan-for-grant' and the other the tax for profit' scheme. In line with the loan-for-grant' reform, SOEs have to apply for loans from the banks and pay interest, while following the tax for profit' reform, SOEs have to pay taxes like any other enterprise and losses are not automatically written off by the state.

GROWING FINANCIAL FRAGILITY

Assessments of China's SOE and SOB reforms have produced mixed results. Economists disagree on the productivity performance of the SOEs during the reform period, on the causes of the worsening financial conditions and on the direction of further reform (Huang, Woo and Duncan 1999).

Researchers have found an amazingly wide range of total factor productivity (TFP) growth rates. High TFP growth rates were estimated by a number of influential studies, including Chen *et al.* (1988), Jefferson *et al.*

(1992), Groves *et al.* (1994) and Perkins (1995). Most of these studies analysed adjusted input data or reconstructed input price indices. Meanwhile, there is also a growing body of literature finding insignificant or even negative productivity growth. These include researches by Xiao (1991) applying city level data in 1984–5, by McGuckin *et al.* (1992) employing National Industrial Census data for the period 1980–4, by Woo *et al.* (1994) on data from 300 SOEs and by Huang and Meng (1997) using a survey dataset of 967 SOEs covering the period 1985–90.

Leaving aside the controversies about productivity performance, economists agree that SOEs' financial performance deteriorated during the reform period. Following the loan-for-grant' reform, SOEs' debt–equity ratio rose dramatically from 23 per cent in 1980 to 367 per cent in 1997 (Table 10.1). Free capital was no longer available; even newly-established SOEs had to rely exclusively on bank loans. High liability-to-asset ratios are not a problem in themselves, but they become an important burden on enterprises' balance sheets when profitability is too low to cover interest payments.

While SOEs in aggregate made profits totalling RMB60–80 billion in the second half of the 1980s, they are making a net loss in the late 1990s.

An important feature of China's reform strategy has been to maintain the state sector but to facilitate the development of the non-state sector. The

Table 10.1 SOE financial performance and SOB policy loans

	Debt–equity ratio of SOEs (%)	SOE net profits (RMB b)	Total amount of policy loans (RMB b)	Share in total loans (%)
1980	23.0	n.a.	33.4	13.8
1981	n.a.	n.a.	43.2	15.6
1982	n.a.	n.a.	52.5	17.2
1983	n.a.	n.a.	56.9	16.6
1984	n.a.	n.a.	126.6	28.6
1985	n.a.	0.6	185.8	31.5
1986	n.a.	63.5	234.0	30.8
1987	n.a.	72.6	277.7	30.7
1988	122.2	81.0	328.7	32.1
1989	138.1	56.3	425.1	35.2
1990	140.4	3.9	545.9	37.0
1991	153.2	3.5	678.2	38.5
1992	159.7	16.6	741.1	35.2
1993	253.4	36.5	932.3	36.0
1994	301.6	34.6	1148.5	35.4
1995	287.6	12.5	1416.0	36.1
1996	354.5	-30.9	1644.0	34.7
1997	367.3		1986.2	38.1

Sources: Institute of Economics (1998); Huang (1999); and information directly collected from the People's Bank of China and the State Economic and Trade Commission.

government thus faces dilemmas in its reform. The state wants to transform all SOEs into independent and efficient enterprises on the one hand, but on the other hand, it cannot afford to bankrupt all the loss-making SOEs. In the financial sector, the ideal model is for SOBs to become true commercial banks, but the government appears unable to stop burdening them with policy responsibilities.

For reasons of ideology and social stability, the government usually steps in with fiscal subsidies or bank loans to save the sinking SOEs. The soft budget' problem persists and the SOEs have developed the unique behaviour of autonomy without discipline'. While there has been an expansion of enterprise autonomy, new disciplinary mechanisms were not put into place. In a centrally planned economy, enterprise disciplines are enforced by administrative controls (such as removal of managers) while in a market environment, competition rules (such as bankruptcy) are in place. The failure to institute new disciplinary mechanisms was reflected in the emphasis on the responsibilities' of the enterprises when introducing the contract system in the mid-1980s and the focus on monitoring' by the state when implementing the shareholding system in the mid-1990s.

As a result, SOEs evolved into insider-controlled firms, with the owner's (the state) interest largely ignored (Aoki 1995). The profit–capital ratio of SOEs fell sharply, from 17.7 per cent in 1985 to 0.7 per cent in 1995 and to −1.5 per cent in 1996. This is largely because SOEs continued their massive investment in fixed assets and paid substantial increases in wage bills. The value of SOEs' fixed assets grew at 16 per cent per annum in the period The loss-making SOEs have tended to destabilise the economy through two channels: the first was through the state budget and the second through the banking system. Direct subsidies to loss-making SOEs rose from RMB18.2 billion in 1988 to RMB84.4 billion in 1993. These represented 1.2 per cent and 2.4 per cent of GNP, respectively.

The behaviour and health of the banking sector were heavily influenced by SOE reform. In the loan-for-grant' reform of 1983 and 1984, the government transferred its responsibility for supplying funds to SOEs from the state budget to the SOBs. Reforms were also introduced to transform the SOBs into independent commercial banks. There has been no clear sign of the success of this reform as yet, as illustrated by lending decisions revealed by survey data (Table 10.2). Of the sample of 421 SOEs that applied for new investment funds from the banks in 1994, 200 were loss-making and 221 were profitable. There was almost no difference in approval rates and approved loan sizes between the loss-making and profitable enterprises.

The lack of risk assessment in lending decisions was partly due to the fact that SOBs are merely another set of SOEs – and managers thus care little about the value of banks' assets and the long-term development of the banks – and partly due to the implementation of government policy. During the reform period, fiscal capacity has declined in relative terms, with the share of budget revenue in GDP falling from 35 per cent in 1978 to 11 per cent in 1997. The government turned to the banks for financial resources. In the early 1980s, policy loans accounted for less than 20 per cent of total bank loans. In the 1990s, this proportion rose to nearly 40 per cent (Table 10.1).

The proportion of non-performing loans of the SOBs is understood to be very high, although comprehensive information is not available. According to one study, in early 1997, the proportion of non-performing loans was about 24 per cent and the proportion of bad debts was about 6 per cent (Li 1998).[3] According to another survey of SOEs, the average ratio of overdue debts to total debts increased from 24.5 per cent in 1991 to 31 per cent in 1995 (Table 10.3). The proportion of bad debts in this sample of SOEs was 6 per cent. Given that SOEs borrowed mainly from the SOBs and that more than 70 per cent of SOBs' loans are to the SOEs, these surveys confirm the high proportion of non-performing loans and bad debts in the SOBs. It is clear that most SOBs are technically insolvent.

Table 10.2 Investment funds applied for and approved by SOEs, 1994

	Number of sample SOEs	Investment funds applied for (RMB '000)	Proportion of approved loans (%)	Amount of approved loans (RMB '000)	Proportion of firms denied (%)	Net Value of fixed assets in 1994 (RMB '000)
Loss-making firms	200	14,941	47.9	6,061	22.1	25,146
Profitable firms	221	11,997	52.4	7,918	19.0	30,346
Total	421	13,393	50.2	7,037	20.5	27,880

Note: Information derived from a sample of 421 SOEs in six industries: food processing, textiles, building materials, chemicals, machinery and electronics.

Source: Survey data of the Chinese Academy of Social Sciences (Huang and Woo 1998).

Table 10.3 Overdue debt ratios of a sample of SOEs by province, 1991–5 (per cent of overdue loans to total loans)

	Jilin	*Sichuan*	*Hunan*	*Jiangsu*	*Total*
1991	33.3	21.9	27.6	15.8	24.5
1992	33.8	23.7	26.7	17.0	25.0
1993	36.6	26.3	27.4	15.7	26.3
1994	38.5	29.6	31.2	17.2	29.1
1995	42.6	31.5	31.2	18.9	31.0

Note: The total numbers of valid sample firms are 631 for 1991, 645 for 1992, 699 for 1993, 712 for 1994 and 711 for 1995. Sample firms were roughly equally distributed among the four provinces surveyed.

Source: Survey data by Yuan (1999).

The non-performing loan problem has been exacerbated by other weaknesses in the financial system. Although most of the SOBs' capital adequacy ratios reached the 8 per cent minimum requirement before the end of 1998 through the issuance of treasury bonds, a large proportion of bank assets are believed to be non-performing. All the four large SOBs, except PBC, made losses in recent years if uncollected interest payments are excluded from the revenue side of the financial reports. Supervision of financial institutions is both insufficient and unprofessional. The large international trust and investment corporations are on the edge of bankruptcy, partly illustrated by the recent closure of the Guangdong International Trust and Investment Corporation (GITIC) with US$4 billion outstanding debts.

PREPARING FOR CAPITAL ACCOUNT LIBERALISATION

Such a vulnerable domestic financial system would likely not survive the opening up of the capital market, especially if there was any kind of financial crisis. China successfully unified its dual exchange rate system in 1994 and realised RMB convertibility under the current account in 1996. It was planned to liberalise the capital account in 2000. The plan has recently been postponed indefinitely as the government realised that the many necessary conditions for capital account opening were still not in place (Song 1998). While free access to the international capital market is welfare enhancing in principle, the recent East Asian financial crises demonstrated that premature liberalisation of the capital account might be accompanied by negative results: banking crisis and capital flight.

SOBs suffer from heavy financial burdens (such as non-performing loans and non-performing assets), vaguely defined (state) ownership and frequent government intervention. Continuation of these conditions would disadvantage the SOBs in competition with new or foreign financial institutions in terms of interest rates, loan/deposit conditions and related services. As a result, good customers would leave but bad customers would stay. This adverse selection problem would lead to a rapid rise in the proportion of non-performing loans and the balance sheets would deteriorate dramatically.

During the past ten years, China has benefited from massive capital inflows, mainly in the form of foreign direct investment. But even in those years when capital account control was firmly in place, capital flight (mainly of domestic capital) through informal channels was a significant phenomenon (Sicular 1998; Li 1998). Removal of capital controls now would be almost certain to lead to accelerated capital flight given that growth prospects have dimmed in recent years, the default rate of financial institutions has increased, and the gap between domestic and US interest rates has widened.

A banking crisis and capital flight would have detrimental effects on the economy. Under a more optimistic scenario, living standards would fall sharply, while under a worst case scenario, the economy would collapse and many of the gains achieved during the reform period would be wiped out overnight.

Many studies have discussed a wide range of preconditions for liberalisation of the capital account. These fall into two broad categories: a stable macroeconomy and a healthy domestic financial system (Hanson 1995). A stable macroeconomy can be characterised by high economic growth, price stability, a healthy current account balance, sustainable fiscal deficits and moderate level of debt. Currently, China's macroeconomy can be regarded as healthy, as indicated by its relatively strong growth, current account surpluses, and reasonable levels of budget deficits and domestic/foreign debt. At the same time, there are many signs of problems – price deflation has persisted for almost two years; domestic demand is weak; there is a lack of investment demand, particularly from the non-state sector; and the current account has begun to deteriorate. A key to building a sound macroeconomy in China is to effectively stimulate the economy.

A more challenging task for China is to prepare its financial sector for capital market integration. To develop a well-disciplined financial system, both SOEs and SOBs need to be transformed into true commercial identities – an objective that the Chinese government has pursued in recent years but has yet to be achieved. This requires further reform of state–enterprise relations. There are four necessary steps to be taken for this purpose: resolving existing financial burdens, instituting new ownership arrangements, introducing private/foreign sector competition and strengthening supervision of enterprises and banks.

The first step is to clean up the existing financial burdens for the SOEs and SOBs. From 1996, the government allocated large amounts of funds from the budget every year to write off SOE bad debts. In 1999, it established four asset management companies to deal with bad loans (Bonin and Huang 2000). These are very important measures if SOEs are to become efficient enterprises. The obvious weakness of the current approach is that it only addresses the stock but not the flow problem of bad debts. While the existing non-performing loans can be reduced quickly by directly writing them off from the budget, debt–equity swaps, re-organisation of assets and sale of non-performing assets at discounted prices, new bad debts can accumulate quickly if the fundamental mechanism is not changed. As an important part of the strategy, the asset management corporations should take over not just the non-performing loans but the whole troubled SOE sector. If there is no clear-cut point, no distinction between good and bad customers, the deterioration of banks' balance sheets cannot be arrested. In order to manage non-performing loans, it is necessary to have an enforceable bankruptcy law, apart from the other three reform steps, to be discussed below.

The second step is to strengthen financial supervision of the enterprises, banks and other financial institutions. This will mainly be the responsibility of the PBC. China has taken the first steps in building an independent central banking system and introducing risk assessment mechanisms. Through close supervision, the emerging financial fragility can be eliminated, risky capital movement can be contained, and inefficient enterprises/banks can be disciplined before it is too late. The Chinese Government or the PBC will need to develop a series of indicators for monitoring performance and a set of measures to enforce financial discipline.

The third step is for the state to give up ownership rights to most of the state enterprises. This is the only way to eliminate the soft budget' problem and to build financially sound enterprise and banking sectors. The state must withdraw completely from any decision making at the enterprise level. In SOE reform, this has already started. The government is determined to relinquish a large number of small and medium-sized SOEs within a short period. This process has been delayed due to the current slowing down of the economy. For the large SOEs, reform measures are much more cautious, although the Chinese government abandoned the idea of conglomerates after learning the lessons of the East Asian crisis. The shareholding system is the dominant form of the so-called modern enterprise institution', but, on its own, it is not a guarantee of success. If the state controls the dominant holding of shares and the government body in control lacks the right set of skills and incentives, SOE performance will not improve. The most clear-cut approach is for the state to relinquish ownership of most SOEs. A new measure recently introduced is to convert the debts owed by SOEs to the state into shares. This might relieve the interest payments burden of enterprises in the short term but does not solve the more fundamental governance problem.

Ownership reform of the SOBs is perceivably more difficult. From early 2000, the first non-state bank, Minsheng Bank, will be officially listed on the stock market. Many OECD countries have accumulated a great deal of experience in privatising large corporations such as banks, and telecommunication, transportation and electricity utilities. Gradual privatisation of China's SOBs would also be a rational choice, although it looks highly unlikely at this stage. Only after the close relationship between the state and the banks is formally severed can the banks escape from the policy burdens imposed (such as policy loans).

The final step is to introduce more competition from the private and foreign sectors. It is true that the sudden introduction of massive competition might cause excessive damage to the SOEs and SOBs. But competition is an important measure to help enterprises and banks become efficient. The experiences of some Central European transitional economies show that the presence of foreign banks was the key reason for the improved efficiency of local banks (Bonin and Huang 2000).

In short, to prepare for capital account liberalisation, the state should withdraw from direct involvement in enterprise level decision making and play the important roles of guaranteeing fair competition and monitoring financial risks.

CONCLUDING REMARKS

China's economic reform has been remarkably successful, but enterprise and bank reforms are perhaps two exceptions. SOE and SOB reforms have focused on repositioning the state–enterprise relationship while maintaining state ownership. In the end, full autonomy cannot be realised and responsibilities cannot be enforced. Now SOEs and SOBs represent the major sources of inefficiency and financial risk in the Chinese economy.

China's financial situation was no less fragile than in the crisis-affected East Asian economies, but China avoided the financial crisis primarily because of its strict capital account control and healthy macroeconomic conditions. The domestic financial system was not susceptible to uncertainties of the international capital market and attacks by international speculators.

Capital account control, however, imposes significant welfare costs on the Chinese economy by restricting access to the international capital markets by enterprises and households. Eventually China will need to liberalise the capital account and realise free convertibility of the RMB, particularly in light of China's strong interest in active participation as an important world economic power in international organisations such as the International Monetary Fund (IMF) and the World Trade Organisation (WTO).

But to liberalise the capital account, China has to follow the proper order of reform, as demonstrated by the recent East Asian financial crisis. It must first meet two preconditions: a sound macroeconomy and a healthy financial system.

China needs to take four necessary steps to prepare the SOEs and SOBs for opening up of the capital market. They are: cleaning up the existing financial burdens such as non-performing loans and assets, instituting more effective ownership arrangements such as privatisation, gradually introducing market competition including that from foreign enterprises and banks, and strengthening financial supervision of enterprises, banks and other financial institutions.

China's past reform followed a gradual approach. While some of the above steps may be taken at a faster pace than others, it is likely that a gradualist approach will be adopted in opening the capital account. But reforms in other areas, including China's accession to the WTO, will certainly create pressures for faster capital market liberalisation.

NOTES

1   This chapter is based on a paper prepared for the international conference Reform and Recovery in East Asia: The Role of the State and Economic Enterprise, 21–2 September 1999, Australian National University, Canberra. The authors benefited from earlier discussions with Fang Cai, Wing Thye Woo and Yongzheng Yang and detailed comments by Ron Duncan, Peter Drysdale and Ross Garnaut. The usual caveats apply.

2   The 14 areas specified by the government in 1992 included SOEs' right to make production decisions, output pricing, output marketing, raw material purchase,

importing/exporting, investment decisions, allocation of retained funds, disposition of redundant assets, amalgamation and acquisition, worker employment, personnel management, wages and bonuses, internal organisation and refusing non-regulated levies (Zhang 1996).

3   In the Chinese system, non-performing loans consist of three types: loans overdue (loans not repaid when due or not repaid after extension of the due date), loans of concern (loans that have been overdue for more than two years or where operation of the project has been stopped) and bad debts (loans that have not been repaid after the enterprises' bankruptcy or liquidation) (Bonin and Huang 2000).

REFERENCES

Aoki, M. (1995) Controlling insider control: Issues of corporate governance in transition economies', in M. Aoki and H. Kim (eds) *Corporate Governance in Transition Economy: Insider control and the role of the banks*, Washington, DC: World Bank.

Bonin, J. and Huang, Y. (2000) Dealing with bad loans of the Chinese banks', paper prepared for the American Economics Association annual conference, 7–9 January, Boston.

Chen, K., Wang, H., Zheng, Y., Jefferson, G., and Rawski, T. (1988) Productivity change in Chinese industry: 1953–85', *Journal of Comparative Economics* 12(4): 570–91.

Garnaut, R. (1998) Economic lessons', in R. Mcleod and R. Garnaut (eds) *East Asia in Crisis: From being a miracle to needing one?*, London: Routledge.

Groves, T., Hong, Y., McMillan, J. and Naughton, B. (1994) Autonomy and incentives in Chinese state enterprises', *Quarterly Journal of Economics* 109(1): 183–209.

Hanson, J.A. (1995) Opening the capital account: costs, benefits, and sequencing', in Sebastian Edwards (ed.) *Capital Controls, Exchange Rates and Monetary Policy in the World Economy*, Cambridge: Cambridge University Press.

Hua, S., Zhang, X. and Luo, X. (1986) Restructuring the microeconomic foundation: further on issues and thoughts of China's further reforms', *Economic Research Journal* 3.

Huang, Y. (1999) State-owned enterprise reform', in R. Garnaut and L. Song (eds) *China: Twenty years of reform*, Canberra: Asia Pacific Press.

Huang, Y. and Meng, X. (1997) China's Industrial Growth and Efficiency: A comparison between the state and the TVE sectors', *Journal of the Asia Pacific Economy* 2(1): 101–21.

Huang, Y. and Yang, Y. (1998) China's financial fragility and policy responses', *Asian–Pacific Economic Literature* 13(2): 1–13.

Huang, Y. and Woo, W. (1998) Free to lose', China Economy Paper 98/1 Research School of Pacific and Asian Studies, Australian National University, Canberra.

Huang, Y., Woo, W.T. and Duncan, R. (1999) Understanding the decline of China's state sector', *MOCT-MOST: Economic Policy in Transitional Economies* 9(1): 1–15.

Institute of Economics, Chinese Academy of Social Sciences (1998) Aggregate trend, financial risk and external shocks: Analyses of the current Chinese macroeconomic situation', *Economic Research Journal [Jingji Yanjiu]* 3: 3–14.

Jefferson, G.H., Rawski, T., and Zheng, Y. (1992) Growth, efficiency, and convergence in China's state and collective industry', *Economic Development and Cultural Change* 40(2): 239–66.

Lardy, R.N. (1998) *China's Unfinished Economic Revolution*, Washington DC: The Brookings Institution.

Lau, L., Qian, Y. and Roland, G. (1997) Reform without losers: An interpretation of China's dual-track approach to transition', Working Paper 97-048, Department of Economics, Stanford University.

Li, X. (1998) Looking at China's potential financial risks from the East Asian financial crisis: Analyses of the assets operation of the state-owned commercial banks', *Reform* 3: 31–39 and 86.

Li, Y. (1987a) *Exploration of Economic System Reform*, Beijing: People's Daily Press. (1997b) Capital flows of the Chinese economy in the process of opening up', *Economic Research Journal* 2: 14–24.

Lin, J.Y., Cai, F. and Li, Z. (1997) *Perfect Information and State Enterprise Reform*, Shanghai: Shanghai Sanlian Bookstore and Shanghai People's Press.

Lin, J.Y., Cai, F. and Li, Z. (1998) Fair competition and China's state-owned enterprise reform' *MOCT–MOST Economic Policy in Transitional Economies* 9(1): 61–74.

McGuckin, R.H., Nguyen, S.V., Taylor, J.R. and Waite, C.A. (1992) Post-reform productivity performance and sources of growth in Chinese industry: 1980–85', *Review of Income and Wealth* 38(3): 249–66.

Perkins, F. (1995) Productivity performance and priority for the reform of China's state-owned enterprises', *Journal of Development Studies* 32(2): 414–44.

Sachs, J. and Woo, W.T. (1997) Understanding China's economic performance', NBER Working Paper 5935, Cambridge, MA.

Sicular, T. (1998) Capital flight and foreign investment: Two tales from China and Russia', *The World Economy* 21(5): 589–602.

Song, L. (1998) China', in R. McLeod and R. Garnaut (eds) *East Asia in Crisis: From being a miracle to needing one?* London and New York: Routledge.

Song, T. and Wei, X. (eds) (1996) *Multi-Dimensional Thinking on Promoting State Enterprise Reform by 40 Economists*, Beijing: Economics Science Press.

Woo, W.T., Wen, H., Jing, Y. and Fan, G. (1994) How successful has Chinese enterprises reform been? Pitfalls in opposite biases and focus', *Journal of Comparative Economics* 18: 410–37.

World Bank (1996) *World Development Report 96: From plan to market*, Oxford: Oxford University Press.

Wu, J. (1993) *Large and Medium Size Enterprise Reform: Establishing modern enterprise institutions*, Tianjin: Tianjin People's Press.

Xiao, G. (1991) Managerial autonomy, fringe benefits, and ownership structure: a comparative study of Chinese state and collective enterprises', *China Economic Review* 2(1): 47–73.

Xu, Z. and Li, L. (1996) *Management History of China's Publicly Owned Enterprises, second volume (1966–1992)*, Shanghai: Shanghai Academy of Social Sciences Press.

Xue, M. (1981) *China's Socialist Economy*, Beijing: Foreign Language Press.

Yang, P. (1990) *Contracting System: Inevitable choice of enterprise development*, Beijing: China Economy Press.

Yuan, G. (1999) Nonperforming debts of the state-owned enterprises in China', paper presented at the 11th Annual Conference of the Association for Chinese Economic Studies, 15–16 July 1999, Melbourne.

Zhang, W. (1997) Decision rights, residual claims and performance: A theory of how Chinese state enterprise reform works', *China Economic Review* 8(1): 67–82.

Zhang, Z. (1996) Promoting reform of the state-owned enterprises through understanding coordination, scientific planning and multiple-experiment', in T. Song and X. Wei (eds) *Multi-Dimensional Thinking on Promoting State Enterprise Reform by 40 Economists*, Beijing: Economics Science Press.

Zhao, J. (1998) Review of foreign economy and trade in 1997 and prospects for 1998', in H. Ma (ed.) *Economic Situation and Prospect of China*, Beijing: China Development Press.

Zhou, S. (1996) China's enterprise reform and industrial development', in T. Song and X. Wei (eds) *Multi-Dimensional Thinking on Promoting State Enterprise Reform by 40 Economists*, Beijing: Economics Science Press.

11 Governance in the city-states: Hong Kong and Singapore[1]

Cheng Yuk-shing, Chia Siow Yue and Christopher Findlay

INTRODUCTION

In the 1980s and first half of the 1990s, the determinants of the East Asian miracle were a matter of active debate as academics and policy analysts tried to understand the phenomenon and determine its sustainability and replicability. Neoclassical development economists interpreted the region's success in terms of the efficiency of the market mechanism and economic policies emphasising openness and private enterprise. The World Bank's 1993 study highlighted the importance of getting policies right'. Statists drew a different conclusion, explaining the East Asian success in terms of effective state intervention and good governance'.

The era of high growth in East Asia came to an abrupt halt in July 1997 when, starting with Thailand, country after country succumbed to a currency and financial crisis which deepened into an economic crisis. In explaining the crisis, analysts and critics pointed to poor governance as one important factor in the origin of these problems, and the International Monetary Fund (IMF) rescue packages adopted by Thailand, South Korea and Indonesia included structural and institutional reforms partly aimed at improving governance.

Hong Kong and Singapore were also affected by the crisis, one less than might have been expected and the other more so. We examine some aspects of the governance issues in these two city-state economies. The next section summarises the recovery from the crisis in Singapore and Hong Kong.[2] This is followed by an examination of some of the components of governance in Singapore to help explain why that economy succumbed to a lesser degree to the financial and economic crisis than most economies around it. The Hong Kong experience is interesting in comparison, since the Chinese economies around it performed much better than the Southeast Asian economies around Singapore. The fourth section reports in more detail on critical policy choices made in Hong Kong in response to the crisis, and identifies some factors which exaggerated the impact of the crisis on that economy. The final section summarises the results of the comparison.

IMPACT OF THE REGIONAL CRISIS ON SINGAPORE AND HONG KONG

Singapore grew rapidly in the 1990s. The average real GDP growth was 9 per cent in the 1990–7 period, leading to higher per capita GNP – the fourth highest in the world – low poverty incidence and a low unemployment rate.

The Singapore economy had remained buoyant up to the first quarter of 1998, with a GDP growth rate of 8.0 per cent for 1997 and 6.2 per cent for that quarter. The regional contagion and the global electronics cycle, however, saw growth plummet to 1.6 per cent by the second quarter of 1998 and turn negative in the third and fourth quarters. In addition to a fall in external demand, domestic consumption weakened in the face of plunging stock and property prices, falling incomes and job retrenchments. Excess capacity, economic uncertainties and tight liquidity affected investment. Despite the negative growth in the second half of 1998, GDP growth for the year averaged a positive 1.5 per cent (Figure 11.1).

Recovery in Singapore was relatively rapid. By the first quarter of 1999, the economy had returned to positive growth, with GDP growth rate recovering to 1.3 per cent in the first quarter and 6.7 per cent in the second.

Anyone reviewing the macroeconomic performance of the Hong Kong economy, even as far back as 1983 to just before the crisis, would also have been struck by the high growth rate (just over 6 per cent) and the low unemployment rate (less than 2 per cent).[3] Yet compared with Singapore, the Hong Kong experience is one of a deeper slump in growth after the crisis and a slower recovery. Part of the reason was the speculative bubble in the property and stock markets that formed in the lead-up to the handover of sovereignty to China in mid-1997. The Hong Kong quarterly growth

Figure 11.1   Real GDP quarterly growth, Singapore (year on year, per cent)

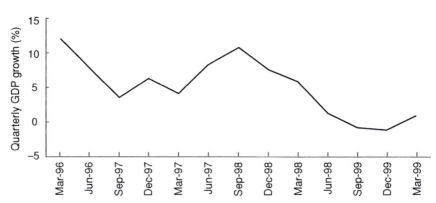

Source. International Economics Database, Australian National University.

experience is summarised in Figure 11.2. At one point, the year-on-year growth dropped to –6.9 per cent in the third quarter of 1998. Growth in Hong Kong only turned positive again after the second quarter of 1999.

One interest in this chapter is the origins of the differences in performance. Factors might include circumstances in their trading partners, their size and character or their stage of development. The impact of the crisis on the surrounding economies appears not to be the source of the difference. Singapore, located in ASEAN, has intense economic relationships with economies affected very deeply by the crisis. Hong Kong is located closer to Northeast Asia. Its neighbours were less affected or appeared to be recovering more rapidly.

Both economies are city states, so the issue of dealing with tiers of governments does not arise as a potential source of difference. Instead, they share common issues in their relationships with their hinterlands. Both are also at similar stages of development and face similar development challenges, including the transition to new roles as their neighbours take over labour-intensive manufacturing processes.

Our focus is on macroeconomic policy choices where there are significant differences, particularly with respect to exchange rate management and associated macroeconomic variables. Figure 11.3 shows the movement in the nominal exchange rate in Singapore since 1996. The real effective rate (that is, trade weighted and adjusted for change in prices) shows much less variation than the nominal rate when plotted over the same range, and some appreciation in the first half of 1999. In Hong Kong, the nominal exchange rate with respect to the US dollar was held fixed. This put more adjustment pressure on other macroeconomic variables. Internal prices had

Figure 11.2   Real GDP quarterly growth, Hong Kong (year-on-year)

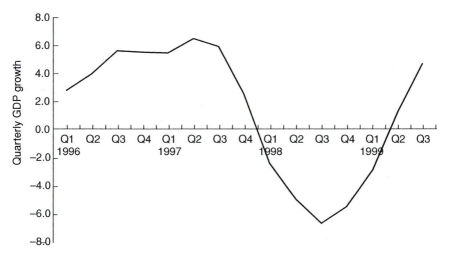

Source: Homepage of Hong Kong's Census and Statistics Department (http://www.info.gov.hk/censtadt/eindex.htm).

to fall to restore competitiveness and, as shown Figure 11.5, Hong Kong's inflation rate fell deeply after the outbreak of the Asian crisis and has been negative since the end of 1998. One set of issues therefore relates to the choice of adjustment mechanism. Another relates to the manner in which the chosen mechanism was actually implemented. We explore these points with reference to the experience of both economies.

POLICY RESPONSES TO THE CRISIS: SINGAPORE

Krause (1987) notes that Singapore has an unusual combination of dirigiste and free trade; this apparent inconsistency reflects a combination of small size, the historical tradition of an entrep t and the views of its political

Figure 11.3   Nominal exchange rate, Singapore ($S per $US as index)

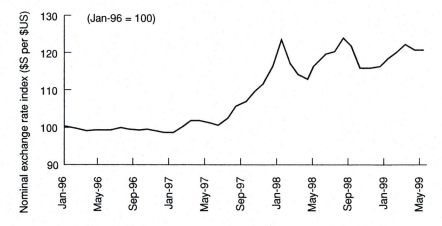

Source: International Economics Database, Australian National University.

Figure 11.4   Real effective exchange rate, Singapore ($S per $US as index)

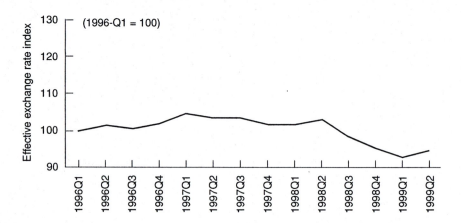

leaders. These features of the economy helped Singapore to escape the full brunt of the East Asian contagion. Its sound fundamentals also reflect one aspect of good governance, efficient and prudent economic management.[4]

In this context, the response to the crisis was not surprising. The Singapore monetary authorities did not intervene in the capital market, although there are some regulatory arrangements affecting capital movements. Singapore continued to allow free capital flows and encourage foreign investments. As the 1998 economic recession was caused largely by the sharp fall in regional demand for goods and services and by the fall in global demand for electronics, and in view of the high import leakage, domestic demand stimulus was largely eschewed. Instead, government policy measures chose to focus on international competitiveness. As we discuss in more detail below, the exchange rate continued to be managed against a trade-weighted basket, albeit with greater flexibility around an undisclosed band, to try to maintain external competitiveness.

Another element of the Singapore response was cost cutting and tax relief to reduce the operating costs of business enterprises so as to help offset the loss in competitiveness posed by the massive depreciation of regional currencies. These responses also helped lower the living costs of individuals and households in the face of falling incomes and job retrenchments.[5] A major feature of the cost-cutting measures was the cut in wages and benefits. The 20 per cent compulsory Central Provident Fund (CPF) contribution by employers was halved and there was also a 5–8 per cent wage cut recommended by National Wages Council (NWC); together they amounted to a reduction in wage costs of businesses of some 15 per cent. Other elements of the cost-cutting package included lower tariffs and user charges of government agencies and tax rebates for businesses and individuals.

Figure 11.5 Composite Consumer Price Index, Hong Kong

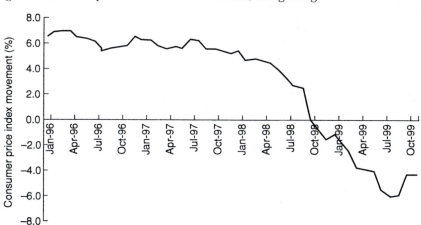

Source: Homepage of Hong Kong's Census and Statistics Department (http://www.info.gov.hk/censtadt/eindex.htm).

Exchange rate policy

The main issue confronting the management of the exchange rate was to reconcile Singapore's ambitions to extend its entrep t role to financial markets and the desire to reduce the risks faced by business in markets for foreign exchange.

The colonial currency board system was retained after political independence to ensure monetary discipline, with the Singapore dollar backed fully by external reserves and fiduciary issues disallowed.[6] The Currency Board issues and redeems currency, while the Monetary Authority of Singapore (MAS) performs other central banking functions.[7] Capital inflows expanded the currency base and subsequently the money supply. Thus, changes in the money supply depend on net capital inflows and on MAS open market (swap) operations in the foreign exchange market to limit the extent of the appreciation of the Singapore dollar. The money supply emerges as a result of exchange rate targeting. Monetary policy is focused on maintaining price stability to secure sustained economic growth. Montes and Tan (1999) note that Singapore's three circumstances of an open trading system, capital mobility, and fiscal surpluses and CPF savings have influenced the objectives, implementation and outcomes of monetary policy, constraining the roles of domestic open market operations, reserve requirement variations, and discount rate variations.

Singapore has been on a managed floating regime since June 1973. All exchange controls were lifted in 1978. Financial liberalisation measures over the years have resulted in almost perfect capital mobility and boosted foreign exchange, money and capital market transactions.[8] The exchange rate policy objective is to achieve a low inflation rate and a strong and stable Singapore dollar. The MAS intervenes in the foreign exchange market to keep the exchange rate within an undisclosed target band. In response to the increased volatility and uncertainty of financial markets, the band within which the Singapore dollar can fluctuate was widened in 1998 (*Economic Survey* 1998). The subdued inflationary environment has also allowed the MAS to manage the exchange rate more flexibly. As evident in Figures 11.3 and 11.4, under this policy, the Singapore dollar weakened against the US dollar, appreciated against most currencies in the region and appreciated slightly against the trade-weighted basket of currencies.

Financial centre development

Since the early 1970s Singapore has sought to develop the financial sector as a key industry in addition to its supporting role in domestic financial intermediation. The Singapore financial centre is dominated by offshore banking. Various incentives have been given to develop Asian Currency Units (ACUs) that deal in the offshore Asia Dollar Market. These incentives include various tax concessions and exemptions from reserve and liquid asset ratios. As of 1997, ACU assets, denominated largely in US dollars, stood at US$479 billion, an amount much larger than the value of assets of the onshore domestic banking system. There is free convertibility of deposits between local and foreign currencies. With interest arbitrage, domestic interest rates are determined largely by foreign interest rates and expectations on the exchange rate. Following the abolition of exchange control in 1978, Singapore residents are free to lend or borrow in ACUs in all currencies except the Singapore dollar. A strong Singapore dollar and balance of payments position and low domestic inflation have moderated fund-switching. Also, exchange rate flexibility allowed changes in the flow of funds to be accommodated through the exchange rate rather than the domestic interest rate.

Various policies have been introduced to insulate the domestic economy from the financial centre's offshore activities. ACUs are strictly demarcated from the banks' domestic operations under domestic banking units (DBUs), enabling the official monitoring of the use of ACU funds, especially the extent to which they are lent to domestic operations. ACU activities are confined to non-Singapore dollar transactions, whereas DBUs are able to engage in foreign currency transactions. The MAS imposes an upper limit on ACUs but not on DBUs, except for banks with restricted and offshore licences whose domestic activities are confined mainly to wholesale banking. Tax and regulatory measures favour ACUs, so banks find it more profitable to book a large part of their business through ACUs rather than DBUs. Foreign residents also prefer to deal with ACUs because of the absence of withholding tax on interest and because of the exemption from Singapore estate and stamp duties.

The Singapore authorities discourage the internationalisation' of the Singapore dollar – lending to non-residents in Singapore dollars is restricted, requiring MAS approval for loans exceeding S$5 million to non-residents or to residents where the Singapore dollar is to be used outside Singapore. Their view is that internationalising the Singapore dollar would make it vulnerable to speculation by international market participants. Montes and Tan (1999) also observe that internationalising the Singapore dollar would make it more difficult for MAS to achieve its objective of price stability and non-inflationary growth. In any case, given the small size of the economy and money supply, Singapore would be hard pressed to meet the funding needs of the region.

There appears to be some relaxation of this restriction on external capital transactions. On 15 October 1996 the Singapore Finance Minister announced a major policy change – as part of the efforts to promote the Stock Exchange of Singapore (SES) and the fund management industry, some forty foreign-currency denominated stocks on SES could apply, subject to certain criteria, to have Singapore-dollar listing. Foreign shareholdings were also allowed in stockbroking firms (*Business Times*, 16 October 1998).

The parameters of the pursuit of Singapore's ambitions as a financial sector and the development of its own financial market have been constrained by its own fiscal policy. Singapore has pursued prudent fiscal policy over many years. The government has had consistent current (operating) as well as overall (operating and development) surpluses since 1975. However, the seven major statutory boards have consistent current surpluses but overall deficits due to high capital expenditures, so that the overall public sector budget has been in deficit. But Singapore is not dependent on external borrowings. Development expenditures are financed from government savings and domestic borrowings. With government spending heavily oriented towards capital projects, the size of intergenerational transfer appears high. The control on fiduciary issues imposes fiscal discipline. The 1993 constitutional amendment, creating an elected president, further constrains the ability of an elected government to use the country's accumulated official reserves to finance budget deficits. Reflecting the demographic structure, annual contributions to the CPF exceed withdrawals. Government surpluses and net contributions to the CPF result in a continual drain of domestic liquidity which is offset by the foreign exchange intervention of the MAS.

Banking supervision and financial market regulatory reform

The regional financial crisis demonstrated that financial liberalisation should be buttressed by a sound domestic financial system and a regulatory framework that both promote high standards of financial and corporate governance. Singapore's financial system is generally sound. There is no deposit insurance (except Post Office Savings Bank deposits guaranteed by the government), but the MAS exercises strict prudential regulation and supervision. Montes and Tan (1999) note that Singapore's financial framework provides explicit walls between different kinds of financial institution and activity. There is a variety of legislation, each element of which contains provisions empowering the MAS to act in areas such as management oversight, capital adequacy, regulation of portfolio and equity, and regulation of offshore markets. This arrangement is not costless: extensive prudential regulation and supervision increases the cost of intermediation as well as the extent of moral hazard.

Details of recent changes in rules applying to banking supervision and of other regulatory reforms in Singapore are reported in the Appendix. Singapore's financial centre has grown in breadth and depth, establishing a wide range of financial markets and services which include commodity trading, futures contracts on goods and financial indices and derivatives. In view of the rapid pace of globalisation and technological change, and market concerns that over-regulation had dampened Singapore's development as a financial centre, particularly *vis-à-vis* the more *laissez faire* Hong Kong, the authorities embarked on a major review of policies pertaining to the regulation and development of Singapore's financial sector in late 1997. The results included moves to a more competitive banking market, a shift in regulation towards assessing asset quality and risk management systems, and actions that led to the development of insurance and funds management industries.

Montes and Tan (1999) highlight some implications of these policy changes. Earlier MAS discipline had obviated the need for detailed public financial disclosure by financial institutions. The reason was that an enormous amount of information about the operations of banks and financial institutions was collected by the MAS and its professional team exercised their discretionary powers within the regulatory framework, contributing to a sound financial system. Following the policy change, financial institutions will have to provide the market with better disclosure of information, such as earnings from different bank activities, and the extent of exposure to and provisions for non-performing loans (NPLs).

Corporate governance

The regional financial crisis demonstrated the need for high standards in corporate behaviour as well as high standards in banking. High-profile business collapses and scandals have raised demands for better stewardship, greater accountability, more skilled risk management, improved codes of conduct and more ethical behaviour. Increased emphasis is now placed on independence of directors to ensure fairness and limit opportunistic abuse by directors. Good corporate governance depends not only on regulations and compliance; it requires the directors to act in the best interests of shareholders and to ensure that business is undertaken responsibly and with integrity.

Transparency and accountability are the pillars of good corporate governance. Transparency is a state of affairs in which organisational goals, standards and decision-making processes in the boardroom are open for review. It is critical to the ethics of the corporation and to the efficient functioning of the capital market on which corporations depend for funds. For accountability of decisions, the board must be self-monitoring and structured such that individuals have direct responsibility over various aspects of the corporation. Accountability is exercised at the annual general meeting, where owners are given a chance to question the board on its handling of the affairs of the company; the annual election process ensures board directors are re-appointed according to how they have served the shareholders' interests.

Phan and Mak (1999) note that corporate governance in practice and philosophy is still relatively underdeveloped in Singapore compared with the United States and the United Kingdom. There is a lower quality of publicly available corporate information in Singapore, even though the Singapore system is based loosely on the Anglo-American model. This deficiency is linked to lack of a regulatory structure (in particular, until recently, the lack of strictly applied accounting standards). One consequence of this situation has been the thin equity capital market, with only about 300 companies listed on the SES main-board. Even among listed companies, equity is tightly held by Singapore investors (government, institutions and individuals), and there are few takeovers. Those that do occur tend to be friendly rather than hostile. In turn, the lack of depth in the equity market has not helped promote the development of better corporate governance.

Some regulatory reform has occurred. Even so, it was only in recent years that the issue became more prominent with the addition of Chapter 9B to the SES Listing Manual aimed at raising the standard of corporate governance among listed companies. Chapter 9B highlights the role of the audit committee, but the provisions were widely regarded as too demanding and rigid. Chapter 9B was removed, and some of the requirements transferred to the revised Chapter 9 of the Listing Manual, while many requirements on the audit committee remained in the Companies Act. In place of Chapter 9B, SES adopts a Best Practice Guide on audit committees and requires the annual report to include how this is complied with, and to provide sufficient disclosure of corporate governance processes and activities. The change moves Singapore from a regulatory system of corporate governance to one that is more driven by market demands for information and transparency, and follows the lead established in Western developed countries such as the United Kingdom and Canada.

A study by Goodwin and Seow (1998) in which they examine the annual reports of ninety-four Singaporean companies from 1994 to 1996 concludes that the disclosure practices fell short of the recommended levels in the Best Practices Guide. They also concluded that, compared with US firms, disclosure practices were poor; for example, in 1996 only 45.7 per cent of companies disclosed whether company directors were executive or non-executive. They also concluded that very little was disclosed concerning the procedures of the board. In the United States, a checklist method is used to ensure that listing prospectuses, proxy statements or other financial information are disclosed in an appropriately comprehensive and consistent manner; further, an industry has developed to collate, interpret and transmit market and company data, thereby increasing the efficiency of information flows. In Singapore there are no such checklists, so the extent and quality of disclosure varies. Phan (1998) argues that the practice of corporate governance must radically change if Singapore companies are to play a role in the global capital and product markets.

POLICY RESPONSES TO THE CRISIS: HONG KONG

Hong Kong had the reputation of being a far more *laissez faire* system than Singapore. However, the scope of the response to the crisis in Hong Kong was constrained by its commitment to a currency board system, or at least apparently so. The nominal exchange rate could not move in the same way it did in Singapore. The management of this system and its implications, we argue, is a key source of difference between the Hong Kong experience and that of Singapore.

Although the currency board system was actually implemented with more discretion than is commonly understood, the employment of discretion in a system that relied on credibility for its operation complicated Hong Kong's response to the crisis. To explain this issue, it is important to examine the operation of the currency board system in Hong Kong in some detail.

The operational mechanisms in Hong Kong differed from those of orthodox currency boards. The government or its monetary authority does not issue notes. Instead, three commercial banks issue notes, but to be able to do so they have to give up foreign currency at the official rate. The effect is that all currency is backed by the foreign exchange reserves that are held by the Exchange Fund. The system appeared to be working well in the 1980s and most of the 1990s, although Hong Kong's increasing role as a regional and international financial centre, where huge amounts of capital can flow in or out overnight, caused tensions in the system, particularly in the form of high interest rate volatility. Such tensions can be magnified or relaxed by the liquidity management system, depending on how it is designed. This has been patently illustrated by the speculative attacks on Hong Kong's currency during the recent Asian financial crisis and the forced changes made by the Hong Kong Monetary Authority.

The Hong Kong version of a currency board

Although there are variants of currency boards, they share some common characteristics. A currency board is a monetary institution that issues base money solely in exchange for foreign assets, at a predetermined fixed exchange rate (Williamson 1995). As it has to follow this monetary rule, it has no discretion in its monetary policy. The monetary base changes only passively with the balance of payments surplus or deficit. A currency board is not allowed to lend to the government and thus cannot create inflation.[9] A currency board thus promotes macroeconomic discipline. In a nutshell, a currency board increases credibility by reducing policy discretion.

As a currency board guarantees the convertibility of domestic currency at a fixed exchange rate and follows the monetary rule, the system involves two automatic stabilisers: a specie flow and cash arbitrage. In the specie flow process, an outflow of capital leads to a contraction in money supply and then to higher interest rates which induce a counter flow of funds. Tsang argues that this mechanism may not be reliable. This is because, he says, if the exchange rate is itself fluctuating and looks insecure, higher interest rates will not necessarily lead to the reverse of the capital flow. He argues therefore that the cash arbitrage mechanism is important in maintaining the exchange rate. If the market exchange rate weakens from the official rate, people can convert their bank deposits into cash, go to the Currency Board to exchange the cash into foreign currency at the stronger official rate, and then sell the foreign currency in the market (Tsang 1999).

As Tsang points out, the Hong Kong Currency Board did not function exactly as intended. Notes and coins are provided by just the three banks and only they can deal with the government at the fixed rate. This feature meant that arbitrage activities were limited and that one of the two stabilisers was almost totally inoperative'. Tsang also points out that the notes arbitrage system was not so effective in an economy with a declining cash base due to technological changes to financial transactions. The market rate actually strayed from the official rate (although by less than 1 per cent).[10]

The Hong Kong government uses various methods to intervene in the market to support the exchange rate. The Hong Kong Monetary Authority (HKMA) has therefore departed from the monetary rule of a currency board. Since the late 1980s, the Hong Kong government started to intervene in the inter-bank market. This was made possible when a new accounting arrangement between the Exchange Fund and the Hong Kong and Shanghai Bank was introduced in 1988. The launch of Exchange Fund Bills and Notes in 1990 and the setting up of the Liquidity Adjustment Facility (LAF) in 1992 further strengthened the ability of the government in influencing inter-bank liquidity. In late 1996, the Real Time Gross Settlement system for inter-bank clearing was introduced. Under this new system, commercial banks keep a clearing balance at the HKMA. During a trading day, settlement takes place on a real-time basis. Towards the end of the day, the LAF opens so banks can initiate overnight repos with the HKMA.[11]

To advocates of orthodox currency boards, these operations are not desirable.[12] From a more practical point of view, provision of overnight liquidity itself does not necessarily create problems. It helps to smooth out any temporary shortage of funds arising in the inter-bank clearing process, a function quite different from the lender of last resort that provides liquidity to insolvent banks. In fact, the aggregate of the clearing balances of the commercial banks at the HKMA (the Aggregate Balance) constitutes part of the monetary base that requires the monetary rule to be observed. It is also through the Aggregate Balance that the specie flow adjustment mechanism takes effect.[13] However, the HKMA did not follow the monetary rule of a currency board in handling inter-bank liquidity. Worse still, it attempted to use discretion to directly influence the interest rate. These actions undermined the credibility of the system.

The problems in this system were revealed in the response of the HKMA to the heavy selling of Hong Kong dollars in foreign exchange markets on 21–2 October 1997. As the spot foreign exchange transactions were settled on a T+2 basis, the impact of these sales on inter-bank Hong Kong dollar liquidity was not felt until 23–4 October 1997. When sellers of Hong Kong dollars looked for Hong Kong dollar liquidity for settlement on 23 October, the inter-bank liquidity was in seriously short supply. The HKMA did not respond on this occasion to the demand for liquidity. It went further. It announced that repeated borrowers in the LAF would be charged penal interest rates, without specifying the definition of repeated borrowers'. This announcement added to the uncertainty about the availability of liquidity from the LAF and triggered a scramble for funds. The overnight Hong Kong inter-bank offered rate (HIBOR) once shot up to 280 per cent, with a closing rate over 100 per cent that day.[14]

In a subsequent attempt to calm the market, the HKMA tried to change its way of handling liquidity. It clarified the definition of repeated borrowers and set up a Reuters screen that indicated the projected level of the Aggregate Balance based on unsettled forex transactions with the HKMA. Even so, the experience of October 1997 and the persistence of uncertainties in obtaining funds from the LAF have made the banks more conservative about lending money, resulting in higher interest rates.

There were two major consequences. First, the credibility of the exchange rate was undermined, because the cost of maintaining it involved high interest rates that could bring the economy into recession. Second, because speculators knew that the HKMA only had interest rates as its weapon, they could exploit that weakness in the system.[15] Cheng, Wong and Findlay (1998) report the swings in interest rates in this period.

From Figure 11.6, we can see that during the crisis, the HIBOR has been substantially higher than the US$ LIBOR rate. The risk premium led to higher interest rates that contributed to slower growth in Hong Kong. While it was reasonable to observe a risk premium for holding HK$ during an episode of currency attacks, it is doubtful that the risk premium needed to be so high.

This adjustment mechanism of the macroeconomic variables involves challenges for banks in terms of the management of their portfolios, and for borrowers and investors in asset markets. One of the good governance' issues is therefore whether alternative routes lead to lower costs of adjustment,

Figure 11.6   Interest rate differential (1-month HIBOR and 1-month LIBOR, per cent)

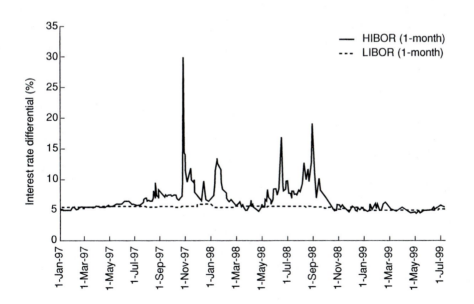

that is, whether the particular form of policy choice is appropriate for an economy like Hong Kong.[16] The choice made in Hong Kong was to maintain the Currency Board. But it also reformed the way the mechanism operated, so as to lower the costs involved in the adjustment process and thereby to maintain its credibility.

Exchange rate mechanism reform in Hong Kong

After the events in the late 1997,[17] there were proposals from academics to improve the system. The first proposal came from Shu-ki Tsang of Hong Kong Baptist University. He suggested that the coverage of the convertibility guarantee should be widened from cash to the whole monetary base, which itself should be enlarged by introducing a deposit reserve system. Such a system, which can be called a convertible reserve system, is similar to the currency boards of Argentina, Estonia and Lithuania.[18] Another proposal was put forward by Alex Chan and Nai-fu Chen of Hong Kong University of Science and Technology. They suggested that the LAF should be reformed so that banks may borrow US dollars at LIBOR from the LAF using Exchange Fund Bills and Notes as collateral and that they be given an option to repay the US dollars borrowed either in US dollars or in Hong Kong dollars at a fixed exchange rate of 7.80. They also proposed that the Currency Board should offer the market an option under which the holder would be compensated by the difference between the spot exchange rate and office linked exchange rate (the exercise price of the option).[19] Nobel Laureate Merton Miller, during a visit to Hong Kong, also proposed that the HKMA should issue special Hong Kong dollar Exchange Fund paper which would be redeemable at the option of the holder either in Hong Kong dollars or US dollars at the exchange rate of 7.80.[20] Besides these suggestions, scholars from the Chinese University of Hong Kong put forward a proposal on the operation of the LAF. They suggested that the HKMA should give up its discretion in the provision of liquidity. This could be done by making a pledge that the door of the LAF would not be shut and the interest rate for any overnight lending followed the market inter-bank rate.[21]

While these proposals may not be perfect and involve some costs and risks, they attempted to address the conspicuous problem of insufficient credibility of the Hong Kong dollar and the associated high interest rate volatility. Yet the HKMA at that time was rather defensive in response to these proposals. In April 1998, it issued a report on the October 1997 experience (Report on Financial Market Review) in which it maintained its position that interest rate is the most potent weapon in the defence of a fixed exchange rate. Also, it attempted to argue that the interest rate hike in the previous months arose from the automatic adjustment mechanism of the Currency Board rather than any measures engineered by the HKMA. That argument simply ignores the announcement effect of the HKMA's threat to punish the undefined repeat borrowers'. In sum, the HKMA was eager to defend the status quo and refused to make any changes to the system.

Extreme measures in the stock market

It was not until August 1998 that the authorities finally acknowledged the links between markets which allowed speculators to gain in the stock index futures. They then took an extreme action. They challenged speculators by intervening in the stock market, where they bought shares to support the index. Their goal was to punish speculators who had short positions.[22] The Hong Kong government spent $US15.2 billion in this intervention. The amount invested by the government was about 15 per cent of foreign reserves. The HKMA's view was that while the intervention ran the risk of some misunderstanding, it was required since otherwise the stability and integrity of our financial markets would be at risk'.

The diminution of foreign reserves was not a problem, as Hong Kong still holds substantial reserves, much more than a currency board normally needs. However, the move generated uncertainty about the philosophy of economic management of the Hong Kong government, which has long been famous for its non-interventionism. The government became the second or third largest shareholder in the economy's thirty-three largest listed companies. This has raised new issues about the disposal of the shares, and concerns about conflicts of interest as the government is now both a regulator and shareholder in these companies. For an economy whose growth had been based on private ownership and the operation of market forces, it was an interesting contradiction that in order to defend the manner of operation of the foreign exchange market, the boundary between the state and enterprise became blurred.

In September 1998, the HKMA announced seven technical measures that addressed directly the weaknesses of the existing system.[23] The measures extended the convertibility undertaking from bank notes to the whole monetary base, which included the clearing account balances of licensed banks at the HKMA.[24] The changes ensured that banks had access to liquidity, provided that they have Exchange Fund paper as collateral. In so doing, the new system contains an element of Tsang's proposal, but it avoids the introduction of a deposit reserve system that would probably be unpopular with the banks. The new Discount Window arrangement has reduced the uncertainty of liquidity provision, as suggested by the Chinese University scholars, but the HKMA has made it consistent with the monetary rule of a currency board by requiring all new Exchange Fund paper be backed by foreign reserves. An earlier move in this direction would have avoided the situation in which the state is now such a large owner as well as regulator of the corporate sector.

In summary, in response to pressures created by globalisation, the Hong Kong response was to reinforce the fixed-rate system. An attempt was made to deepen its credibility and lower the cost of its application. But in the process, the defence of the earlier version of the currency board led the state in Hong Kong to become a very large corporate shareholder. The government is now unwinding this position by floating off its shareholding. Overall, the significant external shock from the rest of the world forced the

Hong Kong government to be more explicit about its actions, and to apply less discretion, in its implementation of foreign exchange policy.

Banking reform in Hong Kong

Issues of policy implementation and risk management are also evident in Hong Kong's banking sector reforms after the crisis.[25] Under prudent supervision, Hong Kong's banking system remained robust during the Asian financial crisis yet, even so, the crisis was followed by substantial reforms.

Although the share of NPLs has risen and profitability has been considerably eroded, no bank has become insolvent. Nevertheless, the HKMA continued its efforts to raise the soundness of the banking sector. In addition, liberalisation of the market for banking services has continued, although the crisis led to a cautious approach to reforms. In 1999, the HKMA released a report on banking reform entitled Hong Kong banking into the new millennium' in which it responded with particular policy reforms following the recommendations made in an earlier Banking Sector Consultancy Study. According to the report, the overall goals are to open up the banking services market, make it more efficient and let market forces play a greater role in determining the number of institutions in the sector while at the same time enhancing safety and soundness' (para 2). Its proposals include:

b)   in terms of market liberalisation
     removing remaining interest rate controls
     relaxing a policy that foreign banks can only have one branch
     increasing access by a variety of financial institutions to the real time
       gross settlement system
     changing the authorisation system for financial institutions (cutting the
       tiers from three to two but not moving to a unitary system)
     reviewing the market entry requirements for a local banking licence in
       2001

b)   in terms of soundness
     studying the issues involved in establishing a depositor protection
       scheme
     clarifying the role of the HKMA as lender of last resort
     developing a more formal risk-based supervisory system in Hong Kong
     conducting a feasibility study on setting up a commercial credit register
       for the banking system (in which all the borrowings by a corporation
       from all lenders are recorded)
     promoting high standards of corporate governance' in the banking
       system (in the process putting more pressure on directors to observe
       their responsibilities)

While the market is more liberalised, there is scope for further reform, and pressure in that direction is likely to come in multilateral services negotiations. We also note that various proposals to increase the soundness of the system mean that the Authority has to deal with new moral hazard issues.

The one branch condition for foreign banks was set up in 1978 when there was concern about excessive competition' leading to a proliferation of branches which might have a destabilising' effect. The HKMA accepts that this rule leads to discrimination against foreign banks and notes the issue was raised in the General Agreement on Trade in Services (GATS) negotiations on financial services. It also notes that the relevance of this rule has been undermined by new technology. Nevertheless, it only committed to allowing foreign banks to increase branches to three. In explanation it cited the concerns of some smaller local banks' who argued that removing the restriction would tip the balance even more in favour of foreign banks'.

Another issue of special interest to foreign suppliers was the proposal to change the licensing policy. The rule is that a locally incorporated applicant for a full banking licence must have been an authorised institution in Hong Kong for ten continuous years and it must also be closely associated and identified with Hong Kong' (para 59). The consultants advised that the ten years should be reduced to three and that the Hong Kong association rule be removed. The HKMA's response was that while it supported a change in that direction, implementation does not appear to be an urgent issue at this stage' (para 61), especially if the rule limiting the number of branches of foreign banks were relaxed. But once again, this restriction will become an issue in the financial services negotiations since it involves a restriction on mode of supply.

An interesting decision was the commitment by the HKMA to study deposit insurance schemes. The consultants said that this was an important issue as the sector becomes more competitive and as the level of risk in the industry increases' (para 62). The HKMA notes a trend in this direction in the rest of the world. The HKMA reports that the larger banks were opposed to the proposal since they were concerned that they would end up subsidising the smaller banks. The other concern of the HKMA was moral hazard. A further issue was how foreign banks should be treated. These concerns led the Authority to decide on a study rather than to commit to such a scheme.

The HKMA has also taken the opportunity to clarify its role as lender of last resort. The role was sometimes thought to be unnecessary in a currency board system. In the context of the way in which the adjustment process worked in Hong Kong, the HKMA notes that during the Asian financial crisis a key concern of the banks was the high level of volatility in the inter-bank market and doubt over their abilities to obtain lender of last resort support if required. This prompted banks to remain as liquid as possible as they were uncertain whether liquidity support would be available from the HKMA. Arguably, this may also have aggravated the credit crunch during the crisis period (para 70).

The HKMA noted that it had introduced a discount window which was designed to provide credit for the end of the day, but it went on to observe that a last resort facility might also be required for banks with more serious funding difficulties. It observed that the specification of a lender of last resort facility must be balanced against the advantage of leaving a certain degree of constructive ambiguity in order to reduce the risk of moral hazard' (para 72). It released a policy statement on these issues (Annex 4) which spells out conditions for lender of last resort support, the instruments used, the extent of support for foreign banks (only for bridging purposes) and how the arrangement could be made consistent with the Currency Board. The latter refers to the ways in which the support would be funded and the HKMA mentions the sale of some of its foreign exchange holdings or borrowing on the inter-bank market.

In light of the expectedly increasing market competition that arises from the liberalisation program and from global pressures, it is foreseeable that some small banks might have to operate in a more competitive environment. Top executives of the HKMA have openly advocated that more mergers and strategic alliances be formed among local banks. They stressed that the HKMA would not mandate consolidations. Rather, it would advocate the idea in public and persuade in private. The regulatory framework will also be altered to give an incentive to banks to think harder about merger and strategic alliances.[26]

SUMMARY AND CONCLUSION

The crisis has led to redefinition of the risks borne by government in both Singapore· and Hong Kong. The impact on the implementation of the Singapore exchange rate regime was small, but the government moved to clarify its role in the banking system. In Hong Kong, the government had to both clarify its role, and limit the extent of its discretion, in the foreign exchange market and in the banking system. The importance of explicit policy statements on the sorts of risks that will be borne by governments, and consistent application of those policies, are key lessons from the regional crisis. They are also lessons that appear to have been learnt in different ways by both Hong Kong and Singapore.

The Singapore experience reported here might be used to suggest that exchange rate flexibility, or even some nominal flexibility managed with a specific real target in mind, is better than none at all. This seems surprising, since it suggests that the capacity for discretion in exchange rate management, with all the risks it entails, might have some advantages. The alternative view is that a rules-based system, which also includes the rule that rates should be determined completely by the market place, reduces risks of distortions from government choices and reduces the costs of adjusting to an external shock.[27]

In fact, the experience reviewed here does not help a great deal. It transpires that the Hong Kong experience is clouded since its currency board was not managed in the manner expected by strict adherents to the currency board model. Instead, the Hong Kong experience actually demonstrates the problems created by having some discretion, at least discretion in the context of a policy system that was based on the assumption that governments were acting without any such discretion. In this case, the market's disappointment about how the system was being managed became excitement when the markets moved to profit from the application of discretion. This led to a crisis of a special Hong Kong type, in which the government became a major owner of stocks in traded corporations, a very interesting outcome given its non-interventionist policy positions elsewhere in the economy. It then led to a round of adjustments to the rules of policy implementation in foreign exchange markets to shift it closer to the strict rules-based currency board model.

Our general theme of policy implementation and risk management is illustrated with respect to banking reform. Here the experience is more uniform. Both economies moved to a more competitive banking market (it was interesting in the case of Hong Kong, with its reputation for non-intervention, that significant reform was still possible). They also moved to stronger prudential regulation which put more focus on the monitoring processes that banks use to manage their own risks rather than prescription of how they should behave.

NOTES

1 This chapter is an edited version of two papers originally presented at the International Conference on Reform and Recovery in East Asia: The Role of the State and Economic Enterprise, organised by the Asia Pacific School of Economics and Management, Australian National University.

2 The original conference paper version of the Singapore paper by Chia contains more details on the impact of the crisis on Singapore. The full text of this paper is available by registering a request at the web site of the conference host, the Australia–Japan Research Centre (*http://ajrcnet.anu.edu.au*).

3 A problem, however, was the relatively high inflation rate. Luk (1998) argues that despite the link with the US$, prices in Hong Kong could move differently from those in the US due to the growth in the size of the service sector in which prices were locally determined (and without local control over money supply in the long term).

4 Apart from the performance of GDP growth, sound fundamentals are seen in the following macroeconomic, financial, and microeconomic performance indicators:

> very high savings and investment rates, with the national savings rate average over 45% of GNP in recent years;

> strong current account surpluses, reaching 15% of GNP in 1997 and a strong balance of payments position, resulting in official foreign reserves which reached US$81 billion at end 1997, among the highest in the world in aggregate and per capita;

> no official foreign external debt after 1994;

> an attractive location for foreign direct investment and multinational corporations;

> strong government budgetary positions with budget surpluses for most years;

> low inflation rate with the Consumer Price Index averaging 2.4% in the 1990s, except for the non-traded property sector which has suffered from an asset bubble;

> low leveraging in the corporate sector with shareholder/debt ratio of 0.25 and high current assets/liabilities ratio of 1.08 for the financial and corporate sectors;

> sound banking system with the Monetary Authority of Singapore maintaining strict prudential and supervisory controls.

5 Three relief packages' were announced in 1998 – the budget delivered in February 1998, the off-budget package in June 1998, and the additional package in November 1998.

6 The system does not work like a classical currency board system, under which the domestic currency is pegged to a reserve currency at a fixed rate set by the authority (see the discussion about Hong Kong below).

7   The MAS is Singapore's *de facto* central bank. It pursues three objectives – to insulate the economy from international financial instability; to protect local banks in domestic banking from excessive foreign competition; and to maintain sound and stable financial institutions. These are achieved through reserve requirements, legislation circumscribing commercial bank operations (Banking Amendment Act 1984), lender of last resort facilities, and organising foreign banks as branches rather than subsidiaries and requiring the parents to make up any shortfall in liquidity on demand.

8   Liberalisation policies in the 1970s decontrolled the exchange rates and interest rates: the 1972 abolition of the cartel system of exchange rate quotation by commercial banks; the June 1973 flotation of the Singapore dollar; and the July 1975 abolition of the cartel system of interest rate setting by commercial banks. The June 1978 measures lifted almost all foreign exchange controls – residents are allowed to borrow/lend in all currencies, including participation in Singapore's offshore Asian dollar market; merchant banks are free to engage in foreign exchange transactions; offshore banks, hitherto restricted to dealing with banks and approved financial institutions, are allowed to deal with resident non-bank customers; and non-residents are allowed to hold Singapore dollar denominated assets. The MAS has argued that Singapore has a degree of foreign participation in the financial sector that is probably unsurpassed in the world (MAS *Annual Report* 1995/96).

9   The empirical evidence of this link is reviewed by Edwards and Savastano. They report that recent empirical work and their own evaluation of methodological issues in that work temper the conclusion that a fixed rate system is better for delivering lower and more stable rates of inflation.

10   Tsang, Sin and Cheng (1999) review a series of reforms to the system that took place between 1983 and April 1998. These reforms, however, did not change the fundamental features of the system.

11   For an analysis of the changes of the liquidity management system in Hong Kong since 1983, see Meredith (1999).

12   See criticism of the Hong Kong system by Schuler (1999).

13   This is discussed by the Chief Executive of the Hong Kong Monetary Authority in the aftermath of the major interest hikes during the Asian financial crisis. See Yam (1998).

14   See the discussion in Meredith (1999).

15   For example, they could borrow and sell HKD in the spot market, leading to higher interest rates and consequently the stock prices and stock futures would fall. People holding short positions would gain.

16   The issue of the choice of regime is also discussed by Cheng, Wong and Findlay (1998). A fixed-rate regime may be preferred by a city state with access to labour from its hinterland and with a economy in which the resource sector is minimal.

17   For details of the experience of Hong Kong in October 1997, see Cheng, Wong and Findlay (1998).

18   See, for example, Tsang (1998).

19   See Chan and Chen (1998).

20   See *Ming Pao*, 20 January 1998, p.B2.

21   See *South China Morning Post*, Business Post, 6 December 1997, p.3.

22   For a defence of the HKMA's intervention in the stock market, see Joseph Yam, Why we intervened', *Asian Wall Street Journal*, 20 August 1998.

23   These seven technical measures announced on 5 September 1998 were:

(1) the HKMA providing a clear undertaking to all licensed banks in Hong Kong to convert Hong Kong dollars in their clearing accounts into US dollars at the fixed exchange rate of HK$7.75 to US$1. This explicit Convertibility Undertaking is a clear demonstration of the Government's commitment to the linked exchange rate system. It is the intention of the HKMA to move the rate of the Convertibility Undertaking to 7.80 when market circumstances permit;

(2) removing the bid rate of the Liquidity Adjustment Facility (LAF). As the improved efficiency of the inter-bank payment system has facilitated liquidity management of licensed

banks, the need for the LAF deposit facility to facilitate orderly inter-bank market activities has fallen away;

(3) replacing LAF by a Discount Window with the Base Rate (formerly known as the LAF Offer Rate) to be determined from time to time by the HKMA. In determining the Base Rate, the HKMA will ensure that interest rates are adequately responsive to capital flows while allowing excessive and destabilising interest rate volatility to be dampened;

(4) removing the restriction on repeated borrowing in respect of the provision of overnight Hong Kong dollar liquidity through repo transactions using Exchange Fund Bills and Notes. Allowing for freer access to day end liquidity through the use of Exchange Fund paper which is fully backed by foreign currency reserves will make Hong Kong's monetary system less susceptible to manipulation and dampen excessive interest rate volatility without departing from the discipline of the Currency Board arrangement;

(5) new Exchange Fund paper to be issued only when there is an inflow of funds. This will ensure that all new Exchange Fund paper will be fully backed by foreign currency reserves;

(6) introducing a schedule of discount rates applicable for different percentage thresholds of holdings of Exchange Fund paper by the licensed banks for the purpose of accessing the Discount Window. This will ensure that the interest rate adjustment mechanism to be fully kicked in when the Hong Kong dollar is under significant pressure; and

(7) retaining the restriction on repeated borrowing in respect of repo transactions involving debt securities other than Exchange Fund paper. No new issues of paper other than Exchange Fund paper will be accepted at the Discount Window. This will prevent significant liquidity to be provided to licensed banks against paper not backed by foreign currency reserves.

24 Note that the convertibility rate for the Aggregate Balance was first set at the level of HK$7.75/US$, which is different from the rate of HK$7.80 /US$ for cash. Later, the HKMA announced that the convertibility rate for the Aggregate Balance would be changed by one pip a day' from 7.75 to 7.80 through 500 calendar days, from 1 April 1999 to 12 August 2000.

25 The conference paper version of this chapter with respect to Hong Kong contains more detail on the extent of reforms affecting corporate governance, which was a set of reforms on securities market regulation.

26 See, for instance, David Carse, Hong Kong banking into the new millennium', speech at the Hong Kong Meeting of the Banking Commission of the International Chamber of Commerce in Hong Kong. 4 November 1999, at http://www.info.gov.hk/hkma/eng/speeches/index.htm.

27 The contrast is exaggerated since the focus here is only on the nominal exchange rate: some adjustment process is always required to external shocks and different economies may make different choices about which routes or markets to use to manage that shock depending on their characteristics.

REFERENCES

Business Times (various issues).

Campos, Jose Edgardo L. and Hilton Root (1996) *The Key to the East Asian Miracle: Making shared growth credible*, Washington DC: Brookings Institution.

Chan, Alex and Nai-fu Chen (1999) An intertemporal currency board', *Pacific Economic Review* 4(2):215–32.

Cheng Yuk-shing, Wong Marn Heong and Christopher Findlay (1998) Hong Kong and Singapore', in Ross H. McLeod and Ross Garnaut, (eds), *East Asia in Crisis: From being a miracle to needing one?*, London and New York: Routledge.

Cheng Yuk-shing (1992) The Role of Institutions in Singapore's Economic Success, Monograph for World Bank Project on the High Performing Asian Economies.

Chia Siow Yue (1999) The Asian Financial Crisis: Singapore's Experience and Response', in H.W. Arndt and Hal Hill, (eds), *Southeast Asia's Economic Crisis: Origins, lessons and the way forward*, Singapore: Institute of Southeast Asian Studies.

Cheng Yuk-shing (January 1999) Singapore's Responses to the Asian Financial Crisis and Globalisation Challenges', paper presented at the AT10 Researchers' Meeting, Tokyo Club Foundation for Global Studies, Tokyo.

Committee on Singapore's Competitiveness (November 1998) *Report*, Singapore: Ministry of Trade and Industry.

Edwards, Sebastian and Miguel A. Savastano (1999) Exchange rates in emerging economies: What do we know? What do we need to know?', National Bureau of Economic Research Working Paper W7228, July.

Goh Keng Swee (1977) *The Practice of Economic Growth*, Singapore: Federal Publications.

Goodwin, Jenny and Seow Jean Lin (August 1998) Disclosure Relating to Board Members: Shedding Light to Build Investors' Confidence', *SES Journal*.

Krause, Lawrence (1987) Thinking About Singapore', in Lawrence Krause, Koh Ai Tee and Lee Tsao Yuan, (eds), *The Singapore Economy Reconsidered*, Singapore: Institute of Southeast Asian Studies.

Luk, Y.K. (1998) Non-Exchange Rate Adjustments in the Asian Crisis: The People's Republic of China and Hong Kong', *Seoul Journal of Economics* 11(4):505–32.

Meredith, Guy (1999) Liquidity Management Under Hong Kong's Currency Board Arrangements', paper presented at the International Workshop on Currency Boards: Convertibility, Liquidity Management and Exit, held at Hong Kong Baptist University, 9 October 1999, http://www.hkbu.edu.hk/~econ/99WS_main.html

Ministry of Trade and Industry (1999) *Economic Survey of Singapore 1998*, Singapore: Ministry of Trade and Industry.

Monetary Authority of Singapore *Annual Report*.
  website, http://www.mas.gov.sg

Montes, Manuel and Tan Khee Giap (1999) Developing the Financial Services Industry in Singapore', in Seiichi Masuyama, Donna Vandenbrink and Chia Siow Yue (eds), *East Asia's Financial Systems: Evolution and crisis*, Tokyo and Singapore: Nomura Research Institute and Institute of Southeast Asian Studies.

Phan, Philip H. (1998) Effective Corporate Governance in Singapore: Another look', *Singapore Management Review* 20(2).

and Mak Yuen Teen (1999) Corporate Governance in Singapore: Towards the 21st century', *Banker's Journal Malaysia*, no. 109.

Schuler, Kurt (1999) The Importance of Being Orthodox', paper presented at the International Workshop on Currency Boards: Convertibility, Liquidity Management and Exit, held at Hong Kong Baptist University, 9 October 1999, http://www.hkbu.edu.hk/~econ/99WS_main.html

Straits Times (various issues).

Tyabji, Amina (1998) Capital flows and macroeconomic stabilisation in Singapore', in C.H. Kwan, Donna Vandenbrink and Chia Siow Yue, (eds) *Coping with Capital Flows in East Asia*, Tokyo and Singapore: Nomura Research Institute and Institute of Southeast Asian Studies.

Tsang Shu-ki (1998) The case for adopting the convertible reserves system in Hong Kong', *Pacific Economic Review* 3(3):265–75.

(1999) Fixing the exchange rate through a currency board arrangement: efficiency risk, systemic risk and exit cost', *Asian Economic Journal* 13(3):239–66.

, Chor-yiu Sin and Yuk-shing Cheng (1999) The robustness of Hong Kong's linked exchange rate system as a currency board arrangement', paper presented at the 54th European Meeting of the Econometric Society held at Santiago de Compostela, Spain, 29 August–1 September 1999 http://www.hkbu.edu.hk/~sktsang/esem99.PDF

Yam, Joseph (1998) *A Modern Day Currency Board System*, Hong Kong Monetary Authority.

Williamson, J. (1995) *What Role for Currency Boards?* Washington DC: Institute for International Economics.

World Bank (1992) *Governance and Development*, Washington DC: The World Bank.
    (1993)   *The East Asian Miracle: Economic growth and public policy*, Washington DC: The World Bank.
    (1994).   *Governance: The World Bank's Experience*. Washington DC: The World Bank.

APPENDIX 11.1

On management oversight, MAS approval is required for the appointment of chief and deputy chief executives and chief dealers. Banks incorporated in Singapore require MAS approval regarding appointment of directors, while foreign banks are required to allow their home country's supervisory authority to carry out inspection of books in Singapore. Finance companies require MAS approval to open new branches, and one criterion in granting approval is the character of management. Insurance companies are required to maintain separate funds for their domestic and offshore activities. As part of management oversight, MAS requires fortnightly and monthly reports – fortnightly reports on capital funds of foreign banks and inter-bank indebtedness with banks outside Singapore (including ACU operations), and monthly reports on loans and advances to bank directors.

On capital adequacy, Singapore banks have capital adequacy ratios (CAR) that well exceed the BIS standard. Banks that operate internationally are required to conform with the BIS capital adequacy standard of 8 per cent of risk-weighted assets, half of which must come from shareholders' funds and minority interests; in practice the banks have higher CARs. Locally incorporated banks must have a minimum of S$150 million in shareholders' funds. Finance companies are subject to a S$50 million minimum capital requirement. Reserve requirements have been set at 6 per cent since 1975. Commercial banks and finance companies are required to keep liquid assets at 18 per cent and 10 per cent, respectively.

Loan regulations imposed on financial institutions are fairly stringent and specific. For banks, credit to any individual or group of individuals cannot exceed 25 per cent of the bank's capital. There are specific regulations on loans for property and car purchases and on unsecured loans of banks, merchant banks and finance companies – unsecured credit (including credit cards) can only be extended to individuals with annual earned income of at least S$30,000 and the loan ceiling is set at two months of a borrower's salary; property loans cannot exceed 80 per cent of the price of the property and car loans cannot exceed 70 per cent of the price of the car. Further restrictions on banks include the following – they are not allowed to possess immovable property worth more than 40 per cent of their capital funds, except when such property is required as operating facilities or staff housing; loans secured by immovable property cannot exceed 30 per cent of a bank's total deposits; banks must maintain internal control over derivatives trading, including segregating trading and back office staff and monitoring exposure limits and the size of off-premises dealings. Further restrictions on finance companies include the following: requirement to maintain a reserve fund, with a proportion of net profits assigned to reserves each year; maintain a minimum amount of liquid assets, based on a list of approved liquid assets; for warehouse financing, loans can only be applied to goods stored in government-approved warehouses. Further restrictions on insurance companies include the following: maximum limits on the distribution of their portfolios, with 35 per cent in equities, 20 per cent in properties and property shares, 20 per cent in foreign currencies and investments, and 10 per cent in unsecured loans. These micro-level regulations help ensure that banks and financial institutions manage their risks prudently, thus containing the incidence of NPLs.

Equity investments of banks are also restricted under the Banking Act. Banks can invest only up to 40 per cent of their capital funds, except for shareholdings in other banks and subsidiaries; MAS waiver can be obtained for investments in corporations deemed critical for economic development. Banks are also not allowed to own more than 20 per cent of any company's capital without MAS approval, except when the ownership results from foreclosure on collateral; even in this case, banks are required to dispose of such shareholdings at the earliest opportunity and MAS approval is necessary for the shareholdings to be kept as an investment. The SES has allowed banks and other financial institutions 100 per cent ownership of stockbroking firms.

The Financial Sector Review Group (FSRG) was formed to chart new directions for Singapore's financial sector aimed at further liberalisation and deregulation. Three committees were formed to work with FRSG – the Stock Exchange of Singapore Review Committee to recommend how the domestic capital market could become more international, competitive and robust; the Corporate Financing Issues Committee to recommend regulation, framework and administrative guidelines for corporate debt markets so as to expand corporate fund-raising activity in Singapore; and the Banking Disclosure Standards Committee to evaluate standards and practices in developed and other Asia Pacific countries and recommend appropriate changes in disclosure practices.

The FSRG has made wide-ranging recommendations to lighten the regulatory environment, but provide for a higher standard of financial disclosure.

The regional financial crisis notwithstanding, the MAS has embarked on a fundamental review of its approach to regulating and developing the financial sector in Singapore.

First, a five-year commercial banking liberalisation package was introduced to provide a more open and competitive environment to spur the development of local banks. This includes:

Increased access for foreign banks take the form of new Qualifying Full
  Banks (QFBs) for those which are strong, well managed and committed
  to growing in Singapore; increased number of restricted banks, and greater
  flexibility in Singapore dollar wholesale business for offshore banks;
Improving the governance of local banks through appointment of capable
  individuals to their boards and key posts. Local banks are required to
  appoint Nominating Committees to ensure this. The MAS retains its existing
  powers under the Banking Act to approve appointments.
Lifting the 40 per cent foreign shareholding limit of local banks. The
  requirement for Nominating Committees and for boards to comprise a
  majority of Singapore citizens and permanent citizens are sufficient to
  ensure local control to protect national interest.

Second, shifting the emphasis from regulation to supervision, from a
one-size-fits-all' regulation towards monitoring and examining institutions
for compliance with laws and guidelines and assessing asset quality and
adequacy of risk management systems. As such, stronger institutions will be
given flexibility to develop and innovate while weaker ones will require
stricter controls. Measures include:

Refining the capital adequacy ratio requirement of local banks. Previously
  local banks had to maintain a CAR of 12 per cent, comprising entirely Tier
  1 or equity capital, which is higher than the BIS 8 per cent , which consists
  of 4 per cent Tier 1 capital and 4 per cent Tier 2 capital. As a higher CAR
  raises the cost of funds to the banks and constrains their flexibility in
  raising capital, with effect from December 1998, local banks are required
  to have at least 10 per cent Tier 1 and Tier 2 capital, and the remaining 2
  per cent made up of Upper Tier 2 capital, defined as perpetual cumulative
  preference shares and subordinated debt.
Using internal models for computation of market risk capital. With effect
  from December 1998, banks are allowed to use internal models for
  calculating market risk capital. Encouraging such use provides incentives
  for banks to improve their risk management systems.
Raising disclosure standards. The MAS prescribes the minimum standard of
  disclosure that banks and merchant banks must comply with effect from
  financial year ending on or after 31 December 1998. They are required to
  disclose, among other things, details on principal sources of income, loan
  loss provisions and off-balance sheet items, aggregate amount of NPLs as
  well as the market value of investments and properties (discontinuing the
  existing practice of maintaining hidden reserves), provide information on
  significant concentration of exposure by geographical regions, industry groups,
  and maturity bands. Banks will also provide in their annual report a financial
  review section covering business description, analyses of results, risk
  management systems, and any other pertinent information.
Setting prudential guidelines for asset securitisation activities. To develop
  the securitisation market, the MAS prepared a set of prudential guidelines
  covering regulatory issues and disclosure requirements.

Reducing minimum cash balances (MCB) of finance companies. To align with changes in MCBs of banks in July 1998, the MCB requirement of finance companies was correspondingly reduced from 6 per cent to 3 per cent in December 1998, while the minimum liquid asset (MLA) requirement was raised from 10 per cent to 13 per cent.

Developing a common risk framework as a consistent platform to establish a general set of principles to enhance effectiveness of financial regulation and supervision by the MAS.

Third, developing the Securities industry, Funds Management industry, Futures industry and Insurance industry.

Measures for the Securities industry include enhancing the competitiveness of the Stock Exchange of Singapore (SES); demutualising and merging SES with the Singapore International Monetary Exchange (SIMEX) to reduce the potential conflict of interests between members who are owners and other users of the exchanges, provide greater transparency and more efficient and flexible funding from the capital markets; develop a corporate fund-raising centre; and establishing a new inspection unit.

Measures for the Funds Management industry include the outplacing of government funds for private management; revamping the CPF Investment Scheme for unit trusts; streamlining the regulation of unit trusts; promoting boutique fund managers.

Measures for the Futures industry include revising the financial requirements for futures brokers; abolishing the minimum commission structure.

Measures for the Insurance industry include reducing capital requirements for captive insurers; granting blanket approval for captives to write certain non in-house risks; enhancing the regulatory framework for investment-linked policies under the CPF Investment Scheme; reviewing amendments to the Insurance Regulations 1997; clarifying regulations on derivatives transactions; reviewing regulations on financial reinsurance; reviewing the distribution of personal financial services.

12 Managing capital flows in East Asia

Dominic Wilson

INTRODUCTION

Old orthodoxies, new heresies

Until recently, prevailing economic orthodoxy held that the free movement of capital was critical to the development process. Capital account liberalisation formed a central part of the so-called Washington consensus of policy recommendations for developing countries, and the International Monetary Fund (IMF) actively sought to enshrine it in its Articles. Over the last two years, this orthodoxy has been severely challenged. The notion that restrictions may be needed, particularly on short-term capital flows, has been canvassed not only by prominent economists (Krugman 1998a; Rodrik 1998) but also by central bankers (Greenspan 1998; McFarlane 1998); speculators (Soros 1998) and the international institutions themselves (IMF 1998; World Bank 1998). The Malaysian government issued a more direct challenge in September 1998, introducing extensive exchange controls against the advice of much of the international financial community.

What has shifted the debate so dramatically, of course, is the financial crisis in East Asia and its transmission to the world economy. The reversal in capital flows to East Asia following the floating of the Thai baht in July 1997 was unprecedented in its speed and scale. The rapid withdrawal of capital has inflicted large real costs on the affected economies, as consumption and investment have fallen to deliver the required current account surpluses. Large parts of the corporate and financial sectors have been crippled by the sudden removal of financing and by the impact of currency depreciations on the real value of foreign currency debt. The Asian financial crisis and its transmission to other emerging markets has highlighted (not for the first time) the risks that large capital movements pose, particularly for developing economies, and has pushed the question of how best to manage them to the top of the international agenda. Governments and international institutions are now examining the issue of how developing economies can reap the substantial potential benefits of access to international capital markets without exposing themselves to unacceptable risks.

The case for free capital movements

The potential benefits of foreign direct investment (FDI) as a means of technology transfer have long been recognised and there is substantial empirical evidence that FDI raises total factor productivity, capital accumulation and growth.[1] While the benefits of FDI are well grounded, the case for full capital account liberalisation receives more of its support from economic theory (Obstfeld 1998). In principle, free access to international capital markets allows countries to borrow abroad to smooth consumption in the face of shocks, or to finance productive investment even when domestic savings are low. And indeed, many East Asian economies, such as Singapore and Korea, have benefited greatly from the ability to borrow abroad to finance investment, particularly during the early stages of their development.

The free movement of capital should also direct world savings to their most productive uses. The ability to trade international financial assets also increases the scope for risk pooling, though evidence that these opportunities are exploited is elusive (French and Poterba 1990). If this leads to an increase in high-yield (but riskier) investment, rates of growth in all economies may be raised (Obstfeld 1994). It is for these reasons that there has generally been agreement among economic policy makers in developed countries that capital account restrictions are damaging.

It is less often acknowledged that these advantages of capital mobility are largely contingent. The notion that allowing free capital mobility increases the efficiency of the allocation of global savings and facilitates risk pooling relies crucially on the absence of distortions in domestic and international financial markets. In cases where domestic markets are distorted, allowing the free flow of capital may magnify existing distortions and worsen the allocation of resources. The concept of immiserising capital flows is familiar from the trade literature (Brecher and Alejandro-Diaz 1977), but the general principle has broader application. In this respect, economic theory creates a presumption that the case for free capital mobility is likely to be stronger for economies with less distorted domestic markets. Capital account liberalisation also introduces new limits on domestic policy autonomy. Since the maintenance of fixed exchange rates, free capital mobility and a domestically oriented monetary policy represent an inconsistent trinity', a move to freer capital movements implies that autonomy with respect to either the exchange rate or monetary policy must be sacrificed. As a consequence, a government's freedom of manoeuvre may in certain situations be curtailed. Shocks in international financial markets that bear no relation to developments in the domestic economy, such as a rise in international interest rates, are also likely to have a more direct impact on the domestic economy. Economies with open capital accounts may thus need greater policy discipline and robustness to external shocks than those that are less liberalised.

These ambiguities in the theoretical case for free capital movements are reflected in the empirical evidence. There are few clear findings relating capital account liberalisation to economic performance and growth. The most rigorous way to investigate these issues would be to compare the path of an economy with and without capital account restrictions in a fully specified model. McKibbin (1998) recently carried out preliminary work in this vein, which illustrates the gains predicted by orthodox theory. But McKibbin himself acknowledges that the magnitudes are highly sensitive and that the model's structure eliminates by assumption many of the market failures that would weaken the case for capital account liberalisation.

Simple regression analyses, which do not rely on assumptions of this kind, give much more ambiguous results. Rodrik (1998) regresses an index of capital account restrictions on GDP growth and finds no clear link between unrestricted capital accounts and growth or inflation performance, after controlling for initial conditions. The World Bank (1998) reports further evidence along similar lines. What neither study notes, however, is the strong negative relationship between black market premiums on exchange rates and growth, and that this relationship is one of the most robust in the growth literature (Lee 1993; Sala-i-Martin 1997). Since these exchange rate distortions are associated with extensive controls on capital and foreign exchange, they indicate the dangers posed by restrictive regimes, at least if the exchange rate is not managed in a way that validates fundamentals.

In practice, the move towards freer capital movement has been based as much on pragmatism as on proof. As international trade has increased, so have the opportunities for disguised capital movements through mis-invoicing and delayed payment. The difficulties of controlling capital flows in open economies were illustrated by a succession of balance-of-payments crises under the Bretton Woods system and helped lead to its collapse (Obstfeld 1998). In developed countries with strong institutions and relatively undistorted markets, the orthodox theory of the benefits of unrestricted capital flows is likely to be reasonably close to the truth. Together with the practical difficulties of restraining capital flows, this creates a powerful case for liberalisation. But in developing economies, where domestic distortions may be more severe, the presumption that full capital account liberalisation is desirable may be subject to qualification.

A distortions approach

Despite the mixed evidence, the debate over the appropriate policies for managing capital flows remains an emotive one and has led to strong, unconditional statements on both sides. In part, this reflects the predisposition in parts of the economics profession to be sceptical of the role of the state to intervene in the market allocation of resources. Yet it is reasonably clear that capital controls can be desirable and effective in some cases. (Who would recommend a speedy capital account opening in China or India?) In any case, the distinction between capital controls', prudential regulations and other policies is less clear than is often pretended. In every country in the world, the flow of capital across borders (and within them) is impeded and taxed by public authorities in various ways, whether in the form of restrictions on foreign direct investment or limits on the balance sheets of financial institutions. Nor is discrimination against foreigners on tax grounds unusual.

What is needed is a framework that helps us to decide when and where various kinds of restriction may be appropriate policy tools, and what are the best available policy options in different circumstances. A logical starting point is to seek to identify the distortions that drove a wedge between the social costs and benefits of decisions in ways that helped to generate the surge and reversal in capital flows in East Asia. An accurate identification of the distortions that contributed to disruptive capital movements in the East Asian crisis is helpful because there is a well-developed theory of how distortions affect welfare and how best to deal with them. The work of Bhagwati (1971) in the trade field emphasised that although trade restrictions might succeed in addressing a range of domestic distortions, there were generally less costly ways of doing so. Similar arguments can be made with respect to current debates over the appropriate management of capital flows. Moving directly to restrict capital flows would almost certainly reduce the incidence of crises, but may also be an extremely costly way of achieving the desired goal.

The general lesson from the trade literature is to tackle distortions as close as possible to their source. As a result, the best solution in efficiency terms is almost always to remove the distortion. In some cases, it may not be possible or desirable to eliminate the distortion itself. This might happen if the distortion arises from a policy that serves another important purpose or from an informational asymmetry that cannot be removed. In that case, there is an argument for second best' policies that alter the cost of the distorted activity in a manner that directly offsets the distortion. In general, the optimal response will seek to influence prices rather than quantities and will fall short of prohibition of the distorted activity. It is important that policy makers consider any additional costs associated with the introduction of the second best' policy. Finally, where the introduction of a second best' policy is costly or complex, or where the initial distortion is very large, it may be preferable to adopt cruder third best' rules prohibiting or limiting certain activities. Martin Weitzmann has illustrated that this may also be the case under conditions of uncertainty (Weitzmann 1974). Once again, any costly side effects of third best' options should be carefully considered.

It is possible to identify a number of distortions that drove a wedge between the social costs and benefits of decisions that helped to generate the surge and reversal in capital flows in East Asia. In some instances, these distortions were the direct outcomes of government policy. In others, they stemmed from market failure that had not been adequately addressed. These distortions took a range of forms. Governments gave subsidies, implicitly and explicitly, to certain kinds of borrowing. There were important externalities in foreign borrowing decisions. And missing or underdeveloped markets, informational asymmetries and the attendant problems of moral hazard compounded the divergence between the private and social costs of lending, particularly in the financial sector. As a result, capital flowed to the wrong places, in the wrong quantities and with inappropriate attention to risk. Many of these distortions arose from the interaction of market failure in the financial sector with other subsidies or externalities. This diagnosis is consistent with the evidence that economies with relatively strong financial sectors (Singapore, Hong Kong and Taiwan) fared better in the recent crisis.

Some of the existing distortions are easily removed by best practice' policy solutions aimed at dismantling subsidies towards certain kinds of borrowing. For other distortions, particularly those related to moral hazard in the financial sector, removing the initial distortion may not be possible, at least in a short space of time. In this case, there is a rationale for policies that raise the private cost of certain domestic and international financial transactions so that they reflect their true social costs. Finally, where distortions are particularly severe, blanket prohibitions or restrictions on certain kinds of activities may be sensible for third best' reasons. The conditions under which these policies are optimal are likely to be restrictive and the associated costs may be large.

Of course, even the elimination of a wide range of distortions will not prevent irrational behaviour in asset markets. Dramatic movements in asset prices and flows will continue. But, as developed country experience illustrates, where distortions are kept to a minimum it should in general be possible to keep the economy robust to these disturbances. Identifying and addressing distortions provides lessons about the appropriate regimes to influence capital flows and to limit vulnerability to crises before the fact. Since governments and international institutions have not had great success in managing and resolving crises, prevention remains the best cure by far. But the use of controls on outflows in emergencies is also back on the agenda (Krugman 1998a). The use of capital controls for crisis management in the light of the Malaysian experience merits some discussion, since some of the objections that are commonly raised to the Malaysian policy have not yet been proved right.

THE RISE AND FALL OF CAPITAL FLOWS TO THE CRISIS ECONOMIES

Capital inflows

The surge in capital flows to East Asian economies between 1991 and 1997 is now well documented (World Bank 1998). Except in Indonesia (and to a much smaller extent Malaysia), FDI was not a significant contributor to rising capital inflows. Instead, the increased inflows took the form of bank lending and also, in the cases of Indonesia and Korea, portfolio investment.

This surge in non-FDI capital flows was associated with various reforms undertaken to liberalise financial markets and the capital account in a number of the region's economies in the late 1980s and early 1990s. In Indonesia, lending ceilings and most interest rate controls were abolished in 1983, and in 1988 required reserve ratios were dramatically reduced (Fane 1998). The Indonesian government progressively relaxed restrictions on direct inward investment and in 1989 liberalised portfolio capital inflows by eliminating quantitative limits on banks borrowing abroad. In the same year Korea loosened restrictions on foreign borrowing, and in 1992 non-residents were allowed limited access to the local stock market (Johnston *et al.* 1997). In subsequent years these limits were gradually raised. In Thailand, the establishment of the Bangkok International Banking Facility (BIBF) in March 1993 greatly eased access to foreign financing and provided special tax incentives for foreign borrowing. The need to remove interest rate and lending ceilings as part of the strategy to promote the BIBF as a regional financial centre spurred financial deregulation. The Malaysian government launched a similar initiative to promote Labuan Island as an offshore financial centre, relaxing regulatory and tax treatment on foreign currency operations for institutions based there.

Financial sector and capital account liberalisation provided the opportunity for increased external borrowing. Stable exchange rates, low interest rates in the United States and Japan, and booming domestic economies across the region provided the incentives. The result was a rapid accumulation of external debt that was particularly dramatic in Korea, Indonesia and Thailand. Much of this debt was short term (over 60 per cent in Korea and Thailand) and the vast majority was foreign-currency denominated. As capital flowed in, pressure on exchange rates was partially offset by sterilised intervention. As a consequence, reserves increased rapidly and interest differentials were maintained, encouraging further short-term inflows. Despite the rapid inflow of capital, indications of future problems were far less obvious than in many previous crises (Radelet and Sachs 1998). Foreign debt to GDP ratios were high in some economies (Thailand, Indonesia), but not unusually so. Debt service ratios were generally low, giving no indication that the level of foreign borrowing was unsustainable. Current account deficits were high in Thailand and Malaysia, though not elsewhere. In contrast to the debt crises of the early 1980s, capital inflows were directed towards investment rather than consumption.

Nevertheless, a number of factors pointed to the underlying fragility of the situation. First, there was evidence that the investment being carried out was increasingly less productive, at least in some economies.[2] There was also evidence that capital inflows were being channelled to a growing extent into more speculative ventures, particularly real estate and equity (Corsetti *et al.* 1998). Bank exposure to the property sector in Malaysia, Indonesia and Thailand was high. The tendency for investment to be directed towards the non-tradeables sector had implications for the sustainability of foreign borrowing, since these sectors would not contribute to revenues for future debt servicing.

Closer inspection of external financial indicators also revealed problems. While the overall quantities of foreign debt did not appear to be unmanageable, the maturity and sectoral distribution was more alarming. Although reserves rose, short-term debt rose faster. As a result, the ratio of short-term debt to reserves rose sharply in several economies, and by 1996 the ratio stood at over one in Thailand, Korea and Indonesia. Since this meant that there was insufficient liquid foreign exchange to repay all short-term debts in full, these economies were in a position where liquidity depended on the willingness of foreign creditors to roll over loans. At the same time, the exposure of some sections of the corporate and financial sectors to currency risk had grown rapidly. The groups that were most exposed varied from country to country. In Indonesia, a large proportion of borrowing was done directly by the corporate sector, which accumulated currency exposure directly. In Korea and Thailand, much of the foreign borrowing was mediated by banks and by non-bank financial intermediaries. In general, Thai banks hedged their foreign liabilities, matching foreign currency borrowings with foreign currency loans to domestic borrowers. It was these borrowers, many of whom were in non-traded sectors, who did not hedge the exchange risk. Their currency exposure then constituted a significant credit risk for Thai banks. In Korea, by contrast, the financial sector appears to have been less cautious in matching the currency profiles of its liabilities and assets, making more loans in domestic currency, principally to the *chaebol*, and building up currency exposure directly. Agreements by Korean merchant banks to guarantee foreign currency loans increased their exposure to currency risk in the event of bankruptcies.

Capital outflows

When the crisis broke, these vulnerabilities were exposed. The rapid exit of capital had a number of interesting features. The most striking was that the largest reversal in capital flows was the result of a cut-off in bank lending, as foreign creditors refused to roll over short-term loans. Bank lending fell from an estimated inflow of US$41 billion in 1996 to an outflow of US$32 billion in 1997. A key to understanding the crisis is to appreciate both the reactions of foreign banks to unfolding events and the vulnerabilities associated with large-scale short-term borrowing.

Another feature of the capital flight is that the withdrawal of capital and the associated currency depreciations unfolded gradually over a substantial period. The third quarter of 1997 saw a large outflow of bank lending to Thailand (over US$10 billion) and a small reversal in Korea, but bank lending continued to increase in Malaysia and Indonesia. The initial depreciation in the baht was not large (around 20 per cent), and while the ringgit and the rupiah fell, the won remained stable until late October 1997. It was only in the final quarter of 1997 that capital flight began in earnest across the region.

Capital withdrawal was sustained and in some cases accelerated following the initial onset of crisis. In Korea and Malaysia, for instance, the largest cutbacks in lending came in the first quarter of 1998 and the most substantial currency depreciations did not occur until January 1998.

The deterioration of the crisis after initial currency movements and capital flight may be partly attributable to a general increase in risk perceptions and to misguided policy responses from domestic authorities and the IMF. But the interaction between currency depreciations and the substantial unhedged foreign currency liabilities that had been accumulated in the affected economies is also vital to understanding the evolution of the crisis. The textbook story is that devaluation of an overvalued exchange rate will restore demand and discourage further capital outflows. But in economies where the corporate or financial sector has large unhedged foreign currency liabilities, this scenario may change. Debt and debt instruments, unlike equity, represent fixed obligations. Where they are denominated in foreign currencies, devaluation raises the domestic currency payments necessary to service them.

Although several analyses of the East Asian crises have drawn attention to the quantity of unhedged debt, its magnitude is less problematic than its maturity and distribution. For small open economies the debt-service burden should not change with devaluation, since export revenues and debt-interest payments ought to rise by equal amounts. As a result, debt-service ratios are only a partial guide to vulnerability, particularly in systems without compulsory foreign exchange surrender. But while devaluation should not increase debt-servicing burdens in the aggregate, individual borrowers may become severely distressed. This is most likely to be true if the institutions that have built up currency exposure are in the non-traded or financial sectors, since the increased burden of debt service will not be matched by increased revenues. Tradeable-goods companies will in general face fewer problems, since devaluation is likely to increase revenues as well as debt payments, providing a natural hedge'. However, even firms with substantial foreign currency revenues may face problems of illiquidity if creditors demand repayment of large quantities of debt at short notice.

As a consequence, though devaluation should not affect the debt servicing ability of the economy as a whole, substantial insolvency and illiquidity problems may emerge if the distribution of gains and losses is sufficiently uneven. Banks will be affected directly if they have built up currency exposure, but will in any case be indirectly affected if there are substantial bankruptcies or defaults by their borrowers. The resulting erosion in bank capital can severely disrupt the provision of credit and the stability of the payments system, particularly in fragile banking systems. These problems were evident in Thailand, Indonesia and Korea in the aftermath of currency depreciations. Exchange rate movements had large consequences for the solvency of companies and banks, particularly since many of the borrowers were only marginally profitable (or outright unprofitable) before the crisis, and since rising non-performing loans had already weakened bank balance sheets. The result was widespread corporate failure and threat of financial collapse.

As these problems emerged, foreign banks, uncertain of repayment, reassessed the credit-worthiness of borrowers in the light of the depreciation, and became increasingly unwilling to roll over debts. The refusal to roll over credit itself prompted insolvency in many cases. Insolvencies and deteriorating financial conditions spread, which in turn fuelled further withdrawal of capital and further depreciations, putting even greater pressure on balance sheets. As the IMF (1998) reported, the ensuing liquidity squeeze created a downward spiral of exchange rate depreciations and credit quality that fed on each other, magnifying price movements relatively long after the initial depreciations'. Widespread uncertainty over the true state of bank balance sheets, and continual upward revisions of the extent of unhedged borrowing and non-performing loans, did not help this vicious cycle of depreciation and capital. In the process, even firms that had borrowed prudently encountered difficulties in maintaining credit.

DIAGNOSING THE PROBLEM

The proximate causes of the East Asian crisis are relatively well understood. According to Greenspan (1998), more investment monies flowed into these economies than could be profitably employed at reasonable risk'. Weak and poorly supervised banking sectors promoted lending to highly risky activities. At the same time, the maturity and distribution of the foreign borrowing that funded many of these loans made economies vulnerable to a reversal in sentiment and subsequent illiquidity. Since borrowers in the corporate and financial sector took on large unhedged foreign currency exposure, depreciating exchange rates magnified the impact of initial shocks, further weakening the banking system. In particular, it is clear that substantial accumulations of short-term foreign debt make economies extremely vulnerable to reversals in sentiment, since investors are in a position to make rapid exits in large numbers. Some theoretical accounts have stressed maturity mismatch (Chang and Velasco 1998), while others have focused on currency mismatch (Krugman 1999). Both appear to have played an important part.

But to say all this still leaves the interesting questions unanswered. Why did banks borrow so much and lend so badly? Why did borrowers expose themselves to exchange risk? Why was bank debt the primary form of capital inflow? Why was short-term debt favoured over longer-term arrangements? Irrationality, greed and myopia almost certainly played some role. But there were also a number of distortions and market failures that meant that individuals making optimal or near-optimal choices nevertheless generated highly undesirable outcomes. These distortions, which tended to drive a wedge between the costs and benefits of certain activities, and between their private and social costs, took a number of forms.

Explicit subsidies to certain kinds of borrowing

A number of the region's economies provided explicit subsidies to foreign borrowing through preferential tax treatment. The Bangkok International Banking Facility gave special tax breaks to foreign currency dealing (Radelet and Sachs 1998) in an effort to promote the Facility as a regional offshore banking centre, as did the Malaysian Financial Centre on Labuan Island. In the Philippines, onshore income from foreign exchange loans was taxed at 10 per cent, as compared with a 35 per cent rate on other loan income. Philippine banks also faced no reserve requirements on foreign currency deposits. These explicit subsidies to foreign borrowing reduced the costs of borrowing abroad relative to borrowing at home and encouraged the accumulation of foreign debt.

Implicit subsidies to the accumulation of foreign debt

In addition to explicit subsidies, institutional arrangements implicitly raised the cost of some kinds of borrowing relative to others. The differential pace at which restrictions on different kinds of foreign borrowing were lifted meant that some forms of funding were easier than others. In general, it has been common practice to loosen restrictions on foreign bank debt earlier and more comprehensively than limits on foreign equity. Thailand and Malaysia, in particular, maintained extensive restrictions on portfolio investments while greatly relaxing restrictions on foreign bank borrowing. In Korea, too, restrictions on bank borrowing were lifted more comprehensively than restrictions on equity purchases by foreigners. Regulations limiting the issues of securities to entities with high ratings also meant that in practice most foreign borrowing was mediated through banks (IMF 1998). Liberalisation of non-FDI capital inflows (both debt and portfolio equity) also proceeded, while extensive restrictions on foreign direct investment remained. As a result, the regulations governing the different types of foreign funding tended to encourage debt over equity and continued to restrict foreign direct investment to particular levels and particular sectors.

The prudential guidelines embodied by the Basle Capital Accord have also been criticised for favouring short-term borrowing over longer-term debt. The Accord sets risk weights for various asset categories against which capital must be held. Since holding capital is costly, loans that attract higher risk-weights raise costs for the lending bank and so are likely to be subject to less favourable terms. Currently, the Basle risk weights are 20 per cent of total asset value for short-term loans to non-OECD banks (and all loans to OECD banks), but 100 per cent for long-term bank loans and loans to the private sector. Some analysts have argued that this creates a distortion that significantly favours short-term bank borrowing (Reisen 1999). The fact that Bank of International Settlements (BIS) banks engaged in substantial short-term lending to the Thai and Indonesian non-bank sectors, although there is no regulatory advantage from short-term lending in this case, suggests that differential risk weights' may not play a large role in explaining the preference for short-term borrowing. This notion is also supported by the fact that there have been large increases in the proportion of foreign debt held in short maturities over the last decade in OECD economies (New Zealand, Greece, Portugal) as well as those outside the OECD.

Exchange rate policy

The combination of stable exchange rates and large nominal interest rate differentials also encouraged foreign borrowing. All of the affected economies pegged or stabilised their currencies to varying degrees. In the face of large capital inflows in the early 1990s, monetary authorities conducted sterilised intervention. Between 1990 and 1997, Thailand, Malaysia, Indonesia and the Philippines maintained large nominal interest rate differentials relative to developed countries, accompanied by only small movements in exchange rates.[3] As a result, effective *ex post* real interest rates on foreign borrowing were between 4 per cent (Malaysia) and 12 per cent (Philippines) lower than on domestic loans. These incentives for offshore borrowing were matched by equally large incentives for portfolio inflows. The yields on $US and yen carry trades', where speculators who had been issued money-market securities in US or Japanese money markets invested the proceeds in local-currency-denominated money-market instruments, were large (IMF 1998).

The differences in foreign and local currency returns suggest that market participants acknowledged a risk of abnormal depreciation. In general, borrowers in the Asian economies did not hedge exchange risk. The important issue then is why borrowers appear to have underestimated or discounted exchange risks and why the failure to cover them was so widespread. One possible explanation is that forward markets were underdeveloped and in some cases suppressed by monetary authorities, which may have raised the cost of covering exchange risk above its perceived value. But one might also argue that borrowers simply accepted the higher risk in exchange for higher returns.

Should this be a matter for concern? If borrowers are myopic, if risk taking (and foreign borrowing) is subsidised in other ways, or if there are external costs to this kind of gamble, acceptance of exchange risk may still be undesirable. Where large parts of the corporate and financial sector are exposed to the same risk (i.e. are taking the same gamble), the systemic consequences of foreign currency borrowing may be severe, even if such borrowing appears optimal at an individual level. This issue will be pursued below.

Despite the tendency to discount exchange risks, economic theory suggests that the actual risk of an eventual failure of the currency peg was large. Fixing exchange rates during a period of rapid capital inflows is a dangerous exercise. Even in the absence of asset price bubbles, the predicted response, both to capital account liberalisation of the kind undertaken in Southeast Asia and Korea and to a rise in perceptions of profitability in the region, is a rapid inflow of capital and then a gradual outflow as returns are repatriated (McKibbin 1998; Blanchard and Fischer 1989). In this case, the equilibrium path of the real exchange rate consists of a sharp initial real appreciation followed by a gradual real depreciation.

With a flexible exchange rate, real exchange equilibrium will be delivered largely by changes in the nominal exchange rate. Where the nominal rate is fixed, however, the initial real appreciation will come through higher inflation. Since the equilibrium path of the exchange rate eventually involves a depreciation, this inflation will eventually need to be replaced by a deflation. If there are rigidities in product and labour markets, reversing a period of inflation may be difficult and costly. In that case, doubts will eventually emerge as to whether the authorities have the capacity to bring about the necessary real exchange rate adjustments through the price level. A high or rising current account deficit (as in Thailand) may be taken as an indication that the necessary depreciation will not be delivered through deflation. If doubts emerge about the sustainability of the peg in the future, there will generally be incentives for speculative attacks in the present.

The difficulties of maintaining exchange rate pegs following capital account liberalisations implies that policies that implicitly subsidise the accumulation of currency exposure are likely to be particularly dangerous at that time. The failure to defend an exchange rate peg may be particularly damaging in emerging markets, since the loss of the monetary anchor may lead to uncertainty about the commitment to price stability, forcing the authorities to choose between substantial depreciation or a costly interest rate signal.

Interaction of foreign capital flows with domestic distortions

If the domestic economy is already subject to distortions to resource allocation, inflows of foreign capital may aggravate them or magnify their scope, leading to larger misallocations of resources than if capital flows are restricted. This argument is a familiar part of trade theory, where there is a long tradition of work on immiserising' capital flows. In the classic case presented by Brecher and Alejandro-Diaz (1977), a situation is described where capital inflows reduce welfare in the presence of import tariffs. The basic problem arises because the existence of a domestic distortion means that foreign capital is misallocated as it flows in.

In East and Southeast Asia, trade restrictions, though important in some sectors, are unlikely to be the most important source of domestic distortions. Nevertheless, other sectoral subsidies have similar implications. In Korea, certain industries, particularly producers of capital-intensive goods and tradeable goods, received implicit or explicit subsidies from the government. When these industries borrowed abroad, foreign capital flowed into areas that were already over-endowed. In addition, related-party' or politically motivated lending was widespread. Since these practices meant that the allocation of resources was not based on intrinsic profitability, they may also have encouraged foreign capital to flow to the 'wrong' places (areas that were already subject to low profitability or excess capacity).

Interaction of foreign capital flows with financial sector distortions

The general problems that arise from the interaction of foreign capital and domestic distortions are not limited to distortions on the production side. Potentially much more important in the East Asian context was the interaction of capital inflows with distortions in the financial system. There is strong evidence that financial systems in these countries were already prone to misallocating resources, particularly towards overly risky projects (Corsetti *et al.* 1998). The inflow of foreign capital greatly increased the scope for financing these projects and almost certainly increased the risks involved. To a large extent, these problems arose because weakly capitalised and poorly supervised banking sectors were subject to severe moral hazard. Under-capitalised banks had little of their own money at stake and so faced stronger incentives to take risks. There was a widespread perception that governments would implicitly guarantee that deposits would be insured and that financial institutions would not be permitted to fail.

Guarantees to financial institutions can be desirable on the grounds of financial stability and the integral place of banks in the domestic financial and payments system. The corollary to government guarantees is that prudential supervision is needed to tightly control the risks that banks take. Prudential supervision was generally inadequate and prudential regulations were poorly enforced (Fane 1998). In Thailand, non-bank financial institutions were allowed to perform many of the functions of banks but were subject to far less onerous regulation. In the absence of proper prudential regulation, deposit insurance and other guarantees that limit liability can act as a general subsidy to risk taking. Uncovered foreign borrowing was one of a number of risky activities that may have been encouraged in this way. The risks associated with moral hazard may be particularly severe after episodes of financial liberalisation. Increased competition is likely to erode the franchise value of existing banks, which if it occurs rapidly may encourage risk taking (World Bank 1998).

Capital inflows increase the potential as well as the means for risk taking. During periods of substantial capital inflow, subsequent real appreciation raises the price of non-tradeable goods, creating fertile ground for temporary (and rational) asset price bubbles. Bubbles may themselves exacerbate the original problem, since risky lenders may be temporarily successful during bubble periods, increasing the value of their collateral in the short term and raising the level of funding they can command (Krugman 1998b).

The problems of capital inflow in the presence of underdeveloped financial markets have been formalised in a number of models. One of the best known is that of McKinnon and Pill (1998). They show how the interaction of liberalisation of the capital account and financial market failures can lead to overborrowing' episodes. In the presence of deposit guarantees, banks effectively discount the lower tails of the distribution of returns and so face incentives to make higher-risk lending decisions. In the domestic economy the scope for overborrowing is limited, since market failure tends to bid up the real interest rate. But with access to international capital markets, the real interest rate is set exogenously. Instead, the effect of moral hazard is to increase the inflow of foreign capital to inefficient levels.

Aizenman (1998) develops a more sophisticated model in the same spirit, in which banks mitigate the problems of excessive risk by engaging in costly monitoring. He finds that, as the riskiness of projects in equilibrium is raised, the higher are the costs of risk monitoring or financial intermediation and the lower are the costs of banks' funds. In other words, economies with inefficient banking systems and poor prudential supervision will engage in excessive risk taking. In this model, for economies where financial market distortions are severe, access to international capital markets may magnify their impact, not just by increasing the level of misallocated investment, but also because, by reducing the cost of funds, such access reduces the level of monitoring and exacerbates the distortion itself.

The problem of moral hazard' is not limited to host countries. There are concerns that international rescue packages that bail out' foreign investors, particularly international banks, following crises, encourage foreign investors to pay too little attention to investment risk. These concerns may well be exaggerated. It is too early to say what final portfolio losses will be, but investors in East Asian bond and equity markets suffered substantial losses, as did some banks. It seems unlikely that the prospect of Korea (or even Thailand or Indonesia) turning to the IMF was high on investors' minds before the crisis broke.

Externalities associated with foreign borrowing

Private and social costs of financial activities may also diverge because of externalities to individual borrowing decisions. For instance, borrowers may not take into account the effect of individual risk taking or individual failure on credit conditions for others, though these external effects may be significant, particularly in the presence of imperfect information. An individual's decision to borrow may also increase the vulnerability of the economy (or at least of other borrowers) to particular events or shocks, particularly in the presence of other distortions. McKinnon and Pill (1998) argue that individual borrowers and lenders are unlikely to take into account the effects of their decisions on the overall stability of the payments system or on the probability of financial crisis. Unless these costs are fully internalised, the social costs of borrowing may exceed their private cost.

The externalities posed by systemic risks are likely to operate regardless of whether economies are open to foreign capital inflows. But foreign borrowing can increase the significance of this kind of externality by raising both the probability of crisis and the costs incurred if it should occur. Chang and Velasco (1998) argue that short-term foreign borrowing may bring efficiency gains by lowering the cost of funds, but that these benefits must be weighed against the risks they bring in terms of increasing the vulnerability of the banking system to runs. If the risks posed by increased vulnerability are not internalised by individual borrowers or lenders, the private costs of short-term foreign borrowing will understate their true social costs. Krugman (1999) makes a similar argument in relation to foreign currency borrowing, arguing that the increased vulnerability to currency movements caused by foreign currency borrowing is unlikely to be internalised.

The divergence between private and social costs will be greater, the larger the costs of a financial crisis. Excessive foreign borrowing may raise the costs (as well as the probability) of financial crisis, since currency and banking crises are likely to occur simultaneously, leading to a deeper impact than either kind of crisis alone. The probability of a bank run prompted by a withdrawal of foreign funds, and the costs of the subsequent crisis, may also be higher than an equivalent domestic crisis, since the central bank in the former case cannot act as a lender of last resort. In domestic financial crises, substantial injections of funds could stabilise the banking sector in the event of a crisis and prevent further withdrawals.

The kinds of coordination failure that lie behind Chang and Velasco's story of illiquidity are most likely to occur with short-term bank debt. Coordination failure arises because, if creditors realise that a borrower is in danger of illiquidity, each individual creditor may have an incentive not to roll over debts, despite the fact that all might be better off if they could act collectively to continue the supply of funds. As a result, small shocks may lead to large reversals in capital flows. Creditors may be particularly inclined to refuse to roll over debt if information about the quality of borrowers or their balance sheet is highly uncertain (Baccheta and van Wincoops 1998) or if bankruptcy procedures make the collection of assets after default costly. Since debt appears to carry special risks, it seems unfortunate that many East Asian countries have favoured the liberalisation of bank borrowing ahead of the lifting of restrictions in equity markets.

It might be argued that creditors should take account of these kinds of risk and impose higher costs on marginal lenders as the ratio of short-term debt to reserves increases, as compensation for additional risk. This is a less likely outcome if creditors face moral hazard problems of their own (for example, from the expectation of domestic or international bailouts), or if information on overall reserve and debt levels is not publicly available or costly to collect.

Imperfect information

A substantial amount of blame has been attached to the lack of transparency in the affected economies, as a cause of investor withdrawal, and many of the recommendations from formal working groups have focused heavily on the provision of information in preventing future crises. If information is costly, herding by investors may be more likely to occur and the ability of investors to assess risk accurately will be limited. Under certain conditions, uncertainty over underlying financial conditions may magnify perceptions of risk when the state of the economy changes rapidly. However, much of the information that indicated fragility was publicly available. Anecdotal evidence suggests that many investors were aware of the risks involved in the positions that they were taking, but attached strong weight to government guarantees and assurances that these risks would not eventuate. In any case, in the absence of other distortions, the rational response to a lack of information would be to charge higher rates or not to lend at all, rather than to continue lending on preferential terms.

Peso problems and perverse incentives

The risk taking in East Asia also suggests that there may be persistent difficulties in discouraging risk taking related to so-called peso problems', where there are small risks of substantial negative outcomes. The pricing of these kinds of risk explains why short-term debt is generally cheaper than long-term debt and why foreign-currency debt is generally cheaper than domestic debt in contracted terms, even if its risk-adjusted cost' is the same. Problems arise because, if the risk does not eventuate, there may be a long period of time when firms that (unwisely *ex post*) fail to cover their risk (say, by borrowing unhedged in foreign currency or borrowing short instead of long) incur substantially lower costs. If the period is long enough, competitive pressures may mean that other firms are forced to join the risk-takers or go out of business.[4] Long boom periods are particularly likely to generate these kinds of perverse incentives for risk taking, since they represent substantial episodes where downside risks do not emerge.

COMBATING MARKET FAILURE

The previous section illustrated that a number of distortions in lending and borrower countries encouraged excessive reliance on short-term foreign borrowing and risky lending practices, which made the East Asian economies vulnerable to crisis. Even if panic also played some role in the unfolding of the crisis, any sensible package of measures to reduce vulnerability to sudden capital withdrawal must address these distortions. In doing this, the general principle should be, as far as possible, to make individuals face the true costs of their decisions. The necessary measures should be seen as part of a broader sequence of financial reform that seeks to align private and social costs and benefits of financial activities.[5]

The developed country paradigm: aiming for 'best practice'

The ideal response to the problems identified above will generally involve removal of the underlying distortions. In the East Asian economies this would require a number of a policy changes. First, favourable tax and regulatory treatment for foreign borrowing should be abolished. This would remove explicit subsidies to accumulate foreign ahead of domestic liabilities. Ideally, restrictions on foreign access to domestic equity markets would not be raised ahead of bank borrowing.

Second, authorities should move towards more flexible exchange rate regimes. By exposing borrowers directly to exchange risk and allowing the exchange rate to appreciate in the wake of capital account liberalisation, the incentives for excessive foreign borrowing are likely to be reduced. The IMF found that increased exchange rate flexibility in Chile after its financial crisis in 1982 was useful in discouraging short-term speculative flows (IMF 1998). Floating the exchange rate is no panacea. Overborrowing episodes have occurred under flexible regimes, and the sharp appreciations that can follow capital account liberalisation will continue to present difficult policy dilemmas.[6] But by eliminating one-way bets' on the exchange rate, a more flexible exchange rate is more likely to equalise the costs of foreign and domestic borrowing and to encourage borrowers to take account of exchange risk (Reisen 1999).[7] The choice of exchange rate regime is likely to be particularly important during episodes of capital account liberalisation.

Third, domestic distortions to the allocation of resources (tariffs, subsidies to different industry groups) should, as far as possible, be removed. By far the most important distortions in East Asia centred on the financial sector. Moral hazard is an intrinsic feature of a financial system in which safety nets are provided to financial institutions. In general, the costs of financial crisis are sufficiently great that in practice safety nets do operate, even where deposits have not been explicitly guaranteed. Without eliminating these guarantees, moral hazard can only be removed (or limited) by prudential regulation.

The traditional regulatory solution mimics an insurance contract (Fane 1998). Minimum capital adequacy ratios operate like the deductible' component of the contract, since the bank loses its capital if it fails, even when deposits are guaranteed. Reserve requirements then operate like the insurance premium, raising the private cost of providing loans to a level that includes the implicit costs of deposit insurance provision. Essentially, the reserve requirement operates as a tax on risk taking activity that balances the subsidy to risk provided by safety-net provision.[8] This implies that reserve requirements are likely to be optimal for all risk taking activities that are subject to moral hazard, not simply for domestic deposits. But the success of tight capital adequacy standards and reserve requirements in limiting moral hazard depends on the ability of prudential authorities to enforce regulations swiftly and actively.

Fourth, the externalities identified in foreign borrowing would need to be internalised. These externalities arose principally from the build-up of short-term foreign currency debts in excess of liquid assets, while the substantial costs of a sudden withdrawal of capital posed substantial risks given the absence of an international lender of last resort. The previous section indicated that external effects were exacerbated by uncertainty over the true financial position of domestic borrowers or by moral hazard in creditor nations. Increasing the provision of financial information and raising the risk weighting on short-term inter-bank lending might give creditors greater incentives to monitor these dangers and price these risks into loans. But although improving disclosure requirements and tightening prudential regulations on cross-border lending in creditor nations could reduce the external costs of currency exposure, it will not eliminate them. To that extent, there is a strong case for raising the costs of accumulating short-term currency exposures relative to other forms of risk.

Applying these remedies to the various distortions would essentially bring the East Asian economies to the position of most developed economies. Developed countries typically do not provide preferential tax treatment to foreign borrowing, or extensive domestic subsidies. They generally operate floating exchange rates.[9] They retain few restrictions on overseas bank borrowing or portfolio equity purchases by foreigners. They enforce strict capital adequacy ratios and reserve requirements, backed up by strong prudential supervision. And, to a growing extent, they require banks and securities firms to hold additional capital against short-term currency exposure (Abrams and Beato).[10] Within the East Asian region, Singapore and Hong Kong broadly conform to this position, though of course in Hong Kong the dollar is pegged through a currency board arrangement.

Undoubtedly, even with these best practice' solutions to existing distortions, large (and possibly irrational) movements in asset prices and capital flows remain possible. But, with the social and private costs of financial activities more effectively aligned, economies can in general be made robust to adverse developments.

Reducing vulnerability: policies for the short and medium term

Implicit in the best practice' recommendations is that their removal is both feasible and does not conflict with other objectives that the economy is unwilling to abandon. The removal of explicit subsidies to foreign borrowing and moves towards greater exchange rate flexibility are easily instituted and have already occurred in most cases in the East Asian economies. But the removal of distortions in the financial sector and the establishment of an effective system of enforceable prudential regulations are unlikely to be possible overnight (McFarlane 1998). Resolving financial sector weakness requires greater technical expertise amongst financial institutions, efficient legal procedures and experienced regulators.

Even if the correct procedures can be introduced, authorities must have the will and the capacity to enforce them. The problem in the Southeast Asian economies was less that the necessary regulations had not been enacted than that they had not been enforced. This is a huge task and, as a consequence, developing economies are likely to continue to have seriously distorted financial sectors, at least over the period in which financial reform can be completed. Where financial systems are weaker, problems of excessive moral hazard will be more severe and the probability and cost of a banking crisis will be higher than in developed countries. As a result, the social costs of various risky financial activities may continue to exceed the private incentives faced by banks even after attempts to institute best practice' measures have been made.

As a consequence, if in the short term these distortions cannot be tackled directly by adequate prudential supervision, there will be a strong second best' case for raising the cost of certain risky activities beyond the levels required in developed countries. The vulnerabilities associated with the East Asian crisis suggest that there may be a particularly strong case for raising the costs of foreign borrowing above domestic borrowing and for raising the costs of short-term and foreign-currency-denominated bank debt relative to other forms of foreign funding. The issue then becomes one of how best to align social and private costs. Direct prohibitions or controls on certain kinds of activity are likely to be an inefficient way of doing this, since they will exclude some transactions where the social benefit exceeds the social cost as well as some where it does not. In general, it will be more efficient to raise the price of these activities so that they reflect their true social costs. In doing this, efforts must also be made to ensure that all those who undertake particular kinds of risky activity are treated equally, or attempts to discourage particular transactions in one part of the economy may simply divert them to another.

A simple way to counter excessive moral hazard in relation to all risky bank-related activities is simply to raise the required minimum capital adequacy ratios (CARs) above the 8 per cent set out by the Basle Accord. Fane (1998) points out that CARs average 16–20 per cent in the top US banks and 17.7 per cent in Hong Kong. By setting minimum CARs of between 15 and 20 per cent, the private costs of engaging in risky activities are likely to be raised to levels that take into account the much greater problems of moral hazard and the large costs of financial crisis in weaker financial systems. Naturally, capital adequacy requirements must be supported by strict arrangements on provisioning for non-performing loans if they are to be effective; new arrangements are currently being introduced in Thailand and Indonesia.

Raising CARs raises the price of risk taking activities generally. But the higher risks and greater external costs imposed by unhedged foreign currency borrowing may justify additional prudential requirements that recognise the additional risks incurred. There are a number of ways to influence the incentives of banks in the affected economies to borrow and lend in foreign currencies and to build up foreign exchange exposure. Best practice' arguments for imposing additional asset requirements on open foreign exchange positions have already been considered and are likely to be reinforced by second best considerations. These would help to limit the build-up of exchange risk by financial institutions themselves.

But these kinds of regulation would not (indeed, did not) prevent financial institutions from borrowing abroad and lending on in foreign currency, transferring exchange risk to the corporate sector, as in Thailand. Measures to discourage on-lending of this kind would need to raise directly the costs of borrowing and lending in foreign currency. Increasing the risk weightings in calculating CARs for foreign currency lending to the private sector would raise the cost of domestic banks' lending to the private sector in foreign currency. At present, a 100 per cent weight is attached to lending to private non-bank borrowers regardless of the currency denomination of lending. It may be desirable to raise the weighting for foreign currency denominated lending. It may also be sensible to investigate ways of keying capital adequacy ratios to the sources of funding, a suggestion advanced by Alan Greenspan (1998). One of the weaknesses of the Basle framework is that it focuses on the asset side of bank balance sheets, paying less attention to the differential riskiness of liabilities. A similar result might be achieved by tightening the risk-weightings for cross-border lending for banks in developed countries, both for short-term inter-bank and private sector lending to developing countries.

Measures along these lines would raise the cost of bank-intermediated foreign currency borrowing. With proper prudential design, non-bank financial intermediaries could also be regulated in a similar fashion. But capital adequacy restrictions will do nothing to prevent direct borrowing or the accumulation of exchange risk by the private sector, although this represented a large part of the problem in some countries. One approach is simply to leave the monitoring of the private sector to the banks that lend to them. If banks both at home and abroad take full account of the risks of lending to corporate borrowers, and if domestic authorities are prepared to allow bankruptcies to occur, this should deliver an efficient solution. Moves to tighten capital adequacy requirements for developed country banks that lend in foreign currency to the private sector in developing countries could help in this regard. The external costs suggest that a *laissez-faire* attitude may be risky. At the other end of the spectrum, strict limits on non-bank borrowing abroad could be maintained. The Czech Republic operates this kind of policy, requiring strict case-by-case approval on non-bank foreign borrowing. This aims to ensure that foreign borrowing is largely mediated by domestic banks that are subject to domestic prudential control. There are presumably costs in such mediation, but these may be worth bearing.

A much-discussed alternative that would raise the cost of foreign borrowing for financial and corporate borrowers alike would be to introduce large compulsory reserve requirements for all foreign loans. The version of this system introduced in Chile, and widely discussed, required that 30 per cent of any foreign loan had to be deposited for one year in non-interest-paying accounts. Less extreme differential reserve requirements for foreign and domestic deposits could still raise the relative cost of foreign borrowing substantially. This kind of requirement is a cruder and more direct form of tax on foreign borrowing than most of the prudential measures described above. The evidence from Chile on the success of this kind of measure is mixed. It appears to have succeeded in discouraging short-term capital flows only after controls were strengthened in 1993, and there is considerable debate over whether their effectiveness has been eroded. Several commentators have argued that the greater stability in Chile's financial sector owes more to improvements in its banking system than the disincentives to foreign borrowing (IMF 1998).

In fact, Chile's experience in this regard is illustrative of the advantages and disadvantages of all of these second best' measures. According to Goodhart's Law', financial regulations that seek to raise the costs of certain kinds of financial activity tend to be circumvented over time. They are best seen as short-term measures that can be justified only alongside vigorous measures to reach the first best' scenario of a prudent and well-regulated financial system. An alternative method of raising the cost of foreign currency borrowing that might be easier to operate would be to limit the tax deductibility of interest on debt denominated in or linked to foreign currencies. Another proposed solution (Feldstein 1999) is for the central bank to accumulate reserves to back' the economy's short-term liabilities. This can be interpreted as an inferior version of the reserve requirement' policy, where the central bank now acquires the reserves (at considerable cost to its own balance sheet). Since, in this case, the private sector does not itself face the cost of reserve accumulation, overborrowing relative to the optimum is likely to continue, though the policy may be easier to implement than the Chilean solution.

Sequencing and prohibitions: policies for the less developed

Although in general, it is better to counter distortions by seeking to raise the private costs of financial activities to the level of their social costs, there are two possible arguments for imposing direct limits or outright prohibitions.

The first arises when the financial sector is so weak, domestic distortions so large and the possibility of effective supervision so remote that very large taxes on foreign borrowing would be required to adequately capture the risks from foreign capital flows. In this case, it may be simpler (and the associated costs smaller) to prohibit certain types of foreign capital inflow altogether. The conditions under which this may prove optimal are likely to be very restrictive. Not only must domestic distortions be severe, but also the prospects for removing them rapidly (a superior solution) must be low. The argument is then essentially one of sequencing. In countries with severe financial weakness, the logical sequence of measures is to reform the financial sector, before liberalising the capital account.

The case for direct controls is most likely to hold for countries with extremely weak domestic institutions that have not opened to foreign capital, and so does not apply in most of the East Asian economies. But for countries such as China and Vietnam, there may be good reasons to work rapidly to strengthen financial systems before greatly liberalising foreign borrowing. Even then, there are huge issues of practicality, particularly as these economies become more open to trade. The risk that continued exchange controls will prove increasingly ineffective and that considerable distortions will emerge as borrowers seek to circumvent them will rise over time. This makes the task of moving to second best' and best practice' regimes more urgent.

The second situation where direct prohibitions may be desirable arises when there is considerable uncertainty about the exact risks of capital inflow or foreign currency exposure and when the costs of a bad outcome rise rapidly. In this case, it can be shown that direct quantity limits are likely to be preferable to attempting to influence decisions by price, using an argument first elaborated by Martin Weitzman (1974). The basic idea is that a policy design based on an underestimate of the wedge between private and social costs could expose the economy to sharply rising risk.

The area where this appears most likely to be relevant is in containing currency exposure. Particularly following episodes of financial liberalisation, financial institutions and regulators may face considerable uncertainty over the risks of foreign currency borrowing. As a result, attempts to influence the cost of taking on foreign currency risk, along the lines already described, might still leave the economy open to considerable risk of overborrowing. This creates an argument for direct limits on foreign currency exposure. Although limits of this sort are being replaced by capital requirements in many developed economies, they still have a role in many developing countries.

Lateral thinking: short cuts to avoiding financial sector distortions

The solutions suggested so far have focused on addressing or counteracting distortions in the financial sector, through prudential regulation or other means. In practice, installing, operating and enforcing these kinds of systems effectively is a demanding task. It may be sensible to consider ways in which distortions and deficiencies in the domestic financial system can effectively be bypassed.

Greater international participation in the banking sector provides one way of rapidly importing expertise and prudent management systems, though it remains one that many of the region's economies (and not just the developing ones) are reluctant to embrace. Through ties to their parents, domestic affiliates effectively have their own private lenders of last resort and, since the parent's asset base will in general be highly diversified, they are less likely to be destabilised by adverse domestic conditions or exposures to particular sectors of the local economy. As a result, a highly internationalised financial sector is likely to be less exposed to risk management problems, and more of the external costs associated with foreign borrowing may be internalised. The regional economies that have come under the IMF's tutelage are moving in this direction already. Malaysia might benefit, too, from greater international involvement in its banking sector. Tough limits on international bank participation have seen the share of deposits held by foreign banks fall from 70 per cent in the early 1980s to around 30 per cent now (Athakurola 1999).

More broadly, the continued liberalisation of foreign direct investment and equity investment and the deepening of equity markets would allow East Asian economies to borrow from abroad in ways that avoid the market failures implicit in their banking system. A greater tendency to use local equity markets to mobilise foreign savings would also limit the exposure to foreign currency risk that is an unavoidable part of bank borrowing.

CONTROLS IN TIMES OF CRISIS: THE MALAYSIAN CASE

Addressing the underlying sources of vulnerability suggests lessons for medium-term choices as to the appropriate regime for managing capital flows. The Malaysian experiment raises the different issue of the role of capital controls as part of crisis response. The rationale behind the imposition of exchange controls in September 1998 was that they would permit a looser fiscal and monetary stance without precipitating a run on the currency. Unsurprisingly, the response to the government's move was generally negative, with most analysts pronouncing it a retrograde step and issuing strong warnings about the penalties that Malaysia would pay and the risks that it was running. Some economists, notably Krugman, argued instead that exchange controls might be an appropriate response to the perverse incentives created in a crisis situation. The dilemma arises where markets demand that a particular policy is needed to signal credibility, but the government believes that this would do great damage to the economy.[11]

It is certainly too early to provide a proper assessment of the Malaysian experiment, but the available evidence suggests that the argument may be quite finely balanced. Real interest rates fell following the introduction of exchange controls to levels lower than elsewhere (by December 1998, real interest rates were 0.7 per cent in Malaysia compared to 3.9 per cent in Thailand and 5 per cent in Korea). Foreign reserves have climbed sharply and inflation is quiescent. According to the latest Deutsche Bank predictions, the Malaysian economy is predicted to grow faster than the Thai economy in 1999 and 2000. The exchange rate peg has kept the real exchange rate well below its pre-crisis levels, avoiding the overshooting that characterised the won and baht earlier this year and supporting more robust export growth than in Thailand or Korea.

Nor is it easy to find evidence of significant costs from the controls. The Malaysian government raised US$2 billion in May in an offer that was three times oversubscribed. Foreign direct investors do not appear to be reconsidering Malaysia on a dramatic scale, though the lack of predictability in Malaysian policy has undoubtedly done damage. The removal of the restrictions on repatriating profits on 1 September 1999 did not prompt significant capital flight, and the Kuala Lumpur Exchange will be reinstated on the Morgan Stanley Capital International (MSCI) stock indices shortly. The standard argument that, once instituted, controls would be hard to remove has proved incorrect. As with the imposition of restrictions in 1994, the Malaysian government has treated controls as a strictly temporary measure. The move to a price-based system was relatively swift (five months after the original controls were announced), and the remaining restrictions involve only a stepped tax on capital gains (ironically rather similar in appearance to the US capital gains tax regime). There has been no suggestion of monetary laxity or fiscal profligacy, and banking sector reform is progressing at a reasonable pace (JP Morgan 1999). Losses have not generally been imposed on investors. Those forced to stay in the Kuala Lumpur stock market have seen it climb by 190 per cent since controls were imposed.

There are of course plenty of explanations other than exchange controls for Malaysia's relatively favourable experience, and it is frequently (and correctly) pointed out that the performances of Korea and Thailand have been strong without such drastic measures. It may also be the case that the reform process has been slower than it would have been under different circumstances. Even a positive judgement does not mean that the Malaysian experiment is a lesson that should be emulated elsewhere. Malaysia's administration has a good record in many dimensions, and its government is better placed to administer controls without problems of corruption or a loss of discipline than governments in most emerging markets. The final judgement may turn out to be that, although the Malaysian experiment has not been overwhelmingly positive, neither has it been clearly negative.

CONCLUSIONS

Until recently, there has been too little acknowledgment that the benefits from free capital movements in terms of superior resource allocation are largely contingent on the absence of considerable distortions in domestic economies. This means that greater care must be taken in assessing the appropriate regimes for capital inflows in developing countries. In particular, the efficiency of the allocation of capital flows and the extent to which they lead to sustained improvements in economic performance will depend heavily on the development and efficiency of the financial system (IMF 1998).

Greed, myopia, irrationality and panic will always be a feature of human behaviour, particularly in asset markets. Nevertheless, the excesses that lay behind the East Asian crisis and the vulnerabilities that they exposed did not emerge without encouragement. A large number of distortions operated that led to substantial divergence between the private and social costs of certain types of financial activity. These distortions were a large contributor to East Asia's problems, and addressing them will be a large component of an optimal policy response.

In general, the ideal solution, and the long-term goal, will be to remove the relevant distortions. This essentially implies further progress towards the developed country' paradigm. Equal tax treatment for particular forms of financial activity, greater exchange rate flexibility and the operation of tough prudential regulations to limit moral hazard (both in developed and developing countries) are the main measures suggested by this approach. Even then, the external costs associated with exchange risk are likely to create first best' reasons for measures to increase the costs of currency exposure, through additional capital requirements, and for higher capital requirements for international bank lending to banks and companies in developing countries.

In the short term, it may prove difficult in many of the East Asian economies to remove distortions completely, particularly those associated with the financial sector. In practice, it takes time for the necessary institutions, practices and culture that support prudent financial management to be established. As a result, measures to raise the cost of certain risky activities, particularly those associated with foreign borrowing, beyond those justified on best practice' grounds may be desirable for second best' reasons. In considering how best to do this, it is sensible to move away from a knee-jerk antipathy to the concept of capital controls', and to acknowledge that capital is already controlled and flows distorted by government policies and market failure. Moves to manage capital flows span a broad spectrum from prudential regulations of the kind operated by developed country financial systems to outright prohibitions on capital movements. The former are in general more likely to provide efficient means for managing capital flows than the latter.

Although it is wise to consider a range of options, changes to prudential regulations in general, and the treatment of foreign currency exposure in particular, would probably go a long way to align the social and private costs of borrowing in the East Asian economies. In combination with increased exchange rate flexibility, removal of preferential tax treatment and the tightening of capital requirements for cross-border lending by developed-country banks, these changes might be sufficient to prevent the worst excesses of foreign borrowing. More explicit taxes, such as the reserve requirements against foreign loans required in Chile, would then be unnecessary.

In the small number of regional economies where financial market weaknesses are particularly severe, even these second best' measures may not be enough. In China and Vietnam, for instance, it is now clear that substantial strengthening of the financial system should precede any significant lifting of restrictions on foreign capital movements. Capital controls are likely to provide only temporary protection in the face of distorted financial sectors. Particularly for economies as open as those in East Asia, the practical problems associated with preventing capital movements or seeking to raise their costs may be large. As a consequence, attempts to raise the cost of foreign borrowing are only worthwhile where they are accompanied by vigorous attempts at financial reform.

The major problem confronting developing economies on this front is the practical difficulty of creating a robust financial system in a short space of time. Many of the East Asian economies have had extensive regulations on paper, but poor enforcement has prevented these regulations from having their desired effect. On this front, the kinds of technical cooperation by regional governments established by the Executive Meeting of East Asian and Pacific Central Banks (EMEAP) group of regional central bankers and the proposals emerging from other international groups will be valuable.

Tackling underlying distortions in a systematic fashion provides no cast-iron guarantee against future crises. But it is likely that countries that are reluctant to address the underlying sources of instability directly will find themselves forced into more drastic and costly remedies for managing capital flows. By tackling the symptom rather than the source of the problems, the risk is that, as governments step in to regulate or tax capital flows, they will fail to do so in the most efficient way, and thereby risk introducing new distortions to replace the old ones.

NOTES

1   Borenzstein *et al.* (1995), for instance, use cross-country growth regressions to demonstrate that FDI raises growth in the host economy, through complementarity with domestic investment and human capital. Similar evidence on the productivity of FDI and its role in promoting domestic investment and growth can be found in country studies (e.g. Warr 1998 for Thailand).
2   Incremental capital output ratios, which measure the amount of additional capital required to produce an additional unit of output, rose between 1987 and 1996 in Korea, Malaysia and Thailand. Thai and Korean stock prices began to fall from early 1996, indicating that expected future earnings were being revised downwards.
3   In Korea, these incentives were markedly smaller. Smaller interest rate differentials were accompanied by significant depreciation of the won.
4   Firms that hedged currency exposure in the Southeast Asian economies (at considerable cost) might have been engaging in sensible risk management, but would have found themselves at a competitive disadvantage to firms that did not, particularly since the risk of substantial depreciation did not eventuate for many years.
5   The notion that crisis prevention involves the removal of distorted incentives that encourage risky lending practices has formed the basis for many financial reforms, including those that followed the Savings and Loans crisis in the US and the tightening of Japanese regulation following the *jusen* crises in Japan.
6   The textbook response to an appreciation that results from a massive capital inflow is to contract fiscal policy. In practice, this may be politically difficult and in some circumstances may induce further inflows by signalling greater credibility of the government's reform programs.
7   Some doubt has been cast (Grenville and Gruen) on the idea that exchange rate flexibility will reduce unhedged foreign borrowing or provide greater flexibility, largely on the basis of Latin American experiences. The Latin American cases, where economies are *de facto* dollarised and so authorities are reluctant to allow exchange rate movements even under flexible regimes, present special problems that do not generally apply in East Asia.

8   The use of prudential regulation to limit moral hazard may arguably be better viewed as a second best' policy. Since moral hazard can be viewed as fundamental' to financial systems, I deal with it here as a distortion that cannot be directly removed.
9   The establishment of Economic and Monetary Union on 1 January 1999 does not invalidate this. All participants will still have floating exchange rates relative to foreign currencies. It will simply be true that they will share a common currency with other participants, where separate currencies previously operated.
10   The EU, for instance, introduced a directive in 1993 that required an 8% capital charge against the overall foreign exchange position of banks and securities firms. France, Germany, the Netherlands and Spain now operate systems along these lines.
11   Why would the market demand such a signal? One answer is that the market is wrong, though this is not the only possibility. Instead, the problem may be one of asymmetric information. The government knows its type (i.e. that it is committed to discipline), but the market does not. The market may then rationally demand a costly signal of discipline, while the government may judge that the signalling costs are not worth incurring.

REFERENCES

Abrams, R. and Beato, P. (1998) The prudential regulation and management of foreign exchange risk', *IMF Working Paper* 98/37.

Aizenman, J. (1998) Capital mobility in a second best world', *NBER Working Paper* no. 6703.

Athakurola, P. (2000) The Malaysian Experiment', in D. Wilson, M. Uzan and D. Dasgupta (eds) *Capital Flows without Crisis?*, Routledge.

Baccheta, P. and van Wincoop, E. (1998) Capital flows to emerging markets: Liberalization, overshooting and volatility', *NBER Working Paper* no. 6530.

Bhagwati, J. (1971) The generalized theory of distortions and welfare', in J. Bhagwati, R. Jones, R. Mundell and J. Vanek (eds) *Trade, Balance of Payments and Growth*, North-Holland.

(1998) The capital myth: The difference between trade in widgets and trade in dollars', *Foreign Affairs* 77(3): 7–12.

Blanchard, O. and Fischer, S. (1989) *Lectures in Macroeconomics*, MIT.

Borenzstein, E., De Gregorio, J. and Lee, J.W. (1995) How does foreign direct investment affect economic growth?', *NBER Working Paper* no. 5057.

Brecher, R. and Alejandro-Diaz, C. (1977) Immiserising capital flows', *International Economic Review:* 317–22.

Chang, R. and Velasco, A. (1998) Financial fragility and the exchange rate regime', *NBER Working Paper* no. 6469.

Corsetti, G., Pesenti, P. and Roubini, N. (1998) What caused the Asian currency and financial crisis?', unpublished manuscript.

Fane, G. (1998) Prudential regulation of financial institutions in the 1997–98 crises in Southeast Asia', in *The East Asian Crisis: From being a miracle to needing one?*, London and New York: Routledge.

Feldstein, M. (1999) A self-help guide for emerging markets', *Foreign Affairs*, March–April: 93–109.

French, K. and Poterba, J. (1991) Investor diversification and international equity markets', *American Economic Review* 81: 222–6.

Greenspan, A. (1998) Remarks' at the 34th Annual Conference on Bank Structure and Competition of the Federal Reserve Bank of Chicago', 7 May.

Grenville, S. and Gruen, D. (1999) Capital flows and exchange rates', in D. Gruen and L. Gower (eds) *Capital Flows and the International Financial System*, Sydney: Reserve Bank of Australia.

IMF (1998) *International Capital Markets: Developments, prospects and key policy issues*, Washington, DC.

Johnston, B., Darbar, S. and Echeverria, C. (1997) Sequencing capital account liberalization: Lessons from the experiences in Chile, Indonesia, Korea and Thailand', *IMF Working Paper* 97/157.

Krugman, P. (1998a) The confidence game', *New Republic*, 5 October.

—— (1998b) What happened to Asia?' unpublished conference paper , January.

—— (1999) Balance sheets, the transfer problem and financial crises' www.mit.edu/people/krugman/index.html.

Lee, J.W. (1993) Trade, distortions and growth', *IMF Staff Papers* 40(2): 299–328.

McFarlane, I. (1998) Speech to financial regulators, Sydney, November.

McKibbin, W. (1998) Some global consequences of financial market liberalisation in the Asia Pacific region', paper presented at ANU Conference on Financial Reform in Japan and Australia, August.

McKinnon, R. and Pill, H. (1998) International overborrowing: A decomposition of credit and currency risks', Stanford University, Department of Economics, Working Paper no. 98004.

Morgan, J.P. (1999) *Asian Financial Markets* Report, 1st Quarter 1998.

Obstfeld, M. (1994) Risk taking, global diversification and growth', *American Economic Review* 85: 1310–29.

—— (1998) The global capital market: benefactor or menace?', *NBER Working Paper* no. 6559.

Radelet, S. and Sachs, J. (1998) The onset of the East Asian Financial crisis', unpublished paper, Harvard Institute for International Development. Available at http://www.hiid.harvard.edu/research/newnote.html#asia.

Reisen, H. (1999) After the great Asian Slump: Towards a coherent approach to global capital flows', OECD Development Centre, Policy Brief no. 16.

Rodrik, D. (1998) Who needs capital-account convertibility?', mimeo, Harvard University, February.

Sala-i-Martin, X. (1997) I just ran 2 million regressions', *American Economic Review* 87(2): 178–82.

Soros, George (1998) *The Crisis of Global Capitalism*, Little, Brown and Company.

Warr, P. (1998) Thailand', in *The East Asian Crisis: From being a miracle to needing one?*, London and New York: Routledge.

Weitzman, M. (1974) Prices *vs.* quantities', *Review of Economics and Statistics* 41(4): 477–91.

World Bank (1998) *Global Economic Prospects*, Washington: World Bank.

13 Building institutions and resolution of the East Asian crisis[1]

Masahiro Kawai

THE CONTEXT FOR FINANCIAL AND CORPORATE RESTRUCTURING

The extraordinary turbulence in East Asia over the past two years has sparked a wide-ranging debate on the causes of the crisis, lessons to be learned and the desirable architecture of the global financial system. Among policy makers, international financial institutions, private organisations, and in academic circles, views are converging that the East Asian crisis was caused by interactions between massive capital inflows and outflows and weak domestic institutions, notably in the financial sector, in the emerging market economies. As a result, discussions are proceeding on how the international financial system and the domestic institutional underpinnings could be strengthened to maximise the benefits of, and reduce the risks posed by, global economic and financial integration.

While debate on international financial architecture primarily covers the ways and means to improve the international economic and financial system, proposals for strengthening domestic institutions in emerging markets include: (a) the need for financial markets to improve transparency and supervision and do a better job in self-regulation and risk management; (b) the need for the authorities to develop effective frameworks for resolving bank and corporate insolvencies at minimum cost and without creating moral hazard; and (c) the need to improve corporate governance through the adoption of international standards and best practices for accounting, auditing and disclosure. A key focus has been on financial and corporate sector improvements. This chapter focuses on issues related to financial and corporate sector improvements.

The East Asian crisis has adversely impacted banks and corporations in the affected economies. Most banks are heavily burdened with large non-performing loans (NPLs), many of which may ultimately have low recovery rates. Many corporations have debt levels beyond their service capacity and inefficient investments that are economically non-viable. The holes in the balance sheets of banks and corporations are huge and it will take several years to write off problem loans and failed investments.

Table 13.1   Key financial and corporate sector statistics

	Indonesia	Korea	Malaysia	Philippines	Thailand
1998 GDP (US$billion equiv.)	$105 b	$309 b	$69 b	$68 b	$121 b
Banking sector's external debt (US$ billion equiv.)	$50.3 b	$72.4 b	$23.0 b	$17.8 b	$46.8 b
Average 1998 banking deposits/GDP	46%	38%	104%	57%	94%
Average 1998 priv. sec. loans/GDP	43%	75%	111%	50%	114%
Total corporate debt (US$ billion equiv.)	$118.0 b	$444.0 b	$120.2 b	$47.5 b	$195.7 b
– of which external debt	$67.1 b	$64.0 b	$40.0 b	$23.3 b	$32.5 b
– domestic debt	$50.9 b	$380.0 b	$80.2 b	$24.2 b	$163.2 b
Debt to equity ratio 1996	200%	350%	110%	140%	240%
Estimated peak NPL[a] % of loans	70–80%	15–25%	20–25%	10–15%	45–55%
Estimated cost of bank recap[a] % of 1998 GDP:					
– Gross	55–60%	10–20%	15–25%		30–40%
– Net	40–50%	5–15%	5–15%		20–30%

Note:

[a] World Bank staff estimates.

Financial and corporate sector restructuring is an essential element of the strategy for recovery in the crisis-affected economies. Without a healthy financial system, incipient economic recovery could be strangled by an inadequate supply of credit or be subject to sudden portfolio shifts by creditors weary of debtors' capacity to repay. Without effective corporate debt workout and operational restructuring, potentially viable corporations will not be considered creditworthy and, more importantly, will not use loans to the most productive ends, with adverse implications for long-term growth. Combined with sound macroeconomic management and an improving external economic environment, financial and corporate sector restructuring will hasten the pace at which market confidence and robust economic growth are restored.

Progress on financial and corporate restructuring has been significant in each of the crisis-affected countries. In the financial sectors in Indonesia, Korea, Malaysia and Thailand, the authorities have intervened in non-viable financial institutions, recapitalised most of the viable institutions, started rehabilitation of weak and/or intervened banks (including the sale of intervened banks to foreign strategic investors), initiated the disposition of assets acquired by publicly supported asset management companies (AMCs), and begun taking steps to improve prudential regulation and supervision. On the corporate side, formal insolvency procedures (bankruptcy, foreclosure and reorganisation) have been strengthened, voluntary restructuring frameworks based on variants of London Rules' have been adopted and many legal impediments to corporate restructuring have been eliminated.

The pace of implementation and the effectiveness of these measures have varied significantly across the countries. While the benefits of reform programs thus far may be reflected in improved macro-financial indicators – currency appreciation, lower interest rates and higher equity prices – the process has not yet resulted in sound, recapitalised banking systems and strong corporate balance sheets, much less a resumption of growth in bank lending and corporate investment. Moreover, the depth of the problems – and their eventual costs – have not been completely recognised.

The halting pace of restructuring in East Asia is not atypical for countries experiencing systemic financial and corporate sector crises. It takes time for governments and the populace to grasp the reality and to build a consensus on how to move forward. Solutions must be found that can gain and hold political support during difficult economic times. The public is usually reluctant to accept the substantial fiscal costs of bank resolution and recapitalisation and/or to bail out rich bankers', and interests that stand to lose from the restructuring process will often try to block reforms.

AGENDA FOR RESTRUCTURING

Financial sector restructuring has been one of the most important policy foci since 1997, the beginning of the crises. It was only in 1998 that corporate sector restructuring became prominent in the policy agenda. Financial and corporate sector restructuring in a systemic crisis is a complex, difficult process that takes time to accomplish.

Strategies for financial and corporate sector restructuring need to be closely linked. Financial sector restructuring must either precede or be carried out in tandem with corporate restructuring. There are several reasons for this. First, the health of the banking industry is ultimately contingent upon successful corporate restructuring and upon achieving a new balance between the roles of the financial sector and corporate sector in credit allocation, credit discipline and driving corporate restructuring activities. Banks' ability to initiate corrective actions with their distressed borrowers is one of the key indicators of a financial system which is properly balanced. Second, the scale of corporate insolvency is so huge and the size of NPLs so large that resolution of bank NPLs cannot be achieved and financial sector health cannot be restored without effective corporate restructuring. Third, if assets of insolvent corporations are not restructured in such a way as to put them back into productive use, the distress in the financial sector will continue, and the costs of debt workout will continue to rise as assets lose value over time and recovery rates fall. Finally, financial sector and corporate sector restructuring can be driven only by the adequate incentives of both creditors and debtors to mutually agree on debt workout.[2]

Financial and corporate sector restructuring must be driven by the incentives of the creditors and debtors.

Financial sector restructuring: resolution, recapitalisation and rehabilitation

The initial priority of financial sector restructuring has been to stabilise the financial system by taking steps to restore the confidence of depositors and creditors. Where a deposit insurance system did not exist, governments have often had to guarantee deposits (and possibly other liabilities) to stem bank runs, capital flight and a potential breakdown of the payments system. Central banks also provided liquidity support to troubled banks and financial institutions.

The next step was to intervene in clearly non-viable and insolvent institutions that would have caused substantial losses to continue. These interventions involved closures (liquidation), mergers with healthier banks, and temporary nationalisation of non-viable banks. Assets of liquidated banks were sometimes transferred to a publicly run asset management company. Forced consolidations and temporary nationalisation of institutions were often accompanied by changes in ownership and management. The governments sold (or have been trying to sell) temporarily nationalised banks by providing incentives to potential strategic investors. The authorities have attempted to put in place a legal and operational basis for these interventions so that the impact restores rather than undermines public confidence in the financial system.

Then, governments developed strategies for the recapitalisation and rehabilitation of weak but viable financial institutions.[3] In most countries, the government strategy included use of public funds to recapitalise weak but viable banks to restore a healthy financial sector and payments system, a fundamental public good that is necessary to accelerate economic recovery and to promote sustained growth in real sector activity. Without recapitalisation, owners of financial institutions would not have an incentive to restructure the NPLs of viable borrowers. At the same time, such public support was often accompanied by recognition of losses on NPLs and costs to existing owners. The strategy also included the carving out of NPLs from the balance sheets of weak banks: NPLs have been managed, either through sale to a centralised government-run AMC as part of the restructuring process or within the bank (through a transfer of NPLs to a wholly- or majority-owned AMC). Different modalities and variations on this approach have been used in each of the East Asian crisis-affected countries.[4]

It is not enough to resolve non-viable financial institutions and recapitalise and rehabilitate weak ones. Capital adequacy, loan classification, provisioning rules, and any improvement in accounting and disclosure rules have been brought, albeit gradually, to international standards so that banks' true financial conditions can be assessed. Prudential regulation and supervision, with accompanying improvement in supervisory agencies, has been strengthened to monitor the progress of bank restructuring and, for the future health of the financial system, to prevent unsound practices that led to the problems in the first place. To the extent that regulatory forbearance is in place, as in most of the East Asian countries, supervision of the banks has been made particularly stringent. Finally, the banks have been encouraged to build a stronger credit culture – sound corporate governance, prudent risk management and sound lending practices. Without these measures, recapitalisation of banks can simply result in a repetition of inefficient capital injections.

Corporate restructuring

Corporate restructuring is a complex process as well. To avoid an unnecessarily long period of uncertainty, slow growth and erosion of asset values in NPLs, governments have tried to establish enabling environments for corporate restructuring; to facilitate both formal and informal debt workouts; to introduce an effective legal, regulatory, accounting and institutional framework for bankruptcy and foreclosure; and to improve corporate governance.

The term corporate restructuring' is used to indicate both corporate debt resolution and corporate operational restructuring. Corporate debt resolution' includes debt rescheduling (agreed roll-over of loan principal and interest payments), debt-to-equity swaps, foreclosure, and forgiveness of principal and/or interest. Corporate operational restructuring' includes asset sales to reduce debt levels, major retrenchment, reduction of production capacity, changing the line of business and closing production facilities.

The first step was eliminating legal, tax and regulatory obstacles to corporate restructuring. The obstacles include tax policies that impede corporate reorganisations, mergers, debt-for-equity swaps, or debt forgiveness; restrictions on foreigners' participation as holders of domestic equity and investors in domestic banks; and labour laws and other existing laws and regulations that could hinder debt restructuring.

The next step was to establish a policy framework that facilitates out-of-court settlements. Given the costs and risks associated with even the most developed bankruptcy systems, out-of-court settlements are considered efficient and less costly. The government can play an effective, yet informal role in facilitating an orderly voluntary workout of debts, sometimes referred to as the London Approach'.[5]

The third step was to introduce effective insolvency (bankruptcy and foreclosure) procedures. Bankruptcy procedures need to be legally enforced and to serve as part of debt-resolution processes to ensure that non-viable firms do not continue to absorb credit and that a creditor can recover the maximum value of the claims to the insolvent debtor corporation. Moreover, the presence of an effective bankruptcy system will create the appropriate incentives for creditors and debtors to reach out-of-court settlements. Enforcement of bankruptcy procedures should be a credible threat as an alternative to out-of-court settlements.

The fourth step has been to use the government-run asset management company as a forceful creditor which has acquired assets from closed banks or distressed assets from weak banks and/or intervened banks.

The last step has been to improve corporate governance. Better corporate governance can help attract investment, improve efficiency and lead to increasing longer-term growth. Based on experience in other countries, corporate governance improves when the extent of disclosure is increased, the power of large inside shareholders is curbed, sizeable outside shareholders are present, and the financial system is competitive and efficient. Broadening ownership by introducing sizeable outside (often foreign) shareholders is likely to be a more efficient structure than one where ownership remains highly concentrated. This has been complemented with reforms in board composition, structure and responsibility as well as improvements in minority shareholder rights in order to ensure effective board oversight of management. Legislative changes have been encouraged to pursue these reforms.

PROGRESS TO DATE AND OUTSTANDING ISSUES: COUNTRY BRIEFS

Countries have followed different approaches to financial and corporate sector restructuring. Aggressive government-led restructuring has been most pronounced in Korea. There, the government has played an active role in bank recapitalisation, NPL carve-out, and corporate debt and operational restructuring because of the need to counter-balance the presence of powerful *chaebol*. Though costly, with inadequate due diligence and potential for moral hazard, the process has been rewarded with strong signs of economic recovery.

Malaysia has also allowed the government-led agencies to take decisive measures to acquire NPLs from banks and to recapitalise banks. Indonesia has followed a hybrid approach involving government agencies as well as a voluntary, market-based framework for corporate restructuring, though the progress has been delayed significantly due mainly to the magnitude of the problem and political uncertainties. The Philippines has followed a decentralised, private sector-led approach, primarily because the country did not encounter a systemic banking crisis. In the case of Thailand, the government intervened in the most badly affected financial institutions and largely relied on private investment for bank recapitalisation, though it introduced a publicly supported recapitalisation plan subject to safeguards. Unlike other countries, Thailand did not opt to establish a centralised, public AMC to carve out NPLs, but instead encouraged individual banks to establish their own AMCs for NPL resolution.

Let us examine in some detail the progress that has been achieved in financial and corporate sector restructuring in each of the five Asian countries affected by the crisis. Appendix Tables A13.1 and A13.2 provide a cross-country summary of progress.

Indonesia

Indonesia's economic crisis was triggered by the depreciation of the rupiah during the second half of 1997. The crisis exposed deep systemic weaknesses in the banking and corporate sectors, which required aggressive and wide-ranging policy measures and institutional reforms. The roots of the crisis can be traced back to 1988 when the government launched premature financial sector deregulation and the number of commercial banks suddenly expanded without adequate banking supervision and transparency. Problems were manifest as early as 1993, when NPLs were estimated to be 14 per cent of total loans. The domestic banking sector was exposed to further vulnerabilities when corporate clients began to borrow actively from foreign banks in the few years leading up to the crisis. Domestic banks would face large-scale NPL problems if these corporations were to become insolvent due to sharp currency depreciation. Indeed, the sharp depreciation of the rupiah that took place in December 1997 – June 1998 had a devastating impact on Indonesian corporations and banks.

Progress in financial sector restructuring

Indonesia's strategy for bank restructuring initially focused on stabilisation of the banking system, resolution (closure, merger, and take-over by the authorities) of non-viable banks, recapitalisation and rehabilitation of weak but viable banks, and enhancement of supervisory and regulatory capacity.

The very first bank resolution was the closure of sixteen insolvent commercial banks in November 1997 (out of a pre-crisis total of 238 in July 1997) in the midst of large bank runs which continued until March 1998. As the public accelerated the withdrawal of deposits following the closure, Bank Indonesia (BI) provided substantial liquidity support, including credits to some large private banks.

In January 1998, the authorities announced a blanket guarantee for depositors and creditors (excluding subordinated debt) of locally incorporated banks; the creation of the Indonesian Bank Restructuring Agency (IBRA); the elimination of restrictions on foreign ownership of domestic banks; and a temporary and voluntary suspension of corporate external debt payment. The blanket guarantee on deposits was designed to stem bank runs and thus stabilise the banking system. IBRA was established to lead the restructuring efforts in the most illiquid and insolvent banks and to manage the assets it acquires in the bank resolution process. For these purposes, Asset Management Investments (AMI) and the Asset Management Units were established within IBRA, with the former responsible for managing equity holdings and the latter intended to acquire NPLs from frozen or merged banks and to manage them. All outstanding liquidity support from BI to the banks (equivalent to 10 per cent of GDP by January 1998) was transferred to IBRA. New risk-based asset classification and provisioning regulations were later announced and all banks were required to have their loan portfolios reviewed by internationally recognised audit firms by end-1998. The Banking Law was amended to give IBRA the powers needed to resolve the problem banks.

The Asset Management Unit (AMU) legally received a total of Rp156 trillion category 5 loans from the ten banks closed in 1998, the seven state banks and four banks taken over by IBRA (BTOs). It received additional loans of newly closed banks and the eight additional BTOs.

In February 1998, fifty-four distressed banks (four state banks, thirty-one private national banks, and eleven regional development banks) were transferred to IBRA's control. In early April, IBRA took management control of seven of these banks, suspending the rights of the shareholders. Another seven were effectively closed. In late May, IBRA took over the management of Indonesia's largest private bank, Bank Central Asia (BCA).

In August 1998, the authorities announced a package of (a) resolution of seven major banks taken over by IBRA in April and May, and (b) resolution of six non-listed state banks. With regard to (a), both BCA and Bank Danamon International (Danamon) would be partially recapitalised by the former owners through the contribution of physical assets and the conversion of central bank liquidity support into equity; two other smaller banks (Bank PDFCI and Bank Tiara Asia) would be offered for sale; and three other banks (Bank Dagan Negara Indonesia, Bank Umum Nasional, and Bank Modern) would be frozen (that is, closed). In each case, the NPLs would be transferred to AMU. With regard to (b), four state-owned banks (Bank Dagan Negara (BDN), Bank Ekspor Impor Indonesia (EXIM), Bank Bumi Daya (BBD), Bank Pembangunan Indonesia (Bapindo)) would be merged into one new bank, which would assume the corporate loan business of another state bank (Bank Rakyat Indonesia). The NPLs of all these five state banks would be transferred to AMU.

The state banking sector, which accounted for 40 per cent of total liabilities of the banking sector assets in 1997, had significant asset quality problems and very weak operations. The Government announced in September 1998 the formal merger of four state-owned banks (BDN, EXIM, BBD, Bapindo) and the corporate business of a fifth state bank (BRI) into a new institution, Bank Mandiri, which was established as holder of 100 per cent of the shares of the component banks. The legal merger, which was completed only in July 1999, created the largest bank in the country with about 25 per cent of total banking sector liabilities. The government then issued the first tranche of recapitalisation bonds in October and the second tranche in December in order to fully recapitalise Bank Mandiri (a total of Rp178 trillion or 14.6 per cent of GDP). The Ministry of Empowerment of State Owned Enterprises (MOSOE) announced interim measures in June 1999 to strengthen

management of the three remaining state banks (BNI, BRI, BTN), and has since developed business plans for these banks. Bank Mandiri and the three state banks will ultimately be privatised.

As a result of thorough portfolio reviews of 128 private banks, completed in February 1999, the government took a major step in March 1999 to resolve weak banks according to the level of capital adequacy ratio (CARs).[6] The authorities would close thirty-eight banks (twenty-one non-viable B' banks and seventeen C' banks, accounting for 5.2 per cent of total banking system liabilities), take over seven B' banks (Duta, Nusa Nasional, Risjas Salim International, Tamara, Pos Nusantara, Jaya Bank International, Rama, accounting for 2.4 per cent), and identified nine B' banks for possible government assisted recapitalisation (11.5 per cent). Of the nine eligible banks for recapitalisation, one could not come up with the necessary capital and has been taken over by IBRA, and the remaining eight would be in a position to obtain public resources for recapitalisation. Of the seventy-four A' banks (the original seventy-three plus a newly upgraded one), fifty-two had been reviewed by May 1999 and twenty-seven were identified as needing changes in their directors and/or management. Bank Indonesia has been monitoring their performance closely.

IBRA announced in July 1999 that eight BTOs (PDFCI, Duta, Pos Nusantara, Rama, BNN, Tiara Asia, Tamara, Jaya) would be merged into Danamon, and another BTO (RSI) was to be merged with BCA. The three surviving BTOs as well as Danamon, BCA and Bank Niaga are expected to be privatised in 2000.

Table 13.2 Summary of bank interventions, Indonesia

Date	Closures		Take-over by IBRA	
	Number of banks	*Market share (liabilities %)*	*Number of banks*	*Market share (liabilities %)*
1 November 1997	16	2.5	–	–
4 April 1998	7	0.4	6	7.9
29 May 1998	–	–	1	12.0
21 August 1998	3[a]	4.8	–	–
13 March 1999	38	5.5	8[b]	4.3
Spring 1999	2[c]	0.3	–	–
December 1999	–	–	1[d]	1.3
Total	66	13.5	Net: 13[e]	Net: 20.7[e]

Notes:
[a] These three banks were part of the six taken over by IBRA on 4 April 1998.
[b] Including Bank Niaga which had qualified for joint recapitalisation, but whose owners declined to participate.
[c] Two joint-venture banks that the foreign partners declined to recapitalise as needed.
[d] Bank Bali, taken over by IBRA following Standard Chartered's withdrawal from its management contract.
[e] After subtraction of the three banks taken over by IBRA on 4 April 1998, and subsequently closed on 21 August 1998.

The estimated cost of bank restructuring has risen to Rp636 trillion (US$88 billion), or over 52 per cent of GDP. About one third of the total cost (Rp218 trillion) is connected with the cost incurred by Bank Indonesia, which incurred losses from past liquidity support to closed banks, BTOs, and a former state bank, and was required to finance payments of claims under the guarantee on the closed banks. Close to half of the total cost (Rp282 trillion) is for recapitalising state banks (Mandiri, BNI, BRI, BTN). Close to one-fifth (Rp108 trillion) is connected with the recapitalisation of twelve BTOs. Private banks account for only a small fraction of total costs. A further increase in total costs may be needed if the operational restructuring and recapitalisation of the state banks and BTOs are delayed and their loan portfolios continue to deteriorate.

These costs are financed through the issuance of government bonds. The government began to issue bonds in May 1999, amounting to a total of Rp500 trillion by the end of 1999.[7] Another Rp140 trillion issuance is expected by mid-2000, to recapitalise state banks and, to a lesser extent, the banks taken over by IBRA earlier in 1999. Bonds are floating rate, fixed rate, and indexed, with floating rate bonds forming by far the largest part of the bonds placed into the banks, since they most closely match the structure of the main payment obligations of the banks, that is, deposits. Interest rates on floating rate bonds are set equal to the SBI rate.

With government-supported recapitalisation, a functioning banking system is expected to be restored. Private banks are in aggregate largely solvent and liquid, though they are operating on narrow margins and would be vulnerable in the event of unfavourable external shocks or a renewed downturn. State banks and BTO banks will continue to be in a fragile condition even after their prospective recapitalisation is completed. This means that banks will have to require widening of margins, substantial operational restructuring and further accumulation of capital.

Bank Indonesia has taken a number of steps in strengthening the banking system and enhancing the organisation of banking supervision. Banks are required to achieve 8 per cent CAR by end-2001, which provides only a minimum standard for bank soundness and may not be achieved just through banks' internal resources. BI needs to monitor closely progress toward these targets. Improved governance in bank management is also crucial to reduce vulnerabilities of the banking sector, through strengthening internal control mechanisms, higher standards of disclosure of financial information, consistent application of international accounting standards, and effective monitoring and analysis by the authorities. Effective regulation, supervision, and examination of banks is critical, including foreign exchange positions, liquidity monitoring, legal lending limits, disclosure in financial statements, debt restructuring operations, connected lending, capital adequacy ratios and regulations on the foreign ownership of banks and on branch networks. The central bank law states that banking supervision will be taken out of BI by end-2002, so that banking supervision will be consolidated with that of

non-bank financial institutions (NBFIs) and the securities markets in a new supervisory institution.

Progress in corporate sector restructuring

In late 1998 corporate indebtedness was estimated to be US$118 billion, of which nearly 60 per cent was owed to foreign creditors and about half of the domestic debt was denominated in foreign currency. As a result, the large-scale rupiah depreciation that took place in late 1997 and early 1998 drove almost half of Indonesian corporations to insolvency and many more corporations to difficulties in meeting debt-servicing obligations.

The Indonesian government's strategy for corporate restructuring contains three elements: the introduction of the Jakarta Initiative and the Jakarta Initiative Task Force, in September 1998, to facilitate voluntary negotiations between debtors and creditors for corporate restructuring and to provide a regulatory one-stop shop' for administrative procedures pertaining to debt resolution; the introduction of a new and improved bankruptcy system and a special commercial court to provide a credible threat as an alternative to out-of-court settlements; and strengthening of the power of IBRA as the largest creditor in the country to maximise asset recovery. To assist the voluntary process the Indonesian Debt Restructuring Agency (INDRA) under the Frankfurt Agreement, in June 1998, was established, to provide foreign exchange cover for Indonesian corporations with foreign currency-denominated debt, once they have reached debt restructuring agreements.

As of end-1999, some 323 firms, with combined external debt of US$23 billion plus Rp15 trillion in domestic debt, have applied to work through the Jakarta Initiative Task Force, and standstill or final agreements have been reached for fifty-eight of them, which account for US$3 billion in foreign debt and Rp2 trillion in domestic debt. The most important corporate restructuring deal agreed in principle to date, involving the Jakarta Initiative Task Force (JITF), concerned Indonesia's largest vehicle manufacturer, PT Astra International, which reached a US$1.2 billion restructuring agreement. Other examples include PT Danareska (US$438 million), PT Lippo Tbk. (US$100 million), and PT HM Soepoerna (US$140 million).

Progress has been slow in comparison to other countries in the region. Only one external debt workout (PT Danareska) has been achieved under the Frankfurt Agreement/INDRA scheme, and the deadline for entry into INDRA was extended from June to December 1999, and again to June 2000. The slow pace of corporate restructuring can be attributed to several factors: creditors (particularly foreign creditors who hold 60 per cent of corporate debt) do not have access to full information on the financial condition of debtor corporations; foreign creditors believe providing a hair cut would induce further strategic defaulting; domestic banks are largely under-capitalised or insolvent and do not have sufficient financial capacity to strike a negotiation deal; and corporate debtors still feel a lack of pressure to take necessary actions because the judicial system has not been functioning as designed and the bankruptcy and foreclosure laws have not been an effective threat to them and because there are not enough economic incentives for debt negotiations. Political uncertainty during the general and presidential elections, the East Timor turmoil, and the Bank Bali incident may also have dampened the pace of debt agreements.

The government has recently taken several steps to accelerate corporate debt restructuring and asset recovery. In particular IBRA, which is now the largest domestic creditor after taking over the assets of failed banks, is playing an increasingly proactive role.[8] First, an inter-agency committee, comprising representatives from BI, IBRA, and the Ministry of Finance (MOF), has been established to implement and monitor the restructuring and asset recovery process. In December 1999, the Financial Sector Policy Committee (FSCP), consisting of key ministers, was established to oversee bank and corporate restructuring. Second, the names of debtors have been made public to induce the borrowers to begin settlement negotiations. All state banks, BTOs, and recapitalised private banks, together with IBRA, published the names of their largest, non-performing corporate borrowers in June 1999. IBRA also published the names of all its 1,689 borrowers together with the amounts owed. Third, since its operating rules were approved in October 1999, IBRA has been playing a growing role in disposing of, restructuring, and foreclosing the acquired loan portfolio. It has extraordinary powers (so-called PP17 powers) to seize assets of non-cooperative debtors and, like any other creditor, is also able to use the normal bankruptcy process. Fourth, the government has agreed in principle to strengthen the role of the JITF. This includes the enhancement of the Jakarta Initiative applied by JITF by adding time-bound mediation procedures and increasing the leverage of JITF by granting referral authority from JITF to the government to the Attorney General for bankruptcy proceedings.

Sustainable progress in corporate restructuring requires the adoption and implementation of a new and enhanced corporate governance framework. Progress has yet to be made in the areas of improved accountability, disclosure, company registration, enforcement of rules on public disclosure, and oversight.

Outstanding issues in financial and corporate sector restructuring

The progress of banking and corporate sector resolutions is slow in comparison to other countries. The focus of resolution of weak banks must shift from recapitalisation to rehabilitation and operational restructuring. The pace of corporate restructuring needs to be accelerated by forcing recalcitrant debtors to come to the negotiation table. Indonesia faces key challenges including:

The bank restructuring process must move from the recapitalisation stage to the rehabilitation and operational restructuring stage. In particular, the recapitalisation of the four state banks (especially Mandiri and BNI) must be completed and operational restructuring carried forward. BTO banks need to be re-privatised. The performance of the seven private banks that were jointly recapitalised must be closely monitored. The soundness of the private banks must be ensured.

IBRA is crucial to achieving the objectives of restoring a sound banking system and promoting corporate restructuring and asset recovery to reduce the public debt. To accomplish these tasks, IBRA needs to be protected from narrow political interests and must be able to play an active role in the work out process with the ability to engage in various forms of debt restructuring.

For non-IBRA-led cases, the role of the JITF needs to be strengthened. The proposed enhanced time-bound mediation procedures for JITF need to be approved and implemented. A procedure must be established which enables the government to direct cases to the JITF and to refer to the Attorney General for the initiation of bankruptcy proceedings those recalcitrant debtors in accordance with the principles and timetables of the new JITF mediation procedures.

Bankruptcy laws must be effectively enforced in the Commercial Court to force the corporate debtors to voluntarily come to the negotiation table.

Disclosure of financial conditions of the debtors has to be enforced to discourage the emergence of strategic defaulters, who are solvent but unwilling to make repayment.

Access to new working capital financing is desirable to induce debtors to come to the negotiation table. For this purpose, introduction of a new Secured Transactions Law is critical to creditors who are potentially willing to provide new working capital to restructured corporations, because it enables registration of a security interest ranking ahead of existing creditors.

Korea

Though Korea began to witness a strong economic recovery in 1999, financial and corporate sector restructuring is far from complete. The country is still struggling to resolve large NPLs in the financial system, weaknesses in the investment trust company (ITC) industry and high debt-to-equity ratios in the corporate sector.

While extensive financial sector problems surfaced in the second half of 1997, the seeds were sown much earlier. These weaknesses were the result of years of bad lending practices and an inadequate supervisory and regulatory framework. Problems included imprudent lending practices, poor credit and funding risk management by both banks and borrowers, and lax or ineffective oversight by regulators. One of the important features was the close relationship between the government, businesses, and the financial sector, particularly through groups of large affiliated businesses known as *chaebol*. These groups are characterised by extensive cross-holdings of equity, intra-group lending and guarantees, and business transactions. With the support of government policies and the banking sector, *chaebol* rapidly developed into many diverse lines of business and played a dominant role in the Korean economy. But due to poor business planning and operations and unsound financial decisions, *chaebol* began to experience serious financial difficulties, even before the outbreak of the crisis.

Though the use of the banking system to support the government's industrial policies had been much reduced in the 1990s, the practice left a legacy of poor risk management and imprudent credit analysis. The structural weaknesses of the Korean banks became increasingly apparent throughout 1997 as a number of major *chaebol* went bankrupt. By the first week of September, six highly leveraged *chaebol* had failed or been placed under bankruptcy protection, raising serious concerns about the quality of bank assets, which are mostly concentrated in manufacturing and trade sectors. Concerns were also raised about the condition of the merchant banks which were heavily exposed to *chaebol* and suffered severe funding difficulties as domestic and foreign lenders reduced their exposures to them.

Progress in financial sector restructuring

In August 1997, the government announced a set of measures aimed at increasing confidence in the Korean financial market. First, official support was provided by the Bank of Korea in the form of special loans and capital injection, in exchange for government bonds, to Korea First Bank. In addition, a special funding facility was created to assist twenty-one merchant banks (of the original thirty) whose exposure to bankrupt companies exceeded 50 per cent of their equity. Second, the government announced guarantees covering the foreign liabilities of Korean financial institutions, including both commercial and merchant banks. Third, a special fund was set up within the Korea Asset Management Corporation (KAMCO), to which the banks would be allowed to sell their NPLs. These measures were perceived by the market as insufficient and international creditors froze or withdrew their credit lines.

Since late 1997, financial sector restructuring in Korea has been designed to meet five objectives: restoring the confidence of depositors, investors and creditors; establishing effective frameworks for resolution of non-viable banks and for recapitalising weak but viable banks; introducing an effective NPL resolution mechanism including the establishment of a centralised asset management company; the introduction of international standards for financial regulation and consolidated supervision; and capital markets development. The following actions have been taken:

First, the government created an independent agency, the Financial Supervisory Commission (FSC), in June 1997 with a mandate to supervise and restructure all banks and NFBIs. This was expanded into the Financial Supervisory Service (FSS) in January 1999 by merging four financial supervisory agencies for banks, non-banks, securities and insurance.

Second, the government removed KAMCO from the Ministry of Finance and Economy (MOFE) and re-established it under the control and supervision of the FSC in November 1997 as a public agency to manage non-performing assets transferred from distressed financial institutions. The government re-oriented its function as a bad bank' to increase efficiency in asset purchase, management and disposition in August 1998. Third, the authorities successfully rescheduled/restructured commercial bank external debt *vis-à-vis* external creditor banks at the beginning of 1998 under a government-led program. This laid a favourable foundation for subsequent bank and corporate restructuring.

Following the results of portfolio reviews of the merchant banks and their rehabilitation programs, in December 1997, the government closed fourteen merchant banks and required the other sixteen to follow a timetable to achieve capital adequacy ratios of at least 6 per cent by June 1998 and 8 per cent by June 1999. A bridge merchant bank, Hanareum Banking Corporation (HMBC), was established to assume all deposits and selected liabilities and to accept in payment the good' financial assets of the suspended merchant banks. Any remaining assets and liabilities after the transfer to HMBC were transferred into bankruptcy, and the court-appointed receiver then sold the NPLs to KAMCO. The government then merged or suspended one merchant bank each, while closely monitoring the remaining fourteen.

In June 1998, five commercial banks (Dongwa, Dong Nam, Dae Dong, Chung Chong, and Kyungki) were deemed non-viable and subsequently acquired by five stronger banks (Shinhan, Korea Housing, Kookmin, Hana, Koram) under purchase and assumption transactions. In October, the Korea Deposit Insurance Corporation (KDIC) injected W5.78 trillion (US$4.8 billion) into these five commercial banks, which acquired one ailing bank each. KDIC later injected an additional W2.26 trillion (US$1.9 billion) into the same five banks, expecting to inject more resources twice in 1999. The seven under-capitalised banks (Korea Exchange, Hanil, Cho Hung, Commercial, Kangwon, Chungbuk, and Peace) received conditional support. These seven banks were required either to merge into healthy banks or to arrange mergers among the undercapitalised banks with government entity assistance and resulting government ownership. Korean Exchange signed a Memorandum of Understanding (MOU) with the FSC and was required either to raise capital or merge to obtain equity capital support. Hanil and Commercial merged and established a new bank called Hanvit. Through its fiscal support, the government became its major shareholder. Cho Hung was planning to merge with Hyundai International Merchant Bank and Kangwon.

In December 1998, two commercial banks in distress (Korea First and Seoul), were intervened and *de facto* nationalised in early 1999. These two nationalised banks were expected to be privatised and MOUs were signed with foreign consortia, Newbridge Capital and Hong Kong and Shanghai Banking Corporation (HKSB), respectively. The agreement was not finalised, as the revival of the Korean economy induced the government to ask for a higher price. In August the FSC announced that negotiations with HKSB for the sale of Seoul Bank has been called off due to irreconcilable differences in the two parties' valuation of the bank's assets. According to the FSC, Seoul Bank was to be declared insolvent and its capital written down prior to another injection of public funds. In September, after ten months of negotiations, the government finally signed a binding agreement to sell a controlling stake of 51 per cent in Korea First Bank to Newbridge Capital. Under this deal the government will take on all NPLs, add to the bank's reserves should its existing reserves fail to meet accounting standards that will be imposed in the future, and take on loans that go bad over the next two years and, for a particularly risky class of loans, for three years.

In July 1999, the near-bankruptcy of the Daewoo conglomerate rocked Korean financial markets, dramatising the importance of immediate action to promote restructuring. Daewoo is Korea's second largest *chaebol*, with businesses in automobiles, heavy industry, electronics, telecommunications, construction, trade, finance, and hotels. With a debt-to-equity ratio of 526 per cent (excluding asset revaluation) at the end of 1998, its domestic debt is about US$40 billion and its officially reported foreign currency debt is some $10 billion. Daewoo remained resistant to change, betting on economic recovery and further borrowing to tide it over its financial predicament. It repeatedly missed the restructuring commitments it made to its creditor financial institutions under its Capital Structure Improvement Plan (CSIP). By July, it could no longer service its debt and hovered near bankruptcy.[9]

Since the outbreak of the Daewoo crisis, the central focus of the government has been to maintain stability in Korea's financial market. In particular, the government attempted to stabilise the ITC sector which had large exposure to Daewoo and experienced substantial redemption of bond funds (a flight of quasi-deposit to quality). Essentially, the government introduced phased redemption of bond funds by allowing individual and corporate investors to redeem their investments in ITCs at differing values depending on the timing of the redemption. The ailing ITC industry required additional public support for stabilisation, and more fundamentally, it needs comprehensive restructuring to restore the health of the industry.

To date, the government has set aside W64 trillion (US$49.2 billion or 14 per cent of GDP) for resolving the crisis in the banking and financial sectors. The amount of public funds injected for the restructuring of the financial system amounted to W79 trillion at end-1999. Of the original allocation of W32.5 trillion (revised later to W20.5 trillion), KAMCO had purchased NPLs from distressed financial institutions with a face value of W56 trillion and at a purchase price of W23 trillion. KAMCO had sold W10.4 trillion and is planning to sell an additional W16 trillion. KAMCO plans to establish joint venture asset management companies to manage NPLs and to form corporate restructuring vehicles to manage NPLs and purchase additional NPLs created through corporate restructuring deals, each with foreign investors. These efforts are expected to accelerate corporate restructuring and asset recovery. Of the original allocation of W31.5 trillion (revised to W43.5 trillion), KDIC had spent W50 trillion through capital injections and loss coverage support.

According to the FSS, NPLs in the Korean financial system (commercial banks and NBFIs), including those acquired by KAMCO, totalled W113 trillion in September 1999. NPLs could rise significantly as further progress is made in corporate restructuring, particularly at Daewoo. Market analysts expect that the government will have to allocate a substantial amount of public resources in addition to the W64 trillion it has already provided for banks. First, loan losses at financial institutions could increase significantly as a result of corporate restructuring, in particular from the Daewoo workouts. Second, at the end of 1999, the FSS implemented new forward-looking criteria for loan classification in the banking sector, which will result in higher provisioning requirements. Large creditors of Daewoo could face substantial new provisioning requirements.

Progress in corporate restructuring

The Korean Government's basic strategy for corporate restructuring consists of three principles: (a) introduce necessary legal and policy changes to allow corporate restructuring without hindrances, (b) take a facilitating role in corporate restructuring and provide policy and administrative guidance for leading banks to act for all domestic creditors of individual corporations; and (c) institute certain agreed measures for structural corporate governance reform.

In Korea sixty-four *chaebol* account for the bulk of corporate debts. The government has relied on a multi-track approach to the restructuring of *chaebol*: (a) court-supervised insolvency procedures for particularly difficult cases; (b) out-of-court workouts under provisions of the Corporate Restructuring Agreement (CRA); and (c) multiple efforts to impose financial discipline on the top five *chaebol*.

The presence of a credible threat of foreclosure and court-supervised reorganisation and receivership has distinguished Korea from other crisis-affected countries in East Asia. While additional reforms are needed, the credible threat of the legal procedure has encouraged corporations to cooperate with creditors in out-of-court restructuring negotiations. Additional insolvency law reforms are needed to facilitate more timely movement of non-viable companies into liquidation and more timely reorganisation of viable businesses.

The top five *chaebol* (Hyundai, Daewoo, Sumsung, Lucky–Goldstar and Sunkyong) have agreed to the CSIPs, under which they would (a) reduce the debt–equity ratio to 2:0 by end-1999, (b) be subject to sanctions if they failed to meet the deadline, and (c) remove existing cross-guarantees between subsidiaries engaged in different lines of business. In addition, the government promoted exchanging businesses with other *chaebol* (Big Deals), and shedding non-core businesses.

Though creditor banks accepted CSIPs of the top five *chaebol*, they have not played their role in the restructuring process until recently. The top five *chaebol* have reduced their combined debt–equity ratio to 386 per cent at the end of 1998, down from 470 per cent at the end of 1997, but failed to meet the 320 per cent target. While the unwinding of cross-guarantees has proceeded satisfactorily, less foreign capital was raised than was planned and the Big Deals' have been slower than initially thought.

The results of the CSIP implementation reviews reveal that Lucky-Goldstar and Sunkyong have shown notable progress since the latter half of 1998, while Daewoo and Hyundai have not. In particular, Daewoo's debt-to-equity ratio increased substantially from 474 per cent at the end of 1997 to 527 per cent at the end of 1998, and continued to rise to 588 per cent in June 1999. Although its debt ratio was reduced from 572 per cent at the end of 1997 to 449 per cent at the end of 1998, and then to 341 per cent in June 1999, Hyundai still maintains a high debt ratio. The two conglomerates responded in May by incorporating more drastic restructuring measures. Hyundai provided more serious restructuring steps, while the response of the Daewoo group was not as broad.

For distressed 6-64' *chaebol* and other large corporations, the FSC has set up an out-of-court workout program to be managed, in large part, by 5–6 lead banks. This program, which seeks to emulate the London Rules' for voluntary extra-judicial workouts, is based on a CRA signed by 210 local banks and NBFIs in July 1998. The CRA provides clear guidelines on timetables for creditor agreement, creditor standstill, the role of the lead bank and creditors committee, and inter-creditor arbitration. The workout process is overseen by a Corporate Restructuring Coordination Committee (CRCC).

By June 1999, ninety companies had applied to the formal workout program in the CRCC framework. About half were subsidiaries of sixteen *chaebol*. Seven of the ninety companies dropped out of the program at some point, leaving eighty-two companies in the workout program. All but two of the eighty-two companies have by now reached agreement on a workout plan.

Small and medium-sized enterprises (SMEs) account for only a small fraction of banks' outstanding loans and, hence, their restructuring has not attracted sufficient attention. The situation is complicated by their close ties with the *chaebol*, on whom SMEs are dependent for their survival. So far, efforts have focused on extending emergency loans of working capital to keep viable and potentially viable SMEs from going bankrupt, thereby gaining time and preserving employment, while allowing non-viable SMEs to go bankrupt.[10] Those that have not gone bankrupt, however, have shed employees to a significant extent. In 1998, SMEs were twice extended a temporary debt moratorium. SME debt workout and operational restructuring are urgently needed.

Korea needs continued corporate restructuring at all levels of the corporate sector. The top five *chaebol* have to reduce debt–equity ratios to 200 per cent by the end of 1999 and to undergo meaningful restructuring. The 6-64' *chaebol* must continue their efforts to implement the CSIPs or to continue workouts with their lead banks. SMEs also have to undergo operational restructuring. Successful conclusion of economic reforms and institutionalisation of the benefits of corporate restructuring now hinges on the implementation of agreed workout plans, adoption of new models of corporate governance and management, and the labour issues not impinging on fundamental change.

Outstanding issues in financial and corporate sector restructuring

The Korean economy has experienced strong signs of incipient economic recovery. However, there is a danger that the pace of reforms in both the financial and corporate sectors may be relaxed and that the remaining structural problems of both sectors may not be adequately addressed. The July 1999 turmoil in financial markets prompted by the near collapse of Daewoo showed that the economy is still vulnerable to sudden portfolio shifts by creditors weary of the debtors' capacity to repay. Successful corporate restructuring now hinges on satisfactory restructuring of the top five *chaebol*. This, in turn, depends on the implementation of agreed workout plans, adoption of new models of corporate governance and management, and the labour issues impinging on fundamental change. The remaining agenda is extensive and complex:

More public funds may be required to restructure/recapitalise the banking sector due, in particular, to Daewoo debt workouts.

KAMCO must expand its capacity to ensure disposition of existing and potential new NPLs as quickly and as efficiently as possible and to limit the fiscal cost of financial crisis resolution. Involvement of private asset managers and restructuring experts is expected to improve asset recovery and to minimise costs.

KDIC needs to design a strategy to sell its existing equity participation in banking institutions in the medium and long term.

The FSS must strengthen institutional capabilities to adopt international standards on prudential regulation, to carry out consolidated supervision and, more generally, to develop a risk-based and quantitative supervision process for the entire financial system.

Capital markets need to be developed with efficiency, safety, transparency and competitiveness. Efforts should focus on the establishment of a new regulatory framework, the strengthening of self-regulatory organisations, redefining the architecture of the securities market and establishing incentives to enhance demand for bonds.

The top five *chaebol* must continue to restructure themselves even though, with the exception of Daewoo, they are in line with their CSIP targets (that is, a reduction of the debt-to-equity ratio to 200 per cent without asset revaluation by end-1999, and a reduction in cross-guarantees). Government-promoted Big Deals' need to be completed.

The agreed workout programs for the 6-64' *chaebol* require new reviews and measures to ensure that they are followed through to completion.

To reduce labour opposition to restructuring, effective action and plans are required to demonstrate adequate protection for workers who may lose their jobs.

Malaysia

The impact of the East Asian crisis on the Malaysian financial system and corporate sector has not been as severe as in neighbouring countries. Several important factors explain the relative soundness of the banking and corporate sectors, including restrictions on foreign denominated borrowings by Malaysian corporations; high statutory reserve requirements in the banking sector; and a well functioning legal system with effective bankruptcy laws. The government's pre-emptive approach to tackling the crisis also limited the damage and restored financial market stability by mid-1999. An institutional framework comprised of Danaharta, Danamodal, and the Corporate Debt Restructuring Committee was quickly put into place with the purpose of removing NPLs from the banking system, recapitalising the weaker financial institutions and facilitating distressed debt workout.

Progress in financial sector restructuring

In mid-1998, the Government created the institutional framework to implement banking sector recapitalisation and restructuring. Danaharta was established as an asset management company in May 1998 to acquire NPLs from banking institutions in order to strengthen their balance sheets and enhance their ability to lend. Danaharta was designed to purchase NPLs from financial institutions whose NPL-to-total loan ratio exceeded 10 per cent. It was also given the power to appoint special administrators to manage the affairs of distressed companies to facilitate and accelerate their restructuring. In July, Danamodal was established as a special purpose vehicle with the purpose of recapitalising financial institutions whose capital adequacy ratios fell below 9 per cent. The last component of the restructuring framework was the Corporate Debt Restructuring Committee (CDRC), which was established in August to facilitate voluntary restructuring of corporate debt outside the courts through voluntary agreements between creditors and debtors.

Progress has been made on these fronts. The objectives of Danaharta are to reduce the level of NPLs in financial institutions to facilitate the credit intermediation process and to maximise the recovery value of the acquired assets. Danaharta acquired and managed RM34 billion face value of NPLs, of a total of RM103 billion (three-month classification of NPLs) in December 1999, about 33 per cent of total NPLs in the system. NPLs in the banking system stood at 24 per cent of total loans (on the three-month definition) and risk-weighted CARs in the banking sector were 12.5 per cent. In October, Danaharta embarked on the secondary carve-out of NPLs from the financial system, although the targeted amounts were considerably less than the amounts acquired in the first round. It has begun to issue government guaranteed zero coupon bonds in four series to finance its requirements. Its recent issue was RM1.05 billion in bonds, whose yield has come down to 5.487 per cent from 7.150 per cent during the first issue in November 1998, reflecting improvements in the economy and the decline in inflation and interest rates. A total amount of RM7.39 billion in nominal value of bonds has now been issued out of a target of RM15 billion.

Danaharta held its first restricted tender of foreign loan assets in August, selling US$85 million (principal value) of foreign assets for US$43 million, a recovery rate of 50.1 per cent. In December, a second sale by tender of US$252 million and fourteen marketable securities was announced, to be closed in February 2000. Danaharta also opened its first quarterly tender in November 1999 for sale of foreclosed property assets, involving forty-four properties. Though Danaharta found buyers for twenty-four commercial and residential properties, it sold only RM18 million out of the indicative value of RM123 million. Unsold properties were transferred to the asset management unit of Danaharta.

Danamodal was created to recapitalise weak banking institutions to increase their resilience and enhance their ability to generate new lending abilities. By June 1999, Danamodal had injected RM6.4 billion in capital into ten financial institutions in the form of Exchangeable Subordinated Capital Loans (ESCL). Of these ten institutions, Danamodal has signed Definitive Agreements with nine institutions for the conversion of the ESCL into permanent Tier one and/or Tier two capital. The capital Danamodal has injected into these financial institutions, an equivalent of approximately 14 per cent of the total Tier one capital of the banking sector at the beginning of 1998, has served to help boost the CAR of the banking system to 12.5 per cent at the end of 1999.

Originally it was anticipated that up to twenty-three financial institutions would become undercapitalised and would require up to RM16 billion in capital injections through Danamodal. However, the government announced that Danamodal would need significantly less. In fact, some of the institutions that received capital injections have begun to repay Danamodal and, as a result, by November amounts due to Danamodal had been reduced to RM4.6 billion through the repayment of part of the ESCLs that the institutions had received. Danamodal's funding is comprised of paid-up capital of RM3 billion provided by Bank Negara Malaysia and RM7.7 billion obtained by issuing zero coupon bonds to fifty-seven banking institutions.

In July 1998, the government announced a plan to bring about a consolidation of the financial industry covering fifty-eight institutions (twenty-one banks, twenty-five finance companies and twelve merchant banks). The purpose was (a) to improve the competitiveness, and thereby ensure the survival, of the domestic banking industry in the face of increasing foreign competition in the future; and (b) to avoid the potentially destabilising consequences of a number of domestic bank bankruptcies under the weight of market forces in an increasingly competitive market environment. Initially the program was formulated around several anchor banks designated by the government. Encountering resistance from the banking community, the government revised its policy in October 1999 to allow the banks' shareholders a greater role in shaping the consolidation of the industry. Under the revised scheme, banking institutions were allowed to choose their own leader in each group to lead the merger process. Banking institutions were required to inform Bank Negara Malaysia by the end of January 2000 of their respective merger groupings. All the merger exercises are to be completed by the end of December 2000.

Progress in corporate restructuring

Three modalities have been used for corporate restructuring in Malaysia: (a) court-supervised restructuring under Section 176 of the Malaysian civil code; (b) voluntary out-of-court restructuring either directly between parties or with assistance of the CDRC along the lines of the London Approach'; and (c) restructuring via the national asset management company, Danaharta.

More than forty companies have filed for reorganisation under Section 176 of the Companies Act. In thirteen cases schemes of reorganisation have been proposed and in another three cases the schemes of reorganisation have been approved. Court-based workouts have proceeded relatively slowly in comparison to CDRC- or Danaharta-led restructuring. Through amendments to Section 176 and the option of creditors to sell their loans to Danaharta, willingness to move restructuring forward has increased. At the same time, the ability of debtor firms to ask for extensions of stay orders against their creditors continues to hamper restructuring efforts.

The main objectives of the CDRC are to restructure the debt of viable corporations by minimising losses to creditors and shareholders and avoiding placing viable corporations in liquidation, thereby preserving employment and productive capacity. The CDRC had received applications from sixty-six corporations with over RM36 billion in debt by December 1999. Of these, fifteen have been either withdrawn by the applicants or rejected by the CDRC for not being viable, while eight cases are being resolved by Danaharta. The debts of fifteen companies amounting to RM13 billion have been restructured.[11] The remaining twenty-eight cases, amounting to RM17 billion, are currently outstanding.

Currently Danaharta has fifty-two companies under Special Administration. Special Administrators are appointed to oversee management of firms under Danaharta control in order to restructure and stabilise the firms. As mentioned earlier, Danaharta held its restricted tenders of foreign loan assets twice and its first quarterly auction of properties.

Corporate restructuring under the CDRC/Danaharta framework has been primarily through rescheduling of debt. The challenge remains to increase the pace of operational restructuring. Reallocation of capital, asset sales, labour rationalisation, mergers, and operational and management restructuring will have to be undertaken.

Outstanding issues in financial and corporate sector restructuring

With an adequate legal system and a well structured institutional framework for bank recapitalisation in place, Malaysia has successfully stabilised its financial system. The banking sector needs to undertake operational restructuring in the consolidation process. While the process for corporate debt resolution is in place, debt workout and operational restructuring through the CDRC/Danaharta have been slow. The key challenge the government faces now is to drive the restructuring process forward at a measured pace that allows the financial and corporate sectors to adjust to lower asset prices without weakening the economic recovery process.

As Danaharta has completed its NPL acquisition phase, it must sharply accelerate the process of disposing of acquired assets, restructuring the acquired loans to viable companies, foreclosing on non-viable debtors and auctioning off their assets. For this, Danaharta needs to enhance its skills in asset management and maximising asset recovery.

All transactions in which Danaharta and Danamodal are involved should take place in a transparent manner in order to maintain public confidence in the impartiality of the operations. Evidence of burden sharing by existing shareholders should be maintained throughout the restructuring process.

The pace of operational restructuring within banks needs to gather momentum to ensure increased efficiency and profitability of the banking sector going forward. Danamodal may use its equity positions in the financial institutions to restructure the operations of banks to achieve successful financial sector consolidation.

The CDRC should speed up its voluntary debt restructuring process; there may be room for more incentives to increase the number and pace of voluntary restructurings. Financial restructuring of corporate borrowers must be accompanied by operational and ownership restructuring.

Section 176 restructurings could also be speeded up by reducing the ability of firms to ask for extensions of stay orders against their creditors.

The corporate bond market needs to be further developed to reduce the dependence of the corporate sector on the banking system and to avoid funding mismatches.

The Philippines

Philippine banks have weathered the East Asian crisis relatively well, reflecting the strong pre-crisis capital positions of banks and lower corporate leverage *vis-à-vis* neighbouring countries. Nonetheless, the banking system – particularly thrift and rural banks – has been weakened by the regional crisis, bank lending stagnated for most of 1998–9, and NPLs rose to 14.5 per cent in October 1999.

Progress in financial sector restructuring

Realising the economy's structural weaknesses, the government has acted to strengthen the banking sector and the supervisory and regulatory framework since the pre-crisis era through, for example, higher minimum capital and stricter provisioning requirements. The preferred approach to insolvencies has been through engineered mergers. While a number of small thrift and rural banks are liquidated annually, there has been forbearance in closing banks, stemming from past (and present) central bank aversion to commercial bank closures, and legal threats to regulators that discourage prompt resolution and liquidation. Thus, the government approach has been to follow a wholly decentralised approach, relying on private markets.

To date, bank restructuring has been limited due to their stronger balance sheet positions compared with other countries. Over the last two years, the authorities have encouraged consolidation through suasion, higher minimum capital and provisioning requirements, and moratoria on bank branching and upgrading licences. During 1999 several bank mergers occurred or were announced.[12] A small thrift bank declared a holiday' on 4 June, faced with a run upon the publication of a stalled merger deal. The government moved to establish a more conducive environment for bank resolution in the event that conditions would worsen. The authorities have committed to privatising the Government's controlling stake in a large commercial bank, the Philippine National Bank, but it requires significant restructuring before seeking a buyer.

The central bank took measures to strengthen banking supervision in 1999, including drawing up a systemic contingency plan, issuing further guidelines for prompt corrective action, stepping up on-site inspections, and improving coordination between Banko Sentral Pilipinas (BSP) and the Philippine Deposit Insurance Corporation in resolving distressed banks. BSP has also stepped up its monitoring of bank groups on a consolidated basis and strengthened early warning systems to detect banking weaknesses.

Progress in corporate sector restructuring

Corporate debt restructuring in the Philippines is usually carried out on an informal or formal basis according to procedures dictated by the existing legal framework for insolvency. When informal debt resolution proves to be impossible, a distressed corporation may petition the Securities and Exchange Commission (SEC) for protection from its creditors. SEC now has the power (a) to impose stays of actions by creditors against corporate debtors; (b) to permit debtors to suspend payments to their creditors; (c) to decide whether a debtor should be liquidated or be permitted to attempt rehabilitation; and (d) to liquidate debtors and appoint receivers, members of management committees and liquidators.

The SEC reports that in 1997 and 1998, fifty-five corporations filed for suspension of payments on debts totaling P109 billion. During 1999 the number of corporations filing for payment suspension has declined dramatically to only twelve in the first ten months of the year and the total debt involved has declined to P19 billion. These numbers indicate that though the crisis did affect Philippine corporations, most corporations have reasonable levels of indebtedness and manageable exposures to foreign currency debt.

Outstanding issues in financial and corporate sector restructuring

Market perceptions on the Philippines have been deteriorating due to the trend towards widening budget deficits, lack of policy direction, and weak governance, slower recovery from the crisis than many neighbouring countries, and slow implementation of economic reforms. Banking sector consolidation is needed to create economies of scale, technology, and regulatory oversight. The corporate restructuring framework needs to be improved by overcoming a number of problems associated with the quasi-judicial process and the way it is administered.

Banking sector consolidation needs to be encouraged with concomitant, effective warning systems to detect banking weaknesses.

The government must resolve the differences in amendments to General Banking Act passed by the House and the Senate concerning foreign ownership of banks, which is currently limited to a maximum of 60 per cent.

The corporate restructuring framework needs to be streamlined including: (a) allowing secured creditors to exercise their contractual rights; (b) establishing clear and coherent rules and time bound procedures; (c) defining the minimum qualifications of individuals appointed as receivers, liquidators, or management committee members; (d) granting priority, in terms of repayment, to lenders willing to provide cash into the business in implementing rehabilitation plans; and (e) allowing the management of companies under the protection of the SEC to obtain fresh funds to avoid unlawful practice of using the proceeds from the sale of goods covered by trust receipts to finance continuing operations rather than using them to repay the creditor whose loan was secured by the receipts.

Thailand

The economic crisis in Thailand was triggered by the baht devaluation in July 1997 and aggravated by the underlying weaknesses of the country's financial system and corporate sector. Prior to the crisis, Thailand had embarked on a comprehensive liberalisation of domestic financial markets and capital account transactions. As a result, financial institutions began to enjoy a more liberal economic environment, including increased business opportunities with the corporate and household sectors as well as favourable funding terms from domestic and foreign sources. However, the financial system was not sufficiently sound nor resilient to cope with problems created by large inflows of deposits and foreign funds as well as the associated expansion of domestic credit. Consequently, the credit boom and bust that preceded the currency crisis comprised a major problem for both the Thai economy and its financial system.

Financial system reform has naturally been a major component of the crisis resolution program. The reform plan included three broad objectives: (a) resolution of non-viable and problem financial institutions; (b) strengthening the financial sector structure; and (c) enhancement of the regulatory and supervisory regime.

In addition to financial system reform, Thailand has also focused on corporate sector reform in order to resolve serious corporate debt overhang and to create a robust corporate sector, thereby helping restore economic health. The reform strategy included: (a) accelerating corporate debt restructuring; (b) strengthening corporate insolvency procedures; and (c) improving corporate governance.

Progress in financial and corporate sector restructuring

Immediately following the currency crisis, the Thai Government adopted a program to stabilise and restructure the financial sector in August 1997. It included a wide range of measures addressing resolution and restructuring of financial institutions, improvements in financial supervision, financial infrastructure reforms, capital market development and corporate restructuring.

The government established the Financial Restructuring Authority (FRA) and the Asset Management Corporation (AMC) in October 1997. These agencies were created to resolve the fifty-eight failed finance companies and dispose of their assets. Of the fifty-eight suspended finance companies, fifty-six were closed down, and their assets taken over to be auctioned by the FRA. The FRA sold assets of intervened finance companies, totalling TB186 billion (US$4.9 billion) in November 1999 – 28.0 per cent of the TB665 billion outstanding principal value. The early auctions that involved non-core assets were considered successful, with 53 per cent of the value of the assets recovered, while the later auctions involving core assets were less successful, recovering only 25.4 per cent of book value. The AMC, as the buyer of last resort, had to purchase business loans at the March 1999 auction for the first time. The FRA has almost finished liquidating the assets of closed finance companies.

After the suspension of the fifty-eight finance companies, the Bank of Thailand (BOT) adopted a market-led approach of recapitalising the remaining financial institutions that formed the core of the financial system. The strategy was based on a progressive strengthening of provisioning requirements designed to prompt financial institutions to obtain fresh capital, supervisors taking over those institutions that would not able to recapitalise. Initially the authorities expected that the increased transparency of financial institutions and tighter prudential rules would attract new investors, both domestic and foreign. The continued difficulties in the real sector and rising NPLs have made potential investors extremely cautious (only two small banks were purchased by foreign investors in 1998). In the meantime, the BOT intervened in four medium-sized banks (Bangkok Metropolitan Bank,

Bangkok Bank of Commerce, Siam City Bank, and First Bangkok City Bank) and seven finance companies. It became clear then that the market-driven recapitalisation would not be sufficient and further government support would be required.

On 14 August 1998 the Thai government announced a Financial Sector Restructuring for Economic Recovery' program for the recapitalisation of troubled financial institutions with injection of public funds (Bt300 billion) subject to safeguards. The recapitalisation schemes consisted of two parts. For Tier one recapitalisation, the government would recapitalise the institution up to 2.5 per cent of capital, provided it adopted up-front the end-2000 LCP rules, fully wrote off NPLs, and fell below 2.5 per cent in its Tier one CAR. Beyond this level, the government would inject Tier one capital by matching private investors' fresh capital. For Tier two recapitalisation, the government would inject capital as the institution wrote off NPLs due to corporate debt restructuring or increased net lending to the private sector.

As part of the program, the BOT intervened in two additional banks (Union Bank and Laem Thong Bank) and five additional finance companies. Merger and restructuring of government-owned entities (Krung Thai Bank and Krung Thai Tanakit) with intervened financial institutions and their restructuring also formed part of the strategy. One bank (BBC) would be liquidated, two banks (FBCB and LTB) would be absorbed by two state banks (KTB and Radhanasin Bank[13]), one bank (UBB) and the twelve finance companies that were intervened would be eventually integrated with a state-owned finance company (KTT), and three banks (RAB, BMB, and SCIB) would eventually be privatised. The mergers around KTB and KTT were achieved and action plans were developed for the eventual privatisation of these two institutions. Work on the privatisation of the three banks is progressing, albeit with some delay.

Siam Commercial Bank applied for Tier one assistance under the 14 August recapitalisation schemes. It raised enough capital in the private market and this was matched by the government. Other private banks have so far remained reluctant to take advantage of the 14 August schemes – particularly the Tier one scheme – that require banks to recognise losses up-front and write down capital, hence diluting ownership. Thai Farmers Bank (TFB), Bank of Ayudhya (BAY), Bangkok Bank (BBL) all raised about TB214 billion in capital by May 1999, particularly in the form of innovative, quasi-equity instruments called Capital Augmented Preferred Securities (CAPS) and Stapled Limited Interest Preferred Securities (SLIPS). However, this may not be enough to move the substantial burden of NPLs off the balance sheets, whether through debt restructuring or transfer to privately owned asset management companies.

The level of NPLs began to decline after reaching its peak in May 1999, though still high at 30.6 per cent for eight private banks and 38.5 per cent for all Thai banks in December 1999. The NPL problem is still serious because these figures exclude NPLs transferred to recently established AMCs. New lending is scarce. The June 1999 deadline for stepped-up loan loss provisioning (60 per cent) placed even more pressure on banks to recapitalise. The government was cautious and did not use large amounts of public resources for recapitalisation or NPL carve-out. Rather, it encouraged access to private market recapitalisation and the establishment of majority-owned AMCs. Bangkok Bank, Thai Farmers bank, and Siam Commercial Bank established their individual, bank-based AMCs to transfer distressed assets.

The government initiated the sales process for the four intervened banks by providing public resources. Nakornthon Bank (NTB) was the first bank acquired by a foreign strategic investor, Standard Chartered Bank, which agreed in September 1999 to purchase a 75 per cent stake for TB12.4 billion. In another transaction, United Overseas Bank of Singapore (UOB) agreed in November to purchase Radanasin Bank (RSB). In these transactions FIDF agreed to share some losses and costs. Bangkok Metropolitan Bank (BMB) and Siam City Bank (SCIB) are expected to be sold under similar transaction structures.[14]

The legal and regulatory framework for supervision of financial institutions is being revised. The government is attempting to strengthen the role of the BOT in the supervision and regulation of financial institutions, including prompt corrective action authority, and put the supervisory regime in line with international standards. BOT supervisory capacity is also being strengthened. As part of financial institutional reform, the Thai government is also preparing a draft deposit insurance law.

Progress in corporate sector restructuring

Since April 1998, the Thai government's strategy of corporate sector restructuring has been three-fold:

Provide tax and regulatory incentives to corporations and banks to create an enabling environment for corporate restructuring, including regulatory (prudential) incentives for NPL resolution for banks;

Strengthen the legal framework for asset recovery and insolvency through court-based bankruptcy procedures, court-supervised reorganisation, or enforcement of security interests;

Provide a well structured out-of-court process for voluntary debt restructuring negotiations in the spirit of the London Rules' approach.

The government provided a full set of tax incentives for corporate restructuring. The initial step was to reduce tax disincentives by providing some temporary relief, between 1 January 1998 and 31 December 1999, on asset sales and debt restructuring by financial institution creditors, and mergers and acquisitions. In August 1998, income tax, value-added tax, specific business tax and duty stamps were exempted in restructuring cases, where debt restructuring would result in imputed income to the debtor. In September 1998, debt write-off was allowed to be considered an expense, thereby reducing a financial institution's tax liability. Similarly, debt restructuring losses were also considered an expense for tax purposes and a tax cut on real estate transfers from 2 per cent to 0.01 per cent has been approved.

Formal court-based bankruptcy and reorganisation procedures have been improved. Prior to 1998, court-supervised rehabilitation was not possible under Thai law. Bankruptcy was used strictly for winding down companies, and was used rarely for large corporations. The Bankruptcy Act was amended in April 1998 to enable reorganisation of potentially viable corporations. The reorganisation amendment proved workable in its early usage, but several problems emerged limiting its utility in resolving large amounts of distressed debt. As a result, in March 1999 after a long period of debate, the Bankruptcy Act was further amended including (a) improved security for new lending to financially distressed corporations; (b) voting by creditor class; (c) rescission of related party transfers; (d) limits to discretion for court action; and (e) conversion of foreign currency-denominated claims. Notably, this amendment lowered the approval threshold for a court-supervised reorganisation plan to 50 per cent of outstanding debt by number and value, plus a special resolution of 75 per cent of the outstanding debt of one creditor class by value. The creation of a specialised bankruptcy court, the Central Bankruptcy Court, was also approved and the Court opened in June 1999.

Through December 1999, thirty-seven petitions for bankruptcy reorganisation were filed. The approval of the bankruptcy amendment has helped speeding the pace of in-court reorganisations, with seven new bankruptcy reorganisation petitions received in the month following the approval compared with only eighteen new filings from April 1998 to April 1999. Of the thirty-seven petitions, twenty-five have been accepted for reorganisation, and eight restructuring plans have been approved by creditors.

In June 1998, the government established the Corporate Debt Restructuring Advisory Committee (CDRAC) to facilitate the voluntary process of corporate restructuring and developed a Framework for Corporate Restructuring in Thailand.[15] The Framework', also called the Bangkok Approach' and endorsed by creditors in September 1998, is an adaptation of the London Approach' to Thai conditions and was developed with the assistance of the Foreign Banks' Association. The Framework' consisted of nineteen principles to facilitate corporate restructuring, which defined the expectations of debtors, creditors and authorities in the voluntary, out-of-court workout process. It emphasised business viability, full information disclosure, and the sharing of restructuring losses among creditors in an equitable manner that recognises legal priorities between the parties involved. It also outlined a thirteen-step timetable for the process.

Relative to the magnitude of the problem, corporate debt restructuring through the CDRAC framework is only slowly beginning to yield results. The CDRAC program monitors 721 target debtors' of which 406 firms have signed the Debtor Creditor Agreement. Unlike most of the East Asian variants of the London rules, CDRAC requires that a plan be confirmed on its second vote, within 6–8 months, or else be sent to court. The value of restructured corporate debt under CDRAC as of end-1999 is TB0.4 billion (out of a total target of TB1.5 billion submitted) or 29 per cent of the target cases.

At the end of November 1999, the BOT reported TB910 billion of corporate debt had been restructured out of total NPLs of TB2360 billion (or 36.8 per cent of total NPLs). This compares with TB680 billion in August. The current restructured amount represents over 150,000 customers. In contrast to other crisis-affected countries, SMEs in Thailand account for more than two-thirds of the aggregate corporate debt; therefore, restructuring requires far more effort.

Outstanding issues in financial and corporate sector restructuring

While macroeconomic indicators have shown improvement, the bank restructuring program in Thailand still faces risks, including a lack of enthusiasm by banks to enter into the 14 August recapitalisation schemes, lack of incentives on the part of debtors to come to the negotiation table, and a prolonged deterioration of the corporate sector cashflows. Relative to the magnitude of the problem, such as the size of NPLs, corporate debt restructuring has only begun to yield some visible results. Commercial banks are undercapitalised and reluctant to absorb losses.

Further government support may be required, in addition to the Bt300 billion 14 August scheme, before the Thai banking sector is restored to health.

State-owned commercial banks, particularly Krung Thai Bank, need to be more decisive in both operational restructuring and NPL resolution.

The legal and regulatory framework for supervision and examination of financial institutions needs to be strengthened.

For the market-based strategy of corporate debt restructuring to work, the right incentives have to be provided to both creditors and debtors so that they can maximise their returns, preserve their asset values, and deploy them efficiently.

The Thai judiciary system must demonstrate determination in enforcing the revised bankruptcy and foreclosure procedures in order to prompt strategic defaulters to resume repaying their bank loans.

With the proliferation of bank-based AMCs, there is a great benefit of coordination among the holders of NPLs to the same borrower by avoiding excessive competition of quick asset disposal which tends to yield low asset recovery.

Mechanisms must be sought to deal with the very large numbers of distressed SMEs.

At the same time, long-term fiscal sustainability is being threatened owing to the sharp rise in government debt, due mainly to the costs of financial sector resolution, which needs to be balanced against further fiscal recapitalisation of financial institutions.

RELAXING CONSTRAINTS ON RESTRUCTURING

To accelerate the pace of financial and corporate sector restructuring, it is important to identify, and relax, existing constraints to further progress.

Corporate restructuring is primarily an issue between creditors and debtors, and the government's primary role is to create an enabling framework that provides both creditors and debtors with sufficient incentives for restructuring. Here, constraints on corporate restructuring from the points of view of the creditors, debtors, and governments and international community are identified, followed by recommendations on how the constraints could be relaxed.

Creditor constraints

The most important constraint on corporate restructuring from the perspective of creditors is their unwillingness to recognise losses on their NPLs. Large NPLs, and the need to make adequate provision for loan losses and maintain the prescribed CARs, make it difficult for creditor banks to work out corporate debts if this entails recognising further losses. Nor can financially weak banks provide working capital financing to restructured corporations. Recognising these losses and recapitalising the banks may result in replacement of management and loss of potential upside gains.

The second important constraint facing the domestic creditor banks is their unwillingness to participate in publicly funded recapitalisation schemes. This unwillingness stems from the controlling shareholders' overriding desire to avoid dilution of ownership and loss of control over bank management. Participation in public recapitalisation schemes almost always requires a dilution of owner equity and control, or management replacement, which the existing owners do not welcome.

The third constraint is the unwillingness of creditor banks to agree on debt workout involving favourable treatment of certain corporate borrowers, such as a hair cut, because this may induce strategic defaulting by other corporate borrowers. Essentially, corporate debt workout with certain borrowers can increase the expectation that other borrowers will receive similar treatment and therefore can reduce incentives on the part of good borrowers to stop repayment. This fear makes creditor banks reluctant even to negotiate on debt workout that may involve debt reduction (a hair cut).

To encourage corporate restructuring, these constraints on creditors must be relaxed.

Recapitalise the banks adequately. It is important that weak banks are adequately recapitalised, by public funds if necessary. There are several ways to recapitalise banks. One way is for the government to purchase subordinated debts or non-voting right equity from a bank using government bonds as payment while the bank keeps the NPLs. An alternative way is for the government to have its AMC purchase NPLs (at market value) from banks in exchange for subordinated or convertible government bonds. The first alternative allows creditor banks to utilise pertinent information about the corporate borrower for successful restructuring; but if the bank does not have the capacity or the incentive to work out corporate debts, the publicly-run AMC has merit. AMCs have been used in Korea, Malaysia and Thailand (in the context of resolution of assets of closed finance companies).

Provide incentives for bank shareholders. Recapitalising banks should be part of a coherent banking reform strategy. The modest response to the Thai Tier one recapitalisation scheme suggests that although the concept of linking corporate debt restructuring with bank capitalisation may be unobjectionable, it works best if there are strong incentives. A fear of ownership dilution discourages banks from raising new capital. The government can give shareholders an incentive to recognise losses fully by injecting capital via instruments that give them an option to purchase the stock back and retain control if the restructuring is successful.

Punish bad borrowers and reward good borrowers. It is important for a creditor bank to clearly distinguish between good and bad borrowers. The establishment of credit bureaux and publicising names of strategic defaulters and non-cooperative debtors may help provide incentives against strategic default.

Debtor constraints

An important constraint to restructuring is the lack of credible threat from the legal/judicial system. Debtors needing no new funds have no incentive to negotiate when they are not servicing the existing debts. Creditors have no effective power to foreclose on the collateral in court. In the absence of the trusted court alternative and of clearly spelt-out rules for a voluntary out-of-court mechanism, the status quo would simply continue, or strategic defaulting would rise with a resulting increase in corporate debt over-hang.

The second constraint is the reluctance on the part of a debtor to dilute ownership and lose control over the corporation. This results in the debtor's resistance to operational restructuring of the distressed corporation because the debtor may be concerned about management replacement, resistance from labour unions and loss of potential upside gains.

The third constraint is the lack of adequate disclosure of financial information on the debtor corporation's (or its group's) balance sheet, especially assets and cash balances. The lack of disclosure by debtors is often raised by external creditors as one of the most fundamental impediments to restructuring negotiations. In the absence of such information, it is difficult to evaluate the debt-servicing capacity of debtors as a prerequisite to corporate debt workout.

The fourth constraint is that the debtor corporation may not be attracted to restructuring without adequate guarantees of working capital financing after restructuring. If debtors know that even after restructuring the corporations' business will not be viable due to lack of working capital financing, they may not have sufficient incentives to agree to restructuring.

For a voluntary process of corporate restructuring to be successful, these constraints must be reduced.

Establish a credible threat of bankruptcy. The alternatives to a restructuring agreement must be clear and credible. In particular, creditors must be able to enforce their legal claims, and this requires courts to function well.

Improvement in the functioning of courts, not just regarding bankruptcy, but especially the procedures for foreclosing on collateral and registering security interests, greatly helps protect creditor rights and provides the debtor with a credible threat to negotiate in good faith. By empowering the creditor, he/she has the incentive to treat the debtor fairly and the debtor has every incentive to abscond.

Provide working capital for restructured corporations. It is crucial that creditworthy corporations have access to adequate sources of working capital finance. One approach would be the formation of a working capital facility available to corporations that have successfully restructured their debt with creditors. Funds from such a facility could be provided on a commercial basis with a first priority collateral position. This would provide sufficient incentives to the debtor to restructure the debt. Debt restructuring, combined with working capital provision, is expected to help accelerate the economic recovery process.

Improve corporate governance. A longer-term, but important, issue is to improve corporate governance. Successful restructuring processes depend on the corporate governance structure of corporations. This should begin now because it takes time. The main task involves broadening ownership by introducing sizeable outside shareholders, improving the quality of the accounting standards and information disclosure, and the wider dissemination of information of interest to non-controlling owners. In the past, neither creditors nor minority/outside shareholders had access to reliable information, and this is being improved by requiring all listed firms to have at least a few outside directors on their board.

Government and international constraints

The first constraint from the perspective of the government is its fear of the mounting fiscal burden for bank recapitalisation. The perception of ever-rising public debt (relative to GDP) during economic crisis makes government even more uncomfortable about acknowledging the size of the problem and to add further fiscal resources for bank recapitalisation. Furthermore, recapitalising banks is politically unpopular because it is perceived as a bailout to rich bankers. Both political fear and concern for fiscal sustainability prevent governments from undertaking effective recapitalisation programs.

The second constraint on corporate restructuring is the lack of capacity or willingness to use an AMC for active corporate restructuring. All countries (except the Philippines and Thailand, which has an AMC only for finance companies) have established public, centralised AMCs to acquire NPLs from banks, but they have not adequately performed their function in corporate restructuring negotiations. In particular, Korea's KAMCO, Malaysia's Danaharta and Indonesia's IBRA have not begun active corporate restructuring. Also, such AMCs often lack human resources and technical capacity for restructuring. This constraint also applies to creditor banks, which lack workout expertise, particularly in relation to the number of borrowers whose loans and operations need to be restructured.

The third constraint is the lack of adequate coordination and information sharing among the stakeholders. This includes: the lack of well balanced burden-sharing of losses among debtors, equity holders, domestic and foreign creditors, and the government; lack of information exchange among creditors about their preferences and strategies; and lack of information sharing about the debtor's financial conditions and about the amount and seniority of other creditor claims. In the absence of such coordination and information exchange, it is difficult for multiple creditors to agree on their stance *vis-à-vis* the debtor and to engage collectively in corporate debt workout and restructuring.

Acknowledge the need for active bank recapitalisation. It is important for the government to acknowledge the scale of NPLs and the costs of problem resolution as soon as possible. A delay of such acknowledgement and action can bring about economic costs in the form of continued losses on the part of commercial banks, protracted recession and foregone output. The governments of the East Asian crisis-affected countries have the capacity to absorb such costs because of the low level of public debt (relative to GDP) in the pre-crisis period.

Use AMCs as possible catalysts for corporate restructuring. The scope for participation of AMCs in resolving corporate debt problems is potentially large. By accumulating NPLs from various debtors to a single creditor, AMCs may become the largest domestic creditor for a significant number of corporations. Thus, the government can use AMCs to demonstrate commitment to corporate restructuring. AMCs may as a result be a major force in corporate restructuring, with considerable influence over reluctant debtors through the threat of bankruptcy.

Strengthen inter-creditor coordination and information sharing. Actions to improve the mechanics of an out-of-court settlement with multiple creditors include close consultation, coordination and information sharing among these creditors. Creditors must make decisions reflecting different preferences, specific conditions, legal and regulatory frameworks. By acting as a clearing house for such coordination and information sharing, the government and international community can reduce avoidable delays.

SUMMARY

The uneven progress of financial and corporate restructuring in the East Asian crisis-affected countries and the detailed explanations above underscore four main lessons.

First, corporate restructuring requires creditors and debtors to have the right incentives to preserve their assets and to manage their businesses efficiently. With such incentives, creditors can judge whether, when and how to restructure their debt claims so that the borrowers will operate the corporations efficiently and repay.

Second, banks must have adequate capital to set the stage for more aggressive restructuring of NPLs on their balance sheets. Government recapitalisation schemes, conditional on some costs to bank owners but without jeopardising their willingness to recognise losses, are essential.

Third, borrowers must be forced to face a credible threat of bankruptcy for a voluntary process of corporate restructuring to work. The alternatives to a restructuring agreement must be made clear and credible. In particular, creditors must be able to enforce their legal claims, and this requires courts to function effectively. Borrowers will have more incentive to agree to a restructuring if working capital finance is available subsequently.

Fourth, governments should acknowledge the scale of NPLs and the necessary costs of problem resolution and take steps to restructure and recapitalise banks more rapidly to avoid delays that will ultimately increase the fiscal and economic costs of the financial crisis. An early infusion of such funds may raise the measured budget deficit initially; but this must be weighed against the likelihood that taxpayer costs could increase further if banks operate with inadequate capital and incentives. Recapitalisation must be accompanied by measures to strengthen bank risk management and supervisory oversight. Coherent strategies for management of NPLs should be developed, including reliance on public AMCs. The legal and judicial framework to support creditor rights must be strengthened and policies to improve corporate governance should be part of the policy package.

NOTES

1   The authour is grateful to Hoon Mok Chung, Bernard Drum, Richard Duncan, Jonathon Fiechter, Dale Gray, Jaques Loubert, William Makr, Gerald Meyerman, Tetsutaro Muraki, S. Ramachandran and Richard Zechter for their contributions. The findings, interpretations and conclusions expressed in this chapter are those of the author and do not necessarily represent the views of the World Bank, its Executive Directors or the countries they represent.

2   Owners of failed or weak banks do not always have sufficient incentive to resolve their NPLs or restructure borrower corporations because, if they realise losses, the resulting write-down of capital may invite government recapitalisation and will force a loss of control of their banks. Similarly, owners of indebted corporations do not always have incentive to agree on debt restructuring because doing so may involve dilution of ownership and loss of control over management.

3   In a non-systemic crisis, the majority of private banks tend to have weak but positive equity and be recapitalised by private investors. The government need only resolve few institutions that are insolvent. In a systemic crisis, the required capital far exceeds that available from the private sector and sufficient private investment to recapitalise the banks may not be forthcoming. In these instances, the government must develop a recapitalisation plan that includes public funds to supplement private funds. Use of public funds can be justified on the ground that the restoration of a healthy financial sector and payments system is a fundamental public good necessary to induce economic recovery and to promote sustained growth in the real sector activity. Bank recapitalisation must require

recognition of losses on NPLs and must first rely on private capital and then public funds to supplement private resources. Public financial support should be provided only to viable institutions where it is most effectively used in restoring the health of the system. It should also be accompanied by costs to existing owners.

4   An important principle of financial sector restructuring is that the longer it takes, the larger the eventual economic costs. Weak banks may continue to accumulate assets that are likely to go bad or owners may lend to connected enterprises in the optimistic expectation that the loans will be repaid some time in the near future. Assets underlying NPLs should be sold in a reasonable time period so that asset markets can clear. Otherwise, depressed asset prices may continue indefinitely.

5   The London Approach' is used to guide voluntary debt restructuring in the United Kingdom. It describes a set of principles under which creditors agree to keep credit facilities in place, seek out-of-court solutions, work together, share all relevant information about the debtor and recognise the seniority of claims.

6   All private banks were classified into three categories: The A-category were those with a CAR of at least 4 per cent of risk-weighted assets; the B-category with a CAR of between negative 25 per cent and 4 per cent; and the C-category with a CAR below negative 25 per cent. The government would assist in the recapitalisation of B' banks which were able to provide business plans demonstrating prospects for future viability. Viable B' banks with fit and proper' owners and management would be eligible to receive up to 80 per cent of the funds required for recapitalisation from the government. C' banks and non-viable B' banks were to be closed.

7   One of the most profound consequences of the crisis has been a dramatic increase in public sector indebtedness. In end-June 1997, public debt which at the time was entirely external debt was a comfortable 24 per cent of GDP. By end-1998, it had reached 60 per cent. But by end-1999, it is estimated to have reached a staggering 95 per cent of GDP – a four-fold increase from the pre-crisis period. About two-thirds of this increase is the expected consequence of the domestic bond issue due to bank restructuring.

8   By mid-1999, IBRA had become the largest non-bank financial institution in Indonesia, assuming responsibility for assets worth Rp433 trillion (about US$60 billion). Of this about Rp220 trillion was in assets transferred from closed banks, Rp110 trillion in assets received from bank owners on settlements of their obligation to pay liquidity support from the central bank, and Rp103 trillion from investment in recapitalised banks and banks taken over.

9   In the face of the Daewoo crisis, the government stepped in to work with creditors to prepare an emergency financing package predicated upon a substantial restructuring plan. As part of the package, Daewoo adopted an accelerated restructuring program, comprising spin-off of affiliates, asset sales, raising of more equity including foreign investment, debt–equity swaps, and the break-up of the *chaebol* into several independent corporate entities. It also put up new collateral of W10 trillion, including W1.3 trillion of Chairman Kim's personal shareholdings, which the creditors would be free to sell if Daewoo fails to live up to its commitments under the agreed restructuring and financing plan. Daewoo's creditor financial institutions set up a Daewoo Restructuring Team in Korea First Bank (Daewoo's lead bank), to be assisted by international advisors. An estimated US$5 billion of the foreign currency debt is due for repayment before end-1999, of which about US$3 billion is held by foreign creditors. Daewoo will need to reschedule some of this debt. Rescheduling discussions with foreign creditors are not yet fully under way and will likely raise difficult issues of guarantees and collateral. Reports indicate that Daewoo will sell off all business outside its core

automotive lines, which if it transpires, will mark the most dramatic restructuring to date in East Asia.

10 Unlike the *chaebol*, a decentralised approach was chosen for SMEs. SMEs were first classified into three categories: viable SMEs (about 35 per cent of total SMEs); potentially conditionally viable SMEs (or conditionally viable after restructuring, about 60 per cent); and non-viable SMEs (about 5 per cent). While no additional credit accrued to non-viable' SMEs as evidenced by a large number of SME bankruptcies (8,200 and 10,500 SMEs went bankrupt in 1997 and 1998, respectively, as opposed to fifty-eight and thirty-nine large corporations in bankruptcy in the same years), lack of credit was never a problem for the top tier of viable SMEs. To protect the credit flows to potentially viable SMEs, the Banking Supervisory Authority (BSA) adopted several schemes to support SMEs: (a) banks were required to roll over SME loans due by December 1998; (b) commercial banks were required to cancel their compensating balances for SMEs between January and November of 1998 to allow credit flows to SMEs; and (c) the relatively larger and stronger 15 commercial banks were required to provide additional loans to SMEs.

11 Such successful restructurings include Renong Bhd with debt of RM8.4 billion, Tongkah Holdings Bhd with debt of RM0.6 billion, Nam Fatt Corp Bhd, Tenco Bhd, Tanco Holdings Bhd, Orlando Holdings Bhd, and a couple of private companies.

12 They included mergers and acquisitions: merger of the PCI Bank with Equitable Banking Corporation; Bank of the Philippine Islands with Far East Bank and Trust Company; and Asian Bank with Pilipinas Bank; and acquisition by Metrobank of two smaller banks.

13 The Radanasin Bank was established in January 1998 under 100% government ownership to participate in sales of the good assets of the 56 closed finance companies.

14 A centralised AMC was used for the first time for the sale of RSB to carve out NPLs from intervened banks. An investor would have an option to either bid for the whole bank and enter into profit and loss sharing agreements with the government, as in the case of NTB, or bid for only its good assets after carving out bad assets to an AMC, as in the case of the sale of RSB.

15 CDRAC has been chaired by the BOT Governor and included five associations (Thai Bankers' Association, Foreign Bankers' Association, Federation of Thai Industries, Chamber of Commerce, and Association of Finance Companies) representing creditors and debtors.

Table A13.1   Progress on financial sector restructuring

	Indonesia	Korea	Malaysia	Philippines	Thailand
I Establish institutional framework	IBRA created and empowered to resolve problem banks, provide guarantees of credit lines, and manage and dispose of frozen bank assets. AMU created to focus on debt recovery.	KAMCO reestablished to manage and dispose of NPLs. FSC created to oversee financial and corporate restructuring. Financial Supervisory Service (FSS) established to supervise and regulate financial institutions.	Danamodal created to recapitalise banks and fincos. Danaharta created to purchase, manage, and dispose of NPLs. CDRC created to oversee voluntary corporate debt restructuring.	Central Bank Monetary Board decides on bank closures. Philippine Deposit Insurance Corporation, established in 1963, is responsible for receivership and liquidation of banks.	The FRA and the AMC established in October 1997 for the resolution of 56 closed fincos and the sale of their assets.
II Resolve non-viable banks **a Liquidate**	16 banks closed in November 1997, 7 closed in April 1998, 3 closed in August, 1998, 38 closed in March 1999, and 2 joint venture banks closed in April 1999.	16 of 30 merchant banks.10 of 25 leasing companies. 28 of 231 mutual savings companies. 128 of 1,666 credit unions. No commercial bank has been liquidated.	None. Malaysia has opted instead for industry consolidation through mergers.	1 commercial bank, 7 thrifts and 44 rural banks under receivership since July 97.	57 out of 91 fincos, 1 out of 15 banks (Bangkok Bank of Commerce).
b Nationalise or absorb into other institutions	6 banks taken over in April–May 1998; 1 bank taken over in May 1998; 8 banks taken over in March 1999; 1 bank taken over in December 1999; 8 BTOs to merge with Danamon; 1 BTO to merge with BCA; and 4 of 7 state banks to merge into Bank Mandiri.	2 commercial banks nationalised, 5 weak commercial banks forced to merge into healthier banks, 7 banks encouraged to merge with government equity assistance. 4 life insurance companies and 7 investment trust companies absorbed by stronger intermediaries.	58 financial institutions are in the process of being consolidated into 10 core banking groups. Earlier, Sime Bank and Bank Bumiputra were absorbed by stronger banks and 16 fincos absorbed by parent banks.	None nationalised; voluntary mergers encouraged.	7 of 15 banks intervened, 1 bank liquidated, 3 banks absorbed (2 by state banks, and 1 by a state finco), 12 fincos nationalised and absorbed by the same state finco. 2 banks already sold, and another 2 likely to be sold. Privatisation of 2 state banks expected to take longer.
III Recapitalise viable banks **a Capital support programs from government**	7 of the 8 banks, identified as eligible for possible government assisted recapitalisation, injected with public funds.	W64 trillion allocated for recapitalisation of which W60 trillion has already been used. Recapitalisation cost could rise substantially due to further corporate restructuring reflecting the Daewoo restructuring.	Danamodal set up in July 1998. RM6.4 billion already injected into 10 financial institutions. Recapitalisation cost initially estimated to be RM16 billion, but after peaking at RM6.4 billion actual injections were subsequently reduced to RM5.3 billion by partial repayments.	None; incentives for mergers.	TB300 billion. Program set up in August 1998 to provide Tier-1 and Tier-2 capital for banks and fincos, in addition to TB1.1 trillion in liquidity support to closed or intervened institutions. Pace of recaps slow. 3 banks and fincos received Tier-1, 3 banks and fincos applied for Tier-2.

Table A13.1   (cont'd) Progress on financial sector restructuring

	Indonesia	Korea	Malaysia	Philippines	Thailand
b Foreign bank or strategic buyers	Foreign and joint venture banks enjoy 10% market share of deposits; no major new investors.	A foreign investor acquired Korea First Bank. Sale of Seoul Bank remains uncertain.	None, but 13 foreign banks enjoy 20% + deposit market share.	None yet; planned for Government stake in the Philippine National Bank (PNB).	2 private banks acquired by foreign banks, gov't majority stake of 2 intervened banks sold to foreigners, and 2 more expected for sale in the future.
c Stop-loss, put-back for strategic buyers	None.	Offered in the case of Korea First Bank. Government to transfer NPLs to a bad bank.	None.	None yet.	Government willing to offer with loss protection to buyers of intervened banks.
d Foreign or domestic equity capital markets	None.	5 banks successful in 1998 in domestic market.	None, banks encouraged to use Danamodal if need capital.	None through mandatory recapitalisation. programs; several commercial banks seeking additional capital via private placements and equity markets.	At least 8 banks have foreign equity (4 controlling shares, 4 minority shares); 3 banks have recently issued Tier-1 capital through a domestic innovative capital instrument (about TB80 billion).
IV Resolve or restructure NPLs a Recognise full extent of NPLs	No, but performed comprehensive system-wide portfolio reviews.	Partially. A new 'forward-looking' system of loan classification introduced in end-1999. Forbearance will allow NPLs to be recognised over 2 years.	In progress, enforcement vs forbearance the key issue.	Yes, but for treatment of restructured loans.	Yes, with implementation of a new set of loan classification rules issued in March 98.
b System-wide carve-out of NPLs	Not yet, but assets and NPLs of closed banks and private banks to be recapitalised have been transferred to IBRA.	KAMCO has used KW20 trillion to purchase KW56 trillion (face value) of NPLs (7% of all bank loans), more purchases of NPLs expected.	Danaharta manages RM34 billion (face value) in NPLs at end-December 1999, acquired from the financial system (banks, fincos and merchant banks), plus another RM8 billion in NPLs from offshore institutions; RM42 billion total.	Not yet; GOP has contingency plans for an AMC.	A boutique approach (in contrast to FRA auctions of closed finco assets). A centralised, publicly-managed AMC not planned for private bank assets despite high NPLs. A centralised AMC set up for state banks.

Table A13.1   (cont'd) Progress on financial sector restructuring

	Indonesia	Korea	Malaysia	Philippines	Thailand
c Restructure viable NPLs	Under the Jakarta Initiative and other voluntary programs, court-based restructuring and reorganisation, and IBRA-led restructuring.	Loans under workouts amount to W35 trillion, due by 6–64 *chaebol* and SMEs, and an additional W60–75 trillion for Daewoo. Debt restructuring options include interest rate reduction, debt to equity conversions, debt forgiveness and longer maturity periods. Government-led restructuring efforts for top 5 chaebol.	Government-led for strategic groups (e.g. Renong); Danaharta to play key role for NPL resolution; CDRC for private sector workouts.	Market-based and bilateral, except for companies filing for suspension of payments with SEC.	Market-based guidelines and incentives put in place. TB762 billion debts reported as restructuring completed (Sept. 99) while TB1.15 trillion on the process of restructuring.
d Tax and other incentives for NPL restructuring	New bankruptcy law, but not effective.	In place (mainly tax waivers and reductions).	In place (capital support, stamp duties waived).	Favorable loan loss provisioning treatment for restructured loans.	In place (tax waivers, Tier-2 capital support).
e Enable/facilitate foreclosure of non-viable NPLs	Exists in theory but not yet enforced in the legal system.	Good framework, but limited use due to unemployment impact.	Good framework. Danaharta Act speeds foreclosures.	Foreclosure possible but slow (delayed by redemption period); framework under review.	New bankruptcy and foreclosure law passed in March 99. Utilisation low.
f Create secondary market for bank NPLs (sale to financial investors)	No.	KAMCO has recovered KW10.4 trillion (face value) of W56 trillion spent to acquire NPLs. Recovery done by issuing debt instruments backed by assets, public auctions, voluntary debt repayments and additional asset acquisitions.	Danaharta to sell or restructure NPLs and underlying assets.	Not yet.	Auction process for US$20 billion of shutdown fincos loans. No centralised mechanism for banks NPLs (only private sector-based).

Table A13.1   (cont'd) Progress on financial sector restructuring

	Indonesia	Korea	Malaysia	Philippines	Thailand
V Revamp regulatory frameworks for banking systems **a Strengthen prudential norms**	Yes new regulations on loan classification, provisioning debt restructuring, connected lending and capital adequacy. Not yet implemented.	New regulations issued on connected lending, loan classification and provisioning, exposure to FX risks, coverage of deposit insurance scheme, and accounting standards. Regulation and supervision are still behind minimum international standards. New 'forward looking' loan classification system put in place at end-1999.	Stronger norms pre-crisis. Initial tightening of NPL definition at the beginning of the crisis was reversed in September 1998, at the peak of the crisis. But BNM continues to publish NPLs, both 3 months and 6 months overdue.	Standards strong and strengthening to close to international best practice.	Process underway to fully revamp the legal and regulatory framework for supervision by 2000.
b Strengthen banking supervision and examination	Not yet, work in progress.	Merger of the four financial supervisory agencies (banking, non-banks, securities and insurance) became effective January 1999.	Good pre-crisis, enhanced by Danamodal and Danaharta.	Fairly good pre-crisis, strengthening with external assistance.	Ongoing reorganisation of BOT with TA provided by donors to build up its supervisory capacity (training and enhancing of supervisory procedures). Draft of new Central Bank Law under review.
c Strengthen enforcement of banking regulations	Implementation key issue.	FSS has received some additional powers to enforce supervision and regulation.	Yes, but forbearance on NPLs.	Regulations enforced, but delays in closure of weakest banks.	Yes with temporary forbearance on NPLs provisioning (to end-2000). The draft of new financial institution law on public hearing.
VI Strengthen bank credit cultures and management **a Encourage/force consolidations**	New willingness to close institutions creates incentives for consolidation.	Encouraged, 3 mergers so far, 5 banks absorbed by stronger banks so far, more likely.	Actively encouraged. 58 financial institutions are to be consolidated into 10 by year-end 2000.	Actively encouraged via merger incentives and higher capital requirements.	Done for 3 nationalised banks and 12 nationalised fincos. Voluntary for others.
b Allow/encourage foreign bank buy-ins	Yes, up to 100% but adherence to reform program, equitable treatment of investors regardless of ethnic origin, political and economic stability are needed first.	Yes, 3 cases (Korea First/New Bridge, Korea Exchange/Commerz Bank, and Kookmin/Goldman Sachs).	New foreign banks not allowed or encouraged.	Yes, but extent and duration under debate.	Yes for ownership limit of more than 49% lifted for a 10 year period.

Table A13.1 (cont'd) Progress on financial sector restructuring

	Indonesia	Korea	Malaysia	Philippines	Thailand
c **Establish CAMEL rating for banks**	Traditionally used, but the willingness and capacity to examine banks and assign ratings based on transparent criteria has been lacking.	Used by BOK and expanded to other financial institutions, FSS focusing now on NPLs, CAR.	Traditionally used by BNM.	Established practice, currently being upgraded to improved CAMELS system.	CAMEL rating already used by BOT, but needs to be upgraded; planned in the reform of supervision.
d **Proper NPL definition, interest accrual, provisioning norms**	Implementation still a key issue.	Partially. New rules define NPLs as all loans in arrears for more than 3 months. A 'forward looking' system that takes into account the borrowers capability to repay was introduced at end-1999.	Put in place in the first half of 1998, except reversion to 6-month NPL definition.	Yes, NPL definition tightened to 3 months in 1998. General loan loss provisioning requirements being phased in; currently slated to rise to 2% by October 1999.	Proper norms have been issued in March 98, classification immediately implemented; interest accrual rules implemented in January 99; provisioning requirement phased-in through 2000.
e **Require credit risk rating/scoring/monitoring systems**	No progress as of yet.	Only minor progress at individual level; entry of foreign banks to help. Some local banks have maintained consulting firms to upgrade the credit monitoring system.	Only at the larger banks.	Risk monitoring systems required of banks.	Only minor progress at individual bank level. Big improvement in banks with foreign control.

Table A13.2   Progress on corporate sector restructuring

1 Establish enabling environment for corporate restructuring

	Indonesia	Korea	Malaysia	Philippines	Thailand
a Legal					
• Removing obstacles for mergers	Not all obstacles removed.	Obstacles largely replaced. Incentives for Big Deal mergers.	Obstacles largely replaced.	(Information not available.)	Need to review tax treatment of non-cash transactions.
• Ease of debt equity swaps	Swaps allowed but impediments remain.	Swaps allowed.	Swaps allowed.	Information not available.	Swaps taking place. Need modification of CCC to legalise.
• Security interests	Regulation on registration adopted in April 1999.	Information not available.	Court administration registers interests.	Information not available.	Need to broaden use and registration of security interests.
b Tax	Mergers are tax neutral but not all obstacles removed. Simplification of tax administration also required.	Tax Exemption and Reduction Control Act (February 1998) provides breaks for CR.	Tax incentives for restructuring available.	Provisions for loan losses not tax deductible unless debtor has filed for insolvency.	Temporary tax relief for debt restructured between 1 Jan. 1998 and 31 Dec. 1999.
c Foreign ownership liberalisation	Few formal restrictions on foreign ownership. Difficult in practice due to attitudes and slow approval process.	FDI and Foreign Capital Inducement Act permits foreigners to take over non-strategic companies.	FDI policies for property and manufacturing sectors relatively liberal. Other restrictions still in place.	Rules on foreign investment and property ownership have been liberalised.	Rules on foreign investment and property ownership have been liberalised.
d Labour market flexibility	A few recent high profile cases of labour unrest.	Some labour union resistance to corporate restructuring despite tripartite agreement.	Not a barrier.	Not a barrier.	Some labour union resistance to corporate restructuring.
e Social and political stability	Uncertainties surrounding political transition.	Tensions with North Korea.	Possible difficulties in political transition.	Reasonable stability.	Reasonable stability.

KEY

Significant progress   Some progress, more needed   Limited progress

Table A13.2 Progress on corporate sector restructuring

		Indonesia	Korea	Malaysia	Philippines	Thailand
2 Strengthen out-of-court mechanisms						
a	**Basic voluntary framework in place**	Jakarta Initiative launched Sept. 1998. JITF advises and facilitates negotiations. But little progress to date.	Lead banks responsible for 'London Rules' type voluntary workouts. Corporate Restructuring Coordination Committee (CRCC) in place.	Voluntary, 'London Rules' style approach, with Corporate Debt Restructuring Committee (CDRC) oversight.	Lead Bank responsible for leading voluntary workout efforts.	Bangkok rules: Bank recapitalisation schemes tied to corporate debt restructuring. (CDRAC) formed to facilitate corporate restructuring.
b	**Adequate incentives to participate**	INDRA established in June 1998, and extended twice to end-June 2000. Used only for 1 corporate restructuring.	Bankruptcy-Law and Fair Trade Act provide ready alternatives, and the government has also intervened directly (e.g. Big Deals) for Top-5 chaebol. Mandated deadlines for standstills.	Functioning Bankruptcy Law and courts provide credible alternative. Government pressure on banks to roll-over/ restructure debt. Allegations of government interference in some cases.	Debtors use fear of SEC's venue for suspension of payments to obtain favorable terms from creditors. SEC grants interim and definitive suspensions of payments; can appoint receivers and liquidators.	Bank recapitalisation schemes tied to corporate debt restructuring, BOT should work more through banks to promote CR.
3 Strengthen bankruptcy and foreclosure systems						
a	**Quality of bankruptcy law**	Bankruptcy Law amended, and a new 'Commercial Court' introduced in August 1998.	Bankruptcy Act, Composition Act, Reorganisation Act passed in February 1998. Considered satisfactory.	Laws satisfactory, with the British legacy of common law.	Bankruptcy law adopted in 1909 has some features of a modern law but does not provide for stays of actions by secured creditors. Since 1976, only liquidation can be supervised by courts.	New Bankruptcy Law passed in March 1999. Separate Bankruptcy Court introduced.
b	**Enforcement and judicial capacity in bankruptcy system**	Bankruptcy cases controversial. Ad hoc judges to be appointed. Training for judges under way. Lack of enforcement is a major obstacle to corporate restructuring.	Increased use of courts; special commission at Seoul court. Business rarely relies on courts, but this is changing.	Judicial system is functions well but specialised skills need to be improved.	Not applicable since courts no longer grant suspensions of payments or supervise implementation of rehabilitation plans.	Initial cases controversial. Training for judges currently under consideration.

Table A13.2 Progress on corporate sector restructuring

	Indonesia	Korea	Malaysia	Philippines	Thailand
c Foreclosure and insolvency procedures	Foreclosure difficult.	Foreclosure is possible.	Foreclosure is possible.	Foreclosure actions can be frustrated by stays issued by the SEC.	Foreclosure laws passed in 1998 and in March 1999.
d Court-based reorganisation procedures	Court-based procedure difficult.	Court-based reorganisation possible.	Court-based reorganisation possible.		New Bankruptcy Law passed in March 1999 includes court-based reorganisation.
4 Improve corporate governance					
a Effectiveness of ownership oversight and boards of directors	Little progress to date in improving oversight.	All publicly traded companies must have at least one non-executive board director, 25% of board seats must be non-executive in 1999.	Malaysian Institute of Corporate Governance (MICG) founded in March 1998 to promote awareness and practices.	Moderate progress.	SET has issued a code of best practice for directors. Requirements of two independent board directors by end-1999.
b Shareholder rights and protection	Legal liabilities for board members clarified in 1997. In practice, considerable self-dealing by insiders and controlling shareholders.	Minimum equity holding requirements for call action suits were drastically reduced from 1% to 0.01%.	In addition to suits by aggrieved parties, Exchange can act against negligent directors.	Exchange can take direct action against negligent directors. Laws allow share buybacks.	Although laws give extensive rights to shareholders, enforcement limited by very weak judicial system.
c International accounting, auditing and disclosure standards	While current auditing and accounting standards largely follow international standards, there is very poor compliance with standards due to lack of enforcement.	Statements of listed companies must be prepared and audited using international standards. Conglomerates must publish consolidated statements as of 1999.	International standards made mandatory. Standards of the Malaysian Accounting Standards Board backed by the force of law.	International standards made mandatory. Standards of the Philippine Board of Accountancy backed by force of law. Small fines for non-submission of reports.	Financial statements of public companies with assets over BT1 billion use international best practices. All listed companies must have an audit committee. Enforcement limited.

14 Shaping East Asia's recovery: post-crisis reform of the international financial system

David Nellor [1]

INTRODUCTION

The systemic reforms taking place in Asia and the international financial system are setting Asia's future course. And their influence will persist far beyond the immediate recovery. The reason is that the rules of the game' of economic relations are being redesigned. These rules of the game comprise the economic constitution governing economic and financial relations both within and across national borders. The broadly defined institutional structure of the international financial system is one important part of this constitution.

The depth and breadth of economic disruption since the Mexico crisis of 1994–5 is compelling *prima facie* evidence of problems in the international financial system. The crisis in the East Asian economies seemed to underline these problems. In lock-step with these damaging developments, a succession of agendas, frameworks, blueprints and new architectures for reforming the international financial system has been tabled. So, why add an economic constitution to this nomenclature? The reason is that the constitutional approach embodies an analytical framework, rather than being simply descriptive. It offers insights into reform of the economic constitution including those parts relating to the international financial system. This framework reflects the observations of Adam Smith, the nineteenth century political economists and, more recently, the public-choice school.

Adam Smith and the early political economists defined markets by the institutional structure in which they operated. The term institutional structure' is defined broadly. It encompasses not only organisations but also the regulations, policies and practices that form the environment in which the private sector and policy makers make decisions. Smith observed that, within an appropriate structure of laws and institutions', individuals following their own interests further the general well-being. Understanding the foundations of exchange – property rights and contract – is central to any analysis once we graduate from the one-person Robinson Crusoe economy. Political economy focused on these broadly-defined institutional structures and asked how effective they were in coordinating individual behaviour. Of course, when attention turns to the global economy, the rules of the game are more complex but the task is the same. It is in the process of formulating the rules of the game that public choice makes its contribution (see, for example, Brennan and Buchanan 1985).

A quick reflection on issues thrust to the forefront by the Asian crisis soon confirms the importance of assessing the institutional structure of markets. Many argue that the crisis exposed significant loopholes in the rules governing domestic financial institutions and corporations. Others suggest that the loopholes were in the institutional structure governing cross-border capital flows, and in the international arrangements to respond to crises. The track record of the global economy says clearly that the rules of the game of the international financial system have a profound impact on whether markets work or fail.

The present review of the international financial system and the defining features of national economies, such as the structure of their financial sectors, are parts of a constitutional convention. This convention is playing out in various forums. At a minimum, there appears to be a consensus that even if the constitution may not need a complete overhaul, elements are either missing or should be re-cast.

This chapter focuses on one aspect of the broader economic constitution, namely the reform of the international financial system. It suggests that the constitutional approach is a helpful way of organising thoughts about reform of the international financial system, and identifies a few important issues that are the focus of the reform discussions. The first part sets out the constitutional approach; the second examines suggestions for strengthening the international financial system to prevent crises; and the third examines the role of the private sector in addressing crises.

AMENDING THE ECONOMIC CONSTITUTION

Constitutional rules guiding the setting of economic policy and governing markets are prevalent. These rules govern national-level economic activity, cross-border transactions, and the international financial system. At the international level, the rationale for an international economic constitution today is the same as that which the Bretton Woods Committee recognised in the 1940s. Establishing institutions to promote mutually beneficial policy, and recognising the implications of an integrated global economy, will strengthen economic performance. An important starting point in reforming these rules is to adopt a constructive constitutional choice setting.

An economic constitution

An economic constitution sets rules to promote mutually beneficial outcomes by shaping economic policy and the choices facing private sector participants. The constitution promotes the positive features of market discipline while, at the same time, discouraging the possible use of monopoly power in markets. It promotes strong economic policy for the benefit of national economies and the mutual benefit of participants in the global economy. A common feature of constitutional provisions related to economic policy is that they do not prescribe policy at any point in time. Rather the provisions are rules of the game within which policy makers act. The precise form of these rules' varies. In some cases, they are broad guidelines and in others binding.

The economic constitution is inherently complex as, like all constitutions, it operates by systems of checks and balances. The inability to resolve the centuries-old question of who will police the police' means that the constitution will be designed to guard against the exercise of monopoly power by market participants as well as national and international policy makers. Thus, for example, some would observe that a loophole in the international financial system, a global externality, calls for a global organisation to autonomously resolve those externalities. However, a proposal to establish an omnipotent global economic authority to eliminate loopholes in the international financial system is not necessarily a desirable constitutional solution; international institutions, too, must be part of the checks and balances that promote a stable and productive international financial system. Garten (1998), for example, proposes a global monetary authority.

The overall economic constitution, of which the provisions governing the international financial system are just one part, sets the context for this chapter. The broadly-defined economic constitution already shapes macroeconomic performance and economic behaviour. This (conceptual) constitution is a compendium comprising elements of national constitutions and laws, regulatory frameworks and international agreements. The following offers a broad-brush overview of some elements of this constitution.

At the national level, policy rules guiding macroeconomic developments are prevalent. Legal restrictions on methods of financing public expenditures are common. In the United States, voters have expressed views on constitutional provisions restricting policy makers' choices on tax policy. Exploring the use of fiscal rules to impose limits on overall fiscal balances and financing is extensive, even if most prominent in Europe because of the Maastricht agreement. Also familiar are efforts to guide monetary policy through establishing independent central banks that set policy within well-defined charters; reforms in this direction are a feature of the reform programs in the Asian crisis countries. Specific constitutional provisions relating to economic transactions are also common. For example, in some federations, constitutions contain provisions guaranteeing free trade across state borders and equality of treatment in trade laws.

Just as national legislation helps define the institutional structure in which domestic economic transactions take place, the interaction of national rules across countries sets the market structure for most cross-border financial activity. This is demonstrated in the behaviour of corporations that are subject to different regulatory, tax and other laws in their home country and elsewhere. The growing focus on offshore centres reflects concerns prompted by the interaction of national rules across countries; in fact, the Financial

Stability Forum (FSF), established by the G-7, is examining offshore centres in this regard. The constitutional convention must assess whether these differences, most apparent in offshore centres, threaten financial stability or the credibility of regulatory efforts. The effectiveness of adopting common international standards (discussed below), for example, may be compromised by offshore centres.

At the international level, which is the focus of this chapter, several multilateral agreements shape economic policy and activity. The Bretton Woods Committee, which can perhaps be viewed as a constitutional convention, established the International Monetary Fund (IMF) as the institutional mechanism to strengthen the global economic environment and to help achieve the mutual benefits possible from globalisation. The experience of competitive devaluation, trade restrictions and other mutually destructive policies contributing to the Great Depression was a costly lesson. Namely, the outcome can be worse for all when countries pursue their own narrowly-defined self-interest. More constructively, countries can all be better off by recognising their mutual interests when setting policy, while time-consistency issues mean that the constitutional provisions must be permanent. The *raison d'être* of the international part of the economic constitution is set out in the Appendix. Other international arrangements, such as the World Trade Organisation, are also important parts of the international economic constitution.

Designing a constitutional convention for the international financial system

Devoting effort to designing a strong constitutional process will pay dividends, both in the form of stronger constitutional rules and in ensuring their legitimacy. Eichengreen (1999) takes the stance of assuming, implicitly, that the process is given. He says that politically unrealistic options should be ignored, in order not to distract from reforms that can be implemented readily. Grenville (1999) says that some bodies are not representative and that the United States calls the shots' in the IMF, even if it has close to universal representation.[2] However, he supports the (defunct) Group of 22 (G-22), an *ad hoc* group of industrial and emerging market economies, although the United States established it and has a major weight. Perhaps more essential to his view is that the G-22 was composed of countries with significant interest in global economic developments. This apparent dissatisfaction with the current international reform process has not been matched by systematic analysis of how the process might be improved.

Economic actors can be seen as making two types of choice, namely constitutional and in-period choices. Constitutional choices involve choosing rules that apply for the indefinite future and set limits on market actions and policies. In-period' choices involve day-to-day economic transactions and policy choices within the environment set by the constitutional choices. Constitutional choices involve two steps. The first step is predicting the circumstances that might prevail in-period, and the second is choosing rules after assessing how they might work in-period. Costly circumstances, such as those arising from contagion or inappropriate policy actions, may arise in only a few of the indeterminate sequence of in-period plays. Nevertheless, constitutional choices are made recognising the need for a constitutional rule to minimise disruptions arising from exceptional as well as typical circumstances.

Minimising distributional or immediate self-interest considerations makes for efficient constitutional choices. This is best illustrated in conventional constitutional choices where distributional influences are reduced by uncertainty about an individual's status in the post-constitution period. Consider the example of individuals making a constitutional choice regarding public provision of social assistance to the poor. If the individuals do not know whether they (or their heirs) will be eligible for the assistance, the preferred choice will be determined by objective considerations. Moreover, uncertainty also has advantages in setting constitutional limits on the types of social assistance program that can be chosen in-period. Individuals do not know if they will become bureaucrats who might benefit from one form of assistance program or another, and therefore identifying the possible types of assistance program will likely reflect efficiency considerations. Thus, when individuals express preferences on constitutional rules without knowing their position in coming periods, their individual interest becomes equivalent to that of the group.[3] Even if it is not possible to conceptualise such an extreme separation between rule making and in-period interests, individuals may be somewhat uncertain about their positions (and perhaps those of their heirs) due to social and economic mobility. Moreover, a lengthy time horizon ensures that individuals are at least somewhat uncertain about their private prospects.[4]

It is self-evident that, in a choice environment involving countries, the difficulty of eliminating self-interest from determining the outcome is enormous. At the same time, efforts to reduce the importance of short-term considerations will strengthen the resulting constitution. Unfortunately, the desirable uncertainty of individual constitutional choices is difficult to imitate when drafting an international economic constitution. While an extended time-horizon applies, lack of mobility in the economic circumstances of countries makes it difficult to conceive of the same uncertainty.

Perhaps more helpful in strengthening the constitutional choice setting is a requirement that rules be general and so apply to all countries. If choices are about generalised' constitutional rules, the chances of providing an objective assessment are more likely, because greater weight will be placed on efficiency considerations and less on distributional factors. To take an example, consider a constitutional decision defining the circumstances when countries are justified in imposing capital controls or standstills on debt payments. The chances of providing an objective assessment are enhanced because details about which countries (or which of their citizens) are winning' and losing' are not known.

Defining all of the possible in-period circumstances poses a difficulty in drafting the constitution. For example, the K ln G-7 Ministerial statement says that all debt should be repaid; yet it also recognises that in exceptional circumstances this is not the case. While these exceptional circumstances must be defined clearly in the constitution, this task is far from easy. In fact, to some, the problem is insurmountable, leading them to suggest that these issues be omitted from the constitution and resolved case by case.

While clearly not a perfect solution, the benefits of constitutional rules still outweigh the alternative of in-period or case-by-case decisions. Constitutional choices apply rules to all, and this reduces distributional conflict. The debate then rests on the differing views of what might be termed the genuine public interest. The alternative of in-period choices means, to take the capital controls example once again, that the identity of a country wanting to use controls is known and those who might lose from their introduction are known. This unbounded case-by-case approach allows distributional considerations to dominate. If defining rules poses an insurmountable problem, at least defining an institutional process to address the in-period situations is important in providing at least some constitutional parameters.

Legitimacy of the constitutional process is essential to effectiveness of rules, and this calls for broad representation in the decision-making process. At present, a tension arises between the interest of large countries, whose well-being is less dependent on the international financial system, and smaller countries, which depend more heavily on international financial markets and trade. It is an understandable reality that any new rules will not be effective without the support of the major economies. At the same time, it is essential to recognise that developments in the global economy have a far greater impact on the economic well-being of many smaller open economies. The constitutional process has to meet the interests of all of these countries, in order to garner legitimacy.

The IMF is the obvious representative forum to discuss the constitution, because its universal membership enhances the legitimacy of its decisions. However, some countries feel that their voice is not adequately heard, either due to the system of constituencies (representation by groups of countries) or because voting is proportional to quotas. Two considerations seem relevant. Mussa (1999) notes that, at the time of Bretton Woods, countries were thought to need quotas in the range of 2 per cent of national income. Given the present deeper involvement of emerging markets in international trade, quotas more in the range of 4 per cent of GDP or higher would, he suggests, seem appropriate. The present quotas of many emerging markets are well under 1 per cent of GDP (Mussa 1999: 34). A second issue addresses more directly the representation of countries whose well-being is affected most profoundly by the health of the international financial system. The present system assigns quotas based on a country's share in the global economy and trade. This might be characterised as a top-down' approach because it starts from the global economy and looks at its parts. Another approach is to start from the country's perspective and define the quota in terms of its relative exposure to the global economy. This bottom up' approach recognises that the citizens of a small open economy are likely to be far more influenced by global economic developments than in a large country dominated by its domestic economic developments.[5] Some balancing of these two approaches would seem appropriate.[6]

PREVENTING CRISES

The economic constitution is intended to make markets operate more effectively by both guiding economic policy and setting the rules for economic transactions. This section looks at several issues that have arisen in discussion on reform of the international financial system. It first describes the specific issue, and then offers some views on the discussion from the constitutional perspective set out above. The specific issues examined are highly leveraged investment institutions (HLIs) and moral hazard; at the adoption of common international standards and capital account liberalisation; and at organisational issues in strengthening surveillance of macroeconomic policy.

Understanding markets

To some observers, understanding the Asian crisis boils down to the rhetorical question, Do markets work? They suggest that the Asian crisis is adequate testimony of market failure. To others, the failure to let markets function contributed to the crisis. From the constitutional perspective, neither conclusion is entirely adequate. Rather, the focus should be on how markets will work more efficiently with different institutional structures and how the economic constitution should help shape those institutional structures. Market versus non-market' views arise on the role of HLIs and on IMF support of the crisis countries, to name just two. Recalling the two-step approach to constitutional choices – first, predicting the in-period circumstances that might prevail, and second, choosing rules after assessing how they might work in-period – is useful in assessing both of these issues.

Highly leveraged institutions

Assertions that HLIs, and in particular hedge funds, triggered large-scale exchange rate changes and capital flight have been prevalent throughout the Asian crisis. These charges – whether right or wrong – resonate with the constitutional approach because they reflect concern about undue exercise of market power. To date there is no definitive evidence supporting these assertions. The Financial Stability Forum is assessing the market dynamics associated with hedge-fund investments, to determine the role of these institutions. The theoretical argument that HLIs may threaten market integrity is based on the speculative attacks and multiple equilibria literature. In one form the argument is that, by moving foreign exchange markets, a lead' investor is able to take a position and then profit on that by leading other investors to a new equilibrium. Central to determining the validity of the argument is that there are investors able to systematically move market prices.

At present, we are therefore still at step one of the constitutional choice process. A stronger understanding of the technical dynamics of foreign exchange markets is needed to define adequately the variety of in-period circumstances that might prevail and need to be addressed by new rules. Only after completing that exercise can the second constitutional choice step, of assessing the operation of various rules, proceed. The Australian Reserve Bank has argued (Reserve Bank of Australia 1999) that

> a strong in principle' argument exists for the regulation of some types of
> hedge fund because they pose a risk to the stability of the financial system
> and to the integrity of financial markets the most effective approach would
> involve three elements: improving standards of disclosure; improving the risk
> monitoring practices of institutions that ultimately provide hedge funds with
> the ability to generate large positions; and removing distortions in the Basle
> capital framework; and, finally, standards of disclosure could be improved by
> the application of higher capital charges to exposures of banks to institutions
> that do not meet specified minimum disclosure standards.

Several reports – both public and private sector – have outlined principles for strengthening supervision of creditors to these institutions, and noted the market discipline that creditors themselves impose. Beyond prudential rules it is not yet clear what additional rules, if any, might be called for.

Moral hazard and IMF-supported reform programs

It is argued that IMF-supported programs create moral hazard by giving investors an implicit guarantee. Investors believe that official support ensures that their investments will be repaid irrespective of the economic difficulties a country may experience. This implicit guarantee results in excessive investment into countries that are expected to receive official support.

The simple possibility of moral hazard does not mean that the economic constitution should rule out international financial support. Setting constitutional rules requires a broader assessment of the operation of alternative rules, rather than a conclusion that one rule is not perfect. Moral hazard is ubiquitous. In public policy discussion on road safety, for example, most judge it useful to adopt at least some road-safety measures, although these measures may lead drivers to take risks they would not otherwise take. It would be easy to eliminate moral hazard by using, as a road-safety measure, the requirement that, instead of an air-bag, every vehicle have a sharp spike protruding from the steering wheel and facing the driver. This would slow traffic dramatically, as the driver would run the risk of suffering the spike if sharp braking were required. This, of course, makes little sense, but it is useful in reminding us that other policy goals make such a safety measure unacceptable and that society accepts some moral hazard in the trade-off between goals.

The economic constitution must design rules to minimise costs, and this applies also to the rules governing the provision of international financial support by the IMF. Economic theory has long examined principal–agent relationships in numerous market settings. The principal (perhaps a company owner) pays the agent (a company manager) to undertake a task (manage the company). The definition of the contractual relation determines whether the agent pursues the owner's interests (the efficient outcome) or pursues other actions in his own self-interest. Likewise with international financial support, the critical issue is design of the incentive structure in the contractual relationship. Mussa (1999) provides a helpful exposition of how moral hazard applies and does not apply in the context of international financial support.

Recognising that rules for international financial support must be designed to minimise cost and that some moral hazard may be deemed justifiable, the constitutional convention must make the trade-off between goals. Those criticising international financial support perhaps do not see this broader picture. A conventional rationale for IMF support is that restoring strong economic performance in a troubled trading partner is in the interests of other member countries. Another reason for international financial support may be to minimise other forms of moral hazard. The international community may wish to ensure that standstills on debt payments – which are more likely to occur without financial assistance – are truly exceptional. The prospect of more frequent standstills (perhaps called by governments with short time horizons) introduces another form of moral hazard, resulting in too low a level of international capital flows. The economic constitution must seek to balance concerns about international financial support with the absence of such support. Neither extreme is likely to be a preferred outcome.

Measures to strengthen the international financial system

Constitutions, by their nature, rely on checks and balances to guide developments away from damaging in-period outcomes. This often means that a difficult trade-off arises. An economic constitution is no different in this regard. Summers observes that policy makers want national sovereignty; financial markets that are regulated, supervised and cushioned; and the benefits of global capital markets (Global Finance Survey 1999). He points out that, in practice, reform must favour two of these goals at the expense of the third. The trade-off between these goals may be constructive from a constitutional perspective because it reflects the system of checks. The trade-off raises difficult challenges in designing constitutional rules on standards, transparency and capital flows.

International standards, transparency and capital account rules

According to Eichengreen (1999), standard setting and transparency is an approach that reconciles national regulation with the needs of strengthening international markets. Progress in developing standards in a variety of areas has been made. The IMF has developed macroeconomic statistics standards in its *Special Data Dissemination Standard (SDDS)*. Upgrading requirements on international reserves, external debt, and procedures for monitoring observance has strengthened this standard. The advantages and disadvantages of including macro-prudential vulnerability indicators in the standard are being considered. A *Code of Good Practices on Fiscal Transparency* has been completed and efforts are underway to encourage countries to assess their fiscal transparency. A *Code of Good Practices on Transparency in Monetary and Financial Policies* has also been developed. Several assessments of countries' compliance with the *Basle Core Principles for Effective Banking Supervision*, based on a draft handbook on the methodology for assessing implementation of the *Core Principles*, have been completed. Standards are also being developed in areas such as securities markets, insurance, accounting, auditing, bankruptcy and corporate governance.

Like standards, transparency is intended to promote positive market discipline on policy makers and market participants. Transparency in decision making has focused on three main areas. The first area is on improving transparency in the IMF, to help ensure greater transparency of policies in member countries. Second, in collaboration with other standard-setting bodies, the IMF has helped develop internationally recognised standards. Finally, the IMF is developing mechanisms to enhance its traditional surveillance role by undertaking assessments of countries' progress towards internationally recognised standards.

A central issue, raised in the context of the crisis, is the appropriateness of capital account liberalisation, including its relationship with domestic financial market liberalisation. While it is generally agreed that financial integration, including liberalising capital accounts, brings substantial benefits, it also brings risks that need to be managed carefully. Capital account liberalisation should be sequenced appropriately, balancing the benefits and risks. It should be fully supported by a consistent macroeconomic framework. The framework would include monetary and exchange rate policies, and an institutional set-up to strengthen the ability of financial intermediaries and other market participants to assess and manage risk and to support monetary and exchange rate policies.

The Financial Stability Forum's working group on capital flows is to develop a risk-management framework. This framework will provide guidance on sound risk management (debt management on the part of the public sector and risk management in the banking sector); risk monitoring and assessment (data issues, role of credit-rating agencies); institution building (market-based incentives); and removal of distortions. IMF surveillance will focus on facilitating orderly capital account liberalisation, and ensuring that effective safeguards are in place to help ensure the resilience of the economy, particularly the financial sector, to possible shocks. Work to improve the reporting and monitoring of capital flows will continue.

Turning to the constitutional perspective, the issues of standards and capital account liberalisation are symbolic of the difficult questions posed in reconciling national preferences with strengthening the international economic constitution. With respect to standards, at the broadest level of principle, adherence to a sound set of standards and transparent reporting of public and private information is intended to strengthen market discipline. The tenacity of this discipline could vary considerably. At one end of the spectrum, standards might be a guideline on best practices': at the other, adherence to standards might become an entry ticket' to the global financial system.[7]

The choice between these options has significant implications for the economic constitution. Supporting a strong international economic constitution, countries would be expected to adhere to rules.[8] This would strengthen the international financial system by ensuring a level playing field and reduce the possibility of competitive' policy setting. Strict adherence to standards benefits citizens of countries. Citizens may recognise that their governments, motivated by short-term political pay-off, may adopt policies that are economically damaging for their own citizens. Standards might prevent governments from adopting such policies. Strict adherence to standards also benefits the global economy. On the other hand, an approach requiring strong adherence to global standards does impinge on national sovereignty to a greater degree than a system where the standards and rules on capital account liberalisation are just guidelines. It is my view that a relatively rigorous set of agreed rules is appropriate, but that countries should have an exit option for occasions when they judge that there are excessive impositions on their national interests.[9] Those choosing the exit option must pay a price, such as incurring a higher cost of access to international capital markets.[10]

Strengthening surveillance through organisational change

This part considers some of the organisational elements of the economic constitution. The structure of organisations should depend on the broader set of constitutional rules, yet it is not clear that proposals made to date have adequately made that link. The broad objective of the organisations is to promote mutually-beneficial outcomes. Efforts in this direction are captured by the term-surveillance of country policy, based on the premise that strong and consistent domestic economic policies promote greater exchange rate stability and stronger global economic performance. Two aspects of these efforts are strengthening the IMF and developing the role of regional groups.

The structure of the IMF

Discussions on reform of the international financial system have thrown up two broad visions of the IMF. One is an organisation with strong political direction and support, achieved through changes in its governing structure. A second vision is of a more independent central-bank-like institution. The choice has implications for the constitutional rules that should guide the IMF and its activities.

Table 14.1 Standards

Proposal/Issue	Developments	Prospects
Macro statistics	SDDS – strengthening data dissemination on reserves and external debt have been adopted. Improved procedures for monitoring observance established.	Subscribing countries to observe new reserves standard by March 2000. Advantages and disadvantages of including macro-prudential indicators of vulnerability to be considered for SDDS.
Fiscal	Code of good practice on fiscal transparency completed and posted on IMF website.	Work on pilot country assessments commenced. Included in country transparency reports.
Monetary and financial policy	Code of good practice on Transparency in Monetary and Financial policies approved.	Supporting documents for implementing the code are being prepared.
Banking supervision	Handbook for assessing compliance with the Basle Core Principles and updating the capital accord.	IMF and World Bank to assess compliance with Basle Core Principles. Revised Basle capital accord (new framework proposed).
Securities markets	International Organization of Securities Commissions (IOSCO) prepared Objectives and Principles of Securities Regulation and Disclosure Standards to Facilitate Cross-Border Offering and Initial Listings by Multinational Issuers.	IOSCO to make recommendations regarding assessing implementation.
Insurance	International Association of Insurance Supervisors (IAIS) has produced compendium of principles, standards and guidance.	Target uniform accounting standards by 2002. Work with World Bank on dissemination and implementation of standards.
Accounting	International Accounting Standards Committee (IASC) has produced a comprehensive set of international accounting standards.	Agreements with IOSCO to develop core set of standards. If IOSCO endorses IASC standards, these could be used for cross-border offerings and listings.
Auditing	International Federation of Accountants has set of standards on auditing.	Work with IOSCO for cross-border offerings and listings.
Bankruptcy	UN Commission on International Trade Law (UNCITRAL) adopted Model Law 997 for cross-border insolvency.	World Bank providing information to governments. Discussions with International Bar Association on an initiative to develop guidelines for insolvency laws.

Table 14.1   Standards   cont'd

Proposal/Issue	Developments	Prospects
Corporate governance	OECD Task Force principles of corporate governance completed. World Bank has undertaken specific country work.	
Payment systems	Committee on Payment and Settlement Systems.	Task force to prepare principles.
Financial sector		Committee on the Global Financial System (CGFS) developing practices to support and deepen forward markets. Institute for International Finance working groups to identify best practices in several areas.
Social policies		A two-track approach with UN to develop basic principles, and the World Bank and other agencies to detail best practices.

The first vision calls for creation of a governing council to replace the Interim Committee.[11] That the IMF should have greater political involvement and endorsement is one lesson drawn by some from the Asian crisis. Proponents of this view say an elevation of the governing body from its present advisory role to an entity with decision-making powers is appropriate, recognising that the IMF is at the centre of the international monetary system. They also note the inevitable drawing of the IMF into sensitive topics such as governance and transparency in fiscal, monetary, and financial and other policies that are seen as central to national sovereignty. More frequent and detailed direct involvement of national representatives at the ministerial level would strengthen IMF decisions in these important areas.

From a constitutional perspective, the case for a governing council would seem to depend on the presumption that there are limited constitutional rules defining the objective and operations of the IMF. In the absence of such rules, more direct and significant accountability of the IMF would be needed. This would justify calling for the political authority noted by the proponents of the council structure. While there are strengths flowing from stronger political leadership under such circumstances, there is the downside risk that a more political council would see distributional considerations dominate decision making. Moreover, the degree of confidence that the political decision making can deliver a stronger international financial system depends also on the Council's composition. Consequently, a central question to resolve, in considering this proposal, is how to arrive at a judgment on whether it is possible to define clearly the objective and scope of operations of the IMF.

A second view on the structure of the IMF is quite different. It calls for greater independence of the IMF from day-to-day political influence. The rationale for the view is the recognition that economic policy making is conducted in a politicised environment and, in the eyes of some, too influenced by large shareholders. Thus proponents of this view have, one way or another, come to the judgment that it is possible to define a set of objectives and guidelines for the IMF as part of the constitution and that its performance against these rules can be assessed. Eichengreen *et al.* (1999) suggest that greater independence is warranted and could be delivered by converting the IMF's structure to something resembling that of a central bank, with executive directors given fixed-term positions to insulate them from the day-to-day political influences.

The role of regional groups

The Asian crisis has sparked calls for a new regional group, to guard against crises and perhaps to alleviate the consequences of the present crisis. The objective of tailoring constitutional rules to meet specific goals might lead the convention to envisage an important role for regional and other sub-global groups.

The integrated global economy means that the primary surveillance function, while constructed from national level analysis, must be a global activity. The discussion, in the appendix, on the establishment of the IMF noted that countries independently adopting their own macroeconomic policies could result in outcomes that made all worse off. Recognition of the need to shape country policy to promote mutually beneficial outcomes was the reason for establishing the IMF as a global entity. The entity undertaking this activity must be global because, for any sub-group of countries, there will always be third countries whose policies affect the sub-group's well being. Thus, for example, an Asian group is likely to be affected at least as much by developments in the US economy as by developments among its own members. Similarly, developments in Latin American financial markets will affect the financing costs of capital to Asian emerging markets. The list of these interactions is lengthy. In fact, if economic interactions were the decisive factors in determining the composition of groups, then it is unlikely that these groups would be geographically regional.[12]

Surveillance is about more than the assessment of policy interactions; it is also about encouraging countries to adopt strong and mutually beneficial policies. At one level, surveillance involves defining the pay-off to various policy options and guiding choices on those options, while recognising their consequences for other countries. This assessment must be done globally, particularly in the integrated global economy that the economic constitution must manage. A second aspect of surveillance is to encourage countries to adopt desirable policies. The issue of how the constitution should make adoption of these policies more likely is a major challenge. It is in this aspect that regional groups can strengthen surveillance through building mutual support and peer pressure.' The effectiveness of neighbourly persuasion is perhaps weakened as group size moves from small to larger and more diverse entities. In observing developments in nation states and formation of groups, some have referred to culture area'. This term refers to groups that have grown from shared experience of history, religious or philosophic beliefs, and may behave similarly long after the events shaping their common culture no longer prevail.[13] These intrinsic links can support a mutual strengthening of surveillance and help to achieve better policy.[14]

Several groups in Asia are now pursuing these types of activities. An important example is the Manila Framework Group. It consists of a fourteen-country sub-set of APEC economies that meets twice yearly to conduct regional surveillance exercises, with the IMF as its technical secretariat. It has been active in regional economic developments. For example, it conducted an extraordinary meeting with the G-7 in mid-1998, focusing on concerns related to the rapid depreciation of the Japanese yen at that time. It has also played a role in developing regional views on reform of the international financial system.

ADDRESSING CRISES – THE ROLE OF THE PRIVATE SECTOR

Constitutional choices require an understanding of the circumstances that might prevail in-period, because only then can appropriate remedies be defined. Defining the in-period circumstances has proved particularly difficult when looking at crisis resolution. One aspect is how to involve the private sector in helping to finance adjustment programs (perhaps in the form of debt rescheduling or write-off). This section focuses on this aspect, namely the contribution of the private sector in resolving crises in an orderly manner while minimising contagion. It also describes developments in this area, before offering some views from a constitutional perspective.

Before moving to crisis resolution, it should be noted that several developments in crisis prevention, related to the private sector, are taking place. Work towards strengthening data monitoring of private external obligations, particularly inter-bank loans, is proceeding. The IMF has assisted several countries establish high-frequency debt monitoring systems to monitor inter-bank lines, and all borrowers are being encouraged to implement such systems. Regulatory distortions are being removed, as evidenced by the Basle Committee's proposed new capital adequacy framework. The proposed new framework seeks to better align capital requirements to underlying risks by raising capital requirements to short-term inter-bank credit lines to emerging markets. Countries are being encouraged to strengthen and perhaps institutionalise communications lines with debtors. Finally, some countries have developed emergency private sector financing facilities. Argentina, Indonesia and Mexico have secured these private contingent credit lines.

The promotion of orderly and effective insolvency systems is increasingly being integrated into IMF-supported programs, and development of guidelines for such systems is an integral part of the work underway on international standards. At the national level, strengthening of domestic bankruptcy and insolvency systems is essential to strengthening markets and private sector involvement. The adoption of orderly and effective insolvency systems allows creditors to enforce legitimate claims, while enabling courts to impose a legally binding settlement on minority dissident creditors. The presence of a sound bankruptcy system can itself offer enough pressure for creditors and debtors to reach negotiated settlements.

Regarding external debt obligations, modification of the terms of international sovereign bond contracts to make international debt restructuring a viable option has gained some support. Inclusion of collective action provisions in new international sovereign bonds, covering majority restructuring and enforcement provisions, are viewed by some as assisting an orderly resolution of financial crises. Collective action clauses enable a qualified majority of bondholders to restrain the ability of a minority of bondholders to undermine a debt-restructuring process. In addition to these provisions, some support the inclusion of representation provisions in international sovereign bond contracts. This provision would authorise a trustee to negotiate on behalf of the bondholders at an early stage of the crisis. Such a provision would address the difficulty of establishing informal contacts with widely dispersed bondholders.

To provide an environment to encourage debtor–creditor discussions, the IMF has revised its policies on arrears and financing assurances. The IMF is now permitted to lend into sovereign arrears to private creditors and into non-sovereign arrears, in situations stemming from the imposition of exchange controls.

Turning to the constitutional perspective, the preceding reforms of constitutional rules to involve the private sector in crisis resolution, are intended to bring about a more orderly adjustment process. Specific concerns in designing these rules are to limit moral hazard, strengthen market discipline, and help emerging market borrowers protect themselves against volatility and contagion. The international community is struggling to define a set of rules to guide such involvement, with the consequence that, in several countries already, a case-by-case approach has been followed. The absence of a clear set of guidelines remains a concern. It could pose unforeseen systemic implications because, owing to the absence of clear criteria for the actions taken, developments in the crisis country will be subject to interpretation regarding their implications for others. Moreover, efforts to resolve crises in some countries might be diverted by distributional considerations. Potential losers in the resolution of the crisis (private sector entities or their country representatives) may lobby (rent seek) to define the case-specific rules for crisis resolution more in their favour.

The main problem is to define clearly the set of circumstances in which capital controls, and the form of those controls, might be justified. Efforts to draw unambiguous lessons on private sector involvement, based on experience, have proved difficult. In particular, the international community has been grappling with questions such as defining the circumstances in which capital controls could play a useful role in reducing the volatility of capital flows. Capital controls cannot substitute for sound macroeconomic policies. However, there may be circumstances where inflow controls – more of a pre-crisis measure – might supplement other policy measures. While evidence on the effectiveness of capital controls is mixed, the Chilean experience suggests that controls can change the composition of inflows toward longer-term flows. The overriding message is that the overall consistency of policy and progress on structural reforms is essential.

Greater difficulty arises in defining the circumstances when partial controls on outflows or the extreme and exceptional cases of comprehensive outflow controls (standstills on payments) might be justified.[15] One view is that controls on capital outflows have rarely been an effective policy in a crisis, and can increase the severity of external adjustment. However, another view is that controls on outflows may play a role, in the context of a broader adjustment effort. The reluctance to support outflow controls reflects a concern that external constraints, probably already difficult in the crisis situation, may become worse. This would mean that the scale of the adjustment burden could become larger owing to loss of access to international finance.

Apart from the country-specific features that might justify the calling of a standstill on debt payments, the process of introducing a standstill in the absence of clear rules could lead to significant contagion effects that precipitate crises elsewhere. Moreover, the lack of a well-defined standstill mechanism could adversely affect investor behaviour. As noted earlier, the prospect of easier' calling of a standstill is likely to discourage unduly otherwise valuable capital flows. At a minimum, it could make flows more volatile, as capital tends to flee at the slightest sign of an emerging crisis. It is thus important to make as much progress as possible in defining specific circumstances for these measures and, at a minimum, to define due process for implementation. In this regard, it would seem appropriate that the IMF articles be modified to address these capital account issues.

CONCLUSIONS

The recent track record of the global economy has shaken faith in the effectiveness of the present rules of the game'. Many argue that recent crises exposed significant loopholes in the rules governing domestic financial institutions and corporations. Others suggest that the loopholes were in the institutional structure governing cross-border capital flows and in the international arrangements for responding to crises. The reforms taking place, both to the rules governing economic and financial relations in Asia and to the international financial system, will guide Asia's course far beyond the immediate recovery.

Viewing these reforms from a constitutional perspective offers guidance both in evaluating the reform process as well as in considering proposals made during the reform discussions. The starting point is to recognise the critical role of the institutional structure of markets. Adam Smith observed that, within an appropriate structure of laws and institutions', individuals following their own interests actually further the general well-being. Of course, when attention turns to the global economy, defining the appropriate structure of laws and institutions is more complex, but the issue is the same.

The rationale for an international economic constitution is to establish rules and institutions to promote mutually beneficial policy, while recognising the implications of an integrated global economy. The present reform of the economic constitution is charged with making markets operate more effectively by both guiding economic policy and setting the rules for economic transactions. The first step is, however, to develop a strong constitutional convention. This requires designing a process that minimises the role of narrowly defined self-interest in making choices and is perceived as legitimate. These issues have been discussed in this chapter, and a case made for developing generalised rules.

Reform of institutional structures to make markets work more efficiently arises in relation to HLIs and to IMF support of the crisis countries. On HLIs, it has been suggested that the constitutional choice process is presently at the first of a two-step process. A stronger understanding of the technical dynamics of foreign exchange markets is needed to define adequately the variety of in-period circumstances that might prevail and need to be addressed by new rules. Only after completing that exercise can the second constitutional choice step, that of assessing the operation of various rules, proceed. On the issue of moral hazard of international support, while recognising that rules for international financial support must be designed to minimise such costs, some moral hazard may be deemed justifiable. The economic constitution must seek to balance concerns about the harmful moral hazard implications of international financial support with the absence of such support, which in itself could involve other forms of moral hazard and be reflected in the loss of valuable capital flows.

Proposals for adopting common international standards in a range of areas, and rules to guide capital account liberalisation are symbolic of the difficult questions posed in reconciling national preferences with strengthening the international economic constitution. With respect to standards, adherence to a sound set of standards and transparent reporting of public and private information is intended to strengthen market discipline and improve policy making. The tenacity of this discipline could vary considerably. At one end of the spectrum, standards might be a guideline on best practices': at the other, adherence to standards might become an entry ticket' to the global financial system. It is my view that a relatively rigorous set of agreed rules is appropriate, but that countries should have an exit option should they judge that there are excessive impositions on their national interests. Those choosing the exit option must pay a price, such as a higher cost of access to international capital markets.

The organisations established by the economic constitution should depend on the broader set of constitutional rules. Recent proposals for the governing structure of the IMF and for establishing regional economic entities have perhaps not made that link adequately. Discussions on reform of the international financial system have thrown up two broad visions of the IMF. One is an institution with strong political direction, and a second vision is a more independent central-bank-like institution. The choice has implications for the constitutional rules that should guide the IMF. The mandate of regional groups should be to strengthen surveillance, both through building mutual support and through peer pressure'.

Constitutional choices require an understanding of the circumstances that might prevail in-period', because only then can appropriate remedies be defined. The international community is struggling to define a set of rules to guide private sector involvement in crisis resolution. The absence of clear guidelines is a concern, because their absence could have systemic implications and see crisis resolution side-tracked by distributional considerations. Consequently, it is important to make progress in defining the specific and exceptional circumstances in which measures, such as standstills on debt payments, are used. At a minimum, it is important to define a due process for such cases.

The constitutional approach to reform of the international financial system has much to offer. It provides guidance about how to work toward sound resolution of the problems faced by the international financial system. Moreover, it emphasises the essential role of rules and institutions in addressing the wide range of in-period circumstances that the international economy may experience. However, the challenges to arriving at these solutions are also significant. A central problem lies in building a constitutional choice setting that encourages countries to adopt an objective vision of reform options.

REFERENCES

Basle Committee (1999) Report of Banking Supervision Working Group.
Brennan, G. and Buchanan, J.M. (1985) *The Reason of Rules: Constitutional political economy*, Cambridge, UK; New York: Cambridge University Press.
Buchanan, J.M. (1991) *Constitutional Economics,* Oxford, UK; Cambridge, MA: Blackwell.
    (1993) Lagged implementation as an element in constitutional strategy', *European Journal of Political Economy* 10: 11–26.
Eichengreen, B. (1999) *Toward a New International Financial Architecture,* Washington, DC: Institute for International Economics.

, De Gregorio, J., Ito, Takatoshi and Wyplosz, C. (1999)   *An Independent and Accountable IMF: Geneva reports on the world economy 1*, CEPR.

Garten, J.E. (1998)   In this economic chaos, a global bank can help', *International Herald Tribune* 25 September: 8.

Global finance survey' (1999) *Economist* 30 January: 3–18.

Grenville, S. (1999)   Financial crises and globalization', speech to the Reinventing Bretton Woods Committee Conference on International Capital Mobility and Domestic Economic Stability, Canberra, 15 July.

Group of Seven (G-7) (1999) Report of G-7 Finance Ministers to the K ln Economic Summit, Cologne, 18–20 June.

International Monetary Fund (1944)   Articles of Agreement of the International Monetary Fund', Bretton Woods.

Mussa, M. (1999) Reforming the International Financial Architecture: Limiting Moral Hazard and Containing Real Hazard', report for RBA Conference on Capital Flows and International Financial System, Sydney, 9 August.

The nation-state is dead. Long live the nation-state', (1995) *Economist*, 23 December.

Olson, M. (1987)   Economic nationalism and economic progress', *World Economy* (UK) 10, September: 241–64.

Rawls, J. (1971) *A Theory of Justice*, Cambridge, MA: Belknap Press of Harvard University Press.

Reserve Bank of Australia (1999) The Impact of Hedge Funds on Financial Markets', paper submitted to the Financial Stability Forum Working Group on Highly Leveraged Institutions, 4 June, Sydney.

APPENDIX

THE RATIONALE FOR AN INTERNATIONAL ECONOMIC CONSTITUTION

The origin of the IMF illustrates the *raison d'être* of the international economic constitution. The experience of competitive devaluation, trade restrictions and other mutually destructive policies contributing to the Great Depression was a costly lesson. Namely, the outcome can be worse for all when countries pursue their own narrowly defined self-interest. More constructively, countries can all be better off by recognising their mutual interests when setting policy. Thus, global integration triggered establishment of the IMF as the institutional mechanism to help achieve this mutual benefit.

To illustrate the case for such constitutional rules, a simplified example of competitive exchange rate devaluation is given on the next page.[16] Countries face a binary choice in a pegged exchange rate environment, devaluing or not. Each cell shows the pay-off from the policy options facing Countries A and B, and represents the change in GDP resulting from the policy selected. The left-hand-side value is the pay-off to Country A, and the right-hand-side value is the pay-off to Country B. These pay-offs show that a country benefits from a competitive advantage if it is able to devalue while others do not. However, none secures a competitive advantage should both countries devalue and GDP is assumed to be unchanged. The resulting matrix is the familiar Prisoners' Dilemma game.

The case for setting constitutional rules to govern policy options is unambiguous. In the absence of such rules, both countries are *always* worse off than potential. Country A can see that it should devalue *whatever* policy Country B chooses. Consider Country A's options. If Country B does not devalue, then Country A can increase GDP by 10 by devaluing and by only 6 if it keeps its rate unchanged. Alternatively, if B devalues, then A will again choose to devalue because the pay-off is 0 versus –2 if it keeps its rate unchanged. The choice B faces also leads it to devalue. These dominant strategies lead to the outcome shown in cell IV, a pay-off of 0 to each country. This solution is clearly inferior to both keeping their exchange rates unchanged (the cell I outcome).

B's policy options

	No change	Devalue
A's policy options — No change	**I** 6 6 (Neither devalues)	**II** –2 10 (A no change; B devalues)
A's policy options — Devalue	**III** 10 –2 (A devalues; B no change)	**IV** 0 0 (Both devalue)

The constitution should establish a rule or mechanism leading to the mutually beneficial cell I outcome. The rule must be designed to eliminate certain policy options (competitive devaluation in the example), in order to prevent an inferior outcome. The constitutional rule must be permanent because the incentive for countries to benefit by devaluing persists irrespective of the rule.

A case for constitutional rules follows from any pay-off matrix having the same ordinal ranking as shown. Nevertheless, the relative pay-off to various options is likely to influence the specific task, and thus design, of the constitutional rule. For example, in some instances, rather than setting a rigid rule, a constitution may coordinate the actions of countries by providing predictability. This is illustrated by modifying the example using different values although leaving the same ordinal ranking. Assume that the pay-off from securing a competitive devaluation is only modestly greater than the pay-off from the mutually beneficial exchange rate stability option (cell I) and that the cost of matching competitive devaluation (cell IV) is high. In these circumstances, and particularly in a repeated game, Country B is less likely to want to devalue if the rule provides confidence that Country A will not devalue.

B's policy options

		No change	Devalue
A's policy options	No change	**I** 6 6 (Neither devalues)	**II** −2 7 (A no change; B devalues)
	Devalue	**III** 10 −2 (A devalues; B no change)	**IV** −6 −6 (Both devalue)

The examples illustrate the rationale for the international aspects of an economic constitution. The constitution promotes mutually beneficial outcomes, including by setting limits that avoid scenarios making all participants worse off. Moreover, the constitutional rules must be crafted to meet the varying needs for policy rules.

NOTES

1   The views expressed are those of the author and do not necessarily represent those of the International Monetary Fund. Max Corden, Christopher Morris, Martin Parkinson and David Vines provided helpful comments but are not implicated by the views expressed.

2   Grenville (1999) is technically correct only in a limited set of decisions that require an 85% majority.

3   In the idealised constitutional choice setting, individuals know the distribution of positions under differing rounds of play under all sets of rules, while remaining ignorant about their own position under any one of those distributions. These choices are made behind Rawls' (1971) veil of ignorance' and satisfy his fairness condition.

4   If decisions are made today to set rules that apply from a point in the future this also helps separate the decision-makers from their own narrowly-defined in-period self-interest. See Buchanan (1994).

5   In an international trade context, Olson (1987: 243–4) refers to this as the mileage rather than the height of tariffs. Trade protection cannot be measured simply by tariff rates, because its significance depends on the size of the jurisdiction. To illustrate, assume the world economy is divided into two countries, one the size of Luxembourg and the other comprising the rest of the world. The height of the tariffs in the large country – whether high or low – has little impact on its economic prospects because most of what is purchased comes from the domestic economy. However, the consequences for the Luxembourg-sized economy of the level of tariffs in the large economy are likely to be profound.

6   The K In Statement of the G-7 Finance Ministers recognises the need to establish an informal mechanism for dialogue among systemically important countries within the framework of the Bretton Woods institutional system'.

7   At present, a middle course has perhaps emerged. Market discipline, IMF conditionality in the case of the Contingent Credit Line facility, and possibly the use of capital requirements on foreign lending based on assessments of adherence to standards may provide an incentive to adopt standards.

8   Some have suggested that rules could be defined to vary according to measures of development or other dimensions, although there is no consensus on the desirability of such arrangements.

9   A strong economic constitution and adherence to rules may perhaps sound more draconian than it really is. As outlined earlier, national constitutions impose constraints on policy making (monetary and fiscal actions). The difference here is that there would be comparable rules across countries.

10   One example is the draft Basle Capital Adequacy standards. The standards use a country's subscription to the SDDS to help determine the cost of lending by banks, through specifying how much capital a lending bank needs to set aside.

11   The proposal in the K In Statement of the G-7 Finance Ministers to change the Interim Committee to the International and Financial and Monetary Committee as well as operational changes was agreed at the 1999 Annual Meeting of the Committee.

12   Even then, as the cross-regional G-22 found, those excluded see their interest overlooked. The G-22 became a group of 33 countries before being abandoned.

13   See The Nation-state . . .' (1995).

14   Many other arguments put forward for new regional entities, in my view, hold little water. The need for liquidity without conditionality is one argument. The run-down of international reserves of Asian crisis countries was about US$80 billion in a *failed* attempt to stave off crisis. Additional funds may have met the same fate. A second argument relates to timeliness. During the 1997 crisis, assistance was provided promptly (The Philippines' request of 11 July was approved on 18 July; Thailand's request of 5 August was approved on 20 August; Indonesia's request of 8 October was approved on 5 November; and Korea's request of 21 November was approved on 4 December). A third argument relates to local knowledge; IMF staff work regularly in all member countries.

15   The K In statement of the G-7 Finance Ministers recognises that such exceptional circumstances might arise but does not define those circumstances.

16   The example is not intended to say anything about the merits of different exchange rate regimes.

Abbreviations

ABC	Agricultural Bank of China
ABRI	Indonesian Armed Forces
ACU	Asian Currency Unit
ADB	Asian Development Bank
AFTA	ASEAN Free Trade Area
AMC	Asset Management Corporation (Thailand)
AMFC	Account for Managing Financial Crisis
AMU	Asset Management Unit (Indonesia)
ASP	ASEAN Surveillance Process
BAY	Bank of Ayudhya
BBC	Bangkok Bank of Commerce
BBD	Bank Bumi Daya
BBL	Bangkok Bank
BCA	Bank Central Asia
BCI	Business Confidence Index
BDN	Bank Dagan Negara
BI	Bank Indonesia
BIBF	Bangkok International Banking Facility
BIS	Bank of International Settlements
BKPM	Investment Coordination Agency (Indonesia)
BLR	base lending rate
BMB	Bangkok Metropolitan Bank
BNM	Bank Negara Malaysia
BOJ	Bank of Japan
BOT	Bank of Thailand
BPI	Bank of the Philippine Islands
BPPT	Agency for Research and Application of Technology (Indonesia)
BRI	Bank Rakyat Indonesia
BSP	Bangko Sentral ng Pilipinas

CADB	China Agricultural Development Bank
CAR	capital adequacy ratio
CBS	Currency Board System
CCB	China Construction Bank
CDRAC	Corporate Debt Restructuring Advisory Committee (Thailand)
CDRC	Corporate Debt Restructuring Committee (Malaysia)
CGFS	Committee on the Global Financial System
CGT	capital gains tax
CIEB	China Import–Export Bank
CPF	Central Provident Fund (Singapore)
CRA	Corporate Restructuring Agreement (Korea)
CRCC	Corporate Restructuring Coordination Committee (Korea)
CRS	contract responsibility system
CSIP	Capital Structure Improvement Plans
DBU	domestic banking unit (Singapore)
DIC	Deposit Insurance Corporation
DOSRI	directors, officers, stockholders and related interests
DPR	House of Representatives (Indonesia)
EDI	Electronic Data Interchange
EPF	Employees' Provident Fund (Malaysia)
ESCL	Exchangeable Subordinated Capital Loans
EXIM	Bank Ekspor Impor Indonesia
FBCB	First Bangkok City Bank
FDI	foreign direct investment
FDIC	Federal Deposit Insurance Corporation (US)
FEBTC	Far East Bank and Trust Co.
FIDF	Financial Institution Development Fund (of the Bank of Thailand)
FIDF	Financial Institution Development Fund (Thailand)
FRA	Financial Sector Restructuring Agency (Thailand)
FSA	Financial Supervisory Agency (Japan)
FSC	Financial Supervisory Commission (Korea)
FSF	Financial Stability Forum
FSRG	Financial Sector Review Group
FSS	Financial Supervisory Service (Korea)
FTC	Fair Trade Commission (Taiwan)
GHQ	General Headquarters of the Allied Occupation
GITIC	Guangdong International Trust and Investment Corporation
GNP	gross national product
HCI	Heavy Chemical Industry

HIBOR	Hong Kong inter-bank offered rate
HKMA	Hong Kong Monetary Authority
HKSB	Hong Kong and Shanghai Banking Corporation
HLII	highly leveraged investment institution
HMBC	Hanareum Banking Corporation (Korea)
IAIS	International Association of Insurance Supervisors
IASC	International Accounting Standards Committee
IBRA	Indonesian Banking Restructuring Agency
ICBC	Industry and Commerce Bank of China
ICMI	Association of Indonesian Muslim Intellectuals
ICW	Indonesian Corruption Watch
IFC	International Finance Corporation
IMF	International Monetary Fund
INDRA	Indonesian Debt Restructuring Agency
IOSCO	International Organisation of Securities Commissions
ITC	investment trust company
ITU	International Telecommunication Union
KAMKO	Korea Asset Management Corporation
KDIC	Korea Deposit Insurance Corporation
KFTC	Korean Fair Trade Commission
KKN	*korupsi, kolusi, nepotisme* (corruption, collusion and nepotism)
KLSE	Kuala Lumpur Stock Exchange
KTB	Krung Thai Bank
LAF	Liquidity Adjustment Facility (Hong Kong)
LIBOR	London inter-bank offered rate
MAS	Monetary Authority of Singapore
MCB	minimum cash balances
MGS	Malaysian Government Securities
MICG	Malaysian Institute of Corporate Governance
MIDA	Malaysia Industrial Development Authority
MIER	Malaysian Institute of Economic Research
MOF	Ministry of Finance
MOFE	Ministry of Finance and Economy (Korea)
MOSOE	Ministry of Empowerment of State Owned Enterprises (Indonesia)
MPR	People's Consultative Assembly (Indonesia)
MSCI	Morgan Stanley Capital International
NBFI	non-bank financial institution
NDB	National Development Bank (China)

NEP	New Economic Policy (Indonesia)
NGO	non-government organisation
NIE	newly industrialising economy
NPL	non-performing loan
NU	Nahdatul Ulama
NWC	National Wages Council (Singapore)
OECD	Organisation for Economic Cooperation and Development
OTC	over-the-counter
PAN	National Mandate Party (Indonesia)
PBC	People's Bank of China
PDIP	Indonesian Democratic Party for Struggle
PKB	Nation's Awakening Party (Indonesia)
PNB	Philippine National Bank
PPP	United Development Party (Indonesia)
PSE	Philippine Stock Exchange
SDDS	Special Data Dissemination Standard (IMF)
SEC	Securities and Exchange Commission (Philippines)
SES	Stock Exchange of Singapore
SIMEX	Singapore International Monetary Exchange
SME	small and medium-sized enterprise
SOB	state-owned bank
SOE	state-owned enterprise
TAC	Total Access Communication (Thailand)
TFB	Thai Farmers Bank (BBL)
TFP	total factor production
TIBOR	Tokyo inter-bank offered rate
TMB	Thai Military Bank
UNCITRAL	UN Commission on International Trade Law
WTO	World Trade Organisation

Index